THE SOURCES OF HISTORY:
STUDIES IN THE USES OF HISTORICAL EVIDENCE

GENERAL EDITOR: G. R. ELTON

Books in This Series

Volumes already published

G. R. Elton	ENGLAND, 1200–1640
T. H. Hollingsworth	HISTORICAL DEMOGRAPHY
C. L. Mowat	GREAT BRITAIN SINCE 1914
Ian Jack	WALES, 400–1542
Kathleen Hughes	EARLY CHRISTIAN IRELAND
Charles H. Carter	THE WESTERN EUROPEAN POWERS, 1500–1700
Walter Ullmann	LAW AND POLITICS IN THE MIDDLE AGES
W. R. Brock	THE UNITED STATES, 1789–1890
David Knight	SOURCES FOR THE HISTORY OF SCIENCE, 1660–1914
Bruce Webster	SCOTLAND FROM THE ELEVENTH CENTURY TO 1603

Volumes in preparation

A. D. Momigliano (with M. Crawford and M. Frederiksen)	ANCIENT GREECE AND ROME
D. J. V. Fisher	ENGLISH HISTORY TO 1189
Martin Biddle	MEDIEVAL ARCHAEOLOGY
H. J. Hanham	ENGLAND SINCE c. 1800
Edward Grant	HISTORY OF SCIENCE TO 1600
Thomas Glick	MEDIEVAL SPAIN
Herschel Webb	THE SOURCES OF JAPANESE HISTORY
S. J. Woolf	ITALY, 1715–1860
Richard Cobb	THE FRENCH REVOLUTION

*Books in this series are distributed through
Hodder & Stoughton Ltd.*

The Sources of History:
Studies in the Uses of Historical Evidence

Law and Politics
in the
Middle Ages

An Introduction to the Sources
of Medieval Political Ideas

by

WALTER ULLMANN

THE SOURCES OF HISTORY LIMITED

Contents

Contents

For
Nicholas

General Editor's Introduction

By what right do historians claim that their reconstructions of the past are true, or at least on the road to truth? How much of the past can they hope to recover: are there areas that will remain for ever dark, questions that will never receive an answer? These are problems which should and do engage not only the scholar and student but every serious reader of history. In the debates on the nature of history, however, attention commonly concentrates on philosophic doubts about the nature of historical knowledge and explanation, or on the progress that might be made by adopting supposedly new methods of analysis. The disputants hardly ever turn to consider the materials with which historians work and which must always lie at the foundation of their structures. Yet, whatever theories or methods the scholar may embrace, unless he knows his sources and rests upon them he will not deserve the name of historian. The bulk of historical evidence is much larger and more complex than most laymen and some professionals seem to know, and a proper acquaintance with it tends to prove both exhilarating and sobering—exhilarating because it opens the road to unending enquiry, and sobering because it reduces the inspiring theory and the new method to their proper subordinate place in the scheme of things. It is the purpose of this series to bring this fact to notice by showing what we have and how it may be used.

G. R. E.

Preface

This book may fairly claim to be one of the first attempts to present the principal sources of medieval political ideas in an integrated and coherent manner. That the study of political ideas in the Middle Ages has been growing in recent years is due partly to the analysis of sources which have not before been considered proper bases or channels for conveying political ideas, partly to the better and more easily available editions of these sources, and partly to the realization that for the earlier medieval period 'political' or governmental ideas were frequently enough embodied in unexpected repositories, such as annalistic records, the numerous *Gesta* of kings, popes, emperors, etc.,[1] inauguration rituals, doxological and symbolic compendia, in sermons, tracts, epistolary communications, no less than in the law and the charters of rulers, municipal statutes, chancery regulations and practices, and so on. If to these are added the formal academic lecture, the severely scholarly commentary, the biblical exegesis, the monographic literature on specific topics, the books instructing young princes in the art of government, one will perhaps realize what an enormous amount of source material is at the disposal of the historian who wishes to extract relevant principles of government from this variegated material.

The systematization of concepts and doctrines which can be

[1] For some excellent observations see G. Melville, 'De gestis sive statutis romanorum pontificum: Rechtssätze in Papstgeschichtswerken' in *AHP* 9 (1971) 377ff. Cf. also H. Diener below, 301 n. 4, and F. Wasner below, 263 n. 1, at end.

abstracted from the concrete manifestations of governments, presupposes some familiarity with the law, its creation and application. For it is increasingly recognized that the so-called political ideas in the Middle Ages are in reality governmental principles conceived, elaborated, applied and modified (or abandoned if necessary) by the governments themselves. It is evident that for the greater part of the Middle Ages government and its underlying principles were considered first and foremost as integral parts of applied Christian doctrines, and thus shared the latter's character of indivisibility in regard to thought and actions. It was the undifferentiated Christian wholeness point of view that indelibly impressed itself upon all modes of thought and imprinted its intellectual complexion upon the chronologically largest span in the Middle Ages. And as far as society and its government were concerned, this wholeness standpoint found its most conspicuous expression in the law and in its (later) scholarly exposition, that is, jurisprudence.[1]

The concept of politics or political science as an autonomous science did not exist within the precincts of the medieval Christian theme of wholeness. Political ideas in the strict meaning of the term could not and did not emerge until matters of government came to be subjected to the full force of Aristotelian thinking. Then indeed the principle of indivisibility of human actions was to give way to atomization, differentiation and the splitting up of human activities into religious, moral, political, etc., categories with their appropriate norms. But this process, which was a result of the absorption of Aristotle, did not come about until the thirteenth century. Although political science then emerged as an autonomous science it still continued to have strong ties with its parent and begetter, medieval jurisprudence. In a word, the wholeness point of view engulfed virtually all public activities and made its appearance in many variegated forms. The em-

---

[1] This point of view of exclusiveness and totality was still common in the fourteenth century. Cf., e.g., Conrad of Megenberg, *De translacione Romani imperii*, cap. 12 (ed. R. Scholz in his *Unbekannte kirchenpolitische Streitschriften* II (1914) at 292: 'Liquidum est religionem christianam quoddam *totum esse*', and hence it was considered all-embracing, comprehensive and indivisible.

barrassingly rich source material finds its ready explanation in the all-embracing claim of the Christian theme itself. It was only when this unipolarity of outlook and action yielded to bipolarity, if not multipolarity, that political ideas and political science could be spoken of as independent categories of thought and action.

Since governmental actions and political ideas cannot be considered in a vacuum but only in close connexion with the actual historical situation, this book furthermore attempts to show the kinds and the growth of the sources in their relation to the historical background. Because in the medieval period reality and ideology cannot be divorced, the one cannot be understood without the other. For every historical contingency produced its own momentum and generated its own ideological dynamics which then found expression in the relevant governmental measures. Hence in order to understand the nature of the sources and their impact adequately, some realization of their historical context is necessary. Although the subject of this book is strictly historical, it is not a history of law, political ideas, or institutions, but an introduction to the principal sources which contained governmental and political ideas. Within its limits the book may perhaps be a modest contribution to the literature and scholarship concerned with politics and may thus possibly add a new dimension to historical-political studies.

It can readily be seen why the almost limitless range of material imposed some fairly drastic restrictions upon me. Having lived with most of the sources for close on four decades, I am in the unenviable position of realizing how much is omitted here. But if this book is to serve its purpose of introducing the main sources on which medieval political ideas rested, some selection is inevitable.[1] The difficulty which has confronted me in writing this

[1] Critics will be right in pointing out certain omissions: the Platonic-Hellenistic sources; the Stoic school; Macrobius; or in the high Middle Ages the Graphia circle; the contribution made by, say, Wazo of Liège, Raoul Glaber, Benzo of Alba; the humanist group of the turn of the eleventh and twelfth century (Hildebert of Lavardin, Marbod of Rennes, etc.); the Franciscan school; William of Auxerre; Praepositinus de Cremona; the Paris circle grouped around Peter the Chanter and Stephen Langton; English and French judicial decisions; sphragistics; different kinds of documentary materials, notably of

book has been how to present this vast mass of varied material. An integrated conspectus of this diversified material has not appeared before. I have therefore tried to marshal it in such a way that the importance and relevance of the sources becomes intelligible to those with a genuine interest in the subject. They will above all wish to know *what* sources there were as well as their characteristic features and contents; *why* they were important; *where* they can be found; *how* they have formed the subject of modern research and how the latter has illuminated their comprehension; and *who* the authors of influential works were. Here and there I have taken the liberty of indicating what topics are in need of scholarly exploration.

In writing this book I have derived some comfort—if comfort it be—from my long-standing familiarity with these sources: this indeed has given me confidence without which I would never have had the courage to embark upon this task. But as the overriding consideration has been to be of assistance to the readers, I have tried to point in the notes to the necessary literature which is as disseminated and variegated as the source material itself. Even so, the extent of the footnotes is only a fraction of the original apparatus: in the last stages I have severely pruned the notes. Since some of the modern literature is of necessity specialized and known to only a few researchers, I considered it a self-evident duty to acquaint students, researchers and readers in general with at least a modicum of this secondary literature. The amount cited appears to me the irreducible minimum for any serious student. Perhaps I may refer to my own experience as a researcher, reviewer and examiner when I have noted how often some very good primary work has been marred by an author's inadequate acquaintance with secondary literature or lack of familiarity with recent advances in research and scholarship. To have further reduced the secondary literature would have been a disservice to scholarship and would have rendered nugatory the very purpose

the papal chancery (letters of grace; letters of justice, the *littera clausa*, etc.); Sicilian, Spanish, Polish and Scandinavian materials, and so on. But this would have needed a multi-volume work, and even this would not have been complete. Completeness cannot be aimed at in this subject.

of the book itself. The sources together with modern literature show how keenly interdisciplinary in character the subject itself is: in the best meaning of the term it is an integrated whole, in no wise different from the original cosmology that produced the material.

More so than on other occasions have I been dependent on the kindness of colleagues, friends and pupils who have sent me over the years their offprints, books and even in some instances special extracts from the sources which I might otherwise have missed. It would be a long list—and would make tedious reading too— were I to name them all individually. What I can do here is to thank them once more for their unfailing kindness and thoughtfulness in sending me copies of their works. I can only hope that they will see how greatly I have profited from their researches. It is moreover particularly gratifying to find that my own previous work has aroused the spontaneous interest of a surprisingly large number of scholars—personally unknown to me and apparently belonging to the younger generation—who have probed into and meritoriously developed topics relative to government and political ideas in the medieval period. With an especially warm feeling of gratitude I would like to mention the stimulus I received from my own research students past and present—and also from some undergraduates—who greatly contributed to my penetration into the sources. My sense of gratitude to my wife is as intense and profound as it has ever been: she has patiently borne with me during all the stages of preparation and gestation of this book, and once again has substantially helped me in the final revision: her realistic critical sense has been of inestimable value to me.

Cambridge   W.U.
Summer 1973

Abbreviations

AA	*Atti del Convegno Internazionale di Studi Accursiani* ed. G. Rossi (1968)
ACDR	*Atti del Congresso Internazionale di Diritto Romano* (1934–5)
ACII	*Acta Congressus Iuridici Internationalis VII Saeculo a Decretalibus Gregorii IX et XIV Saeculo a Codice Justiniano promulgatis*, ed. Pontificium Institutum utriusque iuris (1935–1937)
AD	*Archiv für Diplomatik*
AHP	*Archivum historiae pontificiae*
AUF	*Archiv für Urkundenforschung*
Bartolo	*Bartolo da Sassoferrato: Studi e Documenti per VI centenario*, ed. Università degli Studi di Perugia (1962–3)
BEC	*Bibliothèque de l'école des chartes*
Bibl.	Bibliography; bibliographical
Calasso *Medio evo*	F. Calasso, *Medio Evo del Diritto* (1954)
CC	*Corpus Christianorum* (1954– in progress)
CMH	*Cambridge Medieval History*
CR	*The Carolingian Renaissance and the idea of kingship*, by W. Ullmann (1969)
CSEL	*Corpus Scriptorum Ecclesiasticorum Latinorum*
DA	*Deutsches Archiv*
DAC	*Dictionnaire d'archéologie chrétienne et de liturgie*
DBI	*Dizionario biografico degli Italiani* (in progress)

17

D(D)	*Diploma(ta)*
DDC	*Dictionnaire de droit canonique*
Decreta	*Conciliorum oecumenicorum Decreta*, 2nd ed. by J. Alberigo et al. (1962)
DHGE	*Dictionnaire d'histoire et de géographie ecclésiastiques* (1951– in progress)
Dn	*Digestum novum*
DTC	*Dictionnaire de théologie catholique* (1923–56)
Dv	*Digestum vetus*
ED	*Enciclopedia del Diritto* (1958– in progress)
EHD	*English Historical Documents*, ed. by D. C. Douglas
Epp.	*Epistolae*
ET	English translation
F.-Le Br.	*Histoire des collections canoniques en Occident*, by P. Fournier et G. Le Bras (1931–2)
FT	French translation
gl. ord.	*Glossa ordinaria*
GT	German translation
HBS	Henry Bradshaw Society
HEL	*History of English Law*, by W. S. Holdsworth, new ed. (1924–56)
Hist.	History; historical; histoire; historique
HJb	*Historisches Jahrbuch*
HPT	*History of Political Thought: The Middle Ages*, by W. Ullmann (rev. ed. 1970)
HQL	*Handbuch der Quellen & Literatur der neueren europäischen Privatrechtsgeschichte 1100–1500*, I (1973), ed. H. Coing
HZ	*Historische Zeitschrift*
IRMAE	*Ius Romanum Medii Aevi* (1961– in progress)
IS	*Individual and Society in the Middle Ages*, by W. Ullmann (1967)
IT	Italian translation
J.	*Journal*
JEH	*Journal of Ecclesiastical History*
JR	*Juridical Review*

JTS	*Journal of Theological Studies*
KGD	*Kirchengeschichte Deutschlands*, by A. Hauck, 8th ed. (1963)
KRG	*Kirchliche Rechtsgeschichte*, by H. E. Feine, 4th ed. (1964)
LCC	*Library of Christian Classics*
LdL	*Libelli de Lite*
lit.	Literature
LT	Latin translation
LTK	*Lexikon für Theologie und Kirche* (1957–68)
MA	Middle Ages, Mittelalter, Moyen Age
Mansi	Mansi, J. D., *Sanctorum Conciliorum amplissima Collectio* 35 vols. (Florence–Venice 1759–1998)
Meijers	E. M. Meijers, *Études d'histoire du droit*, ed. R. Feenstra and H. F. W. D. Fischer, I (1956); III (1959); IV (1966)
MGH. AA.	*Monumenta Germaniae Historica: Auctores Antiquissimi*
— *Capit.*	— *Capitularia*
— *Conc.*	— *Concilia*
— *Const.*	— *Constitutiones et Acta publica*
— *DD*	— *Diplomata*
— *Epp*	— *Epistolae*
MIL	*The medieval idea of law*, by W. Ullmann (repr. 1967)
Mirbt	Mirbt, C., *Quellen zur Geschichte des Papsttums und des römischen Katholizismus*, 4th–5th ed. (1932)
Misc. Med.	*Miscellanea medievalia*
MIOG	*Mitteilungen des österreichischen Instituts für Geschichtsforschung*
MP	*Medieval Papalism: the political doctrines of the medieval canonists* (The Maitland Memorial Lectures), by W. Ullmann (1949)
NA	*Neues Archiv der Gesellschaft für ältere deutsche Geschichtsforschung*

NCE	*The New Catholic Encyclopedia* (1967)
PG	*The Growth of papal government in the Middle Ages*, by W. Ullmann, 3rd–4th ed. (1970)
PGP	*Principles of government and politics in the Middle Ages*, by W. Ullmann, 2nd ed. (1966)
PICL	*Proceedings of the International Congress of medieval canon law*
PK	*Papst und König*, by W. Ullmann (Salzburger Universitatsschriften: Dike, vol. III (1966))
P & M	*The History of English law*, by F. Pollock and F. W. Maitland, 2nd ed. (1932)
PGr.	Migne, J. P., *Patrologia Graeca*
PL	Migne, J. P., *Patrologia Latina*
QFIAB	*Quellen und Forschungen aus italienischen Archiven und Bibliotheken*
RAC	*Real-Lexikon für Antike und Christentum* (1950– in progress)
RB	*Revue Bénédictine*
RDC	*Revue de droit canonique*
Reg.	Register
RHD	*Revue d'histoire du droit*
RHDFE	*Revue historique de droit français et étranger*
RHE	*Revue d'histoire ecclésiastique*
Riv.	*Rivista*
RNI	*Regestum domni Innocentii tertii super negotio Romani imperii*
RQ	*Römische Quartalscharift*
RS	Rolls Series
Savigny	F. K. Savigny, *Geschichte des römischen Rechts im Mittelalter*, 2nd ed. (1834–51)
SavZGA; KA; RA	*Zeitschrift der Savigny Stiftung für Rechtsgeschichte: Germanistische Abteilung; Kanonistische Abteilung; Romanistische Abteilung*
SB. Heidelberg	*Sitzungsberichte der Heidelberger Akademie der Wissenschaften*
— Munich	— — *Bayrischen Akademie der Wissenschaften: phil.–hist. Klasse*

— *Vienna*	— — *österreichischen Akademie der Wissenschaften: phil.-histor. Klasse*
SCH	*Studies in Church History*
Schulte	Schulte, J. F., *Geschichte der Quellen und Literatur des canonischen Rechts* (1875–7)
SDHI	*Studia et Documenta Historiae et Iuris*
Stickler	Stickler, A. M., *Historia iuris canonici latini* (1950)
St. Grat.	*Studia Gratiana*
St. Greg.	*Studi Gregoriani*
Stud. Med.	*Studia medievalia*
TII	*Tractatus illustrium iurisconsultorum*, 28 vols. (ed. Venice 1584–6)
TQ	*Theologische Quartalschrift*
Trad	*Traditio*
TRHS	*Transactions of the Royal Historical Society*
TU	*Texte und Untersuchungen zur Geschichte der altchristlichen Literatur*
TUI	*Tractatus universi iuris*, 18 vols. (ed. Lyons 1549)
van Hove	A. van Hove, *Prolegomena ad Codicem iuris canonici*, 2nd ed. (1945)
VI	*Liber Sextus*
WH	Wattenbach, W., *Deutschlands Geschichtsquellen im Mittelalter: deutsche Kaizerzeit*, ed. R. Holtzmann I (1948)
WL	— — ed. W. Levison and H. Löwe (1951–63)
X	*Liber Extra*
ZKG	*Zeitschrift für Kirchengeschichte*

All other abbreviations are self-explanatory.

CHAPTER 1

Introduction

The subject of this book calls for some general observations on the nature and kind of what are called political ideas in the Middle Ages. Concerned as this book is with the sources, it is profitable to realize that political ideas in the Middle Ages had some peculiarities which are perhaps not at once obvious to people in the twentieth century. For politics and the study of political ideas now belong to a branch of scholarship which is autonomous and self-sufficient and which rests on its own laws, premisses and framework. It is as much an independent science as history, philosophy, theology, or, for that matter, law. Another point to be considered at the outset is the public at large. Today and for some time past the public that is engaged in framing, discussing and applying political ideas is to all intents and purposes identical with the electorate, and this in its turn comprises all men and women over a certain age. The presupposition for this is the dissemination of political ideas, whether by books, pamphlets, handbills, sound broadcasting, television, daily and weekly papers, quite apart from speeches by professional politicians. The literacy of, and response by, the public at large are indispensable. There is a virtually constant interchange between the mass media and the public, because the latter has a direct stake in both the major and minor questions of politics. The participation of the public—either directly or indirectly through their own representatives—in the decisions resulting in the law fosters this interchange of ideas and promotes mutual fructification.

Politics, political aims, political ideas, political programmes and the like are not an end in themselves, but are merely means to an end—the end being the law that results from a particular political ideology or even cosmology. Throughout the globe the present age provides daily confirmation of this situation. There is on the one hand the Marxist programme: one of its essential features is the abolition of private property, of the means of production and the dictatorship of the proletariat. As a political ideology this has been argued in literally speaking countless publications and broadcast in thousands of addresses and speeches, all of which amount to a solid political ideology. But political ideologies are not disseminated for drawing-room discussion, but are to serve as foundations upon which the configuration of a society can be shaped. The instrument by which this shaping if not transformation of society can be effected is the law as the binding rule which prohibits private ownership of the means of production and institutes the agencies and organs by which this state of affairs can be administered and enforced. In a word, the law must by its very nature be crisp, clear, unambiguous, easily comprehensible and devoid of jargon. There is therefore some considerable gap between political ideology and its effect—the law. To the voluminousness of the political programme corresponds a brief set of rules. The tangible reality that operates as a force in society is the law, not the ideology which gave birth to the law. It is self-evident that there are considerable shades within the framework of a political ideology which postulate modifications of the existing law. To take an obvious example, the Marxist programme in the hands of Trotsky was not the same as that practised by Stalin—in fact, there is what might be called a whole rainbow of colours from one end of the ideological spectrum to the other.

The capitalist ideology, to take the opposite example, not only makes a virtue of private ownership and especially of the means of production, but supports this also by adequate means: as an ideology this capitalist programme is in no wise different from the Marxist counterpart and is also set forth in books, pamphlets and so on, the common denominator of all of which is the recourse to either a natural law or a hallowed tradition or a psychological or an economic argument. By itself the capitalist ideology is incapable of changing the complexion of society, however numerous and well-argued the means of advocating the system are: what, in conformity with the Marxist ideology, is needed is the law. And the gap between the voluminousness of the ideological writings and the resultant effect, the law, is as striking within the capitalist system as it is within the socialist or communist programme. The distinction between political ideology and the law demonstrates the close interdependence between them.

Yet precisely because they are distinct and separate, ideology and law follow their own principles, their own lines of development and have, in a word, their own autonomous existence based on their own premises. That is to say, the elaboration, amplification and modification of political ideology is the task of the political scientist who in this undertaking can have recourse to a variety of doctrines as well as to observation and experience, and among the relevant matters to be taken into account is also the law itself. The law as the concrete manifestation of a political ideology shows the weaknesses and deficiencies of the latter. On the other hand, the interpretation (as well as application) of the law also follows its own course which is charted by jurisprudential considerations. And yet in the final resort the interpretation of the law also takes into account ideological features. Hence although they are distinct and separate, ideology and law have an undisputable kinship and internal relationship.

For the greater part of the medieval period, however, it cannot be said that law was separated from political ideology if by the latter is understood an articulate system or scholarly aggregate of general and specific themes, premises and theories, based on its own presuppositions. What on the other hand there was, was a science of government which was an integral part of scholarly jurisprudence and therefore had no autonomous character. But even this scholarly jurisprudence did not come about until the late eleventh century. Before then it was the governments themselves, the royal, imperial, papal, and so on, which formulated their own principles of government, embodied them in their own laws, and frequently enough argued in quite a scholarly manner about certain governmental topics in the preambles (the Arengae) of their laws. The historian's task is to extract from the law the governmental maxims and ideas and aims by a process of analysis in depth. Political ideology was built into the law or decree issued by the Ruler. There were no books on political ideology, no pamphlets or other expository means: all there was, was the law which therefore had a far wider scope and framework than has its modern successor. Law in the Middle Ages is one of the indispensable gateways to the recognition of governmental principles and ideology. It should also be kept in mind that these considerations apply with particular force to public law of which principles of government formed an essential ingredient. Until the late thirteenth century the study of political ideas is primarily part of historical jurisprudence with special reference to public law.[1]

Because of the illiteracy of wide sections of the populace which only slowly decreased, the importance of the law in the Middle Ages as the most readily available source can hardly be exaggerated. Moreover, during the early and high Middle Ages the public at large had little say in the weighty matters affecting the common weal, and one of the reasons for this non-participation was in fact the people's illiteracy and a consequent inability to comprehend questions involving general issues. The circle that was at times consulted was exceedingly small, but on the whole well-educated and well-informed: it was an intellectual élite. Elitism was indubitably a feature which the historian meets at every turn throughout the period. This explains partly at least the comparative paucity of literary works relating to the field of government even at a time when education had begun to advance. And this also explains why the law itself assumed a role which it did not possess either in antiquity or in the modern age. The law became the most crucial and vital element of the whole social fabric. It was viewed, quite in consonance with the prevalent Christian theme, as the soul of the body public: the application of the ancient allegory of soul (law) and body (society conceived as the body public) is therefore highly significant.[2] Thereby the idea of

---

[1] Cf. F. Calasso *Medio evo*; H. Mitteis, *Vom Lebenswert der Rechtsgeschichte* (1947); id., *Die Rechtsidee in der Geschichte* (1957); F. Wieacker, *Vom römischen Recht*, 2nd ed. (1961), 288ff; id., *Privatrechtsgeschichte der Neuzeit*, 2nd ed. (1968), 26ff (marred by numerous inaccuracies); H. Kantorowicz, 'Rechtswissenschaft und Soziologie' in *Ausgewählte Schriften* (1962), 83ff.

[2] This goes back to the Hellenistic period. For some sources cf. the passages cited from Isokrates, Demosthenes, Sextus Empiricus in *PK* 37f at note 63.

the rule of law was given concrete shape which is perhaps the most enduring bequest of the medieval period to the modern age.

It is no exaggeration to say that the law has at no other time played such a pivotal role in society as in the Middle Ages, and this at a time when the enforcement of the law presented some virtually unsurpassable obstacles.[1] But—it is advisable to stress this point at the very beginning—it was apparently due to this difficulty of enforcement (a difficulty which concerned communication in all senses of the term) that the law came to be continually re-enacted in order to make the populace aware of it: the constant need for re-enactment was evidently also caused by the general lack of availability of the law: there were no statute books, no public libraries, no record offices to which an ordinary man could repair to acquaint himself with the state of the law. The consequence was that the law survived in an almost unimpaired form, and frequently enough in an exemplary manner: it was transmitted in a great number of copies which are, generally speaking, of very high quality. Further, the vital importance of the law necessitated the steady supply of a trained personnel that was capable of drafting the law and expressing the thoughts of the law-creative organ exactly and faithfully. In a word, it was due to these historically conditioned circumstances and the peculiarities of the contemporary situation that the principle of the rule of law became implanted in the mind as well as in the actions of man.

Considering therefore the fundamental role that was allocated to the law, it is not difficult to see why within the precincts of government the central problem of the Middle Ages was the creation of the law. Who was, to put the question briefly, entitled to create law? Today in civilized communities it is not difficult to give an answer to the effect that it is a representative assembly which has the power to create law and modify or abolish old law, but this has been only fairly recently achieved in the

[1] About this problem in late antiquity see F. Wieacker, 'Zur Effektivität des Gesetzesrechts in der späten Antike' in *Festschrift für H. Heimpel* III (1972) 546–66.

history of the Western world. And the story of this achievement belongs very largely to the history of political ideas, or more correctly, to the history of the science of government.

It is consequently advisable to state at the very outset the two contrasting themes which portray the creation of law.[1] Historically speaking, the one called the ascending theme of government and law, can claim priority and appears to be germane alike to lowly and highly developed societies. Its main point is that law-creative power is located in the people itself (who belongs or does not belong to it, is of no concern in this context): the populace at large is considered to be the bearer of the power that creates law either in a popular assembly or diet, or, more usually, in a council or other organ which contains the representatives chosen by the people. The main ingredient of this ascending theme is that because original power is located in the people, the latter always remains in charge of the direction of its own society. Consent on the part of the populace is a structural element of the theme. Further, the idea of representation is essential to it, that is, that the representatives do not act or speak or treat on their own behalf, but on behalf of the electing populace and are therefore empowered to give consent to legislative measures. Evidently, the Ruler too is no more than a representative of the people, and remains responsible to those who have elected him and they in turn to the people at large. Power ascends, allegorically speaking, from the broad base of the whole people and culminates in a Ruler who has no power other than that which the people have conferred on him. They can depose him or restrict his power or modify it in any way it appears right and proper to them. The right of resistance is built into this theme. This is the state of

[1] This cluster of problems was first expounded in *RHD* 26 (1958) 360ff (book review), and further developed in *PGP* 20ff; *HPT* 12ff; *IS* 30f, 145ff, and for the gradual replacement of the one theme by the other cf. *CR* 174ff. The view still frequently held that in the MA law was 'discovered' or 'found' and not created by a special organ, is one of the myths that dies hard. Cf. on this now K. Kroeschell, 'Rechtsfindung: die mittelalterlichen Grundlagen einer modernen Vorstellung' in *Festschrift f. H. Heimpel*, III (1972) 498ff: the term cannot be found in the sources. See also id. on the direct and indirect sources of the law in his *Deutsche Rechtsgeschichte* I (1972) 21.

affairs that can partly be witnessed in ancient Greece, partly also in republican Rome and especially among the Germanic communities and tribes for which the explicit statements by Tacitus are incontrovertible testimonies.

Opposed to this ascending theme is the descending one according to which original power is located not in the broad base of the people, but in an otherwordly being, in divinity itself which is held to be the source of all power, public and private. The totality of original power being located in one supreme being was distributed downward—or 'descended from above'—so that the mental picture of a pyramid emerges: at its apex there was the Ruler who had received power from divinity and who distributed it downwards, so that whatever power was found at the base of the pyramid was eventually traceable to the supreme head. But, and this is one of the crucial differences from the ascending theme, the office holders are not representatives: they are only delegates of the supreme Ruler. He can therefore withdraw the power conceded to them for reasons for which he has to account on the day of judgment: the people, because it is governed by him, cannot call him to account. Hence there is no *right* of resistance because the officers are appointees and have power as a matter of grace, as a matter of good will, exercised by the supreme head.[1] And just as there are no representatives, consent plays no role within this framework. What enters here is the principle of suitability. Suitability for a particular office can in the last resort be fixed and measured only by the organ that possesses the totality of power and hands part of it on to a lower-placed delegate. Whereas within the precincts of the ascending theme there is, in a strict and dogmatic sense, no necessity for society to be ordered according to rank, a hierarchical order is of the very essence of the descending theme, for there are higher and lower officers according to their office's proximity to, or distance from, the supreme Ruler.

[1] F. Kern, *Gottesgnadentum & Widerstandsrecht*, 3rd ed. R. Buchner (1962) is still fundamental. Special attention should be paid to J. Spörl, 'Gedanken um Widerstandsrecht und Tyrannenmord im MA' in *Widerstandsrecht und Grenzen der Staatsgewalt*, ed. B. Pfister & G. Hillmann (1955) 11ff with copious lit.

The kernel of both themes is the creation of law. Now, for reasons which are irrelevant to this enquiry, during the period of the principate in ancient Rome the ascending theme[1] came to be supplanted by its descending counterpart. To be specific, this descending theme was clothed in the Christian garb which was to set the tone and complexion of society from the early fourth century onwards.[2] The point that is to be made is that Christianity had absorbed a great deal of Hellenism, oriental law and ancient philosophy, notably Platonism.[3] By virtue of its contact with the Roman civilization nascent Christian organizations furthermore came to absorb Roman institutional ideas, of which none was more important than the very concept of law. Here indeed the Bible, notably the Old Testament, and wholly independent of it, the pagan (Roman) law, found a common basis and kinship[4] which explained why the most profound feature of ancient Rome, the law, could, as indeed it did, effortlessly penetrate into the very matrix of the rapidly growing Christian doctrinal body.

The point must be stressed that it was purely private efforts by private writers which in the second and third centuries A.D. began the process not only of assimilating the pagan Roman law to Christian conceptions, but also of infusing the very language, substance and method of Roman law into Christian ideology. That is to say, at the cradle of what later became known Christian dogma stood the Roman law, swiftly to become part and parcel of Christianity itself. One such source was the work of Tertullian,

---

[1] Cf., e.g., C. B. Burns, *Fontes iuris Romani antiqui*, 7th ed. (1909) 120: *Lex Tarentina* (with Mommsen's headnote). Republican Rome sharply distinguished between 'legis*latio*' and 'legis*datio*', the former referring to the 'making' of law ('legem ferre'), the latter to the law given or imposed on dependent communities. Further Th. Mommsen, *Römisches Staatsrecht*, 3rd ed. (1889) II-2, 888ff.

[2] It is regrettable that 'La théologie chrétienne et le droit' in *Archives de philosophie du droit* 5 (1960) contains no historical contribution. For a stimulating study cf. J. Hoffmann, 'Droit canonique et théologie du droit' in *RDC* 20 (1970) 289ff.

[3] Cf., e.g., E. v. Ivánka, *Plato christianus* (1964).

[4] For this ancestral kinship cf. some of the works of D. Daube, e.g., *Studies in Biblical Law* (1947); also 'Princeps legibus solutus' in *Europa e il diritto romano* (1954) II, 401ff.

a Roman jurist of the old stamp.[1] Tertullian (150–230) cast the religious idea into legal forms and shaped the at the time (turn of the second and third centuries) embryonic Christian doctrine by the instrument of Roman law. In particular—and this is especially important in the context of political ideas—he viewed the relations between God and man as legal relations which he conceived as rights and duties. His thought-pattern could easily be pressed into the jurisprudential scheme of the Roman law. It is quite astonishing how easily Roman law conceptions flowed from his pen when he tried to explain difficult religious and biblical themes. For example, the idea of the *corpus* which was to assume a fundamental importance in later governmental ideology when the full Pauline cosmology came to be harnessed to the service of a governmental programme,[2] was in the first instance utilized by Tertullian so that one could speak of a marriage of the Roman law corporation with the Pauline concept of the corporate body of Christians. Numerous other Roman legal terms and ideas came to be utilized by Tertullian to clothe religious tenets with Roman law garments.

It is in this context that one of the crucial Roman law notions, that of jurisdiction, demands a few observations. This term designated the power to fix in a final manner what is right and just, to determine what is the law. The notion covered what a later age was to call legislation in the technical sense: *ius dicere* was the solemn declaration of the law.[3] In practical terms this meant that

[1] Ed. in *CSEL* 20, 47, 76. For some details cf. L. Buisson, art. cit., below, 41 n. 3, at 150ff; T. D. Barnes, *Tertullian* (1971), esp. 22ff on him as a jurist. See further P. Vitton, *I concetti guiridici nelle opere di Tertulliano* (1934); A. Beck, *Römisches Recht bei Tertullian und Cyprian* (1930); P. Lehmann, 'Tertullian im MA' in his *Erforschung des MA* (1962) V, 184ff. His works are now easily available in *CC* (1954).

[2] Cf. M. Roberti, 'Il corpus mysticum di s. Paolo nella storia della persona giuridica' in *Studi E. Besta* (1939) IV, 37ff.

[3] For this see F. Calasso, 'Iurisdictio nel diritto comune classico' in *Studi V. Arangiu-Ruiz* (1955) IV, 423ff; J. Gaudemet, 'Études juridiques et culture historique' and B. Paradisi, 'Le dogme et l'histoire' in 'Droit et Histoire' in *Archives de philosophie du droit* (1959) 1ff, and 23ff; W. Ullmann, 'Law & the medieval historian' in *Rapports XIᵉ Congrès internat. des sciences historiques* III

the Ruler—in late Roman antiquity the emperor as the *princeps*—disposed of the authority to lay down the law for his subjects. It is advisable to keep in mind that thereby the concept of *gubernatio* (government) received its particular juristic connotation and precision. The *gubernator* (governor) was he who had jurisdiction from which no appeal lay to any higher court. *Gubernatio* was essentially the exercise of *jurisdictio:* that was the foundation stone upon which the development of 'political' ideas in the Middle Ages rested. It will now be comprehensible why until the late thirteenth century jurisprudence and governmental science were indissolubly linked. They could well be seen as the two sides of the same coin.[1]

From the fourth century onwards the society to which jurisdiction and government referred was exclusively Christian. It stands to reason that the ante-legal and hence ante-governmental considerations came to be supplied by the Christian reservoir of thought. It was the religious substance of this ante-juristic doctrine that was to be distilled into the language of the enforceable law. The fusion of Roman law with Christian doctrine and notably the permeation of the Bible with Roman law (to which we shall revert presently) was one of the presuppositions for the ready acceptance of the monarchic theme by both the Christian apologists[2] and the Roman constitutional jurists. As has been persuasively shown, the monotheism of the Christian religion was a very powerful agent in the promotion of monarchic ideas and their wholesale acceptance by the Christians. The monarchy practised by the late Roman emperors seemed singularly well to reflect the divine monarchy and greatly facilitated the settlement by

(1960) 34ff at 36ff; id., 'Historical Jurisprudence etc.' in *Atti del Io congresso internaz. di storia del diritto* (1966) 195ff; K. Kroeschell, 'Recht und Rechtsbegriff im 12. Jhdt.' in *Vorträge & Forschungen*, XII (1968) 309ff; now esp. P. Costa, *Iurisdictio: semantica del potere politico nella pubblistica medievale* (1969); cf. my review in *RHD* 39 (1971) 298ff. See also J. W. Perrin, 'Legatus, the lawyers and the terminology of power in Roman law' in *St. Grat.* XI (1967) 461ff.

[1] Hence the ease with which *gubernator* (*gubernacula*, etc.) fused with *princeps* (*principatus*) from the 4th cent. onwards. Cf. also J. Gaudemet, 'Le régime impérial' in *SDHI* 26 (1960) 282ff; also P. Batiffol, *Cathedra Petri* (1938) at 169ff.

[2] For Tertullian see above, 32f; for Cyprian see his *De ecclesiae unitate*, ed. in *CSEL* 3, 209ff.

which Constantine the Great released the Christian Church from the bondage and the state of proscription in which it had been held. The already mentioned fusion of Roman law and of biblical-religious themes was a very powerful preparatory agent which greatly assisted the process of making the Christian Church legitimate. This legitimization was the legislative measure initiated by Constantine: it can also be viewed as the beginning of a Christian-inspired governmental ideology.[1]

Two points warrant some observations in this context. The first concerns the just mentioned monarchic theme. Late Roman governmental practice was now perceived to be willed by divinity. By himself striking up monotheistic chords, Constantine anticipated the response of the Christians who since the end of the first century had held that a clear distinction must be drawn between the person of the emperor and his governmental power.[2] This view was a concrete application of the Pauline thesis as enunciated in the letter to the Romans. The sharp dichotomy precluded any veneration of the emperor as a divine being: the Christian refusal to pay tribute to the 'divinity' of the emperor led understandably to discrimination, invectives and finally persecution of the Christians. Their stern and uncompromising attitude towards the 'divinity' of the emperor's person sharply contrasted with their equally uncompromising affirmation of the divine origin of the emperor's governmental power. It was this thesis— 'there is no *power* but from God', as St Paul had it—which came to be implemented in a dramatic way in the early fourth century.[3]

This had quite especial significance, because the law as an emanation of ruling power was raised to its highest possible

[1] For the background and constitutional problems see *SHP* 5ff.

[2] E. Peterson, 'Der Monotheismus als politisches Problem' in his *Theologische Traktate* (1951) 45ff is fundamental.

[3] Rom. 13, 1–7. Here was the basic distinction between the *power* of the Roman emperor and his *person*, upon which rested the later distinction between office and person. For an excellent analysis see W. Affeldt, *Die weltliche Gewalt in der Paulus Exegese: Röm. 13, 1–7 in den Kommentaren der lat. Kirche bis zum Ende des 13. Jahrh.* (1969). The influence of Ambrosiaster is marked (cf. below 228). Further, R. Daniel, 'Omnis potestas a Deo: l'origine du pouvoir civil et sa rélation à l'église' in *Recherches de science religieuse* 56 (1968) 43ff (to the 9th

pinnacle. As a person the late Roman emperor was, according to the Christian standpoint, no more than any other human being, but in his ruling capacity he possessed power over his subjects, and this power was not of human but of divine origin. Divinity had manifested itself in the emperor's power, and for this reason the law had to be obeyed. Both power and law were objectively assessable quantities. Hence, law came to be sharply distinguished from the personality of the law-creative organ. It was this detachment of the law as an objective measure from the subjective personality of the law-creator which set the tone in governmental ideology from the fourth century onwards. Differently expressed, the validity of the law in no wise depended on the character or personality of the Ruler. Whether the governor was morally 'good' or 'bad', was wholly irrelevant to the authority, validity or function of his law.

This basic view gave precision to the nascent governmental ideology. The substance of the descending theme of government was easily implemented and in fact strongly buttressed by religious and theological considerations. The attack and ridicule to which the Christians exposed the emperor was accompanied by their insistence on the divine location of his power. By exercising this power the late Roman emperor presented himself, according to the Christian apologists, as the 'minister of God' in the language of St Paul. This nascent ideology therefore strongly supported the monarchic form of government.

Here enters the second point to be considered. The fusion of Roman and Pauline notions relative to the corporation makes the Constantinian settlement governmentally and juristically understandable.[1] Next to the monarchic theme the corporational thesis proved to be all-pervading and was to reverberate throughout the

cent. only). In regard to the early Christians and their attitude towards the emperor see A. Harnack, 'Der Vorwurf des Atheismus in den ersten drei Jahrhunderten' in *TU* 28 (1905), fasc. 4; cf. also Th. Mommsen, *Römisches Strafrecht* (1899) 575ff.

[1] Cf. J. Gaudement, *L'église dans l'empire romain* (1959); *SHP* 5, 7, 23, 29ff. About the incorporation of the Church see A. Ehrhardt in *SavZ. RA* 70 (1953) 299ff; 71 (1954) 25ff; cf. also id., 'Konstantins Religionspolitik & Gesetzgebung' ibid. 72 (1955) 127ff.

subsequent ages. For by conferring upon the Church the status of a corporation, Constantine raised it from its subterranean existence and turned it into a lawful body public. And this governmental measure entirely corresponded to the Pauline conception of the Church as the body of all Christians. The Roman and the Pauline conception of a corporation fused with an ease which was indeed most remarkable. Society came from now on to be viewed as the Christian body public, wherein the accent lay on the 'body'. Government and society—monarchy and the corporational structure of society—formed henceforth the backbone of governmental practice and science, and both manifested Roman and Christian elements to an equal degree. They were a perfect match, a pregnant amalgamation and a fertile combination.[1]

By granting the Church the status of a legal-corporate personality Constantine integrated it into the Roman body public. But this signified that the Church as a body now was subjected to the Roman public law of which the emperor had always been the source. And an essential part of the Roman public law was the so-called *ius in sacris*,[2] that is, the law relative to sacred and religious matters as well as to the administrators of sacred cults (the priests), which indeed was the constitutional basis of the emperor as the *pontifex maximus*. Precisely because the Christians had so strongly endorsed the idea of the law and the divine origin of ruling power and had underscored the corporational character of the Church, the emperor had a legitimate claim to an undisputed supreme constitutional control over the Christian Church. And the utter simplicity of the Constantinian measure—a mere governmental decree[3]—revealed the maturity of thought and the ease of manipulation. The paradoxical situation resulting in a monopoly of governmental power ideologically advocated by the Christians themselves is worth pointing out, because it is hardly ever acknowledged.

[1] B. Biondi. *Il diritto romano cristiano*, 3 vols (1952–4).

[2] See Ulpian in Dig. I, 1.1(2): 'Publicum ius in sacris, in sacerdotibus, in magistratibus consistit.'

[3] Readily available in Lactantius, *De mortibus persecutorum*, c. 48 in *CSEL* 27, 2, 228f.

It was precisely in the exercise of his governing function that not only Christian councils were convoked by imperial decree (e.g. Nicaea in 325)[1] and other measures taken affecting the internal life of the Church, but also that Theodosius I decreed the Christian religion to be the sole recognized religion throughout the empire.[2] Moreover ecclesiastical officers (especially bishops and metropolitans) were appointed public functionaries by the emperor and therefore subjected to the code for the imperial civil service. The greater the public role of the ecclesiastical officers became, the greater was the scope for imperial intervention—for in his monarchic status nothing had changed—and the more insistently the question was asked: by what right, by what title-deed, on what basis, did the imperial government proceed in controlling the Church? How was the appointment, dismissal and transfer of ecclesiastical officers by the emperor justified? Was he entitled to convoke councils and issue proclamations which were to all intents and purposes dogmatic pronouncements? How could all this be squared with the basic assumption that the emperor did not only not stand above the Church, but was very much within the Church (St Ambrose)?[3]

In the Western half of the empire especial functions had been laid upon the Church of Rome, and it was within the local Roman Church that these questions came to be raised. Partly as a result of the geographical and physical distance between the capital of the empire (Constantinople) and the resultant difficulty of communication, partly as a result of a fairly well-developed internal organization of this local Church and its advanced institutional set-up, the Roman Church (which by the fifth century had become known as the papacy) had been made aware of its own importance as well as of its potentialities and standing within the Church universal. There had also developed a respectable doc-

---

[1] Decrees in *Decreta* 4ff.

[2] Theodosius' decree *Cunctos populos* in Cod. I, 1.1.

[3] For this statement see Ambrose in his Ep. 21, c. 36 in *PL* 16, 1007; the emperor was '*intra* ecclesiam, non supra ecclesiam'. About these essentially juristic questions cf. G. d'Ercole, 'Storica antica della chiesa e problematica giuridica' in *SDHI* 29 (1963) 326ff (àpropos P. Brezzi's *Fonti della chiesa* (1962)).

trinal body nourished by Platonic cosmology and its attendant theme of totality or indivisibility according to which no distinction could be drawn between religion, politics, ethics, and so on. Hence Christianity was claimed to seize the whole of man, and his activities could not be atomized into various categories.[1]

According to this wholeness point of view, propounded above all by the papacy in the fifth century, the Church universal was a new society altogether, composed as it was of beings who through baptism had shed their 'naturalness' and had become 'new creatures', 'new men' altogether.[2] By losing their naturalness, they had entered a divinely created society—the Church—which followed its own principles, its own norms; in short, to the 'new creature' corresponded a new society and a new way of life, the *novitas vitae*.[3] Its basis was the Bible. Its members were subjected to the laws as given by divinity and made known through the qualified officers. And one of the conclusions that was drawn, concerned the very question of government. Here it was above all the papacy which was able to call upon a respectable body of scholarly opinion—Tertullian, Cyprian, Lactantius, Jerome, Ambrose,[4] and numerous others—supported as it was by its own governmental manifestations in the shape of decretals which authoritatively claimed that this new society must be governed in accord with biblical precept. The Matthean passage (16, 18f) was from the late fourth century on adduced to show that the new society was to be monarchically governed.[5] Thereby the

---

[1] For this wholeness point of view cf. *PGP* 33f, 97f, 234ff. Cf. the instance in *PG* 20 n. 1.

[2] Cf., e.g. St Paul, I Cor. 2, 14; II Cor. 5, 17; Gal. 5, 24 and 6, 15; Col. 2, 12; Tit. 3, 5.

[3] Rom. 6, 4.

[4] Lactantius: informative account in *DAC* VIII, 1018ff; *DTC* VIII, 2425ff; *LTK* VI, 726ff; cf. J. Speigl, 'Zum Kirchenbegriff des Laktanz' in *RQ* 65 (1970) 15ff; Jerome: *DTC* VIII, 894ff; Ambrose: *RAC* I, 365ff.

[5] Of vital significance was the Pseudo-Clementine Letter transl. from the Greek into Latin in the early years of the 5th cent. Ed. B. Rehm, *Die Pseudoklementinen* (1952) with Greek and Latin texts. Details: W. Ullmann, 'The significance of the Ep. Clementis' in *JTS* n.s. 11 (1960) 295ff; also id., in *Studia Patristica*, IV (1961) 330ff. Cf. also A. Rimoldi, *L'apostolo s. Pietro* (1958).

Bible became an indispensable source of governmental ideas. A reply to the questions asked could also be given, for this new society presupposed that its laws were issued by those who had special knowledge—a further Platonic element—and in fact had special qualifications for government.

The immediate result of this argumentation was that the emperor's role as monopolistic governor of the Church was denied on grounds of insufficient qualification: it was the pope on whose behalf the argument was advanced that as the sole successor of St Peter he alone was entitled to issue laws and to govern the Christian body public at least as far as its basic concerns demanded. It was on the question of governing the Church universal that the imperial government at Constantinople and the papal government in Rome parted ways in the fifth century. The split was to reverberate through the centuries, and was to determine the path of Europe for the subsequent millenium, if not beyond.[1]

The gulf that revealed itself starkly by the mid-fifth century, showed what deep fissures separated East and West, and nowhere was the chasm deeper and more noticeable than in respect of the character of society. For in Constantinople the Roman empire continued as a historic entity, and was therefore governed by the laws and the constitution germane to it. In the West the Church considered itself as the body of Christians and consequently not as a continuation of the ancient Roman empire: it was, and viewed itself as, a new society that was to be governed by the principles germane to it. This meant the abandonment of the ancient foundations of the Roman empire and their replacement by Christian tenets, maxims and aims which because of their divine origin were inaccessible to man's intervention or modification. Government within this thought-pattern concerned itself with the translation of religious precepts into legal precepts, and it was precisely in this very context that the principle of functional qualification entered. None of this applied to the East.

Indubitably, there was some superficial similarity between the

[1] For the background *SHP* 17ff; also *PG* 8ff.

monarchic system as propounded by the papacy and that practised by the empire. Both were the emanations of the wholeness point of view; both considered the individual a subject, and not a citizen with full autonomous rights and endowed with independence;[1] both applied the descending theme of government and law.[2] The similarity which in some instances amounted to a parallelism extending to terminology should not, however, lead to the assumption that there was also identity of meaning. The essential point is that in order to express its own governmental ideas the papacy made large-scale borrowings from the Roman institutions, administration and language, but this did not entail that these Roman institutions and papal institutions bore the same meaning when used by the papacy as a governing organ. The linguistic expression was frequently enough the same, and yet the thing to be expressed differed according to the imperial and papal usage. The difference concerned nothing less than the source or basis of the respective governmental system, and allied to this the purpose, the end, the *telos* or *finis* of the government and its law.[3]

As pointed out, the source of the imperial government's standpoint was the ancient Roman constitution. The basis of the papal government's standpoint was the Bible. The monopolization of the Bible as the source of governmental doctrine and decisions resulted in the tension between Constantinople and Rome growing deeper and deeper because the articulate pronouncements and the attempted application of biblical principles had as a necessary sequel the denial of the emperor's right to govern the Church, of which he was, with great insistence, said to be no

[1] Cf. *IS* 10ff.

[2] O. Treitinger, *Die oströmische Reichs- und Kaiseridee*, 2nd ed. (1956); and now H.-G. Beck, 'Res publica Romana' in *SB Munich* (1970), fasc. 4 concerning the ideas of the Byzantines on matters of public government. For the background see now P.-P. Joannou, *Die Ostkirche und die cathedra Petri im 4. Jahrhundert* (1972).

[3] J. Gaudemet, *La formation du droit séculier et du droit de l'église au IVe et Ve siècles* (1957). For the legal–ideological background cf. L. Buisson, 'Die Entstehung des Kirchenrechts' in *SavZ. KA* 52 (1966) 1ff (a very important analysis). For the legally binding character of canonical rules see P. Fedele in *ED* XII (1964) 871ff.

more than its member, however exalted his public standing and function might have been.[1] As far as the West was concerned— and it is this alone which is of interest in the present context—the Bible began to enter its triumphant career as an inexhaustible source of governmental thought after it had been rendered into Latin by the turn of the fourth and fifth centuries. St Jerome's translation became the Vulgate.[2] It is therefore advisable to make some observations on the Bible as the source of inspiring governmental ideas: it cannot be strongly enough stressed that it was the most influential source of governmental ideas in the Middle Ages, whether in the royal, ecclesiastical, imperial, ducal, or episcopal fields. The Latin Bible fertilized the fallow soil in Western Europe with the very ideas which were to crystallize into governmental principles.[3] The complexion of the society into which the trans- lated Bible was injected assumed a thorough-going Latin quality —in sharp contrast to the East which was and remained Greek.

The resistance to the imperial scheme of government by the West began at exactly the same time as a polished Latin translation from the Hebrew and Greek text of the Bible became available. Resistance was to grow into opposition. The Latin Bible was suffused with notions, ideas and quite specific linguistic expressions which had been taken from the Roman constitution and law. It was the language of the cultured and educated classes of the late fourth century. This infusion of Roman law and jurisprudence into the Bible succeeded all the more easily, as the Old Testa- ment in particular was thoroughly permeated with legalism. The soaking of the biblical text with Roman terminology and ideas conveyed overtones and undertones which quite ostensibly flavoured the very meaning of many crucial passages. Since the Bible was held to be the very fount of all Christian life, the

[1] Cf. the documents assembled by H. Rahner, *Kirche und Staat im frühen Christentum* (1962) 75ff and 205ff.

[2] The Vulgate text to be used is that ed. by Clement VIII and repr. numerous times. The new ed. of the *Vetus Latina* under the direction of Bonifacius Fischer is in progress.

[3] Cf. among many studies R. Manselli, 'Gregorio Magno e la Bibbia' in *La Bibbia nell' alto medio evo: Settimana Spoleto* (1963) 67ff.

government and law that were based on it, exhibited the same traits which have already been mentioned, that is, that the Christian theme as derived from it affected the whole of the body public and the whole being of its individual members.[1] This wholeness point of view had its ostensible source in Christianity as presented by the professional interpreters of the Bible. The 'totality' of the theme was reflected in the totality of the law which governed Christian society. This consideration will make understandable the crucial role which the ecclesiastics were to assume in the course of time: they alone were credited with the correct interpretation of the Bible, because they had the necessary educational and intellectual equipment and also the charismatic functional qualification for laying down the principles upon which the government of a Christian society should proceed. In a word, the Bible, precisely because it was the omnipotent source, created a virtually monopolistic position for the ecclesiastics. In practice this was the higher clergy, to wit the bishops.

The overpowering influence of the Vulgate as a source of governmental principles—hardly acknowledged by present-day medievalists—becomes explicable if three main considerations are adequately assessed. The first is that the earlier Roman occupation of large parts of Western Europe had prepared the soil for the reception of Romanized biblical ideas conveyed as they were in the Vulgate. This factual situation provides so to speak the concrete background and was evidently a presupposition. The second is that Christianity itself first became known to the West in its Latin clothing: even before the full text of the Vulgate became available in the Western regions, individual biblical items had been disseminated in the West in their Latin-Roman form: this feature potently fructified the ground for the view that the Bible

[1] For some details cf. C. G. Mor, 'La Bibbia e il diritto canonico' in *Settimana*, cit. 163ff; W. Ullmann, 'The Bible and principles of government in the MA' ibid 181ff; R. Kottje, *Studien zum Einfluss des Alten Testaments auf Recht und Liturgie des frühen MA* (1964); P. E. Schramm, 'Das Alte und das Neue Testament in der Staatslehre und Staatssymbolik des MA' in his *Kaiser, Könige und Päpste* IV, 1 (1970) 123ff; for the specifically legal contents of the New Testament see J. Duncan M. Derret, *Law in the New Testament* (1970), though this does not deal with public law or government.

was the only book that contained the sum-total of divine wisdom. And this was communicated in Latin terms which transmitted the divine word in a thoroughly Roman guise. It really does not need much historical imagination to visualize the depth of impact which so rich a source was to make on contemporary Western man. For the first time he was confronted by the whole corpus of divine wisdom—and this in a language of which he himself had only a most imperfect command. But to medieval man this was the language of divinity: of the character of the Vulgate as a translation there was no awareness.

The third consideration is that the West, in so far as it can be spoken of as an entity in the early medieval period, had no history and no identity of its own. If due weight is attached to this, one begins to realize the comparative ease with which the Bible conquered the West. For it conveyed not only the divine word, but it was also presented as a book that contained a programme and had a plan according to which society should be shaped if it wished to be Christian. The point to be borne in mind here is that the transmitting organs of the Vulgate, that is the ecclesiastics, were also its interpreters. In the way in which the Vulgate was handled in the West, it skilfully implanted the idea of a society that was held together not by force, but by law. And if contemporary society was to be shaped according to Christian principles, it became evidently necessary to model the law on the Bible. Hence the extremely close reliance on the Vulgate by the chancery personnel: the Marculf Formulae of the seventh and eighth centuries are one such example; the Anglo-Saxon laws are another.[1] The chancery personnel was the human contingent which made use of the Bible to a quite astonishing extent: after all, it was they who had to draft the laws and the charters of the ruling kings and bishops. Because the Latinized Bible was the handbook of government, Western Europe was slowly to acquire an identity of its own, at least in governmental respects, and in course of time was also to have a history of its own. The role of

[1] Details below, 198, 201. See further S. Meurer, *Das Recht im Dienst der Versöhnung und des Friedens: Studie zur Frage des Rechts nach dem Neuen Testament* (1972).

the Vulgate in this coagulating process should be properly appreciated. Despite different physical, geographical, climatic conditions and also divergent social developments in Western Europe, the Bible provided the one common bond between tribes, nations, provinces and regions. Even though the Visigoths were vastly superior in their public government and administration to, say, the Anglo-Saxons or Franks, they all nevertheless spoke the common language of the Bible.

As a source the Vulgate assumes significance also in another respect, that is, as a transmitter of the Roman law. This role of the Vulgate as a harbinger of Roman jurisprudence is another point which is hardly acknowledged: there are many features which become understandable only if this role is adequately appraised.[1] Partly by virtue of the legalism displayed in the Old Testament,[2] and partly by virtue of the Roman legal terminology employed, the Vulgate inconspicuously but all the more effectively fertilized and cultivated the soil for the actual reception of Roman law itself from the eleventh century onwards. If the educated classes had not been familiar with the Vulgate, and therefore had not absorbed its Roman jurisprudential wealth, this reception would not have been as quick, painless and thorough as in fact it was. Roman law was so to speak transmitted under cover of the Bible.[3]

The influence of the Vulgate as a source can be also measured conversely, if one glances at the low state of affairs in regard to Roman law in the Scandinavian countries: Roman influence there was in no wise comparable to that observable in the West and South of Europe. The explanation is that the Vulgate did not become known in the North until very much later than anywhere

[1] Cf. my observations in *Atti Io congresso internaz. di storia del diritto* (1966) 195ff, at 210ff.

[2] See O. Weber, *The groundplan of the Bible* (ET 1959) who rightly points out the wholeness standpoint pervading the Old Testament. See further for the legalism of the Old Testament M. Konvitz in *The Jews, their history, culture and religion*, ed. L. Finkelstein, 3rd ed. (1961) II, 1448ff. ('Judaism is a law-centred religious civilization . . . the procedure in the heavenly court is governed by law as in an earthly court').

[3] Cf. J. Chydenius, *Medieval Institutions and the Old Testament* (=Societas scientiarum Fennica, XXXVII, 2 (1965)).

else: it could not do the spadework. Again, the importance of the chancery personnel—themselves clerics of various ranks—as the actual organs of government charged with the framing of the law must be stressed. In the Bible they found a number of topics which were held to have direct relevance to public government, and these topics appeared as often as not in a Roman law garb. One might well say that the Vulgate received its eventual polish through its legal maxims having been expressed in the terminology of the Roman law. Further, there was also a mutual influence in so far as the later Roman and canon law studies were to flavour the interpretation of the Bible itself.[1]

This Latinized Bible also displayed effects in different directions which are particularly important in this present context. For it was axiomatic within the monotheistic framework that God was the governing organ of the cosmos. But this organ was not accessible to any subjective-human evaluations of a moral order or on a moral plane. What divinity had laid down, enacted, in short created, was unchangeable. There was a singularly unanimous agreement that the cosmos was based on an immutable, objective order, precisely because it emanated from absolute divinity. Consequently, the law that manipulated the cosmos partook of the objective features of the cosmos. On this basis human law could not contradict divine law as demonstrated in the Bible, and in some respects became, when once issued, part of the world order itself. In the last resort this is the explanation of why law in the Middle Ages assumed so crucial and overriding a role and was viewed with a respect which it has never since enjoyed.[2]

The significance of this biblically based standpoint was that law, as a force that regulated society, became independent of the organ that had in the first place issued it, independent of the law-giver himself. The already mentioned very marked objective standpoint advocated by Christian apologists, received precision and

---

[1] Cf. the all-too-brief remarks by E. Franceschini in *Settimana Spoleto*, cit., 13ff; further *F.-LeBr.* I, 91ff. Cf. also G. Le Bras, 'Les écritures dans le Décret Gratien' in *SavZ. KA.* 27 (1938) 45ff.

[2] On this feature cf. Calasso, *Medio evo* 474ff; *CR* 116ff and *PG* 370ff.

unassailable reinforcement as a result of the influence which the study of and penetration into the Bible exercised. And nothing makes for more stable and calm social conditions than the law when divorced from the lawgiver. In this scheme of things the lawgiver is merely an instrument of a cosmology or of governmental ideology. His product, the law, becomes the one integrating force of society which gains cohesiveness. And thereby its corporational character is also brought to fruition. These fundamental conceptions relative to the law, lawgiver and society make understandable the emphasis in the Bible as well as in later medieval doctrine on the objectively measurable *functions*, on the *office* (the usual term was: 'officio fungi') and on the rights and duties of the *gubernator* on the one hand[1] and the virtually negligible importance attributed to the latter's personality which was always accessible to infinitely variable subjective assessments and evaluations. The mature Roman law potently underpinned this biblical standpoint: as a law it focused attention not on the individual, but on the generality, on the *corpus* as a whole.

This strong entrenchment of the idea of law led to the maxim of the rule of law, the idea of the *Rechtsstaat*, perhaps best expressed in the allegorically conceived function of the law as the soul of the body public. Thereby sempiternity was conferred on the idea of law and the idea of society ruled by law: the supreme instance was held to be the message in the Matthean passage (16, 18f) according to which the Church possessed sempiternity, *because* founded on the Christgiven *law*.[2] The seventh-century Visigothic laws declared without much circumlocution that 'the law was the soul of the kingdom'.[3] Hence also the view of the indestructibility of kingdoms, empires, and so on, as long as they

---

[1] For the specifically Pauline background cf. I Cor. 12, 4ff ('different *ministries* . . . diversities of *operations*'); Eph. 1, 23; 4, 11, 16; 5, 23f; Rom. 12, 4 ('although we have many members in one *body*, not all have the same *office*') etc. Cf. also I Pet. 2, 13ff.

[2] Details in *IS* 46ff and *PK* 38ff; *CR* 177f; cf. alxo F. Nikolasch, 'Zur Deutung der Dominus-legem-dat Szene' in *RQ* 64 (1969) 35ff (instructive for the idea of the *Traditio legis*).

[3] *MGH. Leges Visigothorum*, I.2.2. On the implications P. D. King, *Law and Society in the Visigothic kingdom* (1972) 34ff.

rested on the law.[1] In brief, as a result of the influence which the Bible as a source of governmental conceptions exercised, the law was viewed as transpersonal and transhuman; it therefore conferred permanency, stability and order on societies which were ruled by it, and where otherwise there would have been nothing but instability and disorder. However, on the level of humanly created law the idea of the rule of law and of its ensuing stability does not necessarily mean its unchangeability and immutability: what was vital was that the social order rested upon the law.[2]

The idea of justice standing as it does in the ante-chamber of the law, was as strongly marked in the Bible as it was in Roman law. Roman jurisprudence provided the technical tools with which to express the biblical idea of justice in a suitable manner, and it was once more this combination which potently directed the path of the development of governmental principles in the Middle Ages. Since law was the prime vehicle by which government was to be exercised, it had to embody the idea of justice, and since the society in question was Christian the contents of justice were orientated by Christian doctrines and derived, in this respect too, their main ingredients from the Bible. And once again the objective character of justice stood in the foreground. What mattered was the objective validity of the law based on the objectively measurable Christian justice. This biblical foundation of basic jurisprudential concepts brought once more into prominence the principle of functional qualification, and in a roundabout way the governmentally and socially relevant standing of the (higher) clergy. In short, the influence of the Vulgate on the virgin soil of Western Europe culminated in the all-pervading view of

[1] Expressed in such ever recurring phrases as 'regnum (ecclesia) mori non potest'. This led without great difficulty to the view of the corporation as a juristic person. Cf. Maitland's introduction to his translation of Gierke, *The political theories of the MA* (repr. 1938) vii–xlv. Cf. also J. H. Franklin, *Jean Bodin and the rise of the absolutist theory* (1973) 109ff (on perpetuity).

[2] On this cf. H. Krause, 'Dauer und Vergänglichkeit im ma. Recht' in *Sav ZGA* 75 (1958) 206ff; R. Sprandel, 'Ueber das Problem neuen Rechts im MA' ibid., *KA* 48 (1962) 117ff; H. M. Klinkenberg, 'Die Theorie der Veränderbarkeit des Rechts im frühen und hohen MA' in *Misc. Med.* VI (=*Lex et Sacramentum im MA*) (1969) 157ff.

the wholeness of man: Christianity and herewith the law based on it, were to demand the whole of man. It is certainly true that the full implementation of the postulates derived from the Bible and expressed in law had at times an air of unreality which was however merely another manifestation of the deeply biblical-Christian axiom that custom, history, tradition, were to be conquered in their effectiveness by the word—and the law was (and is) little more than the word: 'in principio erat verbum'. Its effectiveness depends on the force with which it is credited.

The biblically engendered legalism had one facet to which special importance should be attached in the present context. The wholeness standpoint also explained the 'openness' of medieval law: in order to accommodate a great many divergent social systems the law had to manifest a corresponding flexibility so that it was if necessary, capable of absorbing alien matter. This capacity for absorption was particularly necessary in regard to non-Christian elements and usages.[1] It was indeed a singularly adjustable law to which the Bible with the help of Roman jurisprudence had given birth—one has but to think of the ease with which the Germanic *Munt*, the Roman *tutela* and the Pauline guardianship could be amalgamated to form one of the most important governmental principles in the Middle Ages.[2]

Yet it would be wholly erroneous to think that the Bible set forth anything like a governmental theory or supplied something approaching a blueprint in regard to matters of public government. True, there were certain topics and themes such as the monarchic form of government and the corresponding descending theme of government and law, the conception of the individual as a subject, the principles of obedience, public necessity and utility, functionalism and the dovetailing of functions within

[1] On this process cf. I. Herwegen, *Germanentum und Christentum* (1932); K. F. Stroheker, *Germanentum und Spätantike* (1955); F. Calasso, *Medio evo* 118 ff; P. Koschaker, *Europa und das römische Recht*, 2nd ed. (1953) 18ff. R. Folz (et al.), *De l'antiquité au monde médiéval* (1972) 86ff.

[2] Cf. H. Löwe in Gebhardt's *Handbuch der deutschen Geschichte*, ed. H. Grundmann, 9th ed. (1970), I, 90ff (with copious lit.); also *CR* 177ff; and W. Ullmann, 'Schranken der Königsgewalt im MA' in *HJb*, 91 (1971) 1ff, esp. 14ff. (Gal. 4, 1f).

a corporate body, the emphasis on the office and on the *ministerium*, and so on. It is at best described as a guidebook or a handy reference book which furnished some basic general principles to be worked out in detail: it provided the scaffolding but was not the building. The elaboration of these general guidelines was left to the governments themselves and to scholarship. It was precisely in this context that biblical principles experienced adjustment and accommodation to the exigencies of contemporary social life.

CHAPTER 2

The Roman Law

Among the legal systems in medieval Europe Roman law assumed an importance superior to all: its impact upon governmental practice and science was without parallel. This is partly because Roman law was a mature expression of the most Roman of all Roman ideas—the idea of law and order; partly because of the influence it exercised directly or through the medium of the Bible; and partly as the instrument that forged social relations, shaped intellectual habits and created a mode of thinking which was unique in the history of civilization. It indelibly imprinted its seal on the physiognomy of what came to be Western Europe and in fact played a major role in its making. The Roman law in the shape it received in Justinian's codification[1]—and it is this which commonly represents Roman law—embodied a great many governmental ideas and principles as they came to be evolved in late republican and especially in imperial times. Whether this Roman law had all the superlative qualities with which some legal historians have credited it may be open to doubt, but what matters is not so much the intrinsic quality of this law, which certainly was very high, but the influence which it exercised on the evolution of governmental practice and theory. Within the ambit of governmental science it is not the technicalities of Roman law as a positive law which demand attention, but the general jurisprudential axioms and principles enshrined in it. As Maitland once expressed it, Europe without the Digest would not be the Europe that we know. The great savant did not mean to refer to the Digest in the technical sense, but to the whole *Corpus*

[1] For a full bibliography of the sources concerning classical and Justinianean law, see P. Stein in *Bibliographical Introduction to legal history and ethnology*, ed. J. Gilissen, sect. A5 (1965); L. Wenger, *Die Quellen des Römischen Rechts* (1953) is indispensable.

Iuris Civilis of which indeed the Digest formed an essential part.[1]

The explanation of how the Roman law exercised this enduring influence on medieval and partly also on modern Europe is intimately linked with the opening up of the fallow Western soil to basic Roman ideas and institutions: it was the missionaries in the late sixth century who brought with them the Roman law which in any case had already been administered in Roman Gaul and especially later in the possessions and patrimonies of the Roman Church in Gaul. Therefrom the principle was evolved that 'the Church lives according to the Roman law' (*ecclesia vivit iure Romano*).[2] In itself it was evidently so superior to the half-barbarian (customary) law of the Teutonic tribes that no worth-while obstacles retarded its progress. In juristic respects it was technically and materially immeasurably in advance of anything the illiterate West had experienced. Moreover, it was written in the same Latin language in which the Christian faith was propagated and conveyed to the educated sections. And there was, as has already been observed, a certain internal and ideological kinship between the Bible and Roman law. These features, together with the high degree of juristic expertise, élan and elegance that characterized Roman law, make understandable why it exercised an irresistible influence in early medieval Europe. At least in ideological respects a great deal of Europe was shaped by the Roman law in its Justinianean codification.[3]

[1] For general surveys cf. H. Dannenbauer, *Die Entstehung Europas: von der Spätantike zum MA*: vol. I: *Der Niedergang der alten Welt im Westen* (1959); G. Astuti, *Lezioni di storia del diritto italiano*, vol. I: *Le fonti: età romano-barbarica* (1953); L. Wenger, *Quellen*, cit. 299ff; P. Koschaker, *Europa und das römische Recht*, 2nd ed. (1954); F. Wieacker, *Privatrechtsgeschichte*, cit. (above, 28 n. 1), 26ff, and id. 'Allgemeine Zustände und Rechtszustände gegen Ende des weströmischen Reichs' in *IRMAE*, I, 2a (1963); A. Momigliano, 'L'età del trapasso' in *Riv. storica italiana* 81 (1969) 286ff.

[2] Stated in the *Lex Ribuaria*, the law for some of the Frankish regions (ca. 741), cap. 58, 1, ed. *MGH Leges* V, 185ff.

[3] For a succinct survey see H. F. Jolowicz, *Hist. Introduction to the study of Roman law*, 3rd ed. by B. Nicholas (1972) 478ff, 505ff; further B. Bondi, *Giustiniano primo principe e legislatore catolico* (1936); now G. Archi, *Giustiniano legislatore* (1970).

This codification was begun in 527-8 by the appointment of a commission under the chairmanship of Tribonian.[1] The finished product (534) consisted of three main parts, of which the Digest and the Code were quantitatively and qualitatively the bulk and core of the whole *corpus*. The Digest or Pandects (meaning the complete body of law) (published 533) contained basic juris-prudential principles and divisions, but overwhelmingly consisted of private law. Strictly speaking, the Digest was a collection which was made up of fragments, snippets and excerpts of varying length from the statements of the jurists of the period between the second and fourth centuries.[2] These excerpts referred to the law of persons and things, family law, the law of inheritance, the condi-tions of men, their status, and the relevant legal transactions which occurred in civilized communities. What, however, was always of prime importance was the so-called general part, that is to say the first books: they dealt with general principles, such as the definition of the law, its divisions and sub-divisions, the law-creative power of public organs in the late republic and early empire, the enforcement of the law, procedural maxims, delictal responsibility, and so on. Almost all of the jurists occupied public judicial positions and many were intimately connected with government, though their views had not the force of law. It was not until Justinian that the thousands of excerpts acquired legal, that is enforceable, character by his specific imperial decree (*Tanta* of 17 December 533, §23). What the historian of law and politics has always to keep in mind is that very few legal details were directly applicable to conditions in medieval Europe, and these could be applied only after the appropriate scholarly inter-pretation. The general juristic principles contained in the Digest were seminal and also fructified other intellectual disciplines. The compilation was divided into fifty books which were sub-divided

---

[1] For all details see L. Wenger, *Quellen* cit. (above, 53 n. 1), 562ff (fundamen-tal); further A. Honoré and A. Rodger, 'How the Digest commissioners worked' in *SavZRA*, 87 (1970) 246ff.

[2] About the jurists of the classical period cf. F. Schulz, *Hist. of Roman legal science* (1946); L. Wenger, *Quellen*, cit. 286ff; H. F. Jolowicz, *Lectures on Jurisprudence*, ed. J. A. Jolowicz (1963) 40ff.

into titles and these into *leges*. There was some attempt to systematize all the sayings of the classical jurists: these ceased to be pure opinion and became enforceable law (the *leges*) by Justinian's Edict of publication.

One or two examples should suffice to show in what ways the Digest exercised influence within the framework of governmental principles. As one of the great medieval problems was the seat of the law-creative organ, the concept of jurisdiction was evidently very much in the foreground because it signified the authoritative fixation of what was right or wrong: the exercise of jurisdiction was equivalent to law-creative power. In this respect, however, jurisdiction was only a species of the wider and generic concept of *imperium* which conferred enforceability on the law. But since in the late Roman empire the *princeps* (emperor) embodied all power, the question that engaged the jurists concerned the basis of his power and authority. Ulpian (d. 228 A.D.), one of the most eminent classical jurists, referred to the so-called *lex regia*, according to which the Roman people had transferred all its powers to the Ruler.[1] In other words, the ascending theme of government and law was said to have been operational in the republican period: the Roman people were said to have voluntarily renounced its own powers and to have handed them over to the prince. That this was a constructive device to soothe troubled juristic consciences seems evident, but the explanation served its purpose well enough. In the medieval period, when the Roman law became the subject of scholarly analysis, this *lex regia* played a very great role and in the hands of the scholars became a major instrument with which to restrict monarchic powers. The power which the Roman people had originally possessed was the *imperium* (which had obviously nothing to do with an 'empire'); it was the sum-total of unappealable governmental, that is, jurisdictional power which served to fix and formulate binding rules in the shape of the law.

Since this *imperium* comprehended the supreme power to lay down the law, by the operation of the *lex regia* the Ruler's will

[1] Justinian himself invoked it in his edict appointing Tribonian and his commission: *Deo auctore* of December 530, §7.

became the essential ingredient of the law. This is exactly what the same Ulpian in the same passage tells us: any statement which the Ruler wished to have the force of law, was universally binding: 'legem esse constat'.[1] 'What pleases the prince, has the force of law' was an axiom that was firmly and explicitly anchored in the Digest. It was not a legislative declaration by a law-creative organ, but an explanation and interpretation by a jurist which Justinian adopted. The binding rules thus created by the Ruler, said Ulpian, were commonly called 'constitutions'. And quite in agreement with this basic standpoint was the sequel that 'the prince was not bound by the laws' as the same Ulpian plainly stated:[2] this expressed nothing else but the personal sovereignty of the Ruler, because he alone was the source of the law and therefore stood outside and above the people: he formed (in medieval terminology) an estate of his own.[3]

There was one more basic topic that exercised great influence on the development of governmental ideas. The so-called *Lex Rhodia*[4] (D. 14, 2, 9) contained the statement that the emperor was the *Dominus mundi*: this was the theme which was to gain ever greater and more topical significance in both Byzantium and the medieval West. Since the Roman emperor was the 'lord of the world' and since for both East and West the same Roman law was the commonly accepted law, it assuredly would have been a contradiction in terms if there had been two lords of the world each claiming universality of jurisdiction and dominion. Yet this was exactly the case once there was a Roman emperor in the West from the ninth century onwards. Scholarship (civilian as well as canonistic) based itself on this passage in the Digest to

---

[1] Dig. 1, 4, 1; also Justinian himself in the edict cit., §7 in fine.

[2] Dig. 1, 3, 1: 'Princeps legibus solutus est.' It should nevertheless be borne in mind that Justinian's compilers omitted the context in which Ulpian had made the statement. But as it stood, the statement could be credited with all the appurtenances of absolutism. For the interpretation at the hands of the civilian glossators, cf. B. Tierney, 'The prince is not bound by the laws' in *Comparative Studies in Society and History* V (1963) 388ff(=*AA* 1245ff).

[3] *HPT* 54ff, 132ff; also *PK* 51ff.

[4] On the law and its background cf. F. M. de Robertis, 'Lex Rhodia: critica e anticritica su D.14.2.9' in *Studi V. Arangio-Ruiz* III (1955) 155ff.

maintain not only the legitimacy of the emperor in the West as the sole 'lord of the world' but also his superiority (=sovereignty) over all other kings and Rulers, including the Byzantine emperor. This passage in the Digest furnishes the explanation on a governmental basis for the ever widening gulf between East and West.

While the topics so far mentioned concerned the totality of the Ruler's power, it should nevertheless be pointed out that the Digest also contained topics which could be utilized, as indeed they were, in the service of restricting the Ruler's powers. For instance, the very prominent place which the Digest gave to the institution of tutorship in Rome was applied to Rulership itself in the medieval period.[1] In practice since the ninth century, and in scholarship since the twelfth, the Ruler was seen as a tutor of the kingdom, and in this function his duty was to preserve the kingdom intact and to keep it unharmed. This function militated against any alienation by the Ruler of goods, estates, rights which were inherent parts of the kingdom (or empire), in other words, which were public. The tutorial function of the Ruler was the most effective bar against irresponsible rulership.[2] The principle of inalienability has one of its roots in the tutor which the Roman law provided for minors under age, orphans, etc. Nevertheless, this adoption and application of the Roman tutorship had additional significance in so far as it shows how a purely private law function was transferred to the public law: the sphere of the Roman tutor was exclusively within the Roman private law. This transfer of private law institutions to the medieval public law was a most noteworthy feature.[3] Yet on the other hand the tutorial function of the Ruler proved itself a rather effective

[1] Dig. 26, 4. 1–5; 26, 8 p.t.; Inst. 1, 21; cf. also Dig. 44, 7. 5(1).

[2] For some details cf. *CR* 176ff.

[3] Ibid., 182ff and additional note 183 n. 1. It should be noted that the prohibition of alienation was, on the same basis, and for the same reasons, transferred to ecclesiastical officers, such as bishops. Cf. Th. Gottlob, *Der kirchliche Amtseid* (repr. 1963) 11ff; W. Ullmann, 'A note on inalienability in Gregory VII' in *St. Greg.* IX (1971) (=Memorial Volume for G. B. Borino) 115ff; id., 'Schranken der Königsgewalt im MA' in *HJb* 91 (1971) 1ff, esp. 15ff. In his article on inalienability in *St. Grat.* XI (1967) 491ff, G. Post is quite unaware of the wider background.

impediment to the release of the people from the Ruler's 'tutelage'. While the tutorial function effectively restricted the Ruler, it did not assist the process by which the people itself attained 'majority', for the very idea of a tutor presupposed a minor under age in whose interests the tutor acted. The more effective the Ruler's tutorial function was, the more conspicuous became the people's 'minority', and therefore the greater were the obstacles which retarded the emergence of the abstract notion of the State.[1]

As far as fundamental jurisprudential concerns come into question, throughout the medieval period the West of Europe was the disciple of ancient-pagan Rome. Next to the Bible, the Digest proved itself the most resilient, creative and influential formative organ to which the still half-barbaric West was subjected, and this in precisely those matters which constituted civilized living together. Since jurisprudential axioms which the Digest embraced shaped the physiognomy and complexion of Western Europe to a hitherto still not fully acknowledged extent, it is not indeed surprising to find that governmental practice and doctrine were unfamiliar with the very concept and term of 'political': the term did not occur in the vast body of the Roman law.

The second large part of Justinian's *Corpus Iuris Civilis* was the Code, divided into 12 books and these again subdivided into titles and individual laws.[2] Its basic difference from the Digest was that while this contained extracts from the writings of the classical Roman jurists, the Code had an altogether different character: the laws in it were either formal imperial constitutions or rescripts despatched by the emperors themselves to imperial officers—for instance, provincial governors—which contained the reply to some controversial point of law or to questions that

[1] For some details cf. W. Ullmann, 'Juristic obstacles to the emergence of the concept of the State in the MA' in *Annali di storia del diritto*, 13 (1969) 43ff (=Memorial Volume for Francesco Calasso). See further L. Ejerfeldt, 'Myths of the State in the West-European MA' in *Myths of the State*, ed. H. Biezais. (=Scripta instituti Donneriani Aboensis, vol. VI (1972)) 160ff.

[2] First published 529, second recension 534; see L. Wenger, *Quellen* cit. (above, 53 n. 1), 569ff, 638ff; further S. Solazzi, 'Costituzioni glosate e interpolate nel Codex' in *SDHI* 24 (1959) 1ff.

had arisen in the actual application of the law. These rescripts were the expression of the imperial law-creative will and were therefore law in any case. And because the emperors had universality of jurisdiction, their laws had universal applicability. What therefore the Code technically transmitted was simply the collection of thousands of relevant imperial legislative measures or excerpts from the sometimes lengthy enactments which were thus made easily available within one volume. While they had legal validity before the codification, the jurists' excerpts as mere private opinions in the Digest were raised to the level of law by special imperial decree of Justinian.

In subject-matter too there was a great difference between the Code and the Digest. The former did not—as the latter did— treat of general jurisprudential principles, but stated the law as given by the emperors down to and including Justinian. In fact, the Code opens with the law by Theodosius the Great which made the Christian religion the sole religion of the empire. This law gave additional proof of the universality of the emperor's jurisdiction and function as the head of the oikumene of which the Church was an integral part. The first book of the Code (the first title of which was 'On the Trinity, the Catholic faith and the prohibition of public discussion concerning the faith') dealt with ecclesiastical matters, such as the qualification and suitability of bishops and clerics for their office, detailed elements of the faith, episcopal jurisdiction, clerical privileges, the nature of heresy and the treatment of heretics, Jews and pagans, the right of asylum, and similar related topics. Other legislative enactments in the first book concern law-creative organs, the judicial machinery, public officers (notably the *defensores civitatis*)[1] and related topics. The other books contain official imperial law relating to all kinds of legal institutions and transactions as well as modifications, clarifications and amplifications of existing law.

Although the first book of the Code contained a great many principles of direct concern to governmental practice and doctrine, here too the very idea of terminology of 'political' or of 'politics' was absent. Yet the principle that pervades the first

[1] Cod. I, 55 p.t.

book (as of course is explicit or implicit in all the other books) is the function and authority of the emperors in ecclesiastical and religious matters. Together with the *Novellae* (to which we will presently turn) the Code was replete with measures which show the emperor as the sole law-creative organ. Although ideologically a good deal can be said in favour of the emperor as a king and priest (*rex-sacerdos*) this standpoint is, if at all, only faintly reflected in the Code. What on the other hand appears far more convincingly in the imperial laws is the constitutional standpoint according to which matters pertaining to the Church were matters falling within the precincts of the ancient Roman *ius in sacris* (or the *ius sacrum*) but this in turn was an integral part of the equally ancient Roman public law,[1] of which the source and fountain was the emperor. Hence the numerous interventions of the emperors in ecclesiastical matters (appointments, transfers and dismissals of high clerical officers, convocation of general councils, imperial jurisdiction over clerics, etc.): all these measures were based on the constitutional position of the (former) Roman emperor who was supreme priest (*pontifex maximus*). The only difference between the former emperor and the one depicted in the Code was that the latter was a christianized edition of the former: he spoke the same language; he employed the same symbolism; in his constitutional position nothing had changed; from his divine mouth poured forth (as of old) the *sacrae* or *sacratissimae* laws;[2] in fact he had increased his authority and weight by having become the kosmokrator—the world's Ruler— and thus the earthly representative of God, the Pantokrator. Hence he emerges in the laws as the *lex animata*, the personified law.[3] In a word, the emperor as depicted in the Code (and the *Novellae*) approached the essence of 'L'état c'est moi'.

[1] H. Siber, *Römisches Verfassungsrecht in geschichtlicher Entwicklung* (1952) esp. 249ff; also C. Nocera, 'Il pensiero pubblicistico romano' in *Studi P. Francisci* II (1956) 61ff; cf. also *SHP* 5ff, 23ff.

[2] Thus in Cod. I. 17, 1(6); his law a 'lex divalis' ibid. X. 35, 2; or as a 'divina sanctio' ibid. VII. 6, 34; imperial laws as 'sacratissimiae constitutiones' ibid. I. 17, 1(9) or as 'leges sacratissimae' ibid. I. 14, 9.

[3] See A. Steinwenter, 'Nomos empsychos' in *Anzeiger der Akademie der Wissenschaften Wien* 83 (1946) 250ff (fundamental).

Evidently, the Code was the place which demonstrated in almost classic form the working of the descending theme of government and law. The emperor was the law-*giver* and the subjects were the recipients of his laws. Law was conceived as a concession by the emperor (principle of concession): it was the means by which the Pantokrator ruled mankind through the kosmokrator. And just as no-one has a right to demand anything from divinity, in the same way the subjects had no right to demand any particular legal enactment. Jurisprudentially, the Code made clear three assumptions: the *will* of the Ruler to *concede* law to his *subjects*.

Terminology is always a good signpost to underlying conceptions. Imperial legislation (both in the Code and the *Novellae*) frequently enough used the term *legem ponere* for the process of creating the law. The term is precise, concise and succinct in regard to the antecedent mental process and the scope and extent of the rule thus enacted. The *lex posita* or the *ius posit[iv]um*— the law laid down—was what through a mistaken copying much later (in the twelfth century) became 'positive' law which should correctly be called posited law.[1] The opposite to 'positive' law was (and is) customary law which was a rule that became binding as a result of usages and practices by a group of people through a more or less well-defined stretch of time. Now the material ingredient of customary law was (and is) the will and consent of the relevant group of people to adhere to a particular practice and thus to turn it into a binding rule. Technically speaking, it was the will of the people (the *voluntas populi* in contrast to the *voluntas principis*) which endowed the usages and practices with legal character. Customary law demonstrated the efficacy of the ascending theme.[2] Consequently, the will of the people could

---

[1] For this see S. Kuttner, 'Sur les origines du terme droit positif' in *RHDFE* 15 (1936) 728ff. About the unfortunate attempt by S. Gagnér, *Studien zur Ideengeschichte der Gesetzgebung* (1960) cf. my review in *RHD* 29 (1961) 118ff; here also many examples of the common usage of *legem ponere* (125f) in early medieval law.

[2] For some details cf. *PGP* 281ff; for the doctrine of customary law in the MA see S. Brie, *Die Lehre vom Gewohnheitsrecht* (1898) (still fundamental); A. Steinwenter, 'Zur Lehre vom Gewohnheitsrecht' in *Studi Pietro Bonfante* II (1930) 421ff; F. Calasso *Medio evo* 181ff; for the relation of the medieval

nullify the law of the Ruler. The stark contrast between the descending and ascending themes of government is here nakedly revealed. 'Positive', that is enacted, law was *given* and understood as the Ruler's concession in the Code; it was a grant. Customary law was *made* by the subjects and came into being as a result of repeated performances and practices; its ingredient was the will of the people.

That the Ruler's law could be nullified by customary law was a contingency clearly envisaged by the Code. In order to defuse this potentially dangerous source of law—dangerous to the imperial-descending thesis—Constantine the Great expressly laid down that customary law could not derogate from positive written law.[1] This Constantinian law remained valid throughout the medieval period. Yet since on the plane of legal reality it was undeniable that customary law was for practical purposes, especially in the medieval period, far more relevant to the population at large, the fiction became law that the emperor had all the laws in his breast[2] which signified that the existing customary law displayed its force precisely because the Ruler tolerated and thus acquiesced in this state of affairs: if he had so wished he could have wiped it out. In a word, he was presumed to have had knowledge of all the valid law which evidently included the unwritten customary law. Later the pope was to apply this fiction to himself.

The governmental and legislative totality of power held by the Ruler as depicted in the Code proved an attraction to medieval Rulers, and in this lies an additional explanation for the longevity of its influence. What is rarely noticed is that the German kings were particularly prone to succumb to the influence of the Roman law, and quite especially the Code, because they held themselves successors of the ancient Caesars, although they had attained the imperial position through the instrumentality of the pope. They began to see the model of a Ruler in the Code and

king (as distinct from the emperor) to customary law see H. Krause, 'Königtum und Rechtsordnung' in *SavZGA* 82 (1965) 1ff, at 52ff, 91ff. See also B. Schmiedel, *Consuetudo im klassischen und nachklassischen Recht* (1966).

[1] Cod. VIII, 52, 2.   [2] Cod. VI, 23, 19.

attempted to emulate the function of the (ancient) Roman emperor as portrayed in this law-book. The imitative role adopted by the German kings as Roman emperors was a somewhat artificial device to assert a universality of dominion for which claim there would otherwise have been no justification. In the position which the Ruler, portrayed in the Code, had assumed towards the ecclesiastical body, lay a further incentive for the imitation of the Roman emperor. The German kings, having undergone a metamorphosis at the hands of the pope and having emerged as emperors of the Romans, persuaded themselves (and a good many contemporaries) that they were the true successors of the ancient Caesars, and hence had every right to call the Roman law their own: the insertion of medieval laws into the body of the Code is convincing witness to this standpoint as is also, from a formal-technical point of view, the beginning of a formal imperial legislation which coincided with the assumption of full Roman emperorship in the twelfth century.[1] Once more it becomes clear that the law, here the Code, played a vital role in the rivalry and conflict between East and West. Yet on closer inspection it is also clear that the Western emperors confused appearance with reality. No doubt, it was due to this confusion that the ideology underlying the Code became part and parcel of governments and strongly influenced the cultural standards of the time.[2]

These considerations are necessary in order to understand fully the process of imitation by the Western emperors. Since Justinian had an unbounded enthusiasm for legislative measures, the termination of his codificatory work in 534 provided only one phase of his legislative development: numerous and very lengthy laws were published throughout the subsequent 30 years of his reign.[3] They are the *Novellae* (=*novae leges*) and as imperial laws

---

[1] Evidently, from the material point of view there had been much imperial legislation before the 12th cent. See H. Krause, *Kaiserrecht & Rezeption* (1952) at 26ff.   [2] For this cf. *SHP* 182ff.

[3] F. A. Biener, *Geschichte der Novellen Justinians* (repr. 1970); also H. F. Jolowicz, *Hist. Introduction*, cit. (above, 54 n. 3) 496ff (important for transmission); especially L. Wenger, *Quellen*, cit. 652ff.

dealt with virtually all contemporary issues affecting the 'universal' empire. This supplementary legislation was in fact necessary, since Justinian had prohibited all interpretation of the laws. There never had been in the history of mankind a law that foresaw and provided for all contingencies which always made interpretation of the law a necessary by-product of any legislation, thus supplementing the law itself. But because he was the sole source of all law, he prohibited commentaries and demanded that all doubts concerning the application of law be referred back to him, so that formal supplementary legislation in the shape of his *Novellae* became a necessity.[1] Although laws in every sense of the term, they are more than that, because on closer inspection they are a mixture of law, legal instruction and legal philosophy to which should also be added a not inconsiderable amount of theological speculation set forth in the Arengae, that is, the very lengthy preambles to the individual laws. Some of them are extensive tracts and extend over a number of chapters. What strikes the reader of this source is Justinian's crucial concern with the twin concept of *Romanitas* and *Christianitas*.[2] Hence a disproportionate amount of the *Novellae* deals with purely ecclesiastical questions: they show the emperor in his function as source of the public law of which the (formerly so-called) *ius in sacris* formed an essential part. The universality of Roman jurisdiction and domain combined with the universality of the Christian idea of the sole monarch, the kosmokrator. The recurrent theme in the *Novellae*

[1] See his constitution *Tanta*, §21, where he took the opportunity of restating that solely the imperial majesty could settle doubts, since 'cui (scil. augustali maiestati) soli concessum est legem condere et interpretari'. In his own compilation he saw nothing but *consonantia* and *harmonia*. The concession principle was here widely extended. For some details see J. Gaudemet, 'L'empereur interprète du droit' in *Festschrift E. Rabel* (1954) 169ff.

[2] Cf. B. Biondi, 'Religione e diritto canonico nella legislazione di Giustiniano' in *ACII* I (1935) 99ff; also F. Wieacker, *Vom röm. Recht*, 2nd ed. (1961) 224ff; further G. Archi, *Giustiniano legislatore*, cit. (above, 54 n. 3) 105ff. Special attention is to be drawn to O. Treitinger, *Die oströmische Reichs- und Kaiseridee* 2nd ed. (1956) and E. Ivánka, *Rhomäerreich und Gottesvolk: das Glaubens-, Staats-, und Volksbewusstsein der Byzantiner* (1968); and H.-G. Beck, *Res publica Romana* cit. (above, 41 n. 2).

was that the emperor had the care and protection of the oikumene, its control and solicitude. His legislation provided the foundation for some of the basic views on the relations between the *imperium* and the *sacerdotium*.

The sixth *Novella*—altogether there are 168—can be called a basic constitutional law. In it Justinian amplified the reason for his control of the ecclesiastical organism and in so doing gave precision to the ancient point of view of the emperor as the fount of public-sacral law.[1] Since, according to him, both the *imperium* and the *sacerdotium* proceeded from one and the same source, there was nothing of greater concern to him than what he called 'the probity and good repute' of the priests. Hence the principle of suitability found here a very early concrete expression. It is impossible to exaggerate the importance and influence of this *Novella* which throughout the medieval period served as a classic model of how a secular government should proceed in managing a Christian society. With legal precision the power of the secular Ruler in ecclesiastical matters was here fixed.[2] It is nevertheless worth remarking that medieval doctrine and practice were oblivious of the actual Byzantine background of the *Novellae*. One is justified in saying that pure law divorced from its historical framework exercised potent influence in one of the most sensitive areas in the Middle Ages.

The significance of this source for the development of governmental ideas is only heightened if due consideration is given to the incorporation of numerous extracts from the *Novellae* into the body of the Code by later medieval scholarship, mainly at Bologna. The jurists inserted fragments into the appropriate places of the Code. This unofficial supplementation served how-

[1] This was a further reason for his ecclesiastical legislation. On this cf. also H. S. Alivisatos, *Die kirchliche Gesetzgebung Justinians* (1913); I. Balan, 'Leges Iustiniani de haereticis' in *ACII* I (1935) 481ff; G. Archi, 'Le classicisme de Justinien' in *RHDFE* 46 (1968) 579ff.

[2] Additional documentation in H. Rahner, *Kirche & Staat im frühen Christentum* (1961) 281ff; J. Gaudemet, *L'église dans l'empire romain* (1958); E. Schwartz, 'Zur Kirchenpolitik Justinians' in *Gesammelte Schriften* IV (1960) 276ff; L. Wenger, *Quellen* cit. 868ff, also 302 and 567. For some interpretative details cf. also *PG* 32ff.

ever as an example for the Staufen emperors to decree the insertion of their own laws into the Code as laws of the Roman emperors. Hence not infrequently the user of the Code will find sandwiched between a law of, say, Constantine and Valentinian a law issued by Frederick I—and unwary readers might well be forgiven for thinking that Frederick I preceded Valentinian. A fiction—that of the German emperor as a successor of the ancient Caesars—had been translated if not into reality, at any rate into the appearance of reality, by the vehicle of the law: assuredly this is one of the most fascinating phenomena in any historical jurisprudence and science of government. It was to a not negligible extent this fiction which stood at the cradle of what later became known as 'The Reception of Roman law in Europe'.

The last part of Justinian's work can be dealt with quickly. The *Institutes* were an officially decreed text-book of Roman law and had the force of law as the expression of the imperial legislator's will. It was very brief—four books only—and contained the main general principles relative to jurisprudence: it was the law book primarily intended for students of the law. From the legal point of view it set forth nothing that was not in the Digest or in the Code. As a 'source' of law it did not understandably exercise much influence, although it was the subject of lectures and commentaries by medieval scholars.

The actual transmission of the text of Roman law deserves a few remarks. The designation of Justinian's work as *Corpus Iuris Civilis* was not the emperor's, but conferred by medieval scholarship on the codification. He himself and his contemporaries considered each part as an independent whole, and this original plan was also reflected in the transmission, especially in the manuscripts, and to some extent also in the teaching methods at the medieval universities.[1]

---

[1] For modern students of medieval Roman law only the editions of the 15th to 17th centuries should be used, because they were derived from the Vulgate. These editions also contain, apart from the text upon which the commentaries and lectures were based, the *Authenticum* (see below, 69) as well as feudal law, both of which are absent from the textually superior Mommsen-Krüger edition of the *Corpus* (1872ff).

The only surviving manuscript of the Digest was written most likely about 600, in the Byzantine part of Italy. It was carefully collated with, and corrected on the basis of, an original text of the Digest, since lost. This extant manuscript was in the possession of Pisa (hence the manuscript is called the *Pisana*) until the fifteenth century, when the Florentines captured Pisa and also took possession of this priceless jewel (hence also called the *Florentina*).[1] There is very little evidence that the *Pisana* itself played a great role in the transmission of the Roman law before the end of the medieval period. What did play a role—and perhaps the most crucial role in the transmission of any legal work—was a copy of the *Pisana* which was made in the late eleventh century and found its home in Bologna. It was this copy of the *Pisana*, and not the *Pisana* itself, which formed the basis of teaching and of the influence of Roman law in the Middle Ages. This so-called Vulgate text of the Digest (or *Littera Bononiensis*) was copied over and over again and disseminated throughout medieval Europe. Only very rarely did the *Pisana* come to be consulted, and this not before the fourteenth century. It is needless to say that the Vulgate, because it was a copy, contained numerous errors and textual variants: they became of concern to the humanists and Renaissance scholars who desired a restitution of the uncorrupted text. In the medieval period it was the offspring of the *Pisana* which dominated the lecture hall, the courts, and legal practice.[2]

The Code of Justinian is very much less well transmitted than the Digest. Part of the explanation may be that Justinian had not made it a compulsory subject of legal instruction; hence it was never intended to be taught in any law school, the probable reason for this curious situation being that Justinian had for-

---

[1] There is a photocopy of the *Florentina* (formerly *Pisana*) issued by the Roman 'Commissione ministeriale per la reproduzione delle Pandette', produced between 1902 and 1909 and comprising 10 fascicles. There is a reproduction of this priceless monument in the University Library, Cambridge.

[2] For details see H. Kantorowicz, 'Ueber die Entstehung der Digestenvulgata' in *SavZRA* 30 (1909) 183ff; 31 (1910) 14ff (fundamental); L. Wenger, *Quellen* cit. 594ff.

bidden all interpretation of imperial law. A palimpsest of Verona, probably a production contemporary with the *Pisana* text, embodied the text of the Code, though with some omissions. Since the Code contained the official imperial law, it was copied several times, but in the West without the last three books because they were considered irrelevant: they dealt with the public law relative to the Byzantine administration. Yet in the twelfth century the whole Code, including the last three books, was copied in Bologna, and most lectures dealt with the whole work. Like that of the Digest the text itself was very faulty and an adequate text was not produced until the humanists interested themselves in it. From the point of view of substance and the principles enshrined in the Code the textual deficiency made less difference than the present-day editorial critic would suppose: for purposes of constructing governmental principles the axioms and general tenor of the enactments in the Code were perfectly plain. And they proved amply adequate.

The supplementary legislative measures of Justinian—the *Novellae*—were abridged and made available in summary form by one of the great jurists in the imperial court, Julian of Constantinople, who around 556 composed an abstract of 124 *Novellae* which as *Epitome Juliani*[1] enjoyed great popularity throughout the medieval period. In the early twelfth century however another collection of Justinian's *Novellae* became known which contained 134 *Novellae*, partly in the original Greek, and partly in Latin translation: these 134 pieces had obviously been copied from an authentic source, and for this reason the jurists in Bologna (and other sees of learning) called this collection the *Authenticum*. It was divided into nine books (or *collationes*) and it was from these that the excerpts and fragments were taken which legal scholarship inserted into the appropriate places in the Code. As already mentioned, this example was followed by the Western emperors, especially the Staufens, who ordered that excerpts from their own laws should be sandwiched as *authenticae* between the appropriate (Roman) imperial *leges*.

Neither the *Epitome Juliani* nor the *Authenticum* should be

[1] Ed. G. Haenel, *Iuliani Epitome latina novellarum* (1873).

underestimated in their role as very significant sources which inspired a distinctive and highly matured governmental ideology. The monarchic government of the Ruler in a Christian society was their main theme: the Ruler's law was the *sacra lex*, as nearly every preamble proclaimed. His divine mouth promulgated the law which thus became 'our eternity' (Nov. 11, epilogue); the monarch's law was to be preserved inviolate for all time (Nov. 58, epilogue)[1] or was declared to be immortal (Nov. 47, c.1); 'our will should be recognised by all as a divine precept and as (positive) law' (Nov. 13, epilogue). That universal governorship was the underlying theme of these and numerous other legislative expressions, went without saying: God had given the monarch the leadership of all nations, in the Orient and Occident and the *tuitio* of all divine things (Nov. 9, pref.; 24 pref.; 47 c.1; etc.): hence also the role of the Ruler as the organ endowed with the protective care of all mankind; it was the emperor who referred to his own eternity (Nov. 11, epilogue). These are just a few examples to show the ideological opulence of the Justinianean *Novellae*: they constituted a veritable reservoir for all matters falling within the precincts of government. And this consideration is all the more relevant when due weight is attached to the fiction that the Western Roman emperors in the medieval period held themselves the successors of the Constantines and Valentinians and Theodosians—and Justinians. To this source of Roman law influence far too little importance is attached by present-day scholarship.

In order to exercise influence a legal system needs a fertile soil. This presupposes security of social conditions, a minimum of educational standards in at least the upper strata of society, and absence of external threats to this society. Above all, for any legal system to prove itself influential it must appear to contemporaries as worthy of imitation, assimilation or accommodation, because its intrinsic qualities must be recognized and its superiority to the

---

[1] In the promulgation edict he declared that the laws in the Code and Digest were to be valid *in omne aevum*: they were eternal, see *Tanta* §23; cf. also his constitution *Omnem*, epilogue (both precede the text of the Digest in the editions).

existing legal order must be acknowledged. None of these pre-suppositions were there in the period in Europe after the reign of Justinian. The period between the second half of the sixth and late eighth centuries was, as far as Europe as a cultural unit was concerned, a period of gestation.[1] It was not until the ninth century that Europe emerged as an ideological entity, but even in this same century the peaceful progress of Europe was checked by the onslaught of the Vikings, Saracens and Normans. Their attacks delayed the progressive influence of Roman law for nearly a century that is, until the revival of the idea of a Roman empire in the West.

From the sixth to the eighth centuries the links of Western and Northern Europe with Rome were on the whole rather tenuous. And when strong ties were knitted in the mid-eighth century, they were with ecclesiastical Rome which, in the eyes of the Northern Germanic tribes, had absorbed ancient Rome: the papacy symbolized Rome. It is therefore important to bear in mind that it was the papacy from the mid-eighth century onwards which acted as the transmitter of Roman law and of Roman principles of government. In this capacity the papacy was a very effective bridge builder between the mature, ancient Roman civilization and the virgin, fallow youthful Germanic societies, and in the present context this means one thing—the transmission and implantation of the idea of the rule of law.[2] It was in fact as a result of the welding together of heterogeneous forces—Germanic, Roman and Christian—that the ninth century saw the replacement of the geographical concept of Europe by the idea of Europe as an entity that had its own complexion and sustained itself by its own inner momentum. The coalescence of Franks

---

[1] For the fate of the Justinianean work in the early MA see the masterly exposition by E. Genzmer, 'Die justinianische Kodifikation und die Glossatoren' in *ACDR* I (1934) 354ff. The period 'zeigt einen traurigen Tiefstand' (365). For an excellent general survey see R. Folz (et al.), *De l'antiquité au monde médiéval* (1972) esp. 86ff, 289ff.

[2] Cf. also H. E. Feine, 'Vom Fortleben des römischen Rechts in der Kirche' in *SavZKA* (1956) 1ff; G. Le Bras, 'L'église romaine au service du droit romain' in *RHDFE* 44 (1966) 193ff. See also below, 73f.

and papacy was not only to be fundamental for the future ideological map of Europe, but was also the indispensable condition which enabled the Roman law to play its effective role in moulding the character of medieval government. The 'imperial' idea fostered and consistently advocated by the papacy in the West concretely expressed the fusion between the old and the new, between the papacy as the symbol of the ancient Roman world, and the Franks as the most gifted people of the Germanic peoples. Lastly, certain parts of Europe, such as Italy and the South of France, had never ceased to apply at least the rudiments of Roman law to their own social conditions.[1]

At this juncture reference must be made to some special circumstances. The first—to which some attention has already been drawn—is the principle that wherever clerics lived and whatever functions they performed, they became in actual fact the personal purveyors of the Roman law, because 'the Church lives according to Roman law'. This was particularly important in the regions in which the Roman Church possessed large estates, such as Gaul. These patrimonies were enclaves which became germinating centres radiating Roman law unobtrusively into neighbouring regions. They thus potently cultivated the ground for later systematic fertilization with the Roman law.

In proximity to this circumstance stand certain public functions of the clerics in the Western regions. The actual drafting of documents relative to legal transactions was done by notaries who were clerics and trained in the fundamentals of the law which was none other than Roman law. It is therefore essential to refer to the notaries (the Roman *tabelliones*) who applied Roman law to the exigencies of legal transactions in a most practical way from the sixth century onwards. They must be classed as vital agencies for the diffusion of the Roman law itself and for conditioning con-

---

[1] Some details in C. G. Mor, *Appunti sulla storia delle fonti romani giuridiche da Giustiniano ad Irnerio* (1937); J. Gaudemet, 'Le bréviaire d'Alaric et les Epitome' in *IRMAE*, I, 2b, ααβ (1965); also E. Meyer-Marthaler, *Römisches Recht in Rätien im frühen und hohen MA* (1962), 69ff. For the practical utilization of Germanic, Roman and canon law in the famous letter to the Bulgars by Nicholas I (about which see *PG* 193ff), see B. Paradisi in *St. Grat.* XI (1967) 211ff.

temporaries in the Roman sense.[1] In all likelihood it was the notaries who were the compilers and authors of the very necessary and useful formulary books which reflected the most common type of legal transaction and supplied the formularies to be applied to legal business. It should nevertheless be also mentioned that the formularies contained a good deal of dead legal matter: Roman law was applied to an agrarian economy and society which was vastly different from the mediterranean and above all urban conditions with which Roman law primarily concerned itself. Furthermore, copyists sometimes misunderstood certain legal terms or expressions which nonetheless went into the formulary books and caused considerable confusion later when the original meaning of terms had been completely forgotten.[2]

The third circumstance that deserves some attention here is the influence exercised by the laws of the Visigoths. The topic has not yet attracted as much attention as it quite obviously deserves. The paradox emerges that the legal enactments of the Visigoths in Spain—the conquered and subjugated and to all intents and purposes extinct Germanic people—began to exercise influence upon legal and governmental thought among the peoples North of the Alps, notably the Franks. There is substantial evidence concerning the impact of the Visigothic laws in France from the eighth century onwards.[3] That this influence was so strong in the West-Frankish portion of the Carolingian inheritance was due to the refugees from Arab oppression who literally speaking transported their law-books across the mountains. Further, the extremely high standards and juristic expertise of the Visigothic draftsmen and the resultant first-class formulation of legal principles fell on fertile soil in Francia. Of all the Germanic law codes the Visigothic Code had achieved the acme of juristic dexterity

[1] Cf. F. Calasso *Medio evo* 243ff with further lit. For the importance of the notary cf. L. Wenger, *Quellen* cit. 719, 753ff, and for the importance of the notariate as an institution in the high MA see esp. W. Trusen, *Anfänge des gelehrten Rechts in Deutschland* (1962) 69ff.

[2] For some telling examples see Savigny I. 403 at n. 14. See also below, 194.

[3] For some remarks see F. Calasso *Medio evo* 614ff; also *CR* 69f, 130. For the Visigothic laws see now esp. P. D. King, *Law and Society in the Visigothic Kingdom* (1972).

and polish, and it achieved it because its makers had intelligently and sagaciously absorbed Roman law. No other Germanic tribe had the same standard of legal education and culture as the Visigothic royal (and episcopal) chancery personnel.

The most effective preparatory circumstance in the diffusion and influence of Roman law as a source of governmental conceptions was the imperial idea with which the papacy began to operate from the late eighth century onwards. In the course of the ninth century the creation of the so-called Emperor of the Romans in the West by the papacy became vitally important for the fate of Roman law as a governmental source in medieval Europe. However much this papally created Roman emperor was conceived to be an instrument of the papacy in its policy towards Constantinople, the idea and the fact of Roman emperorship wholly accepted as it was in the West, had necessarily far-reaching ideological and juristic repercussions. There was the propagation of a universal empire—for only the Roman empire could be universal—with the consequence that the Roman law was in course of time to be raised to the level of a universally applicable law. The inescapable sequel was that on the basis of juristic and governmental considerations the emperor in Constantinople was denied the role of a *Roman* emperor and was held (by the West) to be no more than a Greek king or prince. It should be realized that this imperial programme was embraced by both the Carolingian Rulers in the ninth century and the papacy; this 'political' programme must be seen against the background of the Latinization of the soil of Western Europe by the Vulgate, Roman liturgy and the numerous other attendant features of Roman provenance, all preparing and cultivating the ground for the full-scale impact of Roman law.[1]

The period between the last years of the ninth and the second half of the tenth century was one of stagnation at least in regard to the transmission and influence of Roman law as a source of

[1] For some lit. see above, 71 n. 1, 2; also *CR* 135ff. See F. Ganshof, 'Les traits généraux du système d'institutions de la monarchie franque' in *Settimana Spoleto* IX (1962) 91ff; G. Tessier, *Diplomatique royale française* (1962). For the *Capitularia* see below, 203ff.

governmental principles. The reasons for this state of affairs need not be investigated in this context. With the resumption of the Roman-imperial theme by the Saxon dynasty in 962 the Roman law as a source of governmental practice and doctrine came gradually to be realized. For governmental purposes the Ottonians and their circle actively promoted not only the study, but above all the practical application of the Roman law. This stimulus was an important landmark in the development of Roman-law based governmental doctrines and themes. What, furthermore, must be stressed is that it was in precisely this period of the ninth and tenth centuries that Roman law made a noticeable and indelible impact upon the ecclesiastical canon law. Since the ecclesiastics were the chief bearers of the intellectual development this feature is not difficult to understand.[1] Above all, the imperial government at once realized the ideological potentialities of Roman law, and none was more adept in this than Otto III who in his governmental actions proved himself an imitator of Justinian.[2]

The conditions for a full-scale deployment of Roman law in the eleventh century were therefore particularly favourable. As in so many other respects the Investiture Contest also assumes here crucial importance. The conflict appears once more as a watershed in the medieval period. Although the proprietary church system was the ostensible target of attack by the papacy and the hierocratic party the real target was the manipulator of this system, that is, royalty and in a wider sense the laity. Yet, the basis of the system was a hitherto unquestioned custom and one that was of indisputably Germanic origin. The paradox emerged that in order to parry the attack on this Germanic customary law,

[1] See C. G. Mor, 'La recezione del diritto romano nelle collezioni canoniche dei s. IX–XI' in *ACII* II (1934) 283ff. A detailed and excellent survey in van Hove 220ff.

[2] Cf., for instance, the decree on inalienability of ecclesiastical estates (of 20 Sept. 998) which is called a '*sacra lex* domini *piissimi* imperatoris' to be valid *in aeternum* (*MGH. Const.* I. no. 23, p. 50; cf. Justinian himself above, 70). The signature is particularly revealing. Similarly the decree about justices (21 March 996, ibid. no. 22, p. 48): 'hac lege omne per aevum divinitate propicia, valitura edicimus'.

the royal and anti-hierocratic party harnessed the Roman law to their aid: an alien law that within the precincts of governmental conception was neither of Germanic nor of Western provenance, but of Roman and of Eastern parentage, became now from the second half of the eleventh century onwards one of the main supports of the royal side. The significance of this was that the character of Rulership came in course of time to be shifted from its Germanic to a Roman base. The repercussions of this were far-reaching; they are hardly recognized by modern medievalists. Yet, some of the polemicists of this era on the papal side also made use of the Roman law, but never to the extent to which the royalist side had recourse.[1]

What above all made the invocation of Roman law particularly palatable was that it was the law of lay Rulers. And as a result of harnessing the Roman law to the government of the German kings, the issues in the Investiture Contest became more clearly crystallized, and the immediate topic of the controversy—the proprietary church system—was relegated to a secondary place. For the issue became focalized in laity *versus* clergy: it was the confrontation of the *regnum* with the *sacerdotium*. Another development went hand in hand with this crystallization. For a great many questions came to be lifted out of their historical context and were turned into questions of principle. Questions such as obedience to the law, the kind of law to be obeyed, the obligatory character of oaths, the effects of excommunication within society at large, and so on, were seen as properly belonging to public law and were items within the jurisdictional sphere of government. They ceased to be of merely religious import. In the twentieth century it is perhaps a little difficult to realize fully the deep change which this harnessing of the Roman law produced throughout the length and breadth of Western Europe and beyond.

Nevertheless it is apposite to draw attention to the piquancy of

---

[1] For instance, Bonizo of Sutri, *Liber ad Amicum* (ca. 1085–7) ed. in *MGH. LdL*, I, 568ff; see also below, 136. Deusdedit, *Libellus contra invasores* (ca. 1090), ed. ibid. II, 292ff (cf. also F.-Le Br, II, 37ff) or Placidus of Nonantula, *Liber de honore ecclesiae* (ca. 1110), ed. ibid., II, 566ff (also F.-Le Br. II, 53).

the situation in the eleventh century when the most powerful European king came to the sombre realization that he had at his disposal no law with which to meet the hierocratic challenge to his own position. This weakness of the German monarchy should not pass without comment. Yet on the other hand the attempt to apply—as was done—the hallowed Roman law to the German king can only be seen as a further paradox in the situation. For the Roman law knew of no king, but only of an emperor of the Romans, yet in the Investiture Contest the imperial question was never an issue. The only feature that was of concrete value to the German side was that the Roman law was the law of lay Rulers.

The first professional use of Roman law in the service of royalty was made by one of the Ravenna Masters, Peter Crassus, who indeed was the first to realize the potentialities of the Roman law in the defence of lay power. His tract, *In defence of King Henry*, is a source of the greatest importance: it introduced the Roman law into the arena of 'political' conflicts from which it was not to disappear until long after the Reformation.[1] With the help of the Code as well as of the Digest Crassus tried to build up what later was to be called the sovereignty of the king in his domain; and this jurisdictional sovereignty of the king embraced the clerics including the pope. The further significance of this tract as a source lies in that it was clearly aware of the need of a body that was self-sufficient, autonomous and lived on its own laws—the State, but for this the Roman law was bound to prove itself an inadequate source. For Roman law was attuned to conditions entirely different from those prevailing in the late eleventh century; and Roman law amply showed the characteristic manifestations of the descending theme of government and the theocratic premisses, embedded as they were in ecclesiological presuppositions. In other words the Roman law, notably the Code, embodied a great many principles of which the papacy was the acknowledged contemporary interpreter and expositor.

Yet from a wider perspective the harnessing of Roman law had

[1] 'His treatise announces the entry of Roman law into medieval political thought', C. N. S. Woolf, cit. in *PG* 382 n. 2.

effects which were clearly not realized at the time: it proved itself as a source which in due course led to the secularization of government and of the governmental idea itself, releasing it from its theocratic and theological encrustations. This effect was observable in the policy of the Staufen dynasty between the mid-twelfth and mid-thirteenth centuries. Roman law became a source of inspiration, imitation and accommodation, and one of the most conspicuous results was the strong accentuation of the Roman base of government and the concomitant abandonment of the hitherto unquestioned Germanic and customary bases.[1] This effect was comparable to an avalanche. The fertilization of the ground was the joint work of government and scholarship, so that by the end of the twelfth century most of Western Europe was in the grip of Roman principles of government supplied as they were by the law of the Romans. The European landscape had undergone a transformation in the wake of this bloodless revolution, the like of which it had not known before and for which the modern age affords but few examples.

The presupposition for an application of Roman law was, however, that a number of obstacles had to be overcome. To begin with, in its transmitted form it contained enactments that were made over a long period of time, to wit from the second to the sixth centuries. It stands to reason that there were numerous contradictions and irreconcilable statements. Further, there were legal and governmental institutions in the *Corpus* of which the world of the eleventh and twelfth centuries knew nothing, and vice-versa there were contemporary institutions wholly alien to Roman law. The precondition for a useful deployment of Roman law was the solution of the contradictions and the accommodation of Roman law to the contemporary situation. Each needed an extremely high interpretative skill, technique and scholarship. None of these existed to any appreciable degree in the late eleventh century. It was this peculiar situation which gave rise to the growth of special law schools, first at Ravenna and shortly afterwards at Bologna. The growth of universities was

[1] Details in *SHP* 185ff, further W. Ullmann, 'Von Canossa nach Pavia' in *HJb* 93 (1973) 265ff.

directly conditioned by the Investiture Contest and specifically by the need to study Roman law professionally and in depth. The scholarly examination of Roman law in its entirety was the first academic discipline in the history of Europe. To this extent, then, the emerging scholarship of Roman law was the response to a challenge. And since the kernel of the Investiture Contest was jurisdiction, it was clear that the jurists alone were professionally qualified to pronounce on this. It was they who laid the foundations of the (later) study of political ideas. From the point of view of concrete influence the teachings and writings of the civilians (i.e. the scholars of Roman law) were more important immediately than the *Corpus* itself. It is time we turned to some of the significant features of this scholarship which as a source is far from being fully appreciated. For civilian scholarship played a vital and indispensable part in the dissemination and application of Roman law itself as well as in the intellectual fructification of Western Europe. At no other time did pure scholarship affect society and government to the degree that the civilians—and later also the canonists—did in the centuries between the Investiture Contest and the Reformation. It was only in combination with scholarship that Roman law attained the all-pervading influence which it actually commanded.

CHAPTER 3

The Scholarship of Roman Law

The growth of the archetypical University of Bologna was directly related to the profound social, religious and intellectual upheaval which the Investiture Contest occasioned. This university—the citadel of all legal studies throughout the medieval period—was in its beginnings and for the first decades of its existence a lay and purely private academy consisting of laymen who taught laymen the science of law. The one and only subject which formed the topic of academic instruction—down to 1365 when theology was added—was Roman (and a little later canon) law: the Roman law was now available in its totality, that is the Digest, the Code, the Institutes, and the *Novellae*. It is impossible to exaggerate the significance of the emergence of this seat of learning—and of its academic satellites—and of the kind of advanced education it provided, for the intellectual complexion of Europe for several generations. The growth of this institution was spontaneous and conditioned by the gruelling conflict that affected the very foundations of contemporary society and of its government. From the social as well as intellectual standpoint, Bologna and its offsprings may well be considered powerhouses of the central medieval period. They assumed a parental function in regard to medieval (and to a very considerable extent also modern) Europe especially when from about 1140 onwards canonistic jurisprudence came to be established next to its civilian counterpart. The universities, notably their law faculties, were so to speak living sources of contemporary governmental developments. The very fact that the universities and law faculties soon proliferated throughout Western Europe reflected the needs of contemporary society for the scholarly pursuit of jurisprudence (which included the science of government) no less than the need for a personnel that was properly trained in the matters which fell into the orbit of government. The law that was primarily studied (and this applies with equal force to canon law) exhibited an unadulterated monarchic system of government the hallmark of which was the descending-theocratic theme in relation to the creation of the law.

Specifically in regard to Roman law one must bear in mind that first Ravenna,[1] but quite pronouncedly Bologna, were outspokenly on the side of the German Rulers, not because they were German kings, but because they were held to have established a kind of right to Roman emperorship. This was one, though by no means the sole consideration which assisted the growth of Bologna.[2] One of the first and most influential scholars at Bologna, Irnerius[3] (who indeed may have been a German: Wernerius or Guarnerius), was the counsellor of the Emperor Henry V and *amicus curiae* in the literal meaning of the term, even sharing the

[1] For Ravenna see P. S. Leicht, 'Ravenna e Bologna' in *ACDR* I (1934) 277ff. It would seem that the Digest was not taught there (286f). See further A. Sorbelli, *Storia della Università di Bologna* (1944) 42ff; F. Calasso *Medio evo* 281ff.

[2] The study of Roman law is so intimately linked with the history of universities that it is impossible to treat of the one without the other. The literature is too large to be quoted here. Apart from H. Rashdall, *The Universities of Europe in the MA*, ed. F. M. Powicke & A. B. Emden (1936) I, 87ff, cf., e.g., *Contributi alla storia dell'Università di Pavia* (publ. on the occasion of the 11th centenary 1925) (Archbishop Lanfranc taught there); R. Cessi, 'Lo studio bolognese e le studio padovano' in *AA* 149ff; for the older lit. see F. Calasso *Medio evo* 510 n. 15; further G. Ermini, *Storia della Univ. di Perugia* (1948); U. Gualazzini, *La scuola giuridica reggiana nel medio evo* (1952); E. M. Meijers, 'L'université d'Orléans au XIIIe s.' in *Études* III (1959) 3ff; id., 'L'université de Toulouse au XIIIs s.' ibid. 167ff, to be supplemented by D. Maffei, 'Qualche postilla alle ricerche di E. M. Meijers sulle scuole di Orléans, Toulouse e Montpellier' in *RHD* 36 (1968) 387ff (much relevant and unknown manuscript material); R. Feenstra, in *Actes du Congrès sur l'ancienne université d'Orléans* (1963) 45ff (best recent account of Roman law influence). For Vacarius see H. Coing in *HQL* 39ff and below, 97, and for Cambridge in the 13th cent. cf. M. B. Hackett, *The original statutes of Cambridge University* (1970) 30ff, 230f; but cf. my review in *JEH* 22 (1971) 134ff.

[3] 'Mit Irnerius beginnt etwas Neues'—the words of no lesser authority than Erich Genzmer about this *lumen iuris*: 'Die justinianische Kodifikation & die Glossatoren' cit. 367 (above, 71 n. 1). For the half century preceding Irnerius (who after all was only a 'Magister in artibus') see esp. C. G. Mor, 'Legis Doctor' in *AA* 195ff (a number of them had been at Ravenna).

emperor's excommunication by the pope.[1] The Western imperial government displayed a benevolent interest in this university from the early stages of its development. It has already been pointed out why the Roman law in its transmitted form was very much in need of interpretation, adjustment and adaptation. And the imperial theme—largely fostered by Roman law—was similarly in need of professional treatment and interpretation, especially as the Western Roman emperors called the law of the ancient Caesars their own. It will be recalled that in the first instance the Roman law was paradoxically enough employed for purposes for which it was certainly never intended, that is, the defence of a German king. Nevertheless, the ideological opulence of this Roman Corpus proved irresistible, because it embodied jurisprudential principles which with some adaptation could be utilized for the service of the Western Roman emperors in their function as universal lords (the *domini mundi*). Hence the evident interest which the imperial government showed towards the University of Bologna. At any rate, the papal challenge was focused upon the law—hence the recourse to the only available law of lay Rulers in the shape of the Roman law (upon which indeed a great deal of the papal law also was based). The overall effect of the study of Roman law was the hitherto hardly acknowledged secularization of institutions and above all of governmental principles themselves. They began to be, so to speak, released from their religious encumbrances.[2]

The teachings of the civilians concerned the interpretation of

[1] Cf. W. Holtzmann in *Neues Archiv* 50 (1934) 301ff at 317 and 319 (list of excommunicates): 'Gwarnerius Bononiensis legis peritus.' Further G. Cencetti, 'Studium fuit Bononie' in *St. medievali*, 3rd s., 7 (1966) 781ff at 795ff; B. Paradisi, *Storia del diritto italiano*, 2nd ed. (1967) II, 84ff; P. Weimar in H. Kantorowicz (with W. W. Buckland), *Studies in the glossators of the Roman law* (repr. 1969) 333 n. 97 (earliest documentary evidence of Irnerius: 28 June 1112). See also art. cit., above, 78 n. 1.

[2] For some details cf. *SHP* 185ff. This process gained momentum in the Staufen age when certain notions came to the foreground, such as *imperatura* (as coined by the Staufen chancery in *RNI* 14) or the *honor imperii*. About the latter cf. G. Wolf, 'Der honor imperii als Spannungsfeld von lex und sacramentum' in *Misc. Med.* VI (1969) 189ff.

whole *Corpus* of Roman law.[1] The vehicle of instruction was the lecture, that is, reading of the legal text (hence *legere→lectura*) and its explanation which was supplemented by interlinear glosses inserted between the lines of the text itself. The explanation was at first naturally concerned with parallel passages in other parts of the *Corpus*, but above all with the solution of contradictions. Evidently, the space between the lines soon became too crowded and the interlinear gloss gave way to the marginal gloss. The next stage in the technical development of interpretation and exegesis was the so-called *Apparatus*, that is, a complex of several glosses by different authors on a particular point or theme, which in course of time became too unwieldy and necessitated the literary species of the *Summa*: this treated specific points in a more or less systematic way, not necessarily following the original text, but selecting topics or themes. For purposes of instruction some special kinds of literary genres emerged which were divorced from the legal text and dealt with a particular problem in the form of a *Quaestio*.[2] This was a favoured mode of enquiry because the topic could be dealt with in some considerable depth. Another way of transmitting doctrine was by the so-called *Reportatio* which was in reality a course of lectures written up either by the Master himself or more usually by a pupil who had attended the lectures. The species of *Notabilia* served instructional purposes of a non-advanced kind: they were abstracts from a number of glosses on a particular point.

[1] For the working methods, scientific advances and the gradually proceeding comprehension of the whole Corpus see the magisterial exposition by E. Genzmer, op. cit., 345ff, esp. 388ff; B. Brugi, 'Il metodo dei glossatori bolognesi' in *Studi Salvatore Riccobono* (1937) I, 23ff. See further P. Weimar, art. cit. (below, 91 n. 1) and G. Otte, *Dialektik und Jurisprudenz: Untersuchungen zur Methode der Glossatoren* (1971); H. Coing, 'Trois formes historiques d'interprétation du droit' in *RHDFE* 48 (1970) 521ff, at 534ff. See above all the subtle analysis by B. Paradisi, 'Osservazioni sull' uso del metodo dialettico nei glossatori del XII' in *AA* 619ff; F. Calasso, *Medio evo* 345ff remains classic. For further details see now P. Weimar in *HQL* 129ff and A. Carccaterra in *SDHI* 38 (1972) 277ff.

[2] H. Kantorowicz, 'The quaestiones disputatae of the glossators' in *Rechtshistorische Schriften*, ed. H. Coing et al. (1970) 137ff is basic. See also *DDC* VII, 461ff.

None of the great achievements of the civilians (or for that matter of the canonists) would have been possible without the so-called scholastic or dialectical method of enquiry which proved an indispensable condition for the success of the new scholarship. In a way this was a special application of the general mode of enquiry prevalent at the time, that is, the deductive method which started from a general principle and 'deduced' subordinate principles. The dialectical method applied to theology as well as to philosophy, but was of quite especially practical concern to jurisprudence because it combined pure theory with concrete application. Indeed, law was the point where life and logic met (Maitland). The scholastic method was dialectics brought to perfection: it was a method by which the numerous contradictions in the *Corpus* of the law were to be solved by the mental operation of a distinction and if necessary subdistinctions and subdivisions, until a common denominator of the contradictory passages was found. This resulted in the complicated and finely woven texture of numerous distinctions which makes it so difficult for the modern reader to penetrate into the matrix of medieval governmental ideas profitably. Within civilian jurisprudence the distinctive feature of this method was the triad consisting of the *positio* (one standpoint or one interpretation or one legal enactment) contradicted by the *oppositio* and the *solutio* which deduced the elements which were common to both the *positio* and the *oppositio*. It was this method which the civilian (and canonistic) glossators practised in the twelfth century.[1]

The great variety of literary species evolved testifies to the intellectual liveliness of the expositions and to the need for them. This variety also demonstrates the range of subjects covered and the growth of the university population. Admittedly, the first Doctors at Bologna possessed some magnetic and dynamic

---

[1] See E. Seckel, *Distinctiones glossatorum* (repr. 1956); E. Genzmer, 'Vorbilder für die Distinktionen der Glossatoren' in *ACII* II (1935) 343ff. Abelard was particularly influential in regard to academic disputations: Pillius (below, 100) heavily relied on him. For additional remarks on this topic see now S. Kuttner in *St, Grat.* XV (1972) at 61ff.

qualities in their teaching and instruction.[1] Yet the attractiveness of a lecturer is of no avail if the subject is not considered interesting and useful. Both criteria were quite obviously amply fulfilled.[2] The rapidity of Bologna's growth shows how ready the soil was for cultivation with jurisprudential thought, and above all how relevant jurisprudence was considered for contemporary society. There is still a great need for detailed research into the glossatorial school in Bologna—and its offsprings—during the twelfth century, since so few of their literary works have been adequately edited. The work called *Dissensiones Dominorum* is an example which (despite its excellence of editorial workmanship) is barely a fragment of the vast glossatorial output, but it persuasively indicates the fine juristic acumen of the scholars.[3]

The new scholarship attempted to combine pure theory with social and governmental reality. The writings of the scholars constituted one of the major sources of governmental science which laid the foundations of the later political science: in importance the teachings of the jurists ranked in no wise below that of the *Corpus* itself. In fact when after a century of intensive interpretative work on the Roman law the great Accursius was to compose an *Apparatus* of glosses on all parts of the *Corpus* in which he incorporated most of the relevant teachings of the antecedent century, his work was almost at once accepted as the *glossa ordinaria*[4] and given the status of a standard work which

[1] See the survey of the sources in B. Paradisi, *Storia*, cit. II, 307ff.

[2] Cf. the penetrating observations by P. Koschaker, *Europa & das röm. Recht* cit. (above, 49 n. 1) 68ff.

[3] Ed. G. Haenel (1834). The *ius singulare* and its relation to the *utilitas communis* had a direct bearing on governmental science, cf. V. Piano Mortari, *Ius singulare e privilegium nel pensiero dei glossatori* (1958). See now also *HQL*, 243ff.

[4] The *gl. ord.* is in the margins of virtually all sixteenth- and seventeenth-centuries editions of the Corpus. For Accursius as glossator cf. P. Fiorelli in *DBI* 1, 121ff; V. Piano Mortari, 'Cultura medioevale e principio sistematico nella dottrina esegetica accursiana' in *Studi medievali*, 6 (1965) 289ff and the relevant contribution to the *AA*, notably on his European influence (Genzmer 779ff), H. Gilles 1027ff (France); M. J. Almeida Costa 1053ff (Portugal); R. Feenstra 1083ff (Netherlands); A. Vetulani 1293ff (Poland) etc. For the working method of Accursius exemplified by one Digest title cf. P. Stein, ibid. 699ff.

in authority sometimes eclipsed the text of the Roman law itself. The new intellectual juristic discipline rapidly advanced and was to leave its mark on very many non-juristic intellectual pursuits, but above all on the science of government. Under the umbrella of legal science in the narrow meaning of the term this jurisprudence contained unadulterated governmental doctrine. As a source of major dimensions civilian jurisprudence is not yet fully appreciated by modern scholars. A short reflexion will suffice to see the practical relevance of juristic scholarship when one realizes that from the mid-twelfth century on the personnel in the chanceries consisted of the graduates of the universities who in their official capacity attempted to translate their academic knowledge into the reality of government. And the same consideration applies to the advisors and counsellors in the entourage of Rulers, no less than to the justices and notaries and public functionaries of the cities.

It was through the writings and teachings of the civilians that the ancient Roman idea of universality became one of the most favoured public law maxims. This idea was able to gain a foothold all the more easily as it conspicuously tallied with the Christian idea of universality. By fusing the contemporary Roman emperor with the ancient Roman Caesars civilian doctrine applied directly to the former what the law said about the latter. This claim to the universality of the Roman law and hence of the emperor of the Romans should not be understood in modern terms: the claim signified that Roman law and the governmental themes based on it should become the 'common law' (the *ius commune*)[1] of the Western world, its common legal order, so

See further G. Moschetti, 'Eticità della glossa di Accursio sotto l'aspetto della libertà di uomo' in *SDHI* 35 (1969) 23ff (a very valuable study of one particular topic throughout the glossatorial age).

[1] See F. Calasso, *Introduzione al diritto commune* (1951); id., 'Citramontani, ultramontani e il problema storico del diritto commune' in *Europa e il diritto romano* (1954) II, 33ff; Ch. Lefebvre, 'La glose d'Accurse, le Décret et les Décrétales (vers le ius commune)' in *AA* 247ff; id. 'Le droit canonique dans les additions à la glose de Justinien: le ius commune' in *St. Grat.* XII (1967) 329ff (with most useful tables of concordances). See further K. Kroeschell, 'Recht & Rechtsbegriff im 12. Jahrh.' in *Vorträge und Forschungen* XII (1968) 309ff.

that the old thesis that the Roman *lex* was *omnium generalis* could become legal reality: the Roman law was to be the general and basic norm applicable to all mankind. None professed this unity of legal order or the wholeness point of view more succinctly than the author of the twelfth-century *Quaestiones de juris subtilitatibus* when he declared *unum esse ius, cum unum sit imperium*.[1] Again the realization of this aim was—at least within civilian (and also canonistic) jurisprudence—facilitated by the meaning that was attached to the term 'Roman'. The term greatly assisted the attempt at creating a 'common law' of Europe, for since the mid-eighth century a 'Roman' had been identical with a Western Christian (i.e. one who accepted the claims of the Roman Church and hence rejected those of the Church of Constantinople).[2] A purely religious thesis was utilized by scholarship to apply ancient concepts to medieval conditions. That indeed some of the Western Roman emperors, such as Henry VI in the late twelfth century, were determined to translate the ideological substance of the universal Roman rule into reality, can hardly be blamed on the jurists. The scholars were clear in all their writings and teachings that a distinction should be made between a *de facto* and a *de iure* overlordship of the emperor. The view that Roman law and Roman emperorship were 'universal' bore one meaning only: it was ideologically conceived and directly derived from the law of the Romans.[3]

That the civilians dealt at great length with the substance of Rulership and considerably deepened the theme of theocratic Rulership, is not therefore surprising. Quite in agreement with Justinian's standpoint they held that the emperor was a direct appointee of divinity. This was a theme that was constantly re-

[1] Ed. by H. Fitting (1894) and attributed to Irnerius. There is no certainty about the author of what Calasso once called *operetta giuridico preciosissima* (*Medio evo* 370). The lit. is vast. For the present state of research cf. P. Weimar in H. Kantorowicz, *Studies* cit. (above, 85 n. 1), 181ff, 346 n. 293. The ed. by Zanetti (Florence 1958) was not accessible to me.

[2] Cf. *PG* 61ff. For some remarks on the background cf. W. Ullmann, 'On the "Romani" in the earlier MA' in *St. patristica* II (1957) 156ff.

[3] See G. de Vergottini, *Il diritto pubblico italiano nei sec. XII–XIV* (1954) 187ff.

iterated; it thereby challenged the papacy on its own ground. For the civilians were virtually unanimous in their view that the papal intervention, notably the coronation of the German king as emperor of the Romans by the pope, was a mere formality and a pageant that did not confer any rights which the king-emperor did not already possess. However much support this juristic thesis had from the sources, it hardly tallied with reality which had indeed changed quite drastically since Justinian. In this interpretation the jurists showed themselves—as did most of their contemporaries—oblivious of historical developments: the period between Justinian and the age of the Staufens in the twelfth or thirteenth centuries was, historically speaking, short-circuited. Nowhere in the whole body of Justinian's law was there any statement that the emperor was crowned by the pope or that after scrutiny the German king was selected as future emperor by the papacy. Indeed, as far as the pure law went, the thesis set forth by the civilians, was correct: but this law had the respectable age of some seven hundred years, and far-reaching changes had taken place in the meantime. Nevertheless, the civilian thesis, expressed very forcibly by such eminent men as Azo (d. 1220),[1] the already mentioned Accursius,[2] or a little later by Cynus de Pistoia,[3] reflected the purely jurisprudential state of affairs which, though it tallied badly with actuality in the twelfth and thirteenth centuries, nevertheless provided an important platform for the constitutional development in the fourteenth century: jurisprudence and reality were then to march together again.[4] More than that, the civilians' theses formed a

---

[1] For details see P. Fiorelli in *DBI* IV (1963) 774ff, bibl. 780ff. His *Summa Codicis* (and *Institutionum*) has frequently been printed (anastatic reprint 1966). For his glosses on the middle portion of the Digest see G. Dolezalek, 'Azos Glossenapparat zum Infortiatum' in *Ius Commune* 3 (1970) 186ff. For newly discovered glosses see id. in *SavZRA* 85 (1968) 403ff. For the civilian *Summa* in general see E. M. Meijers, 'Sommes, lectures et commentaires' in *Études* III (1959) 211ff, to be supplemented by P. Weimar, 'Die legistische Literatur und die Methode des Rechtsunterrichts der Glossatorenzeit' in *Ius Commune* 2 (1969) 43ff.

[2] For his views see W. Ullmann, 'Dies ortus imperii' in *AA* 661ff.

[3] See *MIL* 177f, 179, also below, 106f.

[4] Reference is made to *Licet iuris* (1338) and the *Golden Bull* (1356), below, 289 n. 1.

bridge to the late medieval and modern conception of sovereignty possessed by the lay Ruler.

Because of the emphasis they had given to the descending theme of government, the civilians also greatly contributed to the doctrine of law creation and the theme of obedience to the law no less than to its limits. These theses were developed with a wealth of supporting material and can without exaggeration be called the first methodical jurisprudential exposition relative to the law-creative process. It was precisely in this connexion that the idea of the rule of law came to find a permanent habitat in the writings of the civilians, as also did the thesis of the emperor's legal sovereignty epitomized in his being the *lex animata*.[1] No less significant was their contribution to the obligations of the Ruler concerning the (divinely entrusted) kingdom or empire of the Romans: the principle of inalienability of public rights worked out in association with the tutorial function of the Ruler was a theme that fitted exceedingly well into the framework of the rule of law. This view was in the final analysis based on the Roman law conception of the *respublica* as a minor under age that was in need of a tutor.[2] Despite its beneficial effects in regard to the limitations which the thesis imposed upon the Ruler, it proved a considerable hindrance to the development of the concept of the (autonomous, independent) State.

The close liaison of the jurists, especially at Bologna, with the imperial government[3] deserves further observations in view of the

[1] See above, 61, and H. Krause, *Kaiserrecht & Rezeption* (1952) who rightly points to the vital role played by Roman law in the accentuation of the imperial plenitude of power. For Frederick I and Roman law, see H. Appelt, 'Friedrich Barbarossa und das römische Recht' in *Römische Hist. Mitt.* 5 (1962) 18ff; id. in *SB. Vienna* 252 (1967). But cf. art. cit., above, 78 n. 1.

[2] Roman law: Cod. II, 54, 4 (Diocletian); XI, 29, 3; Dig. 39, 2, 17 pr; 26, 1, 1; 44, 7, 5(1). The lectures and commentaries on these passages dealt with these and related themes. A great deal of work has to be done on this topic.

[3] For the following see H. Koeppler, 'Frederick Barbarossa and the schools of Bologna' in *EHR* 54 (1939) 577ff; W. Ullmann, 'The medieval interpretation Frederick I's *Habita*' in *Europa e il diritto romano* (1954) I, 101ff. A. Marongiu in *AA* 97ff and my riposte ibid., p. CXVIf; id., 'La costituzione Habita di Federico I' in *Clio*, Jan. 1965, 3ff (of the offprint); G. Cencetti, art. cit. (above, 85 n. 1), 781ff, at 819ff, and art. cit., above, 78 n. 1.

strong and active support which the Staufen Frederick I gave to the university of Bologna. The fifties of the century were a critical period for the university because by then the new canon law school had grown up next to the civilian university. The programme and ideology advocated by the canonists was in many respects at variance with that disseminated by the civilians. This would probably not have been of decisive importance, but what was of crucial significance was that the students (and doctors) of canon law were effectively protected in regard to vital interests in ways which were not available to the civilians. The former were clerics who by virtue of their status enjoyed certain fundamental privileges, whereas the students of civil law were laymen who were exposed to all kinds of vicissitudes, extortions, tolls, reprisals and above all to jurisdictional uncertainties—the very things in which the clerical students enjoyed immunity, protection and certainty. The practical result was, as the Doctors of Bologna vividly presented the case to the Emperor Frederick I at the Diet of Roncaglia in 1158 that the influx of civilian students to Bologna was beginning to show unmistakable signs of decrease. This was clearly information of the greatest significance to a government which held itself to be a successor of the ancient Caesars: in order to realize their governmental aim fully, the Staufen government needed an adequate supply of properly trained personnel, and this training could evidently be had only at the advanced level provided by Bologna. In order therefore to make sure of a continued supply of properly trained jurists and in the long run to save the study of Roman law from extinction, Frederick issued a decree (*Habita*) which gave to the students of Bologna (in practice the decree was of concern only to the lay students) precisely the same privileges which the clerical students already possessed. Among these were immunity from taxes and tolls during the voyage to Bologna, freedom from reprisals[1] and,

---

[1] That is liability for debts and damages incurred by members of the same nation. It was a kind of collective liability, in so far as one member of a nation was responsible for the others. The universities, it should be remembered, were organized on the principle of nations. In the last resort the principle of reprisals went back to the corporational theme.

above all, the special jurisdiction conferred on the teacher of the student.[1]

This Frederician decree proved itself very beneficial for Bologna's civilians and students of civil law. In fact, this decree became virtually a basic source of most European university statutes which either straightforwardly copied it or modified it according to local conditions. The specific academic court made its first appearance in this decree which was the source of all later special university jurisdiction.[2] And because *Habita* was inserted into the Code, it necessarily also formed the subject of academic lectures. This privileged position of the lay scholars potently assisted the study of Roman law as well as the growth of universities in the subsequent decades; it also explains the ease of mobility of the professors of civil law. This decree ranks as a vital source not merely of university history in all Western countries, but also of an ideology that was thoroughly Roman and monarchic. Lastly, it embodied the supreme function of the Ruler, that is, that of protection of his subjects. It also persuasively illustrated the continuity of the Roman imperial idea best shown in the designation of this law itself as a *lex sacra*,[3] not surprising since Frederick as 'Roman' emperor often enough referred to his predecessors as *divi reges et imperatores*.[4]

Perhaps nowhere can the significance of Roman law scholarship as a source of governmental conceptions in the West be more convincingly shown than in the constitutional adaptation which Frederick I's empire experienced. The inspiration could only come from the arsenal of civilian jurisprudence. Although dutifully

[1] The decree is incorporated in Cod. IV, 13 as an *authentica* and is the last item of the title. Ed. H. Koeppler at 607 and repr. by A. Marongiu in *AA* 112 (the ed. in *MGH Const* I no. 178, p. 249 is faulty). For some general remarks cf. P. Classen, 'Die hohen Schulen und die Gesellschaft' in *AKG* 48 (1966) 155ff at 173ff.

[2] For details see my art. cit. at 117ff.

[3] The much improved text by Koeppler has *lex sacra*. In the Arenga Frederick spoke of the 'divinarum atque sacrarum legum professores' who can be none other than the civilians. In imitation of the 'divi imperatores' he referred to 'our sacred palace' (*sacri palatii nostri*).

[4] See *PGP* 132 n. 1; the passages could easily be multiplied.

recorded in the usual text-books, the significance of calling the Roman empire (in the West) 'the sacred Roman empire' (*sacrum (Romanum) imperium*) from the winter of 1157–8 onwards is hardly realized.[1] Yet the innocuous looking addition was highly significant: it brought into clear relief the approximation of the function of the emperor to that of his supposed predecessor, the ancient Caesar. Obviously acting upon the suggestion of his professionally trained juristic advisers, through the new designation of the empire Frederick I adopted the ancient Roman principle according to which the emperor was the final authority in 'sacred matters', since the *ius in sacris* was part of the public law. Hence the empire was 'sacred', and not *sanctum*, which clearly demonstrated to alert contemporaries that the emperor had supreme jurisdiction over the ecclesiastical body. Indeed, law was the supreme instrument of government. This end—the control of the ecclesiastics—was quite obviously not thought capable of attainment without the adoption of the Roman public law principle of the *ius in sacris*. This simple legal device entailed, furthermore, that the Germanic basis of Rulership changed now into a fully-fledged Roman one. The thorough-bred juristic scholars became thereby the begetters of the constitutional device which shifted the jurisdictional control of the clerics from the realm of a vague customary law into that of the precincts of the hallowed Roman law.[2] The title was to remain unchanged until 1485 when it became 'the holy Roman empire of the German nation'.

That royal and imperial chanceries were staffed by professional jurists has been mentioned before. In this connexion attention must be drawn to sources which precisely because they emanated

[1] First occurring in the letters to the German princes summoning them for the campaign against Milan (Whitsun 1158): Otto of Freising, *Gesta Friderici*, II, 50 (ed. *MGH. SS. RR. GG.* at 158). For some details W. Ullmann, 'The pontificate of Adrian IV' in *Cambridge Hist. J.* 11 (1955) 233ff. It should be recalled that anything connected with the (Roman) emperor had sacrality, hence the *sacrum consistorium*, the cabinet of the Byzantine emperor (later adopted by the papacy for the College of Cardinals).

[2] The years immediately following substantiate Frederick's intentions. For the background cf. *SHP* 192ff, and W. Ullmann, 'Von Canossa nach Pavia' in *HJb* 93 (1973) 265ff.

from a chancery and from practising civilians, deserve consideration. It was in the heated period between 1162 and 1165 that some letters were produced which clearly foreshadowed not only a permanent schism between the empire and the papacy—indeed there had been a schism since September 1159—but also a separation of the whole of the empire from the papacy and the establishment of a Church in Germany where Trier (as the oldest German see) was to become what Rome had been.[1] The importance of this source is only heightened when one considers that shortly afterwards governmental measures were announced in England which pursued not at all dissimilar aims. During the height of the conflict with Becket Henry II issued decrees bidding fair to sever his English dominions from any connexion with the papacy. Here, too, the professional skill of a trained jurist was conspicuous. And when one bears in mind that in addition to the similarity of juristic substance, Henry II's legates had been in Würzburg in 1165 and that he himself had in August 1165 suggested the canonization of Charlemagne (actually done at Christmas),[2] there can be little doubt that lines of communication existed which in view of this source material are yet to be explored. Once more, these sources make abundantly clear that the principle and extent of jurisdiction was the very core of a highly charged 'political' conflict.

These considerations should not lead to the conclusion that the study of Roman law and of its governmental themes was of importance to the medieval 'Roman' empire only. Nothing would

[1] Ed. W. Wattenbach, 'Iter Austriacum' in *Archiv f. Kunde österreichischer Geschichtsquellen* 14 (1855) 85ff. The provenance of these letters is still not settled. They are symptomatic of the 'political' trend and the strong pull of the Eastern governmental system. Cf. art. cit. 245, and N. Höing, 'Die Trier Stilübungen' in *AD* 1 (1955) 257ff, and 2 (1956) 125ff; W. Goez, *Translatio imperii* (1958) 105ff whose arguments in regard to the dating are convincing. Cf. also *KGD* IV 263f. In this context reference should be made to the important entries in the collection of letters analysed by G. Hödl, 'Die Admonter Briefsammlung' in *DA* 25 (1969) 347ff, esp. 426ff, and 26 (1970) 150ff.

[2] These Henrician decrees are now ed. by A. Duggan, M. D. Knowles et al. in *EHR* 87 (1972) 758ff at 764ff; about the canonization cf. R. Folz, *Le souvenir et la légende de Charlemagne* (1950); id., 'La chancellerie de Frédérick I et la canonisation de Charlemagne' in *Moyen Age* 70 (1964) 13ff.

be farther from the truth. To the unparalleled impact which the academic pursuit of Roman law studies had throughout Western Europe from the twelfth century onwards too little modern research has been directed. In actual fact, the contact between the civilians and internal German circles was very tenuous in the twelfth century and only slowly increased in the thirteenth. On the other hand, there were some most influential migrations of Bolognese scholars not only to other Italian places destined to become radiating sees of legal scholarship, but also to southern France, for instance, by the Bolognese Master Rogerius in the mid-twelfth century, or by another Bolognese teacher, Placentinus in the latter half of the century to Montpellier, where his stimulating influence gave rise to the establishment of a flourishing law university.[1] It was also in the mid-twelfth century that the Lombard Vacarius migrated to Oxford, transplanting, so to speak, Bolognese wisdom to the virgin English soil.[2] It is not generally known that Vacarius was also a theological writer of considerable calibre and thrust.[3] In the early thirteenth century the great Azo[4] taught in Provence for a time.[5] And as the thirteenth century advanced, the mobility of the famous law professors increased in proportion to their fame. Then indeed the incipient German institutes of higher education came into view, but no less

---

[1] Cf. P. Tourtoulon, *Placentin, sa vie, ses oeuvres* (1896); A. Gouron, 'Les juristes de l'école de Montpellier' in *IRMAE* IV, 3a (1970) 28ff (doctrines); id. in *St. Grat.* XV (1972) 219ff; cf. also P. Stein in *AA* at 706f; excellent survey in *DDC* VII, 1ff (esp. 5ff on his conceptions). Cf. also below, 99f.

[2] Ed. of his *Liber Pauperum* by F. de Zulueta (Selden Soc. 44, 1927) which contains little of interest in the present context. It has mainly excerpts of glosses and of texts; the title indicates the purpose of the work. The best modern authority considers that the work 'non rappresenta il punto massimo della scienze dell'autore,' Ilarino da Milano, *L'eresia di Ugo Speroni nella confutazione del Maestro Vacario* (=*Studi e Testi*, 115 (1945)), 90; rich bibl. at 80f; cf. also J. de Ghellinck, 'Mag. Vacarius: un juriste théologien peu aimable pour les canonistes' in *RHE* 44 (1949) 173ff. He acted sometimes as a papal judge delegate, cf. S. Kuttner in *Trad.* 7 (1951) at 287 n. 18.

[3] Cf. Ilarino da Milano, op. cit. who discovered this interesting and badly neglected tract; ed. ibid. 481–583.

[4] About him above, 91 n. 1.

[5] For Orléans cf. E. M. Meijers, *Études* III (1959) 3ff, esp. 27ff.

than those in Spain, France, the Low Countries and to some extent also England, where at a later date Alberico Gentilis found a home at Oxford.[1] This easy mobility no less than the—by contemporary standards—rapid migration of the literary expositions of the civil law must be properly assessed, if the influence of juristic scholarship on the practice and theory of government is to be fully appreciated. The writings of the great jurists exercised an influence which was for all practical purposes mightier than that of the *Corpus* itself, because their views were directly relevant to contemporary society.

The century between Irnerius and Azo may be called the golden age of juristic scholarship at Bologna. That is why at least a few remarks on some of the outstanding scholars may be appropriate here.[2] Of the glosses which can with certainty be ascribed to Irnerius, there are not many, but that he glossed widely is beyond dispute.[3] The first famous Doctors of Bologna were almost all his pupils; like him, they were laymen whose private lives did not always match up to their public fame. Of these early Doctors there were four who were particularly outstanding: Bulgarus,[4] Martinus,[5] Jacobus and Hugo.[6] The heyday of their influence was

---

[1] See W. Holdsworth, *HEL* V. 52ff. For some details cf. also W. Ullmann, 'St Bernard and the nascent international law' in *Citeaux* 10 (1959) 277ff; id. in *Bartolo* (1962) I, 64ff and for a very instructive survey E. Rathbone, 'Roman law in the Anglo-Norman Realm' in *St. Grat.* XI (1967) 255ff.

[2] The lit. is too large to be quoted. For details Savigny's vols. IV and V are still indispensable. Additional lit. in P. Weimar in H. Kantorowicz, op. cit. (above, 85 n. 1) in the Appendix, and V. Piano Mortari in *ED* XIX (1970) 625ff.

[3] G. Pescatore, *Die Glossen des Irnerius* (1888); id. 'Die Stellung des Irnerius zu einer lehnsrechtl. Frage' in *Mélanges Fitting* (1908) II, 161ff; E. Besta, *L'opera d'Irnerio* (1896); A. Rota, *Lo stato e il diritto nella concezione d'Irnerio* (1954).

[4] For his glosses see P. Torelli, *Scritti di storia del diritto italiano* (1959) 95ff; for his *Apparatus de regulis iuris* (ed. F. G. C. Beckhaus (1856)) see P. Stein in *AA* 699ff, and *Regulae iuris* (1966) 134ff, 155ff; P. Weimar, loc. cit., additional notes at 333f.

[5] His glosses on the last part of the Digest have recently been discovered: G. Dolezalek, 'Der Glossenapparat des Martinus Gosa zum D.n.' in *SavZRA* 84 (1967) 246ff. Cf. now also P. Legendre (ed.), *La Summa Institutionum 'Justiniani est in hoc opere'* (1973) which may be a work belonging to the school of Martinus.

[6] For some of their glosses see P. Torelli, *Scritti*, cit. 167ff.

in the middle years of the twelfth century when they acted as counsellors to the imperial government as well as to other public functionaries. Only fragments of their glosses are edited. In order to appraise the glossators' achievements we should recall that there had been no scholarly exposition of the vast *Corpus* before them and that they alone and without any model had to chart a path through the labyrinth of one of the most mature legal works that had been produced in Europe.

The glossatorial school—distinguished by a refreshing clarity of thought, severe scholarship, exact references to the sources, attention to minute detail, linguistic and dogmatic exegesis, excision of all non-jurisprudential material or considerations—literally opened up a new world.[1] Evidently, the merits of the school harboured also their demerits: the subject-matter itself set limits to this kind of analysis and necessitated a somewhat broader approach. The need was fulfilled by the literary species of the *Summa*, of which the oldest was that of Rogerius on the Code which is fortunately edited.[2] Neither the date of its composition nor of its author's death can be fixed with certainty, but it was probably in the sixties or seventies. This *Summa* is a model of clarity, succinctness and mastery of penetration into the complex matter of the Code; his approach was direct and to the core of the juristic point; above all, Rogerius had a sharp eye for the exigencies of governmental reality. He was also author of one of the most valuable collections of juristic controversies in the schools: the so-called *Dissensiones Dominorum* enjoyed great reputation in the Middle Ages. This is evidenced by the number of extant manuscripts.[3]

One of the most attractive lecturers in the second half of the twelfth century was Placentinus, a native of Piacenza, probably of very low parentage, who always drew large crowds of students to his lectures, whether at Mantua or Bologna or in his native

[1] For a general assessment see F. Calasso *Medio evo* 503ff, esp. 521ff. See also P. Legendre, 'Recherches sur les commentaires pré-accursiens' in *RHD* 33 (1965) 353–428.

[2] Ed. J. B. Palmieri in *Biblioteca iuridica medii aevi*, 2nd ed. (1914) I, 47ff.

[3] Ed. G. Haenel, *Dissensiones Dominorum*, cit.; Rogerius at 71ff.

town, or in Montpellier where he died in 1192. As attractive as his lectures was his literary work, of which his *Summa* on the Code was (and is) an outstanding juristic effort characterized by subtlety and acumen in the interpretation of legal and governmental items, but above all by directness of style and elegance of expression.[1] A contemporary of Placentinus deserves a brief mention, because he was eminent in a special way. Pillius, who died after 1207, not only continued the *Summa* of Placentinus by commenting also upon the *Tres Libri* (i.e. the last three books of the Code)[2] but was also one of the first to write extensively on the feudal law and to gloss it.[3] It is not commonly known that Pillius was counsel for the monks of Canterbury in their quarrel with Archbishop Baldwin (for whom Peter of Blois acted) when the matter came before the pope, Urban III, in 1187.[4]

The link between the 'founder generation' and the new generation in the following century was provided by Johannes Bassianus,[5] a pupil of Rogerius and a teacher of Azo, whose *Summa* on the *Authenticum* has survived in many manuscripts, which testify to its popularity.[6] Azo's own contribution—within our present context—lies in his *Summa* on the Code (written 1208–10) which became one of the most popular and frequently cited works (Bracton relied on it heavily) and which was also glossed and

[1] *Summa Codicis* (ed. Mainz 1536; anastatic repr. 1966). He also wrote a *Summa Institutionum* of which several prints exist. His *Summa in Tres Libros* remained unfinished and was continued by Pillius. Placentinus had influence in England, see P. Legendre, 'Misc. Britannica' in *Trad* 15 (1959) at 492 n. 0.

[2] Pillius' *Summa: Cum essem Bononiae* (repr. 1967), but this too remained a fragment. Details in Savigny IV, 312ff and Ch. Lefebvre in *DDC* VI, 1499ff. An interesting tract was discovered by P. Weimar, 'Tractatus de violente possessore . . . a Pilio Medicinensi composito' in *Ius Commune* 1 (1968) 61ff, ed. 84ff.

[3] A. Rota, 'L'apparato di Pillio alle "Consuetudines Feudorum"' in *Studi e Memorie per la storia dell'Università di Bologna* 14 (1938), 1ff.

[4] See the notes in Savigny, IV, 324 e–g.

[5] Not to be confused with his contemporary Johannes Bazianus, a layman who became a cleric and the first Iuris utriusque Doctor: Schulte, I, 154, and F. Liotta in *DBI* 7 (1965) 313ff. About the civilian see U. Gualazzini in *DBI* 7 (1965) 140ff.

[6] Repr. 1966 as *Summa Novellarum*. Details in *HQL*, 213.

amended by later jurists. The quality of this *Summa* was uni-
formly high, 'sound' and avoided all abrasiveness by side-stepping
'hot' controversial issues, although he did not conceal his detachment from the papal cause. Because of its inner cohesiveness it
was the most frequently used manual down to the sixteenth
century.[1] Azo left not only his influential *Summa*, but also a whole
crop of nearly a dozen most eminent pupils who became *lumina*
in both Roman and canon law (Accursius, Roffredus,[2] the canonists Goffredus de Trano,[3] Martinus de Fano,[4] to mention just a
few).[5] In fact his pupil and later colleague Accursius is usually
taken to mark the end of the glossatorial period. He wrote nearly
100,000 individual glosses. His name would probably have been
consigned to oblivion, had he not in a diligent, conscientious,
though not always original way written his *Apparatus glossarum*
which was almost immediately accorded the accolade of the
standard gloss: it became the *glossa ordinaria* which was, as already
indicated, of quite unparalleled influence for the following two
centuries.[6] Its value does not lie in its scholarly contributions, but
in keeping alive the names and works and opinions of scholars
who might never have been transmitted to posterity. The longevity of the gloss was explicable by its ease of use and handiness
as a work that could be consulted alongside the actual text of the
law itself. It cannot be said that its overall effect was altogether
beneficial: there was a great temptation not to go beyond the

[1] Above, 91 n. 1. Azo's *Lectura* on the Code (also repr. 1966) is in reality a
reportatio by a pupil (Alexander de s. Aegidio) and does not attain the level of
the *Summa*. The few prints are faulty, Savigny, V, 20ff.

[2] For Roffredus see Savigny, V, 184ff. At one time an intimate counsellor
of Frederick II he turned later to the other side; he wrote almost wholly on
private law.

[3] For Goffredus see van Hove 473, 476. See also below, 173.

[4] Ibid., 485, 489.

[5] E. Genzmer, 'Die justinianische Kodifikation', cit. at 390f.

[6] See above, 88. For problems of ed. and related questions see the magisterial
exposé by G. Astuti, 'La glossa accursiana' in *AA* 287ff; and for all biographical
details with numerous hitherto unknown documents see P. Colliva, *Documenti
per la biografia di Accursio* (1963); see also R. Feenstra, 'Quelques remarques sur
le texte de la glose sur le D.v.' in *Atti IIo Congresso internaz. . . . di storia del
diritto* (1972) 205ff.

gloss which obviously harboured the danger of stultification. But this is a danger which high-powered text-books even present nowadays.

The ease of mobility of the academic teachers, together with the quick dissemination of their works and the relevance of legal scholarship for contemporary governments, accounts for the rapidity of influence of civilian scholarship in Europe. There is Spain: the Universities of Valencia and Salamanca, shortly to be followed by Lérida, were faithful copies of the Bologna model. The *siete partidas* of King Alphonse X conspicuously shows the influence of governmental principles derived from Roman law.[1] Similar observations can be made about France where the governmental themes worked out by scholarship came to be adopted as well as adapted. Capetian legislation from the turn of the twelfth and thirteenth centuries imitated the law-creative process and ingredients which scholarship had outlined, while French jurisprudence went so far as to eliminate the names of the Caesars from law-books and replaced them by French kings.[2] The reason for this curious procedure lay in the susceptibilities which the contemporary Staufen government, nourished as it was by juristic scholarship, had aroused: the inherent claim to universal dominion on the part of the (Western) emperor of the Romans was always viewed by the French (as by the English) with apprehension. This resulted in some developments which are of direct interest here.

The one was the French assertion—partly anticipated by an English canonist teaching at Bologna,[3] partly assisted by Innocent III[4]—that *Rex in regno suo est imperator*. The significance of this assertion is that the concept of sovereignty was expressed in terms of the Ruler which juristic scholarship had elaborated. Supreme and inappealable governmental power could be viewed only in terms of Roman emperorship. Despite its juristic flaws the formula was born which began its influential career and had

---

[1] For this Calasso *Medio evo* 614ff.   [2] Some examples in *PGP* 202ff.
[3] Below, 174 n. 5.
[4] In X: IV, 17, 13 (anno 1203); cf. M. Boulet-Sautel, 'Encore la bulle "Per Venerabilem"' in *St. Grat.* XIII (1967) 371ff.

reverberations well into the modern period. The other development—in some ways complementing the first—was the royally
inspired papal decree by Honorius III in 1219 which forbade the
study of Roman law at the University of Paris, because 'the
Roman laws are not used'.[1] Philip Augustus was most sensitive
to the thesis of universal dominion: to have the Roman law and
still more the themes derived from it, propounded in his capital
and in the university which owed so much to him, was understandably unacceptable. This step however deprived Paris of
professional juristic studies for more than 400 years (canon law
also suffered, because it could never be profitably pursued without
a firm grounding in Roman law). The other French seats of learning, such as Montpellier, Toulouse and especially Orléans, rose
proportionately in importance. In France the practical and
theoretical development of the concept of the crime of *lèse
majesté*—treason—followed the lines demarcated by civilian
jurisprudence: this was one more issue of sovereignty which was
understood in terms of jurisprudence. Exactly the same observation applies to the law-creative capacity with which scholarship
endowed the French king in the thirteenth century. And of no
lesser significance—in the present context—was the increase in
the constitutional power of the king who appropriated for the
French legal system the Roman-law based inquisitorial system
which was to become a powerful weapon in the hands of the
French monarchs in defence of their monarchic status.[2] Other
kingdoms showed developments very similar to those in France,
though perhaps in not so conspicuous a way. That there was
less practical influence of Roman law in England was partly due
to the resistance to the claim of universality inherent in Roman

[1] In X: III, 50, 10. Cf. W. Ullmann, 'The prohibition of Roman law at
Paris' in *JR* 60 (1948) 177ff; but cf. S. Kuttner, 'Papst Honorius III und das
Studium des Zivilrechts' in *Festschrift Martin Wolff* (1952) 79ff; further lit. in
PGP 199 n. 4. For the threat to France by the emperor (Henry VI) see Roger
of Hoveden, R.S. III, 301 (ad annum 1195): 'Notum erat regi Angliae quod
praedictus imperator super omnia desiderabat ut regnum Franciae Romanorum
imperio subiaceret.'

[2] For this *PGP* 195f.

law (hence the various royal steps taken to forbid the study of the *leges*)[1] and partly due to the peculiar strength which the feudal law had developed.[2]

The decline of the glossatorial school in the first half of the thirteenth century was accompanied by the rise of scholars who commented in a more or less systematic manner on the whole *Corpus*. They were called Commentators or Postglossators and set the tone down to the sixteenth century.[3] They became a veritable intellectual force on a global scale which was not merely due to their writings, but also to the proliferation of universities in the thirteenth and fourteenth centuries. The Postglossators became a cohesive intellectual élite, far more so than the theologians or philosophers.

Externally, the advantage of their commentaries lies in that to a very large extent they exist in prints of the late fifteenth and sixteenth centuries. Nevertheless these 'editions' must be used with caution, because the printers were careless in their transcriptions from the manuscripts; they also omitted or abbreviated sometimes

[1] Both England and France declined any subjection to the jurisdiction of the (universal) emperor of the Romans. The threat to English independence from Staufen quarters was by no means negligible: in fact at exactly the time when the very position of the English king underwent changes (below, 218f). Archbishop Siegfried of Mainz made a speech at the Fourth Lateran Council (1215) which left no doubt on this 'imperial' score: S. Kuttner & A. García, 'A new eyewitness account of the 4th Lateran Council' in *Trad.* 20 (1964) 115ff, at 128 lines 167ff, and 159f.

[2] For further reasons of why Roman law exercised little influence in England, cf. *PGP* 170ff, and esp. T. F. T. Plucknett, 'The relations between Roman law and the English common law' in *Toronto Law J.* 3 (1939), 24ff. Cf. further, H. G. Richardson, 'The Oxford law school under John' in *LQR* 57 (1941) 323ff. That Henry II's legislation showed considerable traces of Roman law, is evident, cf. *P & M* I, 478f; *PG* 385 n. 4; *PGP* 127. For Glanville, see now J. C. Russell, 'Ranulf of Glanville' in *Speculum* 45 (1970) 69ff. The authorship of *De legibus Angliae* (ed. and ET by G. D. G. Hall in Nelson's Medieval Texts, 1965) is still open.

[3] For the Postglossators see W. Engelmann, *Die Wiedergeburt der Rechtskultur in Italien* (1938); H. D. Hazeltine's Introduction to *MIL*; and for the literary species developed by them see N. Horn, 'Die juristische Literatur der Kommentatorenzeit' in *Ius Commune* 2 (1969) 84ff; see now id. in *HQL* 261ff which is a model exposition of a difficult theme.

or even added to the text.[1] A great deal of research work needs to be done to establish a reliable text. This is all the more difficult as the Postglossators tended to be prolix and diffuse and prone to accumulate 'authorities' which does not always make pleasurable reading for the modern student. Most of the commentaries were in fact lectures (and some of them were designated as such) which mirrored the strength and weakness of the scholar. A deterrent example of the thirteenth century is Odofredus (d. 1265) who was a pupil of Hugolinus and of Accursius, and had a teaching career of some four decades at Bologna. His lectures are repetitive, verbose, long-winded, so that their perusal is tedious for a modern scholar. He above all liked to play to the gallery, his jokes are flat and testify to a mind devoid of wit. Although he lectured on all parts of the Corpus, the contribution to knowledge is not overwhelming. The language is barbaric and uncouth. It is gratifying to note that some contemporaries were clearly aware of the gross deficiencies of one of the most celebrated professors of Bologna. But there are some compensating features even in the case of Odofredus: he frequently quotes older teachers whose glosses or other works are lost, and despite the diffuse presentation there is the one or the other new interpretative point; he also likes to refer to contemporary events in order to illustrate his juristic themes; and he refers to otherwise unknown academic matters. However unpalatable the presentation, the views of Odofredus must be taken into account: there are, especially in his commentaries on the first book of the Code and on the early part of the Digest, many governmental themes which no researcher can afford to omit.[2]

Almost the exact opposite of Odofredus was Jacobus de Arena (d. 1298), a pupil of the famous Guido de Suzaria;[3] he taught at

---

[1] A particularly telling instance is that of Bartolus' works which incorporate statements made by other authors foisted on him: see M. Ascheri, *Saggi sul Diplovatazio* (1971).

[2] *Summa Codicis*, ed. Lyons 1552 (and other eds.).

[3] Guido de Suzaria (d. ca. 1290): professor at Padua and Bologna, whose pupil was Guido de Baysio (below, 180). For a short time he was in the service of Charles of Anjou but was courageous enough to oppose openly the execution of the young Conradin. Cf. Savigny, V, 390; *SHP* 264 and A. Nitschke,

Padua and Bologna and was the master of Ricardus Malumbra[1] and Oldradus,[2] both eminent civilians, the latter also a canonist entering papal service at Avignon.[3] Jacobus was terse, succinct and clipped in his exegesis of the Code, with valuable doctrines on public law, especially the relations between Ruler and kingdom (empire).[4] Another Postglossator of the late thirteenth century was Dynus de Mugellano who taught at Bologna and Rome and assisted in the compilation of the very important and influential title *De regulis iuris* appended to the law-book published by Boniface VIII which became later the subject of independent commentaries. One of these—and perhaps the most influential—was composed by Dynus himself who demonstrated a first-class juristic mind. He died soon after 1300:[5] his most famous pupil was Cynus de Pistoia.

Cynus was a many-sided and gifted scholar, a jurist as well as a poet, a close friend of Dante and Petrarch. He had not only studied under Dynus and Lambertinus de Ramponibus[6] at Bologna, but travelled also in France[7] where he familiarized himself with the teachings of the two outstanding contemporary

'Der Prozess gegen Konradin' in *SavZKA* 42 (1956) 25ff. Of his commentaries on the Digest and Code I know of no print, though there are many manuscripts. Some of his tracts were published separately.

[1] Died 1334, had taught at Padua and Bologna, and was charged with heresy (he was a follower of Louis IV). None of his exegetical works is printed.

[2] Taught at Padua and Siena, and migrated to Montpellier after a brief spell at Perugia. Bartolus was one of his pupils.

[3] About his important role there see below, 186.

[4] His *Commentaria in universum ius civile* (ed. Lyons 1541) (and also later) have greater value than they have commonly been credited with.

[5] For his *regulae iuris* on the Sext see P. Stein, op. cit. 148ff. His *Commentaria in regulas iuris pontificii* (ed. Lyons 1557) are important.

[6] Died 1304. Details in Savigny, V, 624ff. For a wrong ascription of a work on the *D.v.*, see R. Feenstra, 'Une édition inconnue des Distinctiones super *D.v.* de Lambert de Salins' in *Recueil de mémoires et travaux . . . du droit écrit* 7 (1970) 185ff.

[7] Cf. the observations by B. Paradisi, 'La scuola di Orléans: un epoca nuova del pensiero giuridico' in *SDHI* 26 (1960) 347ff (à propos E. M. Meijers' *Études* III (1959)).

French jurists, Jacobus de Ravanis[1] and Petrus de Bellapertica.[2] Above all, Cynus was a fervent Ghibelline and became an assessor of the Emperor Henry VII at Rome in 1310, which brought him into closest contact with governmental business. The achievement of Cynus in the realm of jurisprudence[3] and governmental principles lies in that his main works (the Commentary on the Code and the Lectures on the first books of the Digest)[4] show a felicitous combination of sound practical common sense with originality in the interpretation of the sources and the adjustment of pure theory to the governmental exigencies of the time. This combination as well as the full and intelligent discussion of most recent literature—which had almost fallen into disuse as a result of the soporific effect of the *glossa ordinaria*—enabled Cynus to chart new paths: he began what might well be called the comparative study of law by juxtaposing Roman law with contemporary

[1] Jacobus de Ravanis taught at Toulouse, was later auditor of the Rota. His *Lectura Codicis* (ed. Paris 1519) (wrongly attributed to his pupil Petrus de Bellapertica: rare copy in Caius Coll., Cambridge) reveals an extremely subtle and original mind. Cf. also the observations by G. Chevrier, 'Jacques de Revigny et la glose d'Accurse' in *AA* 979ff; above all, E. M. Meijers, III, 59ff. See now also G. d'Amelia in *RHD* 40 (1972) 43ff. About him as a feudist see below, 217 n. 3.

[2] The statement by Bartolus that he was a pupil of Jacobus de Arena must be a misreading for Jacobus de Ravanis: *Comm. ad Cod.* (ed. Turin 1577) on Cod. VIII, 52, 2, fo. 115 va, no. 20. Died in 1308 as royal chancellor, had taught at Toulouse and Orléans. Powerful juristic mind, as shown in his *Quaestiones aureae* (ed. Lyons 1517), also wrote a tract *De feudis* (ed. in *TII* X. 2). Details in E. M. Meijers, *Études* III, 95ff with an appendix of important texts from him, Jac. de Ravanis and Lambert de Salinis. About his fragmentary *Lectura* on the Institutes cf. P. Weimar, 'Die Erstausgabe der sog. Lectura Institutionum des Pierre Belleperche' in *RHD* 35 (1967) 284ff (also contains some lectures by Jac. de Ravanis).

[3] For the part he played in the creation of forensic medicine, see H. Kantorowicz, 'Cino da Pistoia ed il primo trattato di medicina legale' in *Rechtshistorische Schriften* (1970) 287ff.

[4] His *Summa Codicis* (ed. Frankfurt 1578) is bound up with his *Lectura in Dig. vetus*. New discovery of another Lecture on the *D.v.* by D. Maffei, *La Lectura super Dig. veteri di Cino da Pistoia* (1963). For his independent approach to the *gl. ord.* cf. his *glossae contrariae* made known by M. Bellomo in *RHD* 38 (1971) 433ff.

statute law (mainly municipal) as well as with the French and English law. He also demonstrated the relevance of judicial decisions for the interpretation of the 'common law' of Europe. With him also began the intelligent reference to classical authors. His genuine contempt for the canonists was the Ghibelline's language, although this did not disturb his close friendship with the most eminent canonist of the time, Johannes Andreae. Cynus attempted to combine the ascending with the descending theme by declaring that the institution of the empire was divine, although the emperor himself had his roots in the people (*Imperium a Deo, sed imperator a populo*)—a point of view that exquisitely reflects the scholar's dilemma. Cynus still lacks an up-to-date full-scale exposition.[1]

The seminal character of the teachings of Cynus bore full fruit in his pupil, the great Bartolus, 'the immortal master of Perugia'. Bartolus de Sassoferrato[2] forged ahead on the paths delineated by Cynus. He had the same breadth of learning, the same realism and the same freshness of approach which are the distinguishing marks of his master. His jurisprudential theme was hewn of one block and still awaits its present-day professional expositor, although spade work has been done by Cambridge scholars.[3] Here is not the place to speak of his reputation: it must suffice to state that his opinions had legal force in Spain and in Portugal where most of his works were translated into the vernacular. At Padua a special chair was created in his memory, the incumbent of which was charged with the 'lectura textus, glossae et Bartoli'. In Germany copies of his works proliferated from the date of his

---

[1] Cf. also the notice in *Studi medievali* 12 (1971) 1104.

[2] His other teacher was Jacobus Butrigarius (ca. 1274–1348) whose *Lectura in Codicem* (ed. Paris 1516) (at Caius Coll. Cambridge) is sound without being outstanding in any way; it nowhere attained the standard of Cynus.

[3] J. N. Figgis, 'Bartolus and the development of European political ideas' in *TRHS* (1905) 156ff; C. N. S. Woolf, *Bartolus of Sassoferrato* (1913) (seminal); W. Ullmann, 'Bartolus on customary law' in *JR* 52 (1940) 265ff; id., 'Bartolus and English jurisprudence' in *Bartolo* I, 47ff. For biographical details see J. L. J. van de Kamp, *Bartolus de Sassoferrato* (1936); F. Calasso, in *DBI* 6 (1965) 5ff (posthumously published).

death in July 1357,[1] and in both England and France the surviving manuscripts surpass those of other eminent jurists, and his works were among the first juristic books to be printed (1470).[2] His tomb in the small Franciscan church at Perugia bears a plaque with the simple inscription *Ossa Bartoli*.

There was hardly a topic in jurisprudence that was not fructified by Bartolus, whether in substantive or in procedural,[3] in criminal or civil, in private or public law—in his commentaries on all parts of the *Corpus* and in his tracts one finds the same conciseness and brevity of expression.[4] Bartolus was one of the first, if not the first, who devoted special monographs to 'political' problems. This is exemplified by his tracts on tyranny, on the Guelfs and Ghibellines, on municipal statute law, on treason, on the government of the city-state, and similar topics. His conception of sovereignty—a mighty step forward in the understanding of the involved problem—was a classic instance of applying Roman law to contemporary conditions. Perhaps nowhere is Maitland's thesis of 'life and logic' more appropriate than in Bartolus' sovereignty theme. For his *civitas sibi princeps* was the juristic demonstration of state sovereignty expressed in current jurisprudential and governmental terms. It marks a turning point in the view of the law-creative capability of the people—the ascending theme, here employed with dexterous juristic devices, made its formal entry into juristic precincts. He used the *lex regia* and customary law as instruments and thus arrived at state sovereignty and the principle of representation epitomized in

[1] E. Casamassima, *Codices operum Bartoli de Sassoferrato recensiti: iter Germanicum* (1971). A. Garciá, *Iter Hispanicum* (1973), ed. 'Istituto per la storia dei Post-glossatori e Commentatori' by Bruno Paradisi.

[2] For all details concerning his influence in virtually all European countries, see the contributions to *Bartolo*, above all the brilliant inaugural lecture by F. Calasso, I, 1ff and the equally brilliant concluding lecture by B. Paradisi, I, 387ff.

[3] For comparative purposes see W. Ullmann, 'Medieval principles of evidence' in *LQR* 62 (1946) 77ff.

[4] There are numerous 16th-cent. eds. of his works (e.g. Turin 1577), incl. the Commentary on the *Tres Libri* and the *Authenticum*; one volume contains his *Consilia et Tractatus*.

the Bartolist formula of 'Concilium repraesentat mentem populi'.[1]

Subsequent political ideology owes a very great deal to Bartolus' influence. The conciliar movement is one such obvious instance which derived its juristic ingredients from his sovereignty thesis. Indeed, an echo of the thesis of representation can be heard in the constitutional troubles in France and also in seventeenth-century England. Moreover, through the Bartolist elaboration the principle of *utilitas publica* (the public interest and well-being) an ancient Roman principle gained a new lease of life. The doctrine of Bartolus concerning the division of statute law into *statuta realia, personalia,* and *mixta* was to imprint itself on the jurisprudence of the fifteenth and sixteenth centuries and is, to this day, a fundamental part of international private law.[2] In a way, this was an offshoot of his theme of sovereignty. In the exiled Perugian jurist at Oxford, Albericus Gentilis, Bartolist principles gained an unexpected hearing in English academic quarters. The Bartolist school dominated the lecture halls in the fourteenth- and fifteenth-centuries universities until superseded by humanist jurisprudence.[3]

In singling out Bartolus the impression should not be conveyed

[1] Clearly he was not the first to do so, but he did it better than others. One of the first jurists to have employed the *lex regia* for constructing the ascending theme seems to have been Petrus de Bellapertica, cf. the lengthy passage cit. in *MIL* at 48 n. 5; see also Cynus above, 108. Cf. now the perceptive study by J. Quillet, 'Universitas populi et représentation au XIVe s.' in *Misc. Med.* 8 (1971) 186ff. For his views cf. E. Betti in *Bartolo* II, 37ff; J. Baskiewicz, 7ff; M. David, 'Le contenu de l'hégémonie impériale' ibid. 199ff; W. Ullmann, 'De Bartoli sententia: Concilium repraesentat mentem populi', ibid. 705ff. C. N. S. Woolf remains the standard work: *Bartolus of Sassoferrato,* cit.

[2] Cf. A. Checchini, 'Presupposti giuridici dell'evoluzione storica dalla "bartoliana" teoria degli statuti' in *Bartolo* II, 61ff; G. Luther, 'Der Einflus von Bartolus auf das deutsche internationale Privatrecht' ibid. II, 309ff; P. Vaccari, 'Utrum iurisdictio cohaeret territorio? La dottrina di Bartolo' ibid. 735ff. Economic points are dealt with by R. Trifone, ibid., 691ff.

[3] For this cf. D. Maffei, *Gli inizi dell' umanesimo giuridico* (1956); M. P. Gilmore, *Humanists and jurists* (1963). For the effects see esp. the most stimulating study by D. R. Kelley, *Foundations of modern historical scholarship* (1970), 116ff, 151ff, and 183-214.

that the numerous other jurists populating the many universities in Italy, France, and, in the fifteenth century, also Germany and Poland, deserved no consideration. But hardly any spade work has been done on them and their works which have been available in print since the late fifteenth century. A particularly notorious example is Baldus de Ubaldis, the pupil of Bartolus. By any standards his output is quite astonishing, and the level of attainment is in no wise below that of his master, and yet he has not found a modern expositor to present his teachings in their totality.[1] Baldus was one of the most versatile, talented, widely read, fruitful and original thinkers in medieval jurisprudence.[2] He was not only a civilian, but also a canonist of well-deserved reputation as well as a feudist, that is a commentator on the feudal law. In all his exegeses he combined the civil with canon law and never lost sight of municipal statute law: it is this panoramic view on the law which gives his works their attractive complexion as sources.[3] His versatility was indeed outstanding, as he lectured on all three systems of law: in fact his lectures on the first three Books of the *Liber Extra* belong to the best canonistic commentaries of the fourteenth century. No less than Thomas Aquinas and lesser luminaries he had read and digested Aristotle and worked his ideas into his own jurisprudence (whom Bartolus had still scorned). A perusal of his writings makes the wide range of his sources amply clear.

What in fact makes the study of his enormous output a source of real pleasure is the combination of a fine penetrating juristic mind with a philosophic bent. His work is one of the few examples in which positive law does not amount to a justification

[1] The commemoration volume of 1901—*L'opera di Baldo*—does not fulfil this demand.

[2] Cf. E. M. Meijers, 'Balde et le droit international privé,' in *Études* IV (1966) 132ff; W. Ullmann, 'Baldus' conception of law' in *LQR* 58 (1942) 386ff; N. Horn, 'Philosophie in der Jurisprudenz der Kommentatoren: Baldus philosophus' in *Ius Commune* I (1968) 104ff; id., *Aequitas in den Lehren des Baldus* (1968); cf. my review in *RHD* 37 (1969) 280ff; J. A. Wahl, 'Immortality and inalienability: Baldus de Ubaldis' in *Med. Studies* 32 (1970) 308ff (lacks historical background).

[3] For a useful conspectus of Baldus' sources see G. Chévrier in *DDC* II, 41ff.

of each and every act by superior authority. That immediately succeeding generations made him a peer of his master was only right and proper. His works continued to be printed well into the seventeenth century.[1] Some 2060 *Consilia* testify to his international reputation as a jurist.[2] Whereas Bartolus died at the early age of 43, Baldus lived nearly 80 years (d. 1400) having occupied academic posts for more than 50 years in Perugia, Bologna, Pisa, Padua, Florence, Pavia, as well as important public positions, such as judge, vicar-general of the bishop of Todi, counsellor and legate of Perugia, and the like. One of his pupils became Pope Gregory XI. The Roman curia under Urban VI asked Baldus for a *Consilium* in the matter of the schism in July 1378; a second *Consilium* jointly with his colleague Johannes de Lignano, came a little later in the same year. Both upheld the legitimacy of Urban.[3] A younger contemporary of Baldus was Raphael Fulgosius whose fame both as a teacher at Pavia and Padua and as a juristic consultant was very great indeed, as is evidenced by his having been appointed *advocatus concilii* at Constance. His work on the Code is distinguished by originality and independence of opinion and judgment.[4] He appears to have been the first jurist who doubted the authenticity of the Donation of Constantine.[5]

Of the many contemporaries of Bartolus and Baldus—quite apart from their numerous pupils—two should receive at least a

[1] All his Commentaries on the Code, the Digest, the Institutes, feudal and canon law were very frequently printed, e.g. ed. Venice 1606; his special tracts in *TII* and his Additions to the 'Speculator' (see below, 180), and the *Repertorium* of Innocent IV's commentary are worth mentioning because they contain much relevant material. All are easily available in early prints.

[2] They too have often been printed. They are in five books.

[3] On this cf. my *Origins of the Great Schism* (new imprint and bibl. 1972) 143ff. Johannes de Lignano was professor of both laws at Bologna (d. 1383). Best known for his tract which concerns international law: Th. E. Holland (ed.), *De bello, de represaliis et duello* (1917). Details in van Hove 495, 506f.

[4] Ed. Lyons 1547. I am doubtful about the view of W. Engelmann, op. cit. (above, 104 n. 3), p. XX that this ed. was a *reportatio* (and not a full-length commentary). Details in Savigny VI, 270ff.

[5] D. Maffei, *La donazione di Costantino nei giuristi medievali* (1964) 262ff; here at n. 5 copious lit. on the question.

passing mentioning. Neither of them was an academic teacher, each was a practitioner of renown, and each exercised great influence. The one was Albericus de Rosciate (d. ca. 1350), a pupil of the famous Ricardus Malumbra and of Oldradus, whose practical work at Bergamo in Northern Italy quite clearly stimulated him to literary activity. In his Commentaries on the Code and the Digest he exhibited a happy combination of theory and practice, basing himself wherever he could, on the actual text of documents which he frequently transcribed in full, so for instance the judgment of Henry VII against Robert of Naples in 1313 or Louis IV's decree *Licet iuris*;[1] he also managed to show how closely linked the creation of law was with the actual historical situation. His most famous work concerned itself with the interpretation of municipal statutes in which understandably a great many governmental and political topics came to be discussed.[2] The other was Lucas de Penna, a Neapolitan, who though a practitioner was also a notable *Privatgelehrter*. He composed one of the most important commentaries on the (last) Three Books of the Code, and his work has several distinguishing characteristics: combination of theory with practice which furnished him with numerous concrete examples and had sharpened his eye for social realities; a very great learning of ancient literature as well as of non-juristic writers, such as Thomas Aquinas; a philosophic bent which enabled him to promote the understanding of public and criminal law conspicuously; his independence of mind in political questions greatly appealed to the (later) French jurists who lavishly quoted him; and lastly his frequent quotation of John of Salisbury's *Policraticus* which he thought was the name of the author: John thereby gained a new lease of life in

[1] Ed. of his Commentaries on the Code and Digest Lyons 1548; many other eds.; his tract *De regulis iuris* ed. Pavia 1515. For the second mentioned document see his comments on C, VII, 37, 3, no. 16, fo. 108vb (he was then staying at the curia) and for the first his comments on C, IX, 8, 5, fo. 189va–190rb.

[2] *Super statutis* (ed. Frankfurt 1606) (and other eds.). For stimulating observations see M. Sbriccoli, 'Politique et interprétation juridique dans les villes italiennes du MA' in *Archives de philosophie du droit* (1972) 99ff (includes also other jurists).

the later medieval and early modern political literature. The style
of Lucas' work is refreshingly free from contemporary deficiencies; it has a certain elegance, shows subtlety and liberality of
mind, and above all reveals great humanity.[1]

It would however be erroneous to think that outstanding civilian scholarship was confined to Italy, France and Naples. There is
at least one scholar whose work deserves a few remarks in the
present context. It is Philip of Leyden, an exact contemporary of
Bartolus, Albericus de Rosciate and Lucas, who belonged to an
old patrician family of Leyden and later became a cleric. His large
book *De cura rei publicae et sorte principantis*[2] is the work of a very
well-trained jurist who attempted to apply Roman law to contemporary social, economic and political problems. Written
over a period of some twenty years (1355–75), the work must be
credited with some originality and independence of approach and
also a certain courageousness on the part of the author, even if the
presentation and organization leave a good deal to be desired. A
strong moralist tone pervades the tract which treats of a number
of topics that usually did not attract the attention of professional
jurists: his wide-ranging horizon scans such varied subjects as
the erection of houses, military arrangements, alleviation of
poverty, the position and standing of agricultural labourers, of
monks, of princes, and he has also a chapter on the 'iocunditas
nuptiarum'. Philip does not wield the juristic scalpel with the
elegance and dexterity of a Lucas or a Bartolus and sometimes
approaches the level of commonplace statements. Consistency
was not apparently his strength, for instance, on such a vital
question as to whether the count of Holland was able to apply to
himself sovereign status and therefore become the object of high
treason;[3] on the location of original public power no sharp contours seem detectable. Yet on the other hand his insistence on the

---

[1] For all details and influence of his work see *MIL*. In addition to the writers
here mentioned, reference should be made to F. Hotman's *Francogallia* ed. cit.
(below, 292 n. 4), at 256, 502, who was obviously familiar with Lucas.

[2] Ed. s'Gravenhage 1900. No MS of the work survives. Ed. princeps 1516 of
Leyden is now repr. (1971) with an introduction by R. Feenstra.

[3] R. Feenstra, *Philip of Leyden* (David Murray Lecture 1970), at 68ff.

priority of *utilitas publica* in any shape or form is a very marked feature of the work.[1] This somewhat unwieldy composition is badly in need of close analysis, if only to show the different approach to identical jurisprudential and governmental problems.[2]

There was an avenue of late medieval juristic scholarship which was peculiar—perhaps unique—to an academic discipline. Through this avenue scholarship was able to exercise a considerable influence both on the law in general, and on governmental practice and theory in particular. This was through the medium of the *Consilia*, which were expert opinions given by the jurists on topics submitted to them from all over Europe. In an inconspicuous way this had begun in the first half of the thirteenth century and from then on greatly increased: the lucrative aspect should not remain unmentioned. It was the wealthy and powerful, the reigning dynasties, the municipalities, the prosperous merchants, the baronial families, no less than monasteries and rich landowners who approached the jurists. Questions of citizenship, its acquisition and loss, taxation, military duties, advisability of undertaking a military campaign, legality or illegality of reprisals, issues of maritime law, the relations of conquered territories to the conquering Ruler, and the hundreds of other problems falling into the precintcs of public law and administration were topics submitted to the academic jurists, not to mention of course the myriads of contentious issues relative to property, inheritance, boundaries, fishing rights, and so on and so forth, which are primarily of interest to the social historian. There are literally speaking thousands of *Consilia* from the thirteenth to the sixteenth centuries; a good many have been printed, but this genre of source material has hardly been touched by modern scholarship. The *Consilia* were first-class means to combine theory and practice. How authoritative the opinion of the jurists was can be gauged from their frequent consultation by the Roman curia,

[1] W. Berges, *Die Fürstenspiegel des hohen & späten MA* (1938) has drawn attention to this (259f).

[2] Lit. in Berges, 249ff, 348f, where all essential points will be found. Supplementary details in R. Feenstra, op. cit.

as well as by individual popes and anti-popes, kings and other Rulers.[1]

From the scholarly standpoint the picture that emerges in the late fourteenth and fifteenth centuries is a considerable shift from the exegesis of the juristic sources to application of the law by means of the *Consilia*. Indubitably, pure scholarship suffered stagnation: there was in fact regression where once there had been sparkling originality, and scholarship was apparently satisfied with the accumulation of 'authority' in the shape of quotations. The resultant yield in regard to the theory of government was extremely meagre. This decline of juristic scholarship was due to the social, political, and especially religious and ecclesiastical instability which gravely affected the universities and hence, understandably, jurisprudence as the foremost of the social sciences. The lecture hall had become as stuffy as the times had become stale. Above all, the monopoly of the jurists in matters of government came to be broken by the rapidly advancing political ideology, based as this now was on the rediscovered Aristotle. This new political ideology began to siphon off a great many ingredients of jurisprudence which had made it the prime governmental science in the Middle Ages. Jurisprudence and political ideology became two autonomous branches of learning. Within the sphere of public government jurisprudence had first to share its place with political science and was in course of time replaced by the latter, though there was to remain a very strong affinity between the two branches of intellectual disciplines.

[1] It would be tedious to enumerate all the *Consilia* the jurists gave. Cf. e.g., Dynus (ed. Lyons 1551); Barthol. Salicetus (d. 1412; ed. Venice 1489); Raph. Fulgosius (d. 1427; ed. Lyons 1548); Ludov. Romanus Pontanus (d. 1439; ed. Lyons 1546); Paulus Castrensis (d. 1441, ed. Frankfurt 1572; for an interesting *consilium* see J. Kirshner, 'Paolo di Castro on cives ex privilegio' in *Renaissance Studies H. Baron* (1971) 227ff); Alex. Tartagnus (in 7 books, ed. Lyons 1585). For Bartolus as a consiliator see H. Coing, 'Die Anwendung des C.I.C. in den Consilien des Bartolus' in *Europa e il diritto romano* (1954) I. 71ff; G. Kisch, *Consilia: eine Bibliographie der Konsiliensammlungen* (1970), but cf. my review in *Renaissance Quarterly* 24 (1972) 530ff; for hitherto unknown *Consilia* by Toulouse Masters (early 14th cent.) see H. Gilles, 'Trois consultations des Doctores Tolosani' in *RHD* 39 (1971) 157ff, with ed. of texts.

CHAPTER 4

The Canon Law

Considering that in the medieval period the most distinguishing feature in public life was the practical application of the Christian faith, the fixation of individual articles of the faith in the shape of the law is comprehensible. This law when formulated by ecclesiastical authority was called canon law. Three points deserve to be stressed in connection with canon law. First, there is the already mentioned legal complexion of the Bible. This is conspicuously true of the Old Testament, but it is also true of the Pauline exposition of the Christian way of life, instanced in the letter to the Romans. Linked with this is the second point which indeed has already been the subject of comment, that is, the explanation of the Christian faith in terms of the (Roman) law by apologists who were jurists of considerable calibre. From its infancy the Christian theme was indissolubly associated with the idea of the law, and Roman law provided the juristic mechanics and the technical equipment for all canon law. One, if not the earliest, example of a source demonstrating the combination of faith and law was the statement made by Pope Clement I which reveals the Roman predilection for law as a means of government, organization and administration.[1] The significance of this letter (written ca. 94 A.D.) lies in its exposition of the theme of subordination and the hierarchical ordering of society and herewith of authority.[2] This source established the link between the

[1] Ed. in H. Denzinger, *Enchiridion symbolorum*, 34th ed. (1967) 18ff ET and commentary in R. M. Grant and H. H. Graham, *The Apostolic Fathers: First and Second Clement* (1965). For the background of the basic passage in Matt. 16, 18f see now J. Kahmann, 'Die Verheissung an Petrus' in *L'évangile selon Matthieu*, ed. M. Didier (1972) 261ff.

[2] On this cf. W. Ullmann, 'The cosmic theme of the Prima Clementis and its significance for the concept of Roman rulership' in *Studia Patristica* XI(= *TU* 108) (1972) 85ff; see also U. Wieckert, 'Paulus, der 1. Clemensbrief und Stephan von Rom' in *ZKG* 79 (1968) 145ff at 149ff.

principles underlying the order of the Roman army and the Pauline arsenal of ideas and resulted in the corporational thesis according to which all Christians formed a body corporate—this was to become the all-pervading medieval theme. Therefrom emerged the thesis—powerfully supported by allegory—that it was the head of the body which directed its path. And that head was conceived in monarchic terms of government. It was within these precincts that, as far as the nascent Christian body public was concerned, the idea of the rule of law—allegorically represented by the relations of the soul to the body—came to have its specific significance.[1]

The third point relates to the actual sources of the canon law, which was essentially ecclesiastical law issued by the appropriate ecclesiastical functionary. There were two principal sources: the one, the papal law which was the expression of the monarchic status of the papacy (as the Roman Church came to be known from the late fourth century onwards), and the other the conciliar or synodal decree. Although the latter was historically antecedent to the former, it nevertheless in the medieval period had less significance in the present context, since basic governmental axioms were rarely set forth there.[2]

I

The medieval papacy, it is advisable to bear in mind, always considered itself primarily as an institution of government which held itself responsible for the authoritative guidance of the whole Church comprising as the notion did clergy as well as laity. The monarchic function of the papacy found expression in the vehicle which it borrowed from the imperial administration: the rescript or the decretal letter. The decretal letter had authoritative and binding force and was the classic example of the intimate connec-

---

[1] Above, 28f.

[2] For fundamental considerations see S. Kuttner, 'Some considerations on the role of secular law and institutions in the history of canon law' in *Scritti Luigi Sturzo* (1953) 1ff. See also H. E. Feine, 'Vom Fortleben des römischen Rechts in der Kirche' in *SavZKA* 42 (1956) 1ff.

tion between faith and law.[1] This connection indeed explains why the decretal (letter) had binding force in the West (which largely acknowledged the primacy of the papacy as the law-creating organ) and why it deployed no binding force in the East (which did not acknowledge the juristic and magisterial primacy of the papacy). In the final resort the decretal was a judicial verdict, hence the name: *decernere→decretum→decretalis epistola*.[2]

The decretal letter addressed either to individuals or to certain groups, to bishops or princes, was the authoritative papal statement concerning a controversial point in doctrine, liturgy or discipline—in short any matter which the papacy considered relevant for the well-being of the whole Christian body public. The decretal created law both in its formal and material respects. The decretals pouring forth from the papal chancery in ever increasing quantities formulated the canon law, and the term 'canon' signified the norm of right living (*norma recta vivendi*). 'Right living' was (and is) a relative concept depending on the kind of society to which it applied. And it was precisely in the context of fixing the norm of right living in a Christian society that the papacy came into conflict first with the imperial government in Constantinople, and later with royal governments in Western Europe. For the point was that the papacy insisted on its being the solely competent and qualified organ which knew 'the canon of Christian life'. This monopolization necessarily entailed conflicts, because both papacy and secular governments claimed the control of the same body public which was on the one side an empire (or kingdom) and on the other the Church (comprising clerics and lay). But by virtue of the wholeness point of view, according to which the Christian's life could not be split up into different compartments (religious, moral, political, etc.) but was one indivisible whole, the papacy claimed to direct the Christian's

---

[1] For this topic cf. *PGP* 95ff.

[2] The background was the imperial rescript or *responsum* (*imperatorum* or *pontificum*), cf. F. Schulz, *Hist. of Roman Legal Science* (1946) 16f, 152. They were collected, e.g. the *Decretorum libri tres* (ibid. 144f and 240); further L. Wenger, *Quellen* cit. 463f.

path in both his individual and his corporate capacity.[1] The monarchic authority, asserted with all the panoply of the Roman constitutional law, manifested itself in an unimpeachable manner: in the decretal letter which constituted law.

The oldest extant decretal, issued during the pontificate of Siricius (in 385), was addressed to the Spanish bishops and was a formidable juristic document settling a number of disputed points authoritatively.[2] From then onwards the output of papal decretals steadily increased, notably under Innocent I who raised the claim that all major causes were to be reserved to the papacy, a central element in all papal government.[3] In conjunction with the thesis of the sovereign status of the papacy this legal standpoint proved a potent handle for intervention in all kinds of matters which bore directly upon the well-being of the Christian body public. In view of the accelerated release of decretals their collection became a matter of practical necessity:[4] what should be kept in mind is that down to the thirteenth century there was no official papal collection of decretals. That before then all collections were private efforts is probably explicable by the usually very well-ordered papal archives which served, so to speak, as the ideological and legal storehouse of the papacy: the institution could thus dispense with officially sponsored collections.

Evidently, the greater the status of the papacy in the public field, the more voluminous its decretal output was and the greater the amount of governmental matter embodied in the decretals. This was quite demonstrably the case in the second half of the fifth century when after the Council of Chalcedon the papacy and the government in Constantinople were in serious conflict, the crux of which was the function and position of the Roman Church

[1] Cf. *PG* 19ff.

[2] Ed. in *PL* 13, 1130ff. For the background J. Gaudemet, *Le formation du droit séculier et du droit de l'église au IVe et Ve siècles* (1957).

[3] Innocent I in his Ep. 2, c. 6 in *PL* 20, 470. For the implications cf. W. Ullmann, 'The papacy as an institution of government' in *SCH* II (1965) 78ff, at 83ff. See now also G. Siegwalt, 'L'autorité dans l'église' in *RDC* 22 (1972) 97ff, esp. 103 and 241ff.

[4] For a survey of the early collections see Stickler 36ff (Spain, Gaul, Italy).

within the Christian world.[1] The papal decretals from Leo I
onwards elaborated the theme of papal monarchy with the help
of the Roman law by explaining the crucial Matthean passage
(16, 18f) in terms of the pope's legal successorship to St Peter:
the pope became his successor because he had inherited the status
and position of the 'prince of the apostles'. The explanation of this
passage thus moved entirely on a juristic level: jurisdictional
power was monarchic power—the centre piece of every papal
decretal throughout the Middle Ages.[2] In particular the Gelasian
decretals refined the Leonine substance by formulating two vital
principles. That of concession transferred a religious theme of
Pauline provenance to public government: the crucial idea that no
Christian had a right to power or public office, which according
to papal reasonings were the effluence of a divine good will, was
clothed in juristic language: the possessor of public power was
designated as the recipient of a good deed or grace (*beneficium* or
gratia). The other principle was that of a division of labour,
according to which the monarch, here the pope, embodied
the sum total of power (the concept and term were actually of
Leonine parentage) and had *auctoritas*, thus giving general binding
directions, while the execution was left to other organs. In itself
this principle was merely a specific application of the descending
theme which the fifth-century decretals crystallized.[3]

[1] Ed. of decrees of Chalcedon in *Decreta* 59ff (both Greek and Latin); the
two decrees which are of direct concern, are 17 and 28 (here at 71 and 75f).
On the council see A. Grillmeier & H. Bacht (eds.), *Das Konzil von Chalkedon*,
3 vols. (1954).

[2] Ed. of Leo I's decretals in *PL* 54, 595ff. For details see W. Ullmann, 'Leo I
and the theme of papal primacy' in *JTS* 11 (1960) 25ff. It should be noted that
despite the monarchic plenitude of power with which the pope was credited
(the idea and terminology of *plenitudo potestatis* are Leonine), he was never
called *pontifex maximus* in the M.A. This appellation became common in the
15th cent. when classical learning was revived, though even then it was not in
official documents, see R. Schieffer, 'Der Papst als Pontifex Maximus' in
SavZKA 57 (1971) 300, at 306ff.

[3] Ed. of Gelasius I's decretals in A. Thiel, *Epistolae pontificum Romanorum
genuinae* (1862) at 295ff. For the development *PG* 15ff and *SHP* 32ff. Discussion
and GT of some documents by H. Rahner, *Kirche & Staat im Frühmittelalter*,
2nd ed. (1962) 205ff; A. S. McGrade, 'Two fifth-century conceptions of papal

Only fragments of decretal output in the sixth century survived, notably the letters of Pelagius I.[1] A most important exception is the Register of Gregory I which is an invaluable source
and proved to be a reservoir for numerous medieval collections.
Its original is lost, but an authentic copy of the eleventh century
has survived and shows the juristic skill and acumen of Gregory.[2]
In pursuit of his policy of bi-furcation[3] the theme of papal
primacy formed the backbone of virtually every decretal dispatched to the West: the full rigour of papal jurisdiction emerged
in them—precisely the theme that was conspicuously absent in his
communications sent to the East. Further, the theme of un-
conditional obedience of the subject (the inferior) to the law issued
by superior authority[4] and the justification of penal measures to
be taken by the papacy against recalcitrant Rulers were other
Gregorian tenets relative to government that reverberated
throughout the medieval period.[5]

With the papacy taking an ever increasing lead in the shaping
of the ideological map of Europe—Gregory I came to be called
Pater Europae—the importance of its decretals increased correspondingly. Canon law was the one written system of law that
was created for contemporaries, grew out of the exigencies of
society and was thus a living law—in this it differed fundamentally

primacy' in *Studies in Medieval and Renaissance History* 7 (1969) 3ff. For borrowing from Roman law in the famous Ep. 12 c. 2 (ed. cit. 351) with its distinction
between *auctoritas* and *potestas* and the pope's responsibility for the whole
Church, see J. L. Nelson, 'Gelasius I's doctrine of responsibility' in *JTS* 18
(1968) 154ff (the model may have been the *actio noxalis*).

[1] Ed. P. Gassó & C. Battle, *Pelagii Papae Epistolae quae supersunt* (1956);
cf. my review in *JTS* 8 (1957) 344ff.

[2] Ed. *MGH. Epp* I and II.

[3] For this see *SHP* 51ff, at 54f.

[4] His *Homilies* ed. in *PL* 76, 1132ff, contain a good deal of hitherto unnoticed
material of which the theme of obedience is just one. The reference is to *Hom.*
II, 26 (col. 1201). See also below, 233.

[5] See *Reg* XIII, 11, ed. cit. II, 376. Gregory VII based himself on this in his
justificatory letter concerning the excommunication and suspension of Henry
IV: *Reg* IV, 2 and VIII, 21 (ed. in E. Caspar, 294ff and 550f). For some aspects
of his influence see J. Gaudemet in *Études Le Bras* (1965) 129ff and C. G. Mor,
ibid. 283ff.

from its model, the Roman law, which by the time of its codification was in many respects outdated. But the canon law—emanating as it did from a real and actively governing monarch—had to take reality into account: it proved itself highly flexible and resilient and absorbed a number of Germanic features into its own system, notably in liturgical, symbolic respects and also in regard to ordeals and even the proprietary church system, so hotly attacked at a later period.[1] Papal canon law was one of the chief instruments by which the amalgamation of Roman, Christian and Germanic elements was effected.

What ensured the eventual success of canon law and herewith also its character as a source of governmental ideas were its repeated re-enactment, the dynamic initiative of the papacy, and its active intervention in the process that eventually shaped Western Europe. Over and above this, there was the ready availability of reference to the well-kept archives and registers in the papal chancery which functioned as the legal memory of the institution. From the papal point of view the decretals were held to be the chief instruments by which the papacy as the law-creative organ 'built' the Church—the realization of the promise in Matt. 16, 18f: in the decretal law the papacy saw the fulfilment of the function for which it had been created in this self-same passage. To a large extent canon law embodying as it did papal ideology had a large share in forming the complexion and the very shape of the medieval social structure; yet it must also be kept in mind that this papal canon law would hardly have achieved this had it not equipped itself with the techniques of Roman law which thus became an indispensable, yet auxiliary tool. An early example of the eighth/ninth century is the so-called *Lex romana canonice compta* which adjusts and also applies Roman law to contemporary contingencies. The work needs closer ideological analysis than it has so far received.[2] The scaffolding provided by Roman law was however merely of technical

[1] Exemplified by the Roman synod of 826 chaired by the pope that endorsed the system: ed. *MGH Concil.* II, 576, c. 21.

[2] Ed. C. G. Mor, *Lex romana canonice compta: testo di leggi romanocanoniche del s. IX* (1927). See also id. in *Études Le Bras*, cit., and Stickler 150, 433.

assistance.[1] The significance of this was that in the realm of law exactly the same features were observable which characterized the essence of Eastern and Western societies, that is, in the former priority belonged to history and tradition to which faith was subordinated; in the latter priority belonged to faith which claimed to subordinate to itself the historical development. The West of Europe did not begin its perceptible historical development until the seventh and eighth centuries, that is, with Christianization and hence with the effect which canon law began to exercise.[2] The official correspondence of the papacy with the new Frankish Rulers (Pippin and Charlemagne) contained a very great deal of matter relative to government in Christian society: it was collected by Charlemagne himself and is known as the *Codex Carolinus*,[3] which is a source of prime importance not merely for general historical purposes, but also for governmental principles, since the papacy had here the first opportunity of presenting some of its basic topics in a concrete manner in its dealings with secular Rulers who were not emperors.

Yet the almost paradoxical situation arose that the more the Christian faith became the leaven of society, propagated as the faith was in the authoritative legal pronouncements of the papacy, the more conspicuous the part became which secular Rulers played in ecclesiastical and religious matters. For by virtue of the theocratic function which they had come to accept as a result of Christian influences, secular Rulers considered themselves entitled and bound to take a hand in the shaping of their kingdoms. After all, as this self-same Christian viewpoint also stated, the kingdoms had been entrusted to kings by divinity. In this respect

---

[1] C. G. Mor, 'Le droit romain dans les collections canoniques des Xe et XIe siècles' in *RHDFE* 6 (1927) 512ff; id. in *ACII* II (1934) 276ff; id., 'Diritto romano e diritto canonico nell'età pregraziana' in *Europe e il diritto romano* (1954) II, 13ff.

[2] For the development *CR* 43ff, 135ff. For the collections from ca. 840 onwards see *F.-LeBr.* I. and Stickler 99ff. For the immediately preceding period van Hove 265ff. For the basic presentation see F. Maassen, *Geschichte der Quellen & Literatur des canonischen Rechts* (repr. 1956).

[3] Ed. in *MGH. Epp* III, 469ff. The collection reaches down to 791. Its analysis from the ideological angle is an urgent task.

they did not differ in essence from the Eastern emperors. Despite the dissemination requested by Charlemagne of a large collection in the Frankish realms[1] there was a recession of papal letters and communications and above all influence in the late eighth and early ninth centuries.[2] The very brisk conciliar activity in the vast Frankish domains[3] was another reason for the diminution of papal material. The Carolingian Renaissance catapulted some first-class minds into the forefront, precisely those who were to dominate the ecclesiastical scene for a century and a half, and were potently instrumental in the implementation of the royally decreed Renaissance itself.

In the ninth century the canon law of the papacy came to be only one of the several legal and governmental sources and had to take its place next to the particular law passed by kings or by councils. The result was a strongly marked legal particularism partly also explicable by the increasing power of the bishops in their dioceses which resulted in the episcopalist system: according to this system the diocesan bishop was to all intents and purposes independent of the papacy. The hallmark of episcopalism was an aversion from a centralized monarchic papacy, the accentuation of territorial lordship personified in the diocesan bishop, and the harmonious co-operation between episcopate and secular Rulers.[4] Episcopalism was underpinned by the proprietary church system, according to which the owner of the land was entitled to build a church on his land and therefore to appoint the cleric to this church which remained the lay lord's property. Technically, the owner conferred a living (the *beneficium*) as well as the clerical function (the *officium*) on the cleric. The system was explicable only by contemporary agrarian and economic

---

[1] Ed. in *PL* 67, 315ff (*Dionysio-Hadriana*); Maassen, 441ff; Stickler 106ff; *DDC* IV, 1131ff; H. Mordek, 'Dionysio-Hadriana und Vetus Gallica' in *SavZKA*, 55 (1969) 39ff.

[2] For this see Ch. de Clercq, 'La législation religieuse franque dépuis l'avénement de Louis de Pieux' in *RDC* 4 (1954)—8 (1958).

[3] Ed. *MGH Concil.* I–II. See below, 152f.

[4] The so-called *Capitula episcoporum* served purely diocesan interests, but are valuable sources of information concerning regional affairs. Survey in van Hove 184f, and Stickler 114ff.

conditions. It was based on customary law which had an enormous governmental potential. Gradually the monasteries came to be engulfed and in course of time the highest ecclesiastical ranks were 'in the gift' of the king. Within this framework traditional, customary and unsophisticated as it was, the papal canon law found little response. As a matter of fact, in 826 the Roman synod under the chairmanship of the pope himself endorsed the system.[1]

Yet opposition to this kind of government of a Christian society was never absent: it was said that it violated basic axioms, because unqualified organs, such as kings, appointed clerics, prompted as they were not by considerations of suitability for the ecclesiastical office, but by considerations which were wholly alien to their office; in any case, no ecclesiastical office should be conferred by a layman. This kind of opposition seems to have been concentrated in or near Rheims and found expression in one of the most influential and largest (quantitatively and qualitatively) forgeries produced in the medieval period: the Pseudo-Isidorian collection.[2] The main aims of the forgers—a single individual could hardly produce this vast concoction—were the abolition of secular control over the clergy, and the elimination of particularism by the centralization of the ecclesiastical government in the papacy; a further object was the reduction of councils to purely consultative assemblies, unless convoked by the papacy or by their decrees having been sanctioned papally, in which case they assumed universal legal character. The means used to achieve these aims were partly the fabrication of decretals and partly the falsification of genuine canonistic material, with the addition of some genuine matter.

The essential backbone was the decretal legislation by the early papacy down to Silvester I which was wholly invented; it began

[1] Above, 125 n. 1.

[2] Ed. P. Hinschius, *Decretales Pseudo-Isidorianae* (repr. 1963). For some deficiencies see Shaffer Williams, *Codices Pesudo-Isidoriani* (1971). On the work itself see now H. Fuhrmann, *Einfluss und Verbreitung der pseudo-isidorischen Fälschungen* I (1972), II (1973); older literature *PG* 177ff. For the view that the notorious Le Mans forgeries possibly applied Pseudo-Isidore specifically, see W. Goffart, *The Le Mans Forgeries* (1966); id., 'Postscript' in *Analecta Bollandiana* 87 (1969) 5ff; cf. M. Wallace-Hadrill's review in *Speculum* 43 (1968) 719ff.

with the spurious letter of Clement I to St James, the brother of Christ, which the forgers could not resist expanding by more than doubling its length.[1] In this first part (comprising 254 closely printed pages in the modern edition) and actually concluding it, was 'incorporated' the forged Donation of Constantine which showed that Constantine had by a constitutional grant raised the position of the pope (Silvester) to the pinnacle of supreme and unappealable power by giving St Peter (unspecified) territories and provinces of the occident, making him the imperial monarch in the West and conferring on him also the imperial status in the shape of the imperial insignia. Of all the enactments in this collection the Donation was certainly the most valuable and useful and deserves special consideration as a source because it dealt in contemporary terms with the concept of Roman-Christian Rulership. The influence of this forgery concocted in the mid eighth century[2] cannot be exaggerated.[3] The two themes monotonously reappearing in almost every 'decretal' were papal primacy,[4] and therefore papal monarchy and its law, and opposition to lay intervention in ecclesiastical matters. The ingenuity of this 'atelier' of forgers (the expression is that of the late Gabriel Le Bras) commands respect. Although the primary aim was the abolition of lay control, the real winner was the papacy.

The ideological substance was not new.[5] What was new was the form, that is, the decretal[6] that was to prove how deviant and

---

[1] For this source see above, 39 n. 5.

[2] See *PG* 75ff and 466ff.

[3] *Ps.-Isidore*, ed. cit. 249ff; also in C. B. Coleman, *Constantine the Great & Christianity* (1914) 228ff; new ed. by H. Fuhrmann in *MGH Fontes iuris Germanici antiqui* X (1968). For actual use in the papal chancery in the 8th cent. see *PG* 59 n. 1, 60, 65 n. 3, 73 n. 3. For the numerous collections which incorporated the forgery see *F.-LeBr.* I, 209ff and *CR* 153ff. For the use by later jurists see D. Maffei, *La donazione di Costantino nei giuristi medievali* (1964); cf. my review in *JTS* 16 (1965) 526ff.

[4] See on this now A. Marchetto, *Episcopato e primato pontificio nelle decretali pseudo-isidoriane* (1972).

[5] See *PG* 177f; now also H. Fuhrmann, *Einfluss* (above, 128 n. 2) I, 65ff.

[6] Cf. also the observations by J. Rambaud-Buhot, 'La critique des faux dans l'ancien droit canonique' in *BEC* 126 (1968) 5ff, at 25ff.

repulsive contemporary governmental practices were. In one form or another this could have been proved by statements from littérateurs, individual popes and even councils and contemporaries, but their statements lacked the crushing weight (quantitatively) and the qualitative stamp of early Christianity and of its pristine authority. Hence the recourse to 'early' papal law which represented the 'norm of right living'. It is always overlooked that Pseudo-Isidore was not forward looking, but was intent on reestablishing a legal and governmental system that had been set aside by wholly non-Christian usages and practices: the 'true' tradition was observable in the law as it was conveyed in their own fabrication. The great appeal of this work lay in its ease of handling: all 'relevant' matter was contained within two stiff covers. Nowhere else could the descending theme have been presented in such concentrated and 'persuasive' a manner as here. If a lemma or rubric had to be chosen for Pseudo-Isidore, it might be: Strict hierarchical ordering of Christian society and the stern implementation of this order through obedience by the inferior to functionally qualified superior authority culminating in the papacy as the one biblically founded monarchic institution.

Very soon after Pseudo-Isidore was finished (853), another collection of equally spurious origin appeared. Its purpose was exactly the same as that of Pseudo-Isidore. The aim of Benedictus Levita[1]—allegedly a deacon of the cathedral of Mainz—was to show that there had been a 'tradition' demonstrated by royal and imperial decrees which long ago had fully endorsed papal primacy and clerical immunity from secular jurisdiction and other controls. As a legal source Benedictus Levita is invaluable for fathoming the interests of contemporary ecclesiastics, but it never reached the wide public which Pseudo-Isidore did. There is still no satisfactory edition of the work. Its value as a source lies in its reflection of the motivations of contemporary clerics, even if these aims had an incomparably more persuasive spokesman

---

[1] Ed. in *MGH Leges* II, 40ff. Lit in *F. LeBr.* I, 202ff; van Hove 237ff; *PG* 184ff. About Roman law in Benedictus see F. L. Ganshof in *IRMAE* I, 2bcc, αβ (1969). See further H. Mordek, 'Une nouvelle source de Bénoit le Lévite' in *RDC* 20 (1970) 241ff.

in Pseudo-Isidore.¹ Whether or not a particular legal collection becomes influential, depends a great deal on favourable external contingencies, among which political stability, social peace and receptivity of the soil for the relevant laws are in the foreground. But these presuppositions only partially existed before the mid-eleventh century. It was not until then that the full impact of Pseudo-Isidore could be witnessed, although many a collector of the 'ancient' law had seen the 'usefulness' of the work earlier.

The collections of canon law in the period between Pseudo-Isidore and the Gregorian age showed a strong particularist, if not regional or local flavour, and many of them still await their editor and interpreter. They came from France as well as the Western and Eastern portions of the Carolingian inheritance no less than from Italy and from what is now Switzerland.² In some of them attempts were made to weave Roman law into the growing canon law and in so doing new governmental conceptions came to be evolved. A good example from the late ninth century is the *Collectio Anselmo dedicata*, of Italian origin, which is divided into 12 books in which an approach to a systematic exposition is made. The work was dedicated to Anselm II, Archbishop of Milan (d. 896). It contains excerpts from papal decretals, notably Gregory I and also intelligently selected passages from Roman law; there is considerable reliance on Pseudo-Isidore. The work emphasized the hierarchical theme and the tenet of the jurisdictional primary of the papacy as a presupposition for orderly ecclesiastical government.³

An entirely different species of canon law is set forth by the work of Regino of Prum, composed in the beginning of the tenth century (about 906). In some respects it was the exact antipode to the *Anselmo dedicata*, representing as it did a marked episcopalist standpoint. The quite voluminous collection—*Liber de synodalibus*

¹ The so-called *Capitula Angilramni* (ed. P. Hinschius 757ff) had not much influence; see *PG* 175f.

² For a survey see Stickler 144ff.

³ Despite numerous preparatory studies, notably by P. Fournier and C. G. Mor, the work is still not edited. As far as I know only Bk. I is ed. by J. C. Besse in *RDC* 9 (1959) 207ff, at 214ff.

causis—have not without justification been called guidelines for the diocesan administrator (H. von Schubert), or seen from another angle 'une expression manifeste des principes de la Réforme carolingienne' (Fournier-Le Bras). Regino gives an excellent account of the episcopal judicial visitations, the 'synodal' means of detecting public crimes and the personnel employed. In the present context the work deserves especial attention as it shows how—in default of an effective royal governmental machinery—the attempt was made to establish public order by the ecclesiastical law and ecclesiastical institutions and procedures, such as the synodal method which Regino advocated. He appears to have reflected the practice of his time. It was the official enquiry, the *inquisitio* of Frankish origins, which when associated with Roman law, had a very great future in public law and became an effective tool of government.[1]

Yet another kind of canon law orientation is represented by Burchard of Worms in his very important and influential *Decretum* from the early years of the eleventh century.[2] It is, probably, the largest of all collections before the mid-twelfth century. The avowed aim of the author was to set forth the canon of the Church in order to show the way to its 'reform' and to a Christian social order. These are indeed the very first distant rumblings of the great Investiture Contest. The work is of veritably encyclopedic dimensions.[3] Freedom of the clergy from lay control was the means to establish 'order' in a Christian society. Hence the barely disguised and all the more effective attack on the proprietary church system. Yet the papal primacy or monarchy played no significant role in the work which, in this sense, still belonged to

[1] Ed. (S. Baluzius) in *PL* 132, 175ff; modern ed. by F. G. A. Wasserschleben, *Reginonis libri duo de synodalibus causis et disciplinis ecclesiasticis* (1840). Admirable analysis in *F.-LeBr.* I, 244ff.

[2] For the dozens of small collections of little significance in the 10th cent. see *F.-LeBr.*: here as within Roman law there was 'pleine régression' (I. 362).

[3] Ed. in *PL* 140, 537–1090. For a very helpful bibliographical note see G. Fransen in *Trad* 25 (1969) 514f; M. Kerner, *Studien zum Dekret des Bischofs Burchard v. Worms*, 2 vols. (1971). For additional material in regard to the transmission of the work see H. Mordek, 'Handschriftenforschungen in Italien' in *QFIAB* 51 (1971) 626ff.

the old episcopalist strain.[1] What was a new departure was that theology was put at the service of the legal order: the nineteenth and twentieth books of the *Decretum* dealt with matters falling within the precincts of juristic theology, notably penance, and were significantly called the *Liber medicus* (XIX) and *Speculator* (XX). The differentiation between sin and crime was taken a step further; the same part also sets forth the remedies to be applied to criminal offenders—the criminal law begins to be seen as part of the public law. The influence of the work can be traced right through to the mid-twelfth century.[2]

However varied in character, depth, scope, and quality canonical collections of this period were, they performed a most valuable service: it was largely through them that the idea of the rule of law as the vehicle for managing public affairs was kept alive. In the general political instability of the time this idea might well have been suffocated. That in the course of the eleventh century the climate of opinion concerning fundamental matters of public life changed rapidly, was in no small measure due to the influence of the collections: they had prepared the ground not merely by cultivating the idea of the rule of law, but above all by constantly stressing the kind of society which could call itself Christian. This latter theme came to be broadcast ever more insistently and with ever greater single-mindedness as the century advanced. The other significant point to be stressed is that the collections showed the need for distilling a purely religious theme into the language of the law. That the great divide—the Investiture Contest—showed the indissoluble link between (Christian) ideology and law is by now generally accepted, but needs to be stressed again in the present context, because it was the many collections of canon law which exercised a steadily increasing influence in wider and wider sections of the populace and thus materially contributed to the changing outlook through the length and breadth of Western Europe. Ecclesiastical law had in this respect a

[1] See the subtle analysis by *F.-LeBr.* I, 388ff; M. Kerner, op. cit. is not always aware of the deficiencies of Burchard.

[2] In general *F.-LeBr.* I, 414ff; further C. G. Mor, 'La reazione al Decretum Burchardi in Italia' in *St. Greg.* I (1947) 197ff; A. Pelster, ibid. I, 321ff.

very great advantage in comparison with the contemporary secular law, which had no such collections dispersed throughout Western Europe. Further, despite all differences and variations, the authors and readers of the canon law collections were clerics who by virtue of their status and function shared a number of fundamental common assumptions and a basically similar outlook.

It was on the strength of the transmitted canon law that the hierocratic party in the mid-eleventh century was able to claim that it did not advance any novel points or aims. What was new was the application of ancient ideology which had by now become traditional, but this latter feature was entirely due to the effect which the many canon law collections had had. The intellectual élite of society had become attuned to this ideology and its manifestation, the law. In the collections was found (or believed to be found) the 'norm of right living'. Hence from the mideleventh century multiformity of collections of canon law began to give way to uniformity of thematic law. In general, therefore, by emphasizing the primatial tenet the rapidly increasing collections of the second half of the eleventh century exhibit a theme, that of papal monarchy. The law as created at the time and as collected, stressed consequently the two presuppositions for any governmental thought: society and its government. And the sources pointed out that this twin concept of society and government was firmly anchored in the Matthean passage according to which Christ had *uno ictu* founded a society (the Church) as well as its government (papal monarchy). Hand in hand with this went the stress on the wholeness point of view which as a fundamental Christian axiom found concrete expression in the canon law. The 'totality' of human contingencies covered by the canon law, could be understood only from this premiss.

The impetus came from Archdeacon Hildebrand in the fifties of the century. He had suggested to Cardinal Peter Damian that he should collect in one small and handy volume all the prerogatives appertaining to the Roman Church.[1] This impetuous demand was not fulfilled by Damian, but by the author of the

---

[1] Peter Damian in *PL* 154, 89.

collection of 74 Titles, which heavily relied on Pseudo-Isidore and thematically pointed up the papal monarchical function.[1] This was one of the earliest thematic law collections to be followed by a spate of others. They were all with one exception private works, and had nothing to do with the curia.[2] The exception is the so-called *Dictatus Papae* of Gregory VII. These are the chapter headings of a lost canonical collection. They summed up the 'prerogatives' of the papacy in a singularly impressive and concise manner and presented the theme of papal monarchy as the only permissible government in a Christian society. The collection to which these 27 headings refer, can thus be regarded as having received official approval.[3] The period of

[1] Ed. in part by F. Thaner, in his ed. of *Anselmi Lucensis collectio canonum una cum collectione minore* (1906–16). A new ed. by J. Gilchrist is soon to appear. The authorship of Humbert is no longer certain; cf. *St. Greg.* I (1947) 65ff; II (1948) 91ff; III (1950) 149ff; IV (1952) 111ff; see now on the whole complex of questions H. Fuhrmann, 'Ueber den Reformgeist der 74 Titel-Sammlung (Diversorum Patrum Sententiae)' in *Festschrift H. Heimpel* (1972) II, 1101ff (with exhaustive lit.).

[2] The main collections were (all relevant details in *F.-LeBr.* II, 20ff also in Stickler 165ff): (a) The *Capitulare* of Cardinal Atto, the bishop-elect of Milan (cf. *SHP* 145) written between 1070 and 1075; ed. in A. Mai, *Scriptorum veterum nova collectio* VI, 2 (1832) 60ff. (b) Anselm of Lucca's collection, ed. F. Thaner (above, n. 1). He was also a publicist of calibre (*LdL* I, 519ff: *Liber contra Wibertum*). Probable date of the collection: 1080–6. Firmly orientated towards the papacy. Biographical details by C. Violante in *DBI* III (1961) 399ff. (c) Cardinal Deusdedit's *Collectio canonum*, ed. W. von Glanvell (1905). One of the largest and most consistent canonistic products. Contains numerous texts otherwise not known; probable date: 1081–7. He too was a publicist of calibre: *Contra invasores et simoniacos* (ed. *LdL* II, 292). (d) The *Collectio Britannica* lives under a heavy cloud of suspicion, see below, 138 n. 1. (e) Of especial importance was Archbishop Lanfranc's collection which was mainly instrumental in integrating the English Church into the framework of the universal Church after the Conquest. The original MS is in Trinity College, Cambridge. For this see the pioneering work by Z. N. Brooke, *The English Church & the Papacy* (repr. 1969). About Lanfranc's connexion with Pavia see N. Tamassia in *Mélanges Fitting* (1907) II, 189ff.

[3] Ed. in Gregory VII's *Reg* II, 55a (ed. E. Caspar in *MGH. Epp sell*, repr. 1955) 201ff. G. B. Borino's study on their character as chapter headings is fundamental: *Archivio della società romana di storia patria* 67 (1944) 237ff; see also K. Hofmann in *St. Greg.* I, 531ff and S. Kuttner ibid., II, 387ff. Analysis

canonistic development that began in the fifties of the eleventh
century, came to an end a little less than one hundred years later
with the work of Gratian.

The present context does not necessitate a detailed enumeration
of the many collections of canon law which appeared in the
interval.[1] Their common feature was the emphatic insistence on
papal primacy as the vivifying principle operative in a Christian
society. This monopolization of the function of the Roman
Church came to be one of the undisputed elements in the canon
law productions of the time. The other was the descending theme
of government and law, the gradation of officers and offices, and
with it the centralization of government. These collections were
strictly legal as well as works which set forth an ideological justification of 'the norm of right living', as instanced by Bonizo of
Sutri's *Liber de vita christiana*: it attempted to show how Christian
life was to be shaped by following the 'canon' of the Church.
What this source made abundantly clear was the indissoluble link
between faith and law: faith in the institution of the papacy as a
divinely established governing organ was the material ingredient
of the canon law. Contrariwise, it was not consent or agreement
given by those to whom law applied, which infused binding
character into canon law. This fundamental tenet of all canon law
formed the focal point of exposition in Bonizo's work.[2]

As a result of this development the papacy came to emerge in a

by K. Hofmann, *Der Dictatus Papae Gregors VII* (1933); B. Jacqueline, 'A propos
des Dict. Papae: les auctoritates apostolicae sedis d'Avranches' in *RHDFE* 34
(1956) 568ff. Background in *SHP* 151ff; for the Old Testament background
of many pronouncements see Ch. Schneider, *Prophetisches Sacerdotium &
heilsgeschichtliches Regnum im Dialog 1073-1077* (1972). For another possible DP
see H. Mordek, 'Proprie auctoritates apostolice sedis: ein zweiter DP Gregors
VII?' in *DA* 28 (1972) 105ff (with edition).

[1] Details in *F.-LeBr.* II, 127ff (Polycarp); the important collection of Alger
of Liège ed. in *PL* 180, 857ff (written in first or second decade of 12th cent.).
On this and the possible influence on Gratian see G. Le Bras, 'Alger de Liège
et Gratien' in *Rev. des sciences philos. et religieuses* 20 (1931) 5ff; also Stickler 192f.

[2] E. Perels (ed.), *Liber de vita christiana* (1930); see U. Lewald, *An der Schwelle
der Scholastik: Bonizo von Sutri & das Kirchenrecht seiner Tage* (1939); W. Ber-
schin, *Bonizo von Sutri: Leben & Werk* (1972).

most conspicuous way as a law-creative organ for contemporary Christian society. Here however two paradoxes must be mentioned in order to make this process understandable. Both are linked with the basic papal assumption that as an institution it desired nothing but the application of law for the right order to be established in a Christian society. Yet, there were many ecclesiastical laws—a short reflexion suffices to make us realize that 'canons' had been used for well over six hundred years—and despite the quantity of canon law there was not much uniform law: there were many collections of law but not one universal law. The papacy's urgent demand for the implementation of the law in fact compelled it to act with ever greater frequency as a legislative organ, with the consequence that the emerging papal canon law had direct relevance to contemporary exigencies and approached the character of a universal law. The disadvantage experienced in the eleventh century by canon law in comparison with Roman law which was a mature, polished and fixed law, was to prove itself a great advantage in the twelfth century, for by then canon law was largely contemporary law, and not, as Roman law was, an overwhelmingly historic law that was in constant need of adaptation.

The second paradox refers to the many contradictions in the collections of canon law. The paradox lies in that the papacy enjoined application of the canon law, but in view of the numerous contradictions it was extremely difficult to follow this postulate. Nevertheless in order to achieve harmony and a smooth management and organization of the universal Church, unity if not also uniformity of law was imperative. The decretals, rules, statutes, canons, declarations, statements, etc. in the collections were frequently hundreds of years old and were issued by authorities of varying standing and often referred to conditions vastly different from contemporary contingencies. If, then, there were several decrees some of which contradicted each other, which one was to be applied? The problem was not unique to canon law, but affected Roman law just as much as theology and philosophy. The answer lay in the development of what came to be called the dialectical or scholastic method: perhaps at no other time than in the late eleventh century was the application of this method more urgent.[1]

Recent research has shown how the dialectical method evolved. Although this research is mainly concerned with Roman law and civilian jurisprudence,[2] its findings are applicable to canon law. The method indicated how contrary statements might be solved. It was generally accepted that laws were emanations of the human mind which was a divine gift incapable of contradicting itself; it was the task of the interpreter to solve contradictions which were only apparent, not real. The instrument to be used to achieve this end was the mental operation of a distinction which separated immutable laws from those which were changeable, because prompted by the exigencies of time, space and person. By applying this method it was possible to achieve the much desired harmony of the intellectual and real worlds. The method was indispensable for a fruitful pursuit of jurisprudence (which was thus able to make use of the teleological argument) and the prerequisite for the canon law's becoming a universally accepted norm of living in a Christian society. The method was one of the means which transformed multiplicity of law into uniformity. As the method was also applicable to Roman law studies,[3] philosophy and theology, it can be said that jurisprudential exigencies once more decisively influenced the development in intellectual spheres.[4]

[1] Urban II's alleged letter (cf. *PG* 371 n. 4) in S. Loewenfeld, *Epp pontificum Romanorum ineditae* (1885) 61f is shown to be a further spurious element in the (by now notorious) *Coll.Britannica*. See on this S. Kuttner, 'Urban II and the doctrine of interpretation' in *St. Grat* XV (1972) 53ff (fundamental). For the unreliability of the *Coll. Brit.* cf. W. Ullmann, 'Nos si aliquid incompetenter' in *Ephemerides Iuris Canonici* 9 (1953) 275ff; Kuttner, art. cit. 74 at notes 70–2, to which should be added J. L. Nelson, 'The problem of Alfred's anointing' in *J.E.H.* 18 (1967) 145ff; see also F. Dvornik, *The Photian Schism* (1948) 324ff.

[2] See above, 86 n. 1, 91 n. 1, for canon law Kuttner cit.

[3] Despite Justinian's bombastic claim in the promulgation edict (*Tanta*) that there was nothing but harmony within the body of his codification, the need for a method to solve the *contrarietates* became at once evident as soon as Roman law was studied professionally. See *Tanta*, preamble and §15.

[4] See the brilliant exposition by J. de Ghellinck, *Le mouvement théologique du XIIe siècle*, 2nd ed. (1948) 60ff.

One of the first to apply the dialectical method in practice was the already mentioned Bonizo of Sutri, and Ivo of Chartres avowedly made the method the central point of his enquiry: he spoke of a 'consonantia canonum' thereby indicating the principle of harmony.[1] His application was all the more important as his scheme was instrumental in reaching a settlement of the outstanding issues between the French king and the papacy in the matter of investitures.[2] Similarly, the works of Bernold of Constance,[3] Polycarp, that is, Cardinal Gregory,[4] and others began to apply the method. The wider significance of the application lay in the initial separation of theology and jurisprudence. This scholarly pursuit also showed how essential a firm grasp of the Roman law was for the fruitful study of canon law, and throughout the subsequent period the study of Roman law formed the foundation of canonistic studies. Furthermore, the application of the dialectical method coincided with the upsurge of Roman legal studies in Bologna in the early twelfth century.[5]

A scholarly study of canon law in the strict meaning of the term had not existed before Gratian, the Camaldunensian monk at Bologna, composed his book in 1139–40.[6] As will be seen in the following chapter, the effect of this book of Gratian's was the establishment of a fully-fledged canon law school at Bologna that was to flourish in company with civilian jurisprudence. From

---

[1] Ivo's *Decretum* ed. in *PL* 161, 47ff; his *Panormia* ibid., cols. 1043ff. ET of the important Prologue to the *Decretum* (selections) in *LCC* X (1956) 238ff (here 240). Lit. in van Hove 361n. 3; Stickler 180ff.

[2] See H. Hoffmann, 'Ivo von Chartres und die Lösung des Investiturstreits' in *DA* 15 (1959) 385ff; also A. Becker, *Urban II* (1964) I, 187ff.

[3] See below, 250.

[4] Only fragments are ed.; for details F. *LeBr.*, II, 169ff. Written between *ca* 1105 and 1107.

[5] See esp. P. Legendre, *La pénetration du droit romain dans le droit canonique classique de Gratien à Innocence IV* (1961). On the other hand the canon law itself evinced great interest among civilians, see B. Paradisi, 'Diritto canonico e tendenze di scuola nei glossatori da Irnerio ad Accursio' in *Studi medievali* 6 (1965) 155ff; and G. Le Bras, 'L'église médiévale au service du droit romain' in *RHDFE* 44 (1968) 193ff.

[6] Commonly called *Decretum* (for the correct name below, 165). Best available ed. by Ae. Friedberg, *Corpus Iuris Canonici* (repr. 1959), vol. I.

the law-creative standpoint the effect of Gratian's book and teaching was equally far-reaching. For the papacy was from now on able to call on a fully trained personnel for its services, and many a student and master reached high positions in the papal curia, including one of the earliest pupils of Gratian, Roland Bandinelli, who after a successful chancellorship became Pope Alexander III. In his pontificate began the quite unparalleled spate of papal legislation from the late fifties onwards. The creation of law became the foremost preoccupation of the papacy.

Indeed, one of the most conspicuous features from the mid-twelfth century down to the eve of the Reformation was that the governors themselves, the popes, were highly qualified jurists. In the history of public government this is assuredly a unique phenomenon. Most of the secular Rulers were hardly able to write a Latin sentence, let alone to argue a difficult juristic case that bristled with complex governmental problems. Yet the popes themselves directly and personally intervened in the multitudinous litigations which now flooded the curia. Although Alexander III himself tried to stem the tide of appellate jurisdiction, Innocent III sat three times a week in consistory and himself chaired the papal tribunal.[1] The result of this spate of litigations and approaches to the papacy was the thousands of decretals pouring forth from the papal chancery.[2]

The decretals dealt with virtually every issue which the papacy considered vital and relevant for the well-being of the Christian body public. In them there was no important item of public law that did not figure prominently—royal elections, episcopal appointments, suspension of public officers, depositions of bishops, kings and other Rulers, sanctions against individuals and corporations (excommunication and interdict), tithes, counter-

---

[1] See *Gesta Innocentii*, c. 41 in *PL* 214 col. LXXXf.

[2] The subsequent two and a half centuries were the ages of the great lawyer popes. The point has often been discussed. Cf. R. James Long, 'Utrum iurista vel theologus plus perficiat ad regimen ecclesiae' in *Med. Studies* 30 (1968) 134ff. Considering that the papacy was an organ of government in the M.A., jurists were eminently suited as popes, see W. Ullmann, 'The papacy as an institution of government' cit. (above, 122 n. 3).

feiting of money, privileges of classes and groups, interpretation of statutes and municipal laws, fixation of crime as a public offence, measures to preserve and enforce the purity of the faith apart from such obvious legislation which referred to monasteries, duties of clerics, liturgical matters, matrimony, and so on. In short it would be only tedious to try to enumerate the multitude of issues legislatively fixed. The basic assumption behind every decretal was papal primacy in the shape of universal monarchic government to be exercised over society which was the Church as the body of clergy and laity alike. In his function as governor the pope did not belong to the Church, but stood outside and above it, the hallmark of true personal sovereignty. He formed an estate of his own, and in his official capacity was immune from judgment.[1] The substance of these decretals which dealt with the scope of public jurisdiction also explains, at least partly, why the concept of the State did not arise: jurisdiction was exercised by specific office holders, including the secular Rulers *within* the Church, and not by incorporeal abstractions, such as the State. It was precisely because the secular Rulers in the West of Europe shared the basic assumptions of the decretals that their opposition to the papacy on individual issues proved to be an excruciatingly difficult task. In a word, the decretal was the vehicle by which the papacy as a monarchic institution attempted to govern Western Europe conceived as the Church, and this government concerned the basic requirements of a Christian society. The lively and relevant legislative activity of the papacy most effectively imprinted the idea of the rule of law upon society.[2]

The large decretal output in the second half of the twelfth century created a serious problem for the practitioners: a ruling given by the papacy for a case, say, in Hungary, had applicability

[1] For this see *PGP* 39, 48ff, 89f; *HPT* 28, 103f; *PK* 26ff.

[2] From the governmental point of view the appearance of the term in papal documents 'Salva sedis apostolicae auctoritate' from the pontificate of Celestine II (1143–4) onwards is most important. For this see J. B. Sägmüller in *ACII* III (1936) 157ff, also separately printed 1937 under the title: *Zur Geschichte der Entwicklung des päpstlichen Gesetzgebungsrechts.*

also in other parts of Christendom, precisely because the papacy considered itself a universal institution of government. But the practitioner who was always enjoined by the papacy to apply the latest ruling could hardly be aware of all the numerous legislative measures. Hence arose the need for a conveniently concise collection of decretals which were called *extravagantes*, that is, 'walking outside' the *Decretum* of Gratian. This was the work of scholarship.[1] The very first official collection of new law (i.e. that issued since Gratian) was that published by Innocent III in 1209–10, which contained however only select decretals of his first twelve pontifical years.[2] Gregory IX on 5 September 1234 published a comprehensive, official law-book which superseded all previous collections; it was called the *Liber Extra* (i.e. the book outside the *Decretum*). Its main contents were decretals officially issued by the papacy since Innocent II, but it also contained some excerpts (or snippets) from the Fathers (e.g. St Jerome, Augustine, etc.) which were endowed with legal force—exactly the same procedure adopted by Justinian when he conferred legal character on the Digest which embodied excerpts or snippets from the classical Roman jurists. Another parallelism between the Roman law, that is, the Code, and the *Liber Extra* is worth mentioning. Like the former, the canon law book also began with the title 'On the supreme Trinity and the Catholic faith'. The division of the subject-matter into five books subdivided into titles and chapters (actually the device of one of the late twelfth century Bolognese canonists) was the model for all later collections.[3] The *Liber*

---

[1] For the collections of decretals after Gratian see S. Kuttner, *Repertorium der Kanonistik* (1938); new ed. in preparation. The annual Bulletin of the Institute of medieval canon law gives information on all relevant canonistic publications. A brief survey now by K. W. Nörr in *HQL* 836ff.

[2] See also below, 169, and Kuttner op. cit. 322ff. Examination of MSS containing the compilations yields much new historical material of some importance. See W. Ullmann, 'A Scottish charter and its place in medieval canon law' in *JR* (1949) 225ff; id., 'The disputed election of Hugh of Balsham' in *Cambridge Hist. J.* 9 (1949) 259ff; id., 'A forgotten dispute at Bridlington Priory and its canonistic setting' in *Yorkshire Archaeological J.* 148 (1951) 456ff (also showing Alexander III's intervention long before the Avranches settlement).

[3] For other details see G. Le Bras, art. cit. (above, 139 n. 5) at 197ff.

Extra (which had 185 titles and 1961 chapters) remained in force as the common law of the Latin Church until Whitsun 1918.[1]

This officially promulgated canon law was the uniform law for all Christendom, at least as far as the papal writ ran. In was universal in this sense and embodied the law as the 'soul' of the Christian body public. The underlying idea was that the papal monarch alone legislated on the topics of vital concern to Christian society. Hence the fixation of the function of the secular Ruler occupied a conspicuous place in the decretals. The function allocated to the secular Ruler corresponded to that allocated to Roman law: that is, each had an auxiliary role. And this assignment was conditioned by ecclesiological and Christian doctrinal considerations. Exactly the same applied to the role which the so-called temporal things played in canon law: they, too, were no more than auxiliary means for the attainment of the Christian's eventual aim, his salvation. The canon law implicitly or explicitly rested on the cosmological thesis that actions, matters and situations in this life were merely preparatory to the life in the other world. Hence the canon law can be said to have brought into clearest possible relief the comprehensive, all-embracing 'totalitarian' Christian standpoint and to have drawn the necessary legal and constitutional implications.[2]

It is not without significance that the very first decretal in the *Liber Extra* fixed the faith by defining it in terms of the law—in a purely formal sense no different from that set forth in Justinian's Code—and that much of the first book concerns itself with general governmental and jurisprudential matters, such as the two titles 'On the constitutions' and 'On rescripts' which were firstrate legal statements relative to the law-creative power of the papacy and the scope and extent of its decretals both in regard to

[1] Best available ed. by Ae. Friedberg, *Corpus* cit. (as 139 n. 6) II, 6ff. Lit. in van Hove 357ff and Stickler 237ff. For Raymond of Pennaforte, the head of the commission charged with the compilation, see *DDC* VII, 461ff, and for Gregory IX as legislator see P. Michaud-Quantin in *Études Le Bras* (1965) 273ff.

[2] See B. Tierney, 'Medieval canon law and Western constitutionalism' in *Cath. Hist. Rev.* 52 (1966) 1ff (presidential address); further S. Kuttner, 'The scientific investigation of medieval canon law' in *Speculum* 24 (1949) 493ff; id. 'Methodological problems . . .' ibid. 30 (1955) 539ff.

persons and things. Together with the following title 'On custom and customary law' these titles are in reality introductory expositions of constitutional jurisprudence. Hence also the law referring to judicial organs, the appointment of and procedure before judges delegate who were judicial officers with delegated papal power to try specific cases.[1] Of particular concern in the present context was the law embodied in the title 'De maioritate et obedientia' which dealt with the relations of the (inferior) subject to (superior) authority.[2] Specifically, this title contained the fundamental declaration of Innocent III in relation to the comprehensive powers of the Petrine commission: the so-called petrinological argument was here raised to a vital governmental principle.[3]

In this connection mention must be made of another genre of source which supplied a good deal of governmental material for the *Liber Extra*. The double election in Germany in 1198 provided the papacy under Innocent III with a unique opportunity of declaring itself on a number of fundamental questions concerning the relations between pope and emperor and especially on the latter's function. Innocent considered the matter so important that he established a special Register exclusively dealing with this conflict which enabled him to formulate some very important 'political' and governmental principles.[4] In his capacity as the creator of the Western Roman emperor and as universal legislator he clarified the position of the so-called *Rex Romanorum* which was the preliminary stage to the fully-fledged Roman emperorship;[5] relying on St Bernard and Hugh of St Victor he explained

---

[1] For details see J. Sayers, *Papal judges delegate in the province of Canterbury 1198–1254* (1971); cf. my review in *JEH* 23 (1972) 181ff. As regards special requirements of the judges delegate see R. Helmholtz, 'Canonists and standards of impartiality for judges delegate' in *Trad* 25 (1969) 386ff.

[2] For some observations see *IS* 12ff, also *CR* 179ff.

[3] X: I, 33, 6. For the concept of petrinology, see *JTS* 11 (1960) at 32ff.

[4] *Registrum de negotio Romani imperii* (*RNI*) ed. F. Kempf (1947). The ed. by W. Holtzmann (1947) is useful for teaching purposes. There is a splendid facsimile reproduction (by W. Peitz) of the *RNI* (1927) which is a good tool for teaching and research purposes.

[5] The significance of this function and title is commonly overlooked, see W. Ullmann, 'Dies ortus imperii' in *AA* 661ff. Further details in 'Von Canossa

with superb juristic skill the nature of the imperial office-holder as one of an assistant; he showed why and how the allegory of soul and body was applicable in a specific way to the relations between pope and emperor—and here Innocent revealed in his thought-processes extraordinary kinship with a very early Christian source (the *Didaskalia*);[1] and how and why the papacy had translated the empire from the Greeks to the Franks (so-called translation of the empire)[2] and why the future emperor had to be approved by the papacy; and many consequential questions were here authoritatively solved by Innocent III with the superiority of intellect and legal knowledge which few, if any, other medieval popes could equal. Very many excerpts from this Register made their way into the *Liber Extra*, and thus became common law.

Due to the large decretal output by Gregory IX, Innocent IV and Alexander IV, the *Liber Extra* became soon outdated; and the plentiful legislation of the two Lyons Councils (1245 and 1274) added to the accumulated weight of decretal material. On the model of Gregory IX Boniface VIII appointed a commission which produced the so-called *Liber Sextus*,[3] meaning the sixth book as an addition to the five books of the *Extra*. In method and substance it followed its predecessor (it had 77 titles and 447 chapters). In it the mature papal-hierocratic ideology had reached its apogee. These two large law-books of the thirteenth century are indispensable sources of governmental ideas. By the thirteenth century the papacy had become to all intents and purposes the focal point of Western Europe—hence the proliferation of decretal

nach Pavia' in *HJb* 93 (1973) 265ff. The crucial negotiations between Celestine III and Henry VI in 1196 cannot be explained without taking into account the function of the *Rex Romanorum*, cf., e.g., G. Baaken, 'Die Verhandlungen zwischen Heinrich VI und Coelestin III in den Jahren 1195-97' in *DA* 27 (1971) 459ff, esp. 502ff.

[1] *PGP* 93f has the details. It can safely be assumed that Innocent had no knowledge of this early Christian source.

[2] *RNI* 18, 29, 62, etc. Innocent did not invent this translation theory but as so much else perfected it by his conciseness and succinctness of diction. This became the universal law. For lit. see W. Goez, *Translatio imperii* (1958).

[3] Ed. Ae Friedberg (as 139 n. 6), II, 935ff. For some collections between Gregory IX and Boniface VIII see van Hove 362ff, Stickler, 251ff and *MP* 201ff.

output and the ramifications of the papal canon law into all segments of public life. There is hardly any other instance in European history which mirrored a government at work as faithfully as the thirteenth-century canon law. The function of the papal monarch as the *Speculator* (overseer: the term is biblical) of Latin-European Christendom is here depicted in its full maturity. The value of this canon law as a source is only heightened by the consideration that the Ruler himself (the papal monarch) was a fully trained jurist and sometimes (such as Innocent IV) a juristic scholar of European renown, who always had a highly professional personnel at his disposal. No other European government in the thirteenth or fourteenth centuries had such a cosmopolitan galaxy of talent, learning and practical experience as the papacy.

The last part of the *Corpus Iuris Canonici* consisted of a selection of decretals issued in the latter years of Boniface VIII's pontificate, mainly by Clement V and the Council of Vienne (1311). This part was intended as *Liber Septimus* and is commonly known as *Clementines*: Clement V's material takes up the largest part, and he also prepared its publication which was however undertaken by his successor John XXII in 1317.[1] It followed the patterns of its two predecessors, but in reality was merely an appendix to them (it had only 108 chapters). These three parts of the *C.I.C.* (totalling 2516 chapters) were to remain the official canon law until superseded by the modern *Codex Iuris Canonici* in 1918.

The consideration of canon law as a source of governmental ideas necessitates some remarks on a feature with which the modern world is not unfamiliar. The elimination of activities held to be subversive of the existing social order is a governmental activity in a number of modern societies. In the Middle Ages the extermination of heretics was of profoundest concern to virtually all Western governments, precisely because in the overwhelming majority they were built on theocratic foundations. Hence attacks on these bases by unorthodox views publicly expressed affected the very core of Rulership. The sources relating to the public prosecution of heretics are of a varied nature, but most are easily

---

[1] Ed. in Ae. Friedberg, II, 1132ff.

accessible in governmental decrees by emperors, popes and kings. These legislative measures might be termed applied governmental jurisprudence. Leaving aside Justinian's example of burning books by decree, there were the legislation of the Lateran Councils,[1] the joint imperial-papal decree of Frederick Barbarossa and Lucius III in October 1184,[2] the legislative measures taken by Innocent III,[3] and the edicts issued by Frederick II in November 1220.[4] The important substantive point was the juristic conception of heresy as high treason.[5] The procedural measure—the Inquisition —was partly the extension of the ancient episcopal visitation, partly the adaptation of late Roman procedural principles, and partly rested upon the conception of heresy as a public crime.[6] What needs stressing in this context is that these sources reveal the character of society and its government far better than any learned tract could have done: they show that the custody of the ideologically cementing bond of society lay in ecclesiastical hands which only goes to show the ecclesiological substance of society. The secular power within the Church (be it now the emperor or a king) had to act as a police force in exterminating the

---

[1] II Lateran, cap 23 (in *Decreta* 178) and IV Lateran, cap 3 (ibid. 209ff).

[2] The decree is in Mansi, XXII, 477; also in X: V, 7, 9. For background see *SHP* 202, 252; now G. Baaken, 'Unio regni ad imperium' in *QFIAB* 52 (1972) 219ff, esp. 227ff.

[3] *Vergentis* in *Reg* II, 3; X: V, 7, 10.

[4] His coronation edicts in *MGH. Const* II, 85, pp. 107ff.

[5] See W. Ullmann, 'The significance of Innocent III's Vergentis' in *Études Le Bras* 729ff.

[6] Burning of heretics first decreed by the early Capetians in 1017, decree in Mansi XIX, 373. Later the inquisitorial powers of the king and of his servants were put on a constitutional basis, see *PGP* 195ff. For the actual Inquisition and its procedure see Bernard Gui, *Manuel de l'inquisition*, ed. G. Mollat, 2 vols. (1926-7) (early 14th century); for verbatim reports see, e.g., J. Duvernoy (ed.), *Le régistre d'inquisition de Jacques Fournier 1318-1325*, 3 vols. (1965); for a late medieval case see K. V. Selge, 'Heidelberger Ketzer in der Frühzeit der Hussitischen Revolution' in *ZKG* 82 (1971) 167ff, at 183ff (with some questionable premisses in regard to the inquisition, 178ff). For general principles see W. Ullmann's Introduction to H. C. Lea's *Inquisition in the M.A.* (1962); H.Maisonneuve, *Études sur les origines de l'inquisition*, 2nd ed. (1962); id., 'Le droit romain et la doctrine inquisitoriale' in *Études Le Bras* 931ff.

heretics. The Pauline view that 'princeps non portat gladium sine causa' was brought to full fruition within criminal law. These sources also reveal why within this ecclesiological ambit the conception of a State could not arise.

Both from the point of view of governmental continuity as well as governmental ideology and practice a well-kept archive is always necessary. And within the exercise of the papal government the papal archives had always been efficiently organized repositories. It was the papal Registers as records of papal decisions and legal measures taken which not only greatly facilitated the papal government at work but also made the actual compilation of canon law a task that proved not too difficult. The papal Registers[1] are compendia which contain copies of official documents despatched to a variety of recipients by the chancery which acted as the nerve-centre of the government. (In parenthesis the difference between a Register, a *Regestum* and a Cartulary should be noted: the *Regestum* (or Calendar) usually denotes a summary of the contents of a document; the cartulary has copies of documents issued by different authorities for one recipient). Of the early papal Registers only fragments have survived, such as Gregory I's[2] or John VIII's[3] and Stephen V.[4] The oldest extant original Register is that of Gregory VII.[5] Virtually all other Registers

[1] For an excellent introduction to the papal Registers see now L. E. Boyle, *A survey of the Vatican Archives and its medieval holdings* (1972), esp. 103ff (*V*atican, Avignon and Lateran Archives).

[2] Ed. *MGH. Epp* I–II. For some problems of transmission see P. Meyvaert, 'The Register of Gregory the Great and Bede' in *RB* 80 (1970) 162ff.

[3] Ed *MGH Epp* VII, 1–272 (the copies of 314 Letters from the last six years of his pontificate). See D. Lohrmann, *Das Register Papst Johannes VIII.* (1968). For Leo IV's fragments see W. Ullmann, above, 138 n. 1.

[4] Ed. in *MHG. Epp* VII, 334ff. As a source of the highest quality must be mentioned the series entitled *Papsturkunden* concerning papal documents in European countries before 1198 as well as the *Italia Pontificia* and the *Germania Pontificia*, all publ. by the 'Akademie der Wissenschaften' in Göttingen, ed. A. Brackmann, P. Kehr, W. Holtzmann, J. Ramackers, C. Erdmann, et al. (1902–). See further J. Pflugk-Hartung, *Acta pontificum Romanorum inedita* (to 1198), 3 vols. (repr. 1958).

[5] *MGH. Epp sell* (as 135 n. 3). Further material in H. E. J. Cowdrey, *The Epistolae Vagantes of Gregory VII* (1972). For some details on the main Register see

have been lost before the time of Innocent III[1] from whose pontificate onwards the almost complete papal Registers begin. According to conservative estimates there are more than 300,000 official
documents enregistered between Innocent III and the outbreak
of the Great Schism in 1378, and nearly 700,000 for the period
down to 1502.[2] The Registers are preserved in the Archivio
segreto of the Vatican.[3] The thirteenth-century Registers have
now been edited,[4] whereas of the several hundred volumes of the
Avignon Registers only special parts or entries relative to special
countries have been published. For the reconstruction of governmental ideas the consultation of the full Registers is indispensable,
for the canon law itself contained only tiny fragments of the
official legislative output (and not even this was registered in its
totality).[5] In the present context the instructional books for the

PG 276 n. 2, and further lit. at 472, to which should be added: L. Santifaller,
Quellen & Forschungen zum Urkunden-und Kanzleiwesen Gregors VII. (in *Studi e
Testi* 190 (1957)).

[1] They are in *PL* 214-16. New ed. in preparation by the Austrian Institute in
Rome: vol. I (1964) and indices (1968). For his letters to England see C. R.
and M. G. Cheney (eds.), *The letters of Innocent III concerning England and
Wales* (1967). For details of his Registers see F. Kempf, *Die Register Innozenz'
III.* (1945); id., 'Zu den Originalregistern Innozenz' III.' in *QFIAB* 36 (1956)
86ff. About the *RNI* above, 144 n. 4.

[2] K. A. Fink, 'Neue Wege zur Erschliessung des vatik. Archivs' in *Festgabe
für K. Adam: Vitae et veritati* (1956) 187ff, at 189; for the Avignonese Registers
and the Registers in the 15th cent., see H. Diener, 'Die grossen Registerserien im
Vatik. Archiv' in *QFIAB* 51 (1971) 305ff (very helpful), and esp. L. E. Boyle,
A survey (above, 148 n. 1) (most useful).

[3] See K. A. Fink, *Das vatikanische Archiv*, 2nd ed. (1961); M. Giusti, *Studi
sui registri di bolle papali* (1968) (Vat. and Lat. Registers); now above all L. Boyle,
op. cit.

[4] By the *Écoles françaises d'Athènes et de Rome*, with the exception of the
Registers of Honorius III which are ed. by P. Pressuti (1888) and of Clement V
which are ed. by the Benedictines (1885-1957).

[5] See, e.g., the important decree of Eugenius IV concerning the status of the
cardinalate (*Non mediocri dolore*) discussed by W. Ullmann, 'Pope Eugenius IV,
Cardinal Kemp and Archbishop Chichele' in *Essays Aubrey Gwynn* (1961)
359ff. It is necessary to keep in mind the incompleteness of the Registers. The
exact principles of registration are still not clear.

papal chancery personnel deserve attention and for the same reasons as their secular counterparts.[1]

The conclusion of the medieval canon law in the early fourteenth century also reflects the state of the papacy and its standing in Europe. Especially the papacy's sojourn at Avignon from 1307 to 1378 severely curtailed the function of the papacy as a law-creating organ, and the following forty years of schism inflicted enormous and, as it proved, irreparable damage on the authority of the institution. The papacy began to recede in its function as the governmental, ideological and religious focus of Europe. For from the late thirteenth century onwards forces had also come to the fore which were cosmologically fundamentally different from those upon which the papacy was built. And with the decline of the papacy went the decline of the authority of its law as a vehicle of public government. More and more was it compelled to withdraw to those tasks and functions which contemporary thinkers, governments and reflective men considered germane to its vocation—the purely religious field or what was called the *forum internum*, and disciplinary matters. Public government in the sense in which the papacy and medieval Europe had understood it, became more and more the exclusive task of the organs of the State. But the State was conceptually built on foundations different from those of the Church and the papacy. The uniformity of the ideological presuppositions gave way to multiplicity of premisses—unipolarity yielded to multipolarity. The mental category of politics had entered the arena of discussion, with the consequence that law and politics were seen as two separate, though interdependent branches. Public government had become a matter of politics and had no necessary conceptual

---

[1] See below, 200ff. Apart from the *Liber Diurnus*, ed. Th. Sickel (1889), see, e.g., in the 13th century the papal dictator Thomas of Capua, ed. E. Heller, *Die ars dictandi des Thomas von Capua* in *SB Heidelberg* 1929, fasc. 4; P. Herde, 'Papal formularies for letters of justice' in *PICL* II (1965) 320ff; id., 'Ein Formelbuch Gerhards von Parma' in *AD* 13 (1967) 225ff, ed. at 264ff; Marinus of Eboli's two tracts (he was vice-chancellor of Innocent IV) ed. P. Herde in *QFIAB* 43 (1964) 119ff, at 196ff (82ff of the offprint); H. Diener, 'Ein Formularbuch aus der Kanzlei der Päpste Eugen IV. & Nicolaus V.', ibid. 42 (1963) 370ff.

connection with religion or faith which was the very core of the medieval canon law.

II

The conciliar decree emanated from a properly convened synod or council[1] and constituted canon law in every sense of the term. The synod as an institution was prominent long before the papacy had reached its monarchic status and the papal decretal become an instrument of papal monarchy. Before the turn of the fourth and fifth centuries the synod was the assembly which decreed on dogmatic, disciplinary and liturgical topics. The part played by the papacy in the early synods (which were primarily local Roman assemblies) was certainly not in any way suggestive of the leading and determinative role which it was to play later. As far as the law as a vehicle of government was concerned, the great councils of Christian antiquity, beginning with Nicaea in 325 and ending with Chalcedon in 451, did not appear to assume great significance. Their importance lies in the field of doctrine and organization and in the formulation of basic articles of the faith, and only partly in their disciplinary decrees. They were convoked by imperial edict and were therefore essentially imperial assemblies in which the Western churches, including the Roman Church, played no leading part.[2]

The emergence in the fifth century of the papacy as a monarchic institution acting through the instrumentality of the decretal, was of crucial significance for the function of the synod as a law-creative organ, for the descending theme of government advocated by the former would not brook a reconciliation with the ascending theme represented by the latter. Hence as law-creative organs the synods never assumed anything like the importance of the

---

[1] For all details concerning medieval councils see C. Hefele-H. Leclercq, *Histoire des conciles*, 8 vols. in 15 to the end of the medieval period (1909–1917). A new *Konziliengeschichte* ed. W. Brandmüller & R. Bäumer in 30 vols. (for the MA) is in preparation.

[2] Ed. of decrees in *Decreta* 1ff (Nicaea); 17ff (Constantinople); 33ff (Ephesus); 57ff (Chalcedon); here also details of Schwartz' ed.

monarchic papacy. Throughout the medieval period there were numerous provincial, regional or local synods in the Western parts of Europe, but they cannot be said to have enacted decrees of importance in governmental respects before the ninth century.[1] Part of the explanation is that these councils, notably the Frankish in the eighth century, were royally convoked assemblies which concerned themselves with issues of general concern to the Frankish realm. Similar observations can be made about the Visigothic synods in the seventh and early eighth centuries.[2] These latter show an extremely high intellectual standard which is not surprising in view of the advanced educational standard of the hierarchy. Both early Frankish and Visigothic councils exhibited two significant features. First, to a great extent they were instruments of royal policy: for their enforcement the decrees needed royal approval and confirmation. Without the latter they constituted merely internal regulations for the clergy. Second, they exhibited a very lively concern for matters of public and social welfare. The decrees show a heightened awareness on the part of the synodists for the needs of the socially inferior sections of the populace. Since very many of these Frankish and Visigothic decrees were transmitted to the Middle Ages in numerous canon law collections, they must be given the credit of parentage for a great many medieval social welfare institutions.[3] The participation of laymen in many early councils is noteworthy.

During the Carolingian age in the ninth century conciliar activity was brisk, for the councils were the main instruments by

---

[1] Ed. in *CC* (1963) (Gallic councils 314–695) and *MGH. Conc. aevi merovingici et Karolini* I–II, Cf. Ch. de Clercq, *La législation religieuse franque de Clovis à Charlemagne* (1936); id., as above, 127 n. 2.

[2] Ed. *MGH. Leges Visigothorum*, at 472ff (supplementa). Further *PL* 84, 303ff, and J. Vives, *Concilios visigóticos e hispano-romanos*, I (1963). On the subject itself cf. P. D. King, *Law and Society in the Visigothic Kingdom* (1972) 53ff, 125ff and H. H. Anton, 'Der König und die Reichskonzilien im westgotischen Spanien' in *HJb* 92 (1972) 257ff.

[3] W. Ullmann, 'Public welfare and social legislation in early medieval councils' in *SCH* VII (1971) 1ff; for Merovingian councils see now also J. Champagne et R. Szramkiewicz, 'Recherches sur les conciles des temps mérovingiens' in *RHDFE* 49 (1971) 5ff.

which the principal aims of the Carolingian Renaissance were to be implemented. They formed a powerful ecclesiastical platform for the dissemination not merely of abstract ecclesiological theories, but above all for translating abstract religious themes into the concrete language of the law. Since the Carolingian Renaissance was of an ecclesiological substance, Rulership as expounded in the numerous decrees now began to be strongly inclined towards the theocratic idea: the 'King by the grace of God' was the point of departure for the councils. Hence the strong religious and ecclesiological complexion of the decrees relating to Rulership, its scope and extent, as well as to the delineation of clerical and secular functions, and the numerous other topics falling within the precincts of governmental doctrine. The synodal decrees of this age made a substantial contribution to the science (and practice) of government and greatly promoted a unified Europe, one of whose features was the idea of law as a vehicle of government, the very idea instilled by the canons of the synods.[1] The participants were almost all members of the higher clergy.

In its succinctness, its quantity and quality, this Frankish conciliar (and royal) legislation was one of the most valuable sources of medieval governmental ideas.[2] In it a virtually comprehensive system of Christian governmental principles was set forth. Theocratic Rulership had all the makings of absolutism, and yet, it was the synodists of the Carolingian age who not only clearly perceived this, but also in their decrees took steps to nip this development towards royal absolutism in the bud. Conciliar law declared the Ruler to be subjected to a higher law: in other words, the idea of the rule of law had made its concrete appearance. With it came also the sequels, such as the fusion of Roman, Christian and Germanic governmental ideas which was to yield one of the most fruitful governmental principles, that is, the tutorial function of the Ruler. The clipping of the secular monarch's absolutist wings was a major achievement largely carried through by means

[1] For some details CR 23ff, 134, 176f; for procedural questions see H. Barion, *Das fränkisch-deutsche Synodalrecht des Frühmittelalters* (1931).

[2] Since conciliar decrees became frequently part of the royal law, they were often incorporated into the Capitularies, ed. *MGH Capitularia* I–II.

of the canons of the synods in the ninth century. And this law became an essential part of the (later) universal canon law, because the individual decrees were again transmitted in numerous collections to later generations.[1] And papal decretals too came to absorb a good deal of these basic ideas expressed in Frankish conciliar law.

It is undeniable that the tenth and early eleventh centuries were periods of stagnation in intellectual respects, but this should not lead to the erroneous assumption that conciliar activity and legislation also stagnated. The councils and their decrees had, however, primarily local and provincial importance, and their contribution to governmental principles was small. There is, however, a notable exception, and that is the synod of Hohenaltheim in 916. This in fact was the first large and important ecclesiastical assembly in the East-Frankish realms which were the nucleus of later medieval Germany.[2] This synod conspicuously manifested the influence of Pseudo-Isidore, above all in the decrees relating to government; the influence of the Visigothic councils upon Hohenaltheim was similarly noticeable.[3] On the threshold of medieval Germany this synod symbolized, so to speak, the fusion of the tenets of the Carolingian Renaissance with those of Pseudo-Isidore.

In the Italian peninsula the synods convoked by the papacy demand special attention. Although these papally convoked synods were no more frequent or important than any other assembly between the eighth and the eleventh centuries, they became the nucleus of a significant development in the eleventh century, that is, from the pontificate of Leo IX onwards. Out of these synods developed partly the more or less regular meetings of the cardinals and the pope as well as the large plenary assemblies usually held during Lent which became the forum for issuing universally valid decrees. These plenary meetings to which many non-Italian bishops and abbots came, were the immediate

[1] See the appendix to the *MGH Conc.* II, 885ff.

[2] Ed. *MGH Const.* I, 618ff. Details and lit. in *CR* 128ff.

[3] Details also in M. Hellmann, 'Die Synode von Hohenaltheim' in *Die Entstehung des deutschen Reiches* (1956) 289ff.

precursors of the great Lateran Councils which were ecumenical.

On the model of the imperial senate at Constantinople the meetings of pope and cardinals were called consistories, but they were purely consultative assemblies without any legislative powers. In some respects the Lateran Councils—so-called because they were held in the Lateran, the pope's episcopal church in Rome—continued the ancient imperially convoked councils, with the difference that they now were summoned by the pope, and therefore claimed universal legislative powers. This presupposition was an application of the pseudo-isidorian tenet that only the pope could summon general councils. The four Lateran Councils (1123; 1139; 1179; 1215) were all summoned for the discussion of important, topical issues.[1] Next to these four there were in the thirteenth century the two Councils held at Lyons (1245 and 1274) which dealt also with topical problems.[2] In the fourteenth century the assembly at Vienne in 1311–12 was the last great ecumenical council[3] before the large assemblies in the early fifteenth century.

In regard to the subject-matter the decrees passed in the seven councils did not materially add to the growth of governmental principles.[4] This is understandable if the concept of papal monarchy and plenitude of power is given proper consideration. By and large the decrees relative to governmental ideas spell out details of already formulated principles in decretals. Some of the decrees of these general councils were nevertheless sources of governmental ideas, such as the introduction of the numerical

---

[1] Ed. in *Decreta*: I Lat., at 166ff; II Lat.: 173ff; III Lat.: 187ff; IV Lat.: 206ff. For details of the latter see S. Kuttner & A. García y García, 'A new eyewitness account of the Fourth Lateran Council' in *Trad* 20 (1964) 115ff, ed. 123ff, and commentary 129ff.

[2] Ed. in *Decreta* 259ff; 285ff.   [3] Ed. ibid. 336ff.

[4] This evidently applies still more to the regional councils, although they are vital sources of social history and in a wider sense of public and governmental ideas. There is a valuable survey of literature and sources by J. Sawicki, *Bibliographia synodorum particularium* (1967) which is not free from deficiencies and errors, cf. my review in *JEH* 20 (1969) 127ff. Supplements in *Trad* 24 (1968) 508ff; 25 (1969) 471ff; *Bull. of med. canon law* 2 (1972) 91ff.

majority principle in papal elections;[1] the definition of heresy;[2] the role of the secular power in the extermination of heretics; the precise juristic reasons for deposing an emperor. Yet each of these could have been issued by the pope alone, since the conciliar decree had no more weight than a decretal. The juristic difference between a decretal and a decree lay in the method of publication. The former was addressed to specific recipients, while the latter was promulgated at open sessions of a large assembly and distributed afterwards. Further, whereas the decretals dealt with specific legal points that arose in connection with special cases, the conciliar decree fixed the law in a general way and was thus to all intents and purposes statute law, not addressed to special persons.

The councils were intended to be primarily debating assemblies presided over by the pope. Their decrees in any case needed papal confirmation. Of specifically juristic interest was the terminology chosen for the promulgation of some decrees: '... de consilio fratrum nostrorum et hoc approbante concilio *decrevimus* ...' which did not indicate any application of an ascending theme of government but suggested that the substantive ingredient of the decree was the papal will which had the support of the council, since the subject of the decree had been deliberated upon by both pope and cardinals. The council served as a platform for the publication of specially important measures which were assured of their dissemination by the participants.[3] In consideration of the general

---

[1] For the background *SHP* 228f. The usual majority required was not numerical, but qualitative, that is, the so-called *pars sanior*. The development is too little studied. For some recent works see, e.g., L. Moulin, 'Sanior et maior pars: note sur l'évolution des techniques éléctorales dans les ordres religieux du VIᵉ au XIIIᵉ siècles' in *RHDFE* 36 (1958) 368ff; id. in *Studi politici* 6 (1959) 364ff; A. Petrani, 'Génèse de la majorité qualifiée' in *Apollinaris* 30 (1957) 430ff; K. Ganzer, 'Das Mehrheitsprinzip bei den kirchlichen Wahlen des MA' in *TQ* 147 (1967) 60ff (with further lit.). For the requirement of unanimity see P. Grossi, 'Unanimitas: alle origine del concetto di persona giuridica nel diritto canonico' in *Annali di storia del diritto* 2 (1958) 1ff.

[2] For the claim to their infallibility cf. B. Tierney, *Infallibility* (1972) 45ff.

[3] For the difficult textual transmissions of I Lyons see esp. S. Kuttner, 'Die Konstitutionen des 1. allgemeinen Konzils von Lyon' in *SDHI* 6 (1940) 70ff; and of II Lyons id., 'Conciliar law in the making' in *Misc. Pio Paschini* (1949) II, 39ff. For Vienne see E. Müller, *Das Konzil von Vienne 1311–1312* (1934) (fundamental).

council's being a 'representative' embodiment of the whole of Christendom Innocent III enlarged its composition by convoking also the secular powers (as well as abbots and provosts), and he can thus be said to have paved the way for the conciliar movement. Indeed, the Fourth Lateran Council was the first truly universal council of the Middle Ages, and all subsequent councils were 'universal' in this same sense until the Fifth Lateran Council in 1511 restored the pre-1215 practice which has remained the norm down to the present century.[1]

The large councils of the fifteenth century and their decrees reflected the victory of conciliarism over the papal-descending theme of government. Conciliarism was the application of the ascending theme to ecclesiastical government and was conditioned by the unsatisfactory constitution of the Church that led to the Great Schism.[2] The decrees of these Councils (Constance; Ferrara–Basle–Florence)[3] breathed the essential spirit of conciliarism which was based on three strands of thought: the Marsilian view of the people's political sovereignty;[4] the canonistic corporation thesis;[5] and the Bartolist view of the people's legislative sovereignty.[6] The relevant decrees of the so-called Reform Councils therefore set out from the premiss that totality of power rested in the Church universal which acted through its 'representative' general council. Consequently all officers in the Church,

[1] For this Innocentian development see A. Hauck, 'Rezeption und Umbildung der allg. Synode im MA' in *Hist. Vierteljahrsschrift* 10 (1907) 465ff.

[2] See *HPT* 219ff; *SHP* 296ff.

[3] Ed. in *Decreta* 381ff (Constance); 431ff (Basle-Ferrara-Florence). Details J. Gill, *The Council of Florence* (1959); id., *Constance et Bâle-Florence* (1965); for Constance in particular see H. Finke, et al. *Acta concilii Constantiensis,* 4 vols. (1896–1928); for Basle, J. Haller, et al., *Concilium Basiliense,* 8 vols. (1896–1936); for Florence, G. Hoffmann, et al., *Concilium Florentinum,* 5 vols. (1940–1953). For some interpretative details see P. Ourliac, 'Sociologie du concile de Bâle' in *RHE* 56 (1961) 5ff and A. Black, *Monarchy & Community* (1970) 90ff, esp. 108ff (Basle).   [4] See below, 282f.

[5] Zabarella's tract *De schismate* ed. S. Schard, *De iurisdictione, auctoritate et praeeminentia imperiali* (Basle 1566) 688ff, and in his own *Commentaria in Decretales* (ed. Venice 1602), after I, 6, 6, fo. 107ff. See also below, 173, 187.

[6] W. Ullmann, 'De Bartoli sententia: Concilium repraesentat mentem populi' in *Bartolo* II, 705ff.

including the pope, derived their power from the council to which they all remained responsible. The Council of Constance was one of the classic instances in which a thesis propounded by scholars found a virtually complete expression in legislative acts. The conciliarist theme and the decrees exercised influence far beyond the medieval period. The outright condemnation of tyrannicide revealed the conciliarists' adherence to a positivist conception of the rule of law.[1]

But the decrees of Constance also assume importance as clear barometers of the sensitivity of the conciliarists to a number of widely propagated political theses which even the otherwise radical conciliarists felt constrained to condemn. To this extent the decrees are first-rate sources of the state of mind of the higher clergy assembled at Constance which despite its opposition to the papal monarchy nevertheless showed itself the custodian of the traditional standpoint in political respects. The solemn condemnation of a number of explosive theses propounded by John Wyclif and Jan Huss were at the same time also indications of how far some theologians were prepared to advance radical, if not revolutionary theses that appeared to their contemporaries to harbour dangerous aims. The condemned theses show how far a purely subjective point of view could be taken in such matters as the qualifications of the Ruler for his office, the reasons for depriving him of it, the right to withhold tithes, not to pay taxes, the moral conditions for the pope's fitness to be the vicar of Christ, the refusal to obey the papal law if the pope was 'a bad man', the moral qualifications for holding property. Yet these same decrees also reveal that by censoring the individualistic-subjective theses, the conciliarists inadvertently supported the papacy which had always been a staunch and consistent advocate of the objective standpoint in public law.[2]

The subsequent councils in the fifteenth century (Ferrara–

---

[1] Advocacy of regicide was called a 'doctrina perniciosissima' in the decree of Constance (session of 6 July 1415), condemning the proposition of Jean Petit, the Parisian Master: *Decreta* 408.

[2] Ed. *Decreta* 405ff. For some details on these points which herald the new outlook, see *PGP* 104ff; *IS* part 3; *SHP* 326ff.

Florence–Basle) passed a number of decrees very few of which had much relevance to governmental principles and in any case were of an *ad hoc* nature. The decretal output of the papacy too rapidly declined and again few decretals embodied governmental ideas— one of the exceptions being the fixation of the status of the cardinalate by Eugenius IV and the prohibition of appeals to a general council by Pius II[1]—though the papacy attempted to assert its function as a universal institution charged with the pursuit of peace among the nations as evidenced by the envisaged but abortive congress of European States. The overall picture concerning the canon law as a source of governmental principles is that its material ingredient—faith—had gravely suffered and was drastically reduced in its efficacy, with a corresponding diminution of canon law output. This ingredient had come to be replaced by consent which is only another way of saying that the place of the descending theme of government and law was taken by its ascending counterpart. In regard to the substance of the law, notably that issued by the Council of Constance, the observer witnesses vacillation but above all the corrosive effects of doubt which were detectable on all fronts on the eve of the cataclysm that was to rend into two the hitherto one and unified Europe.

[1] For the former see his *Non mediocri dolore* ed. in *TUI* XIII, 1, 190ff; and details in art. cit. above, 149 n. 5; for the latter see his *Execrabilis* of 18 Jan 1459, ed. in *Bullarium Magnum* (ed. Lyons 1692) I, 386; similarly Julius II in his *Suscepti regiminis*, of 2 July 1509, ed. ibid., I, 511f.

CHAPTER 5

The Scholarship of Canon Law

Canonistic scholarship in the strict meaning of the term could not and did not come into being until two conditions had been satisfied. The first referred to the method of solving the many contradictions to be found in the numerous collections of the ecclesiastical law, while the second referred to the proper grounding in general jurisprudential matters which could be had only by a professional training in analysing juristic concepts: this was made available in only one mature legal system—the Roman law. Both conditions were fulfilled by the thirties of the twelfth century. There was no such thing as a scholarship of canon law before then: what there was, was intelligent amateurism, and no more. Professional canonistic scholarship was intimately linked with the youthful civilian jurisprudence.

The significance of canonistic scholarship as a source of governmental principles is twofold. First, canonistic scholarship took a vital part in making and developing the canon law itself. There had grown up from the earliest generation of canonists in the mid-twelfth century down to the end of the medieval period an intimate connection between the canonistic schools—quite especially Bologna—and the papacy in its judicial capacity and therefore in its law-creative function. This close link constituted a community of interests which attained a degree of harmonious co-operation unparalleled anywhere else. The official canon law as promulgated by the papacy was the concrete emanation of the abstract and yet very earth-bound canonistic, notably Bolognese scholarship. Pure doctrine came to be distilled into the succinct and precise language of the papal canon law. This feature separated canonistic scholarship sharply from its civilian counterpart, since the imperial legislation never manifested the influence of the theoreticians to that marked degree which distinguished ecclesiastical legislation. And the same observation holds evidently good for royal governments.

Secondly, also from the very beginning of the school at Bologna, the canonistic scholars became the expert interpreters of the very law the underlying ideas of which they themselves had set forth in their lectures and literary productions. The interpretation of the canon law by the canonists was a major source of governmental principles in the high and late Middle Ages, if not also beyond. The canonists exercised influence far beyond their immediate concerns. These are features which are indeed unique. Because there was this circle—canonists, papacy, canonists—scholarship acted something like a self-propelling and self-perpetuating organ, for the professional interpretation by the jurists gave rise to further decretal legislation which in its turn was again the subject of academic teaching. Lastly, the popes and their immediately surrounding personnel were not only graduates, but very frequently also eminent teachers of law and brilliant exegetists and commentators on the canon law itself. It is indisputable that these characteristics can be classed as unique in the history of law, of governmental science and of institutionalized government.

In fact, the beginnings of a canonistic school at Bologna are directly connected with the reverberations of the Investiture Contest, when many of the assumptions which society had taken for granted came to be rather effectively questioned. The lay side had a fully matured legal system, the Roman law, which together with the great advances which civilian jurisprudence had made in the early decades of the twelfth century put the hierocratic side at a severe disadvantage. For the hierocratic side had neither a uniform law nor a scholarship, and the former was not attainable without the latter. But what there was, was a fully matured religious and theological system of thought which when joined to jurisprudence yielded a powerful ideological arsenal. It was what de Ghellinck once called 'une communauté des matières' between theologians and jurists that made the emerging and rapidly growing canonistic doctrine so resilient and incomparably stronger and more realistic than its civilian counterpart.[1]

[1] For this 'juristic theology' see *PG* 365ff; also *F.-LeBr.* II, 314ff and esp. J. de Ghellinck, *Le mouvement théologique du XIIᵉ siècle*, 2nd ed. (1948) 422ff;

It was from the hands of the pure theologian Abelard that the Camaldunensian monk Gratian received the fully developed method of solving contradictions.[1] Without this dialectical method of enquiry it would not have been possible to create what Gratian did create—a text-book of canon law. The juristic equipment Gratian received from the civilians, for without a thorough grounding in Roman jurisprudence this kind of book could not have come about.[2] And mastery of the Roman law and civilian jurisprudence remained an indispensable requisite for all fruitful canonistic scholarship throughout the subsequent period.[3] With every justification has Gratian, who finished his work in 1139-40, been called the Father of canonistic scholarship. It is indeed rare that a text-book has so seminal a character as Gratian's had. Its influence in the Middle Ages is without a parallel: only the number of manuscripts of the Bible surpass those of Gratian's *Decretum* which assuredly was the most successful text-book ever written. For in contrast to earlier works of canon law, his was not intended to be a mere collection of canonical law.

The title which Gratian gave to his work was not *Decretum* (which was the name given to it by scholarship) but *Concordia*

A. M. Landgraf, 'Diritto canonico e teologia' in *St. Grat.* (1953) I, 371ff. This does not of course mean that theologians and canonists were always in agreement, see Y. Congar, 'Un témoignage des désaccords entre canonistes et théologiens' in *Études Le Bras* 861ff.

[1] This has been established beyond a shadow of doubt by H. Denifle, E. Seckel and others, see E. Genzmer, 'Die justinianische Kodifikation und die Glossatoren' in *ACDR* (1933) I, 383 n. 179; 419 n. 320; 422 n. 339; further S. Kuttner, 'Zur Frage der theologischen Vorlagen Gratians' in *SavZKA* 23 (1934) 243ff; *PG* 370ff.

[2] Cf. S. Kuttner, 'New studies on the Roman law in Gratian's Decretum' in *Seminar* 11 (1953) 12ff; id., ibid. 12 (1954) 68f. See also A. Vetulani, 'Encore un mot sur le droit romain dans le Décret de Gratien' in *Apollinaris* 21 (1948) 129ff. See also above, 163.

[3] Cf. also G. Le Bras, 'Le droit romain au service de la domination pontificale' in *RHDFE* (1949) 377ff, and F. Merzbacher, 'Die Parömie "Legista sine canonibus parum valet, canonista sine legibus nihil"' in *St. Grat.* XIII (1967) 275ff; Ch. Munier, 'Droit canonique et droit romain d'après Gratien et les Décrétistes' in *Études Le Bras* 943ff; and P. Vaccari, ibid. 997ff; *DDC* IV. 1504ff.

discordantium canonum, that is, a harmony of discordant canons.[1] He intended to reconcile the many contradictory canons by the application of the new dialectical method. The solution suggested by him was the so-called *Dictum Gratiani*: this constituted a very real advance, because nobody before had even attempted a solution of the 'contrarietates' by this method. In regard to the material used by Gratian no advance can be seen, with the exception of the decrees of the Second Lateran Council (1139): all the other material could be found in previous collections.

The work appeared at the right time and in the right place—Bologna—and became at once recognized as a new kind of scholarship that utilized the collected law in the service of scholarly analysis and synthesis. Its nearly 4,000 chapters relate to virtually every problem in public life that could be encountered in a Christian society.[2] The questions treated range from purely disciplinary canons to sacramental topics, from episcopal jurisdiction to the exclusive (that is, reserved) papal jurisdiction, from the scope of secular law to heresy and apostasy, from consecration of churches to the baptismal font, from prebends, immunities, tithes to appellate jurisdiction, and so on. The first part of the *Decretum*, containing 101 *Distinctions*, was the general jurisprudential section,[3] while the second, dealing with fictive 'Causae' gave plenty of opportunity to display all the subtleties of the new dialectical method. As a text-book it was not, and could not be, an official book and never received official sanction by the papacy.[4]

[1] It is remarkable that the wrong title of the work is still reproduced by Mme Rambaud, art. cit. (as above, 129 n. 6), at 60. On the need for a new ed. of the *Decretum* see S. Kuttner in *Apollinaris* 21 (1948) 118ff. For all details concerning his work and influence see the studies presented on the occasion of the eighth centenary in 1952: *St. Grat.* ed. A. M. Stickler (1953–7) 5 vols. They continue to be published. The best guide in regard to medieval scholarship is still van Hove 338ff, 424ff.

[2] For a competent survey of the contents see Stickler 205ff.

[3] For Gratian's theory of law see L. De Luca, 'La nozione della legge nel Decreto di Graziano: Legalità o assolutismo?' in *St. Grat.* XI (1967) 405ff; and now C. G. Fürst, 'Zur Rechtslehre Gratians' in *SavZKA* 88 (1971) 286ff with copious literature.

[4] Concrete evidence of its perusal in the papal chancery does not emerge until about three decades later: W. Holtzmann, 'Die Benutzung Gratians in

From the governmental point of view in a Christian society Gratian's own thesis was especially influential, for he postulated that the owner of a church, the lay lord, be dispossessed and turned into its patron (its *advocatus*, hence advowson) who had specific duties towards 'his' church. In a word, footing on the respective legislation of the first two Lateran Councils (1123 and 1139), Gratian defused the whole proprietary church system by this comparatively simple juristic device.[1] Furthermore, this patronage was considered an ecclesiastical matter and therefore an issue of exclusive ecclesiastical jurisdiction, because it was annexed to a spiritual thing, the individual church. One of the earliest pupils of Gratian, the later Cardinal Roland and Pope Alexander III, turned this pure theory into law: from the strictly legal point of view the Investiture Contest came to an end with the issue of these decretals which were inspired by Gratian's theory.[2] No less significant for public government was the explicit enumeration of the specific privileges which the clerics enjoyed: the privilege of immunity from taxes and tolls, the privilege of forum (i.e. accountability only before the ecclesiastical tribunal) and the privilege of inviolability. Above all, the theme of papal legislative sovereignty was here unambiguously laid down with a wealth of material and made foolproof by underpinning papal monarchy with numerous quotations. The universality of canon law became legal reality which rested on the thesis expressed by Gratian himself that the individual canons (i.e. decrees) derived their *ius et auctoritas*, that is, enforceable character, from the (explicit or implicit) sanction or approval by the papacy as the supreme monarchic legislative organ.[3] Consequently, the secular law had —not at all unlike the secular Ruler—auxiliary function, provided that it did not contradict the canon law. This became the generally

der päpstlichen Kanzlei' in *St. Grat.* (1954) I, 323ff (earlier use in episcopal chanceries). But cf. now *HJb* 93 (1973) 296 n. 96.

[1] *Causa* XVI p. t. treats of this question.

[2] In X: III, 38, 3ff (*De iure patronatus*). For lit. see *KRG* 397ff, also 263ff. For Roland as one of the originators of the concept of *articulus fidei* in his *Sententiae*, cf. K. J. Becker, 'Articulus fidei' in *Gregorianum* 54 (1973) 517-68.

[3] *Dictum Gratiani*, post cap 16, *Causa* XXV, *quaestio* 1.

accepted standpoint both by the papacy and scholarship, and was understood by the canonist scholars to comprise also the Roman law.[1]

Although wholly unofficial, Gratian's *Decretum* opened the great era of canonistic scholarship first at Bologna, then at most other universities. What the papacy had hitherto lacked—the trained professional jurist—was amply provided from the forties onwards: the canonists were the technicians who worked the machinery by which Christian society in the high Middle Ages was to be guided. Some of the popes themselves, such as Alexander III or Innocent IV in the thirteenth century, had not only been professors at Bologna but also made substantial contributions to the scholarship of canon law, while others happily combined scholarship with practical statecraft, such as Innocent III or Gregory IX or Boniface VIII or John XXII. In contrast to most lay Rulers they could thus speak authoritatively and knowledgeably in matters of government. In no other place but Bologna could this new branch of learning have arisen or have attained the excellence of standard which it did. The reason was that nowhere else had civilian jurisprudence reached such high levels as there. This was to prove beneficial, not merely for the pursuit of canonistics itself, but also in other respects. For the unparalleled increase in decretal output made their collection a necessity, even if only in order to satisfy the needs of the adjudicating courts which wished for an up-to-date body of law. Here the English canonists of the second half of the twelfth century took a leading part in this collecting activity,[2] but the collections soon assumed such proportions that they became unwieldy and thus missed the point

[1] *Dict. Grat.* post cap 6, *Dist.* 10 and *Dict.* post cap 4, C, XV, qu. 3; he refers to the 'constitutiones principum' and in the second passage to the 'leges saeculi', 'leges principum'. For illustrative passages from scholarship see van Hove 461 n. 3 and 462 n. 3. For official papal statements see Lucius III in X: II, 1, 8 and Innocent III ibid. I, 2, 10. Van Hove (462) rightly pointed out that the *Roman* law as such was never officially declared an auxiliary law or a law supplementary to canon law.

[2] See the detailed analysis by Ch. Duggan, *Twelfth-century decretal collections* (1963) to be supplemented by his studies in *SCH* I (1964) 132ff and II (1964) 179ff.

of the exercise altogether. What was needed was systematization of the vast material—and that presupposed juristic professionalism. The Bologna professor, Bernard of Pavia, undertook this task and systematized, categorized and classified the material according to a plan which in its essentials was modelled on the Code of Justinian.[1]

Bernard of Pavia composed (ca. 1190) one large systematic collection out of the great mass of decretals and their collections made in England, France, Spain and Italy. He divided his Compilation into five books, these into titles and the titles into chapters (altogether 927) which were called 'extravagant decretals'.[2] This principle of division followed Justinian's division of the Code, and the very first title of the first book in Bernard's Compilation was literally identical with Justinian's. This division was to become standard in all subsequent private collections, and was also adopted in the official collections, beginning with Innocent III's.[3] The *Liber Extra* was as much the work of scholarship as of practical legislative experience: published on 5 Sept. 1234 it was the first official law-book of the papacy that contained the relevant decretal material issued since Gratian's *Decretum*, and some earlier excerpts which scholarship considered he should have incorporated in his work. Nothing reveals the standing and importance of scholarship better than the method of publication chosen by the papacy for its official law-books. They were dispatched to the University of Bologna (and later also to other universities, including Oxford) because the universities were obviously considered the most

---

[1] This was the *Compilatio Ia*, ed. Ae. Friedberg, *Quinque compilationes antiquae* (1882). Details in S. Kuttner, *Repertorium* cit. (as above, 142 n. 1), 322ff; Stickler 225ff.

[2] For this see above, 142. For the papal rescript in the high MA see W. Stelzer, 'Reskript und Reskripttechnik' in *Röm. Hist. Mitteilungen* 14 (1972) 207ff.

[3] The so-called *Compilatio IIIa*, publ. probably late 1209 (S. Kuttner in *Misc. G. Mercati*, V (1946) (=*Studi e Testi* 125) 621), ed. Ae. Friedberg, *Compilationes* (as n. 1), 105ff. The second official collection (the *Quinta*) was made by order of Honorius III in 1225, ed. Friedberg, 151ff. The other three were private works, that is, apart from the *Prima*, those by John of Wales (the *Secunda*, 1212) which was a conflation of the compilations by Alan and Gilbert, ed. ibid. 66ff; and the *Quarta* (1217) by Johannes Teutonicus, ed. ibid. 135ff. For all this see H. v. Heckel, 'Die Compilationen des Alanus und Gilbertus' in *SavZKA* 29 (1940) 116ff; Stickler 229ff.

appropriate forum for the dissemination of the new law that superseded the old.

The complete Corpus of canon law which took little more than 130 years to complete embodied a system of law that was at once living law born out of the exigencies of contemporary society and a law in the formulation of which scholarship had played an indispensable role. The character of canon law as a living law was an enormous advantage which it had over the Roman law. No adjustment was needed here, and if modifications in the law were required, there was a living monarch who could change the legal situation with one stroke or one decretal letter. On the other hand, it would have been the height of frivolity and irresponsible temerity if a law in the body of Roman law had been changed by a medieval emperor. What therefore was originally a grave disadvantage turned out to be a great advantage. Further, canonistic scholarship itself was as earth-bound as the law which the scholars interpreted. And the papal curia once more profited from scholarship in so far as the young graduates were employed in all kinds of curial business and especially in the legal departments where recent students were always needed for all kinds of juristic tasks.[1]

Trained canonistic scholars were furthermore sought in the episcopal chanceries, in the archidiaconal offices, and in the numerous judicial positions which experienced a mushroom growth from the mid-twelfth century onwards.[2] By applying

---

[1] This was the *Capella* and its members were the *capellani*. See R. Elze, 'Die päpstliche Kapelle' in *SavZKA* 38 (1950) 145ff. See also *KRG* 322f. For the 14th cent. however see B. Schimmelpfennig, 'Die Organisation der päpstlichen Kapelle in Avignon' in *QFIAB* 50 (1971) 80ff. Evidently the chancery and similar departments had great need of canonists. See especially P. Herde, *Beiträge zum päpstlichen Kanzlei- und Urkundenwesen im 13. Jhdt*, 2nd ed. (1967) and his *Audientia litterarum contradictarum*, 2 vols. (1970). Further, B. Barbiche, 'Les scriptores de la chancellerie apostolique sous le pontificat de Boniface VIII' in *BEC* 128 (1970) 115ff and particularly Brigide Schwarz, *Die Organisation kurialer Schreiberkollegien* (1972) (important for curial procedure and the function and status of the officers, ed. of new texts).

[2] For the practical application of ecclesiastical jurisprudence, see W. Trusen in *HQL* 476ff dealing with most of the important officers in the various departments and judicial courts.

what they had learned in an abstract way, the trained canonists came to develop the law itself and herewith also its jurisprudence. In the universities which began to multiply in the twelfth and especially in the thirteenth century in the Western kingdoms, the method of treating canon law and its basic topics was the same everywhere, though in the important questions concerning government there was by no means a dead unanimity or a simple regurgitation of old stale matter. This applies with particular force to the first generation of canonists—the decretists—who were sometimes quite bold in their interpretations and conclusions in regard to delicate governmental issues. The liveliness of regional scholarship, notably French,[1] Spanish[2] and also, in a different way, English,[3] is indeed noteworthy. For there were many governmental problems which were hardly touched at Bologna and yet were vital issues in the kingdoms, such as feudal concepts and practices, the creation of bishops and the role of the king in the process, the relations of royal to ecclesiastical law, the standing of the individual cleric, and many other topical problems awaited their canonistic treatment.[4] The canonists, especially the Spaniards, developed governmental conceptions relative to the

[1] A good example is the *Summa Coloniensis* (written 1169), ed. G. Fransen and S. Kuttner (1969–). Other examples of the French decretist school are the *Summa Parisiensis*, ed. T. MacLaughlin (1952) written about 1170 (excellent juristic piece); the *Monacensis* (Kuttner, *Repertorium* 179ff); the *Bambergensis* (ibid. 206ff). Valuable excerpts of these (and other products of the French school) ed. by J. A. Watt, *The theory of papal monarchy in the 13th century* (1965), svv.

[2] Though evidently some 'regional' scholars worked in Bologna, a notable Spanish example being Laurentius Hispanus as the author of the important *Glossa Palatina*; for identification see A. M. Stickler, 'Il decretista Laurentius Hispanus' in *St. Grat.* IX (1966) 461ff (with numerous passages ed. and relevant in the present context). For Vincentius Hispanus see below, 172 n. 1.

[3] The study by S. Kuttner–E. Rathbone, 'Anglo-Norman canonists' in *Trad* 7 (1951) 279ff is fundamental.

[4] Hardly a beginning has been made. There is a great deal of material relative to government in the glosses written by an Anglo-Norman canonist in Caius College, Cambridge MS 676; for details see Kuttner art. cit. 317ff (circle of John of Tynemouth).

triad of king, bishops and pope.[1] Unfortunately, a very great deal of textual preparatory work has still to be done to make the treasures hidden in all kinds of repositories available to systematic analysis. About their first-rate character as sources of governmental ideas no doubt is permissible.

Academic mobility worked greatly in favour of disseminating canonistic scholarship. Mobility was more marked in the field of canonistics than in its civilian counterpart: the needs of ecclesiastical bodies, such as cathedral chapters, monastic houses, episcopal curiae, and so on, encouraged migration of scholars and the dissemination of 'published' works. Above all, the judicial machinery which the papacy had devized, that is, the so-called delegated system of papal jurisdiction, virtually forced the various chanceries to keep abreast of the state of the current law and contingent doctrines.[2] The highly developed legatine system by which the papacy reached the farthest corners of Western Christendom (and from the early thirteenth century onwards also the former Byzantine empire) similarly demanded men with adequate legal and doctrinal equipment for the most effective presentation of the papal cause.

The escalation of the academic study of canon law within two generations was contingent upon the rapidly developing need for a law that was the right norm of living in a Christian society. The proliferation of the faculties of canon law in the nascent and quickly growing universities of the twelfth and thirteenth centuries demanded more, better and more highly qualified academic staff. This is evidenced in the increase of the Masters who were Doctors of both Laws (the *ius utrumque*) from the mid-thirteenth century onwards.[3] A successful career as an academic canonist frequently secured the highest curial functions: a number of canonists reached the cardinalate, such as, to mention but a few,

---

[1] For some examples see G. Post, 'Blessed Lady Spain—Vincentius Hispanus and Spanish nationalism in the 13th cent.' in *Speculum* 29 (1954) 417ff; see also id., 'Two notes on nationalism' in *Trad* 9 (1953) 281ff.

[2] See above, 168. For 'Legatus' in medieval Roman law see now J. W. Perrin in *Trad* 29 (1973), 357ff.

[3] For details see below, 184.

Goffredus de Trano,[1] Hostiensis,[2] Johannes Monachus,[3] Petrus Bertrandi,[4] Franciscus Zabarella,[5] Panormitanus,[6] Johannes de Turrecremata,[7] Johannes Antonius de s. Groegio,[8] and so on. Similarly, a successful literary activity as teacher and interpreter was one of the recognized avenues to attaining episcopal rank. In fact, the number of academic canonists who became bishops reached the three-figure class. These facts would go to prove convincingly how vitally important a branch of academic activity canonistics had become and how immediately relevant it was to contemporary society. On the other hand, the religious Orders were not strongly represented among the higher echelons of the

[1] Goffredus died 1245. His fame rested on the very handy *Summa decretalium* (ed. Venice 1586) which served as a useful introduction to the living law.

[2] Hostiensis was the senior cardinal as cardinal-bishop of Ostia, his name was Henricus de Segusia, Bolognese student, enjoyed enormous reputation, although he was an academic teacher only for a short while (at Paris); died 25 Oct. 1271. He was one of the most important canonists; wrote the *Lectura in Decretales* (ed. Paris 1512), a most detailed work, and the more popular *Summa* (ed. Venice 1570) which was designed to deal with both laws, though it was primarily canonistic. For details see N. Didier, 'Henri de Suse, évêque de Sisteron' in *RHDFE* 31 (1953) 244ff, 409ff; id., 'Henri de Suse en Angleterre (1236–1244' in *Studi V. Arangio-Ruiz* (1954) II, 333ff; also J. A. Watt, op. cit. (as 171 n. 1), 107ff.

[3] Frenchman, died 22 Aug. 1313 when chancellor of the Roman Church and papal legate to France. Wrote Commentary on the Sext (ed. Venice 1585). His glosses on certain decretals became incorporated into the *gl. ord.* and are in fact semi-official expositions.

[4] Also Frenchman; died 24 June 1349. Wrote many commentaries; of special significance is his *Tractatus de iurisdictione ecclesiastica et civili* directed against Petrus de Cugneriis (see below, 291). The tract *De origine iurisdictionis* is not his, but belongs to Durandus de s. Porciano, see O. Martin in *Mélanges Fitting* (1908) II, 105ff.

[5] A brilliant conciliarist; died as cardinal at Constance 6 Nov. 1417. See below, 187.

[6] See below, 187.

[7] See below, 301.

[8] Influential *lumen iuris* at the turn of the 15th and 16th centuries. His *Commentaria* on the *Decretum* (ed. Lyons 1522) were, judged by the standards of the time, good expositions of juristic and governmental problems, though overloaded with quotations. He died in 1509.

academic profession, although there were members of Orders (Benedictines, Augustinians, Cistercians, Carthusians) who wrote on individual canonistic topics without reaching the standard of their secular brethren. In reverse proportion stood the dozens of academic teachers who were laymen and taught canon law and wrote on it.[1]

There was a vigorous and influential English contingent in Bologna towards the end of the twelfth and early thirteenth centuries. One of the earliest exegetists of canon law was the archdeacon of Richmond in Yorkshire, Honorius, who wrote a *Summa quaestionum* on the basis of the *Decretum*. This represented a new literary species with a great future.[2] A master at Bologna, Alan, wrote highly influential glosses which were both sound and original and contributed greatly to the growth of the properly understood hierocratic idea of government.[3] He, John of Wales, and Gilbert[4] as well as Richard de Mores[5] were other English canonists who not only taught but also composed seminal works, notably the first three who collected the new decretals.[6] There was also a lively native scholarship in the early thirteenth century as is proved by the number of extant manuscripts, and of the study of canon law in the two universities there is ample evidence in the thirteenth century,[7] though this has not yet been made fully available.

That the English canonists in the two universities never reached the level of their Bolognese colleagues finds its ready explana-

[1] See below, 184.

[2] For details see the discoveries by Kuttner and Rathbone, art. cit. (above, 171 n. 3), 304ff.

[3] Details about him in Kuttner, *Repertorium* 316f, 325f; *MP* 147ff; A. M. Stickler, 'Alanus als Verteidiger des monarchischen Papsttums' in *Salesianum* 21 (1959) 346ff.

[4] See lit. in van Hove 429 n. 6.

[5] For identification see Kuttner and Rathbone 329ff; S. Kuttner in *DDC* VII, 676ff; for some of his views *MP* (s.v. Richard de Lacy) 211ff.

[6] See above, 169 n. 3.

[7] For some remarks see W. Ullmann, 'Canonistics in England' in *St. Grat.* (1954) II, 519ff; id., 'The Paleae in Cambridge MSS of the Decretum' ibid. (1953) I, 159ff (conclusion 213ff).

tion in the legal-constitutional position of the country itself. In England, Roman law was in every respect a purely academic subject, and without a lively continuing civilian scholarship canonistics was bound to desiccate. There was, however, something like a revival of canonistic studies in England in the course of the fourteenth century and throughout the fifteenth, though it focused attention almost wholly on the interpretation of English conciliar law. John of Athona, a Doctor of both Laws of Oxford and later canon of Lincoln, commented on the legatine constitutions issued by Otho and Othobono (in 1237 and 1279), and William Lyndwood was a canonist who may well be compared favourably with his continental peers: a Cambridge Master and later bishop of St David's he glossed the decrees of the provincial councils.[1] There is still plenty of unquarried material in Lyndwood's work which despite the author's unconcealed reticence on governmental and 'political' issues (especially those relating to the English law) contains a great deal that needs detailed exploration, just as do the numerous canonistic manuscripts which hibernate in College, cathedral and monastic libraries.

As already indicated, the method of teaching and expounding canon law and the techniques were in all respects identical with those observed in civilian jurisprudence. But there was some difference in so far as the surviving canonistic material is infinitely richer in contents and more varied than that of civilian jurisprudence. Further, some of the canonistic topics prompted the composition of special tracts or monographs to a greater extent than fell within the civilian's ambit. The tracts entitled 'De potestate papae' (or similar headings) are very numerous and in fact became literary expositions of respectable dimensions. For the quick and practical use of canon law the species of the *Notabilia, Repertoria, Margaritae*, gained great popularity, and could be compared with present-day 'Aids to students' or 'Law for the practitioner'. Of a similar kind were the *Flores* (in reality an

---

[1] Athona's and Lyndwood's works are ed. together in one volume (Oxford 1679). ET (1543) ed. by J. V. Bullard & H. Chalmer Bell, *Lyndwood's Provinciale* (1929). On Lyndwood see also C. R. Cheney, 'William Lyndwood's Provinciale' in *The Jurist* 21 (1961) 405ff. He died 21 Oct. 1446.

offshoot of the *Florilegia* of an earlier vintage) *iuris canonici* or from the thirteenth century onwards the *Flores utriusque iuris*.[1]

It is customary to divide the canonistic scholars into decretists and decretalists, the former the interpreters of Gratian's *Decretum* and the latter interpreters of the new decretal legislation. The rapidity with which canonistic studies developed in Bologna is indeed noteworthy: within less than two decades after Gratian there was a canon law university at Bologna and, as indicated, in the French realms which were noted in the twelfth century for their intellectual alertness, there also grew flourishing canon law schools.

In the reconstruction of the ideas propounded by the canonists the historian however faces serious difficulties which are heightened in the present context because of the paucity of easily available original material as well as of secondary works. Vast areas of medieval canonistic scholarship are still unexplored, especially the decretist schools of the twelfth century, where vital information is missing. Only a handful of works are published, and some of the most original and penetrating commentaries, such as the monumental work of Huguccio on the *Decretum*, remain as yet accessible only in manuscripts. Huguccio was also a theologian of calibre, and it is the combination of juristic and theological thought which raises the quality of his work far above any of his contemporaries. His style and exposition have grace and elegance; and in the present context his views reflect the severe juristic standpoint, consonant with the material itself.[2] He was one of

---

[1] For a recent discovery and identification see R. Feenstra, 'Les Flores utriusque iuris de Jean Hocsem' in *RHD* 31 (1963) 486ff. The collection of *Flores utriusque iuris* by Panormitanus was most popular; there are many editions.

[2] For Huguccio (he died as bishop of Pisa in 1210) see the excellent entry in *DDC* VII, 1357ff, with full bibliography. For some of his views see A. M. Stickler in *Eph. iuris can.* 3 (1947) 1ff; also in *Salesianum* 15 (1953) 575ff, at 604ff; *MP* 142ff. (I used Pembroke College MS 72 mainly); G. Catalano, *Impero, regni e sacerdozio nel pensiero di Uguccio da Pisa*, 2nd ed. (1959); J. A. Watt, op. cit. (above, 171 n. 1), 15ff. For a work that may have influenced Huguccio, see J. Keir, 'Apparat au Décret de Gratien "Ordinaturus", source de la Summa Decretorum de Huguccio' in *St. Grat.* XII (1967) 143ff.

the teachers of Innocent III at Bologna. Among the other decretists whose works are however readily available in modern editions and above all are of interest to governmental science, are the *Summa* of Paucapalea,[1] one of Gratian's own pupils, the *Stroma* of Roland (who became Alexander III),[2] the *Summa* of Rufinus[3] and of Stephen of Tournai[4] who combined civil with canon law (he was a pupil of Bulgarus and Martinus), and the *Summa Parisiensis*.[5] There are, however, numerous excerpts of individual glosses available, but the total amount readily at hand in modern editions is small in comparison with the output.[6] The *glossa ordinaria* of Johannes Teutonicus on the *Decretum* of Gratian, later greatly supplemented by Bartholomaeus of Brescia, is printed in the margins of most of the early printed editions of the *Decretum*.[7]

As exegetists the decretists were primarily concerned with the explanation of the text of the *Decretum* including the 'Dicta' of Gratian himself. They kept strictly to the letter of the source and took hardly any account of what was said outside this source. This restricted vision does not make their works as sources of governmental ideas any the less important. On the contrary, their value is increased precisely because they attempted to explain the 'pure law' uncontaminated by material not considered or included by Gratian. Among the topics which the decretists—and this observation also goes for the decretalists—elaborated and presented in almost classic form was the descending theme of government and law and with it the most meritorious differentiation between office and person. Qualifications for Rulership, such as the principle of suitability, were set forth at length in conjunction

---

[1] Ed. J. F. Schulte (1890); see also J. Juncker, 'Summen und Glossen' in *Sav ZKA* 14 (1925) 384 ff, at 419ff.

[2] Ed. F. Thaner (1884). See *DDC* VII, 702ff (uneven, incomplete bibl.).

[3] Ed. H. Singer (1902); also J. Juncker art. cit. (note 1), 428ff; *DDC* VII, 779ff.

[4] Ed. J. F. Schulte (1891). There are very valuable passages in J. Juncker art. cit.; see also id., 'Die Summa des Simon de Bisignano und seine Glossen' ibid. (15 (1926) 326ff.

[5] Above, 171 n. 1. [6] See above, 171, 176.

[7] Johannes died 1245; Bartholomaeus died 1258; the gloss was finished by ca. 1245. Details and lit. in van Hove 430ff.

with the depositions of Rulers by the papacy.[1] The decretists also had ample opportunity of commenting on the principle of division of labour as laid down by Gelasius I whose relevant passage Gratian had taken into his *Decretum*. They also at length discussed the relative functions of the pope and the (Western) emperor. After all, the Donation of Constantine was in part incorporated into the *Decretum*,[2] and arising from their discussions were their views relating to the tutorial function of Rulers, especially in connexion with the inalienability of public rights and goods which gained great practical significance in regard to the government of bishops in their dioceses as well as to other ecclesiastical officers.[3]

Above all, they were the first jurists who propounded a fully-fledged doctrine of canon law based on the general part of the *Decretum*: they could do this, because they had a ready recourse to general jurisprudential expositions, mainly set forth in civilian works. But because canonistic scholarship was in numerous ways intimately linked with the ecclesiastical and religious substructure of the (canon) law itself, the canonists indubitably had a great advantage in comparison with their civilian colleagues: they quite effortlessly accommodated their doctrines of government within the general framework of ecclesiastical subjects including theology and had thus a wider horizon and angle of vision than the civilians were able to enjoy. The canonists did spade-work in every respect, and their jurisprudential doctrines evidently had large-scale repercussions on the science of government, especially in regard to the creation of new canon law itself and its relations with other legal systems. Medieval 'constitutionalism' owes a great debt to the early generation of the canonistic scholars.

In assessing the work of the decretalists—in the present context

[1] Usually in connection with Gregory VII's excerpt in Gratian, XV, 6, 3. For depositions of kings see also K. Schnith, 'Gedanken um Königsabsetzungen im Spätmittelalter' in *HJb* 91 (1971) 309ff.

[2] See D. Maffei, *La donazione di Costantino nei giuristi medievali* (1964); for some further relevant topics see below, 263.

[3] For the background of this neglected topic see W. Ullmann, 'A Note on inalienability with Gregory VII' in *St. Greg.* IX (G. B. Borino Memorial volume, 1972) 115ff.

it is mainly their lectures and commentaries which are of immediate concern—it should be borne in mind (1) that they built on the firm foundations of the decretists' theories; (2) that the law upon which they commented was living law and produced in their own time or in the immediately antecedent generation: it was a law which in all vital respects was decisively shaped by canonistic scholarship; (3) that they were fully aware of the nature of the law as a universally applicable norm of right living in a Christian society; (4) that they were able to draw on the fully developed civilian jurisprudence which had taken into account the decretals as legislative products as well as the canonistic teachings as mature jurisprudential expressions. It was precisely the decretalists' admirable mastery of both laws which enabled them to attain their commanding heights.[1] Far more of their works are extant in early editions than those of the decretists. For instance, to take just a few of the giants of the thirteenth century, there was, apart from the already-mentioned Goffredus de Trano or Hostiensis, Innocent IV who wrote while pope a large commentary on the *Liber Extra* as well as on the Constitutions of the First Lyons Council.[2] The great contribution which he made to doctrine lay in his conceiving a corporate body as a fictive personality: this was the so-called juristic person. He thus powerfully contributed to the corporational theme of society and the institutionalized descending theme of government.[3] There were further-

---

[1] In this context see also G. Le Bras, 'Accurse et le droit canon' in *AA* 217ff; and P. Legendre, 'Accurse chez les canonistes' ibid. 249ff. See also for a general survey of canonists K. W. Nörr in *HQL* 370ff.

[2] Ed. of his *Commentaria* Frankfurt 1570 (and many others) together with the *Additiones* by Baldus. Details in *DDC* VII, 1029ff (uneven, but full account).

[3] See Maitland's Introduction to his translation of O. Gierke's *Political Theories of the Middle Age* (repr. 1938); see also W. Ullmann, 'The medieval theory of legal and illegal organisations' in *LQR* 60 (1944) 285ff; id., 'The delictal responsibility of medieval corporations' ibid. 64 (1948) 77ff; esp. B. Tierney, *Foundations of Conciliar Theory* (repr. 1969) 99ff. For a specific application of the corporation thesis see M. J. Wilks, 'The idea of the Church as "unus homo perfectus" and its bearing on the medieval theory of sovereignty' in *Misc. hist. ecclesiasticae* (1961) 30ff; see also J. A. Watt, op. cit. (171 n. 1), 66ff, and P. Michaud-Quantin, *Universitas: expréssion du mouvement communautaire dans le moyen âge latin* (1970).

more the continuator of Huguccio's *Summa*, Johannes de Deo, a
Spaniard teaching at Bologna;[1] 'Abbas antiquus', that is, Bernard
of Montmirat, a famous teacher at Bologna and Toulouse;[2]
Bernard of Parma whose gloss on the *Liber Extra* became the
ordinary gloss and exercized great influence;[3] the so-called
'Speculator', that is, Guilielmus Durantis, whose *Speculum iuris*
was of encyclopedic dimensions and combined in a very dexterous
way pure theory with practice; there was hardly a contemporary
governmental problem which was not treated in this enormous
work; he also seems to have assisted in the drafting of the decrees
of the Second Lyons Council (1274); that he was also a notable
expert on liturgical symbolism is worth mentioning, however
little modern canonists take notice of this.[4] In the fourteenth
century the canonists' fame and reputation stood in no wise below
that of their civilian brethren. Two Bolognese deserve a passing
remark, because their works proved to be sources of first-rate
importance. Guido de Baysio, commonly known as 'the Archdeacon' (which was his function at Bologna) himself a pupil of the
eminent civilian Guido de Suzaria and teacher of Johannes
Andreae, appeared not only influential but also contributed
greatly to the development of the fully matured hierocratic
ideology. His main works are the so-called *Rosarium*, a very large
Summa on the *Decretum* (which preserved many teachings of
early canonists whose views would otherwise have been consigned
to oblivion) and his commentary on the *Sext*.[5] The other Bolognese luminary was Johannes Andreae, a layman whose prolific
output secured him a most influential place in the later Middle
Ages; his contemporaries called him *fons et tuba iuris*, himself
having been the pupil of most distinguished civilians and canonists, among whom were Ricardus Malumbra and Martinus

---

[1] See Schulte II, 103; van Hove 477.

[2] Van Hove 478 with further lit.

[3] He taught at Bologna; died 1263.

[4] Ed. *Speculum iuris* (Basle 1574, and many other eds.); his *Rationale divinorum
officiorum* (ed. Lyons 1512 and other eds.). He died 1 Nov. 1296.

[5] Ed. of *Rosarium* Lyons 1534; ed. *Commentaria in Sextum* (Venice 1577).
He died 10 Aug. 1313.

Syllimanus as well as Aegidius Fuscararius and 'the Archdeacon'. He was of low birth and extremely poor. A friend of Petrarch and Cynus as well as of high-ranking ecclesiastical officers, he perfected the governmental thesis of the papacy in his large works on the *Sext* and the *Liber Extra*,[1] as well as in his *Additiones* to the 'Speculator's' huge work. Of the native English canonists in the thirteenth century little is known, and they certainly did not materially contribute to the development of governmental ideas. There was William of Drogheda, probably a pupil of Vacarius and teacher at Oxford, who wrote a procedural tract, and Laurence of Somercote, a canon of Chichester, who wrote a short treatise on episcopal elections.[2]

In substance the teachings of the decretalists constitute some of the major sources of medieval governmental principles.[3] They

[1] The *Novella* (so called after his daughter) on the *Liber Sextus* ed. Venice 1504 (and other eds.); for the title see the text cited in Schulte II, 205 n. 3; reprinted 1963–6 with an introduction by S. Kuttner. *Commentaria in Sextum* (ed. Lyons 1550); he drafted the statutes of the university. He became a victim of the plague and died in 1348. He had 9 children, of whom two were illegitimate: both attained high ecclesiastical office, one became a cardinal.

[2] For the former see van Hove 491 with lit. and eds.; for the latter see Schulte II, 114 ('Sumentone'). The tract is ed. by A. Wretschko, *Der Traktat des Laurentius de Somercote* (1907) ed. at 27ff (written in 1254). This tract seems to have been kept up to date as evidenced by the additions in MS. ULC Ii, 6, 17 and Ii, 1, 22 (mid-14th cent.).

[3] In the recent decades a great amount of work has been done on this topic. Only a few references can be given. See, e.g. (apart from the studies already mentioned) A. M. Stickler, 'De potestate gladii materialis . . .' in *Salesianum* 6 (1944) 113ff; id., 'Imperator vicarius pape' in *MIOG* 62 (1954) 166ff; id., 'Die Glosse Duacensis zum Dekret' in *Festschrift W. Plöchl* (1960) 385ff; id., 'Der Dekretist Guil. Vasco' in *Études Le Bras* 705ff; id., 'Der Kaiserbegriff des Bernardus Compostellanus Antiquus' in *St. Grat.* XV (1972) 105ff; *MP* (1949); B. Tierney, 'Some recent works on the political theories of the medieval canonists' in *Trad* 10 (1954) 594ff; id., 'The continuity of papal political theory in the 13th cent.' in *Med. Studies* 27 (1965); id., 'Tria quippe distinguit' in *Speculum* 37 (1962) 48ff; 'Pope and Council: some new decretist texts' in *Med. Studies* 19 (1957) 197ff; J. A. Watt, op. cit.; id., 'The use of the term plenitudo potestatis by Hostiensis' in *PICL* II (1965) 161ff; id., 'Medieval deposition theory' in *SCH* II (1965) 197ff.

also greatly influenced the development in a later age.[1] The accentuation of the monarchic powers of the pope resulting from the doctrinal clarification of his function as vicar of Christ, their detailed ramifications and applications in regard to persons and things, might well be said to be the backbone of canonistic doctrines, and with this thesis was intimately linked the mediatory role of the pope as the point of intersection between heaven and earth.[2] The doctrine of the pope's personal sovereignty in his governing function reached a very high standard, especially in connexion with the relations to secular Rulers who as 'sons' (*filii*) were comprehended as the pope's subjects. This very same theme of sovereignty necessitated the exposition of the pope's own immunity in his governing function and the protection of this immunity by means of the law.[3] This again involved the elaboration and definition of the crime of high treason (*crimen laesae maiestatis*) committed against the pope. The decretalists excelled in subtle and penetrating analyses of the duties incumbent upon the secular Rulers as officers of the Church and brought into clear relief their ministerial functions. In particular, the constitutional principle of inalienability was one which to all intents and purposes they perfected, since this was one of the oldest restrictions imposed on any ecclesiastical officer.[4] And the assimilation of the king to an emperor evidenced in the adage 'Rex in regno suo est imperator' heralded a great future in regard to royal sovereignty: it may have been an English canonist who inaugurated this ideological development.[5] But there was no item in govern-

[1] For some observations see W. Ullmann, 'The medieval papal court as an international tribunal' in *Essays Judge Dillard* (=*Virginia J. for International Law* 11 (1971)) 356ff; also J. Muldoon, 'The contribution of the medieval canon lawyers to the formation of international law' in *Trad* 28 (1972) 483ff.

[2] On this see *PGP* 54f, 59, 76ff, 142ff.

[3] On the relation of faith, tradition and papal sovereignty, cf. the important paper by B. Tierney, 'Sola scriptura and the canonists' in *St. Grat.* XI (1967) 347ff.   [4] See above, 58 n. 3.

[5] Cf. *MP* 145 n. 2 and Appendix H; S. Mochi Onory, *Fonti canonistiche dell'idea moderna dello stato* (1951), esp. 162ff. F. Calasso held that it was Sicilian jurists who initiated the development: *I glossatori e la teoria della sovranità*, 3rd ed. (1957), ed. of Proemium of Marinus de Caramanico's *Liber constitutionum* (scil. Siciliae) at 179ff.

mental doctrine which was not materially fructified by the decretalists in the thirteenth and fourteenth centuries.

No other sphere than that of conflicting jurisdictions over clerics and ecclesiastical matters revealed so clearly the true nature of the 'political' tensions in the Middle Ages, and in no other field was there so intimate a connexion between scholarship, government and law. Since the question in the last resort concerned whether or not a cleric was a subject of the king (or emperor), both civilians and canonists took a lively interest in the problem. It became thorny and very delicate, once concrete issues came into the open, as was the case in England under Henry II and his conflict with Thomas Becket.[1] And the incorporation of the so-called *privilegium fori* (together with the privileges of immunity and personal clerical inviolability) in the *Decretum* of Gratian[2] established the benefit of clergy and made it incumbent upon the canonists to express themselves upon it. There is no commentary or lecture or gloss on the relevant entry which does not at great length expound this clerical privilege embracing as it did criminal as well as civil actions. The topic was perhaps more acute in the kingdoms than in the empire, probably on account of the close link between the national clergy and the king. That the issue was still topical in fourteenth-century England has been proved by the case that went right up to the Rota Romana, the supreme papal court.[3] That this explosive issue involved a number of consequential items, such as the relations of positive enacted law to

[1] For the Becket dispute see, e.g., Ch. Duggan, 'The Becket dispute and the criminous clerks' in *Bull. Instit. Hist. Research* 35 (1962) 1ff; D. Knowles, *Thomas Becket* (1970). For France see R. Génestal, *Le privilegium fori en France du Décret de Gratien à la fin du XIVe siècle*, 2 vols. (1921-4); G. Le Bras, 'Le privilège du clergie en France dans les derniers siècles du M.A.' in *J. des savants* 20 (1922) 163ff, 253ff. For England in general see L. C. Gabel, *Benefit of Clergy in England in the later M.A.* (1929); W. Holdsworth, *HEL* III, 293ff.

[2] Gratian, *Dict.* post cap 47, C. XI, qu. 1; and chapters 8, 42, 43; decretal legislation: X: II, 2, 12; VI: II, 2, 2; III, 2, 1.

[3] W. Ullmann, 'A decision of the Rota Romana on the benefit of clergy in England' in *St. Grat.* XIII (1967) 455ff; here also the Portuguese case as reported by Albericus de Rosciate (462 n. 19). The Rota always had a strong English contingent, mostly Oxford and Cambridge men, ibid., 465ff.

customary law, or secular law to canon law, is self-evident.[1] There is therefore a great need to analyze the decisions of the Rota Romana closely, because this tribunal was a unique forum composed of highly experienced jurists endowed with direct jurisdictional powers. And only the most important cases reached this court, the verdicts of which represent a first-rate source of jurisdictional and therefore 'political' ideas.[2]

Canonistic scholarship began to attract an increasing number of laymen, which once more goes to show how relevant to contemporary social and political conditions this scholarship had become. Clearly, these laymen had already been full doctors of civil law, and the doctorate in both laws (the *Doctor iuris utriusque*) became quite common among the lay scholars from the mid-thirteenth century onwards.[3] One of the first laymen to lecture on canon law at Bologna was Aegidius Fuscararius in the mid-thirteenth century; Dynus de Mugellano was asked by Boniface VIII to assist in the composition of the title 'De regulis iuris' in the Sext;[4] Johannes Andreae, one of the most eminent jurists Bologna ever possessed, also was a layman,[5] but then in the four-

---

[1] The English case was quite instructive in this respect, see 479ff.

[2] For lit. and the problems to be examined see art. cit., 484ff; See further C. Lefebvre, 'Le tribunal de la Rote romaine et sa procédure au temps de Pius II' in *Enea Silvio Piccolomini* (Commemoration volume, ed. D. Maffei 1968) 199ff; further *DDC* VII, 742ff. The oldest collection of Rota decisions is that of Thomas Fastoli, an auditor under John XXII and later bishop of Menevia (died 1361). For details of the Rota and MSS see now G. Dolezalek, 'Die handschriftliche Verbreitung von Rechtssprechungssammlungen der Rota' in *SavZKA* 58 (1972) 1–106; G. Dolezalek and K. W. Nörr in *HQL* 849–56.

[3] For this see B. Kurtscheid, 'De utriusque iuris studio saec. XIII' in *ACII* (1935) II, 309ff; and E. Carusi, 'Utrumque ius—problemi e perspettivi', ibid. 539ff (also important for the development of the idea of a *ius commune*); P. Legendre, 'Le droit romain, modèle et langage: de la signification de l'Utrumque ius' in *Études Le Bras* 913ff and G. Miczka, 'Utrumque ius—eine Erfindung der Kanonisten?' in *SavZKA* 57 (1971) 127ff, esp. 137ff for the several meanings of the term in the 12th century when it frequently designated divine and (human) canon law. For the role which the *ius utrumque* played in creating a unified jurisprudence and law in the later M.A., see W. Trusen, *Anfänge des gelehrten Rechts in Deutschland* (1962), 22ff.

[4] See above, 106. Further *DDC* IV, 1250ff.

[5] Above, 180f.

teenth century there were very many lay-academics at Bologna, Perugia, Siena, and other places who played a conspicuous role in canonistic jurisprudence: Paulus de Liazariis,[1] Johannes de Lignano,[2] Baldus de Ubaldis,[3] Petrus de Ancharano,[4] Antonius de Butrio,[5] Andreas de Barbatia,[6] to mention just a few of the outstanding men. This feature of laymen as exponents of canon law is worth mentioning, since primarily and essentially canon law was ecclesiastical law, but their active participation in its interpretation can be explained by the ecclesiological substance of their society.

It may be recalled that the civilians gave expert opinions on the contentious issues submitted to them from all over Europe. Exactly the same can be said about the canonists who too acted as *consiliatores*. The great authority which in view of their scholarship they commanded, can in fact be shown by their having been consulted on a great many—and sometimes fundamental—problems by popes, cardinals and corporations, especially in the fourteenth and fifteenth centuries. Their *Consilia* are as much neglected as those of their civilian colleagues. Such vital matters as disputed elections, schisms, electoral pacts (the so-called Capitulations), tithes, taxation, and so on, were submitted to them. In the early fourteenth century the Avignonese curia consulted canonists and civilians on no less a problem than the issue of sovereignty. This was the crux of the conflict between the Sicilian king Robert

[1] Bolognese, often employed as an ambassador; died 8 Aug. 1356.

[2] Also Bolognese, very productive author. See above, 112.

[3] Above, 111.

[4] Pupil of Baldus at Perugia, taught at Bologna (simultaneously with Zabarella and Antonius de Butrio). Ed. of his *Lectura* on *Lib. Extra* (Bologna 1581, and other eds.) and on the *Sext* (ed. Lyons 1517). His *Consilia* (ed. Venice 1539). Died 13 March 1416.

[5] Pupil of the latter. Prolific writer; produced eminent pupils, among whom were Zabarella, Johannes ab Imola, Dominicus de san Geminiano. His *Consilia* (ed. Frankfurt 1587) were very important. Died 4 Oct. 1408 in Bologna.

[6] His monographs were important, e.g., *De praestantia cardinalium* (ed. in *TUI* XIV) and his *Consilia* (ed. Venice 1509), one of which dealt with the highly inflammable problem of the electoral capitulations and the restrictions placed on the pope's powers. On this see W. Ullmann, 'The legality of the papal electoral pacts' in *Eph. iuris can.* 12 (1956) 1ff, at 12ff.

the Wise and the Emperor Henry VII in 1313. Oldradus de Ponte consulted by Clement V expressed the view, heavily buttressed by jurisprudential arguments, that the claim to universal jurisdiction and universality of dominion by the imperial government was ill-founded in law, and that the territorial king had full, supreme and inappealable jurisdiction within his domains. As indicated, the thesis that was probably first inaugurated by an English canonist exactly a century earlier, now became the law: supported by the *Consilium* of Oldradus, the eminent Doctor of both laws, the pope issued the decree *Pastoralis cura* which extended the concept of personal sovereignty into a territorial notion. This decree and the scholarship that promoted it, marked the beginning of the territorial fragmentation of Europe in conceptual respects. This happy combination of scholarship and law is a particularly rich source of governmental ideas in the Middle Ages. It is in fact one of the most fertile roots of modern *Staatslehre*.[1]

There were of course numerous other issues though of lesser significance than *Pastoralis cura* which manifested the same impact of scholarship on law and government. The conciliar movement towards the end of the fourteenth century and notably in the first half of the fifteenth was primarily an academic movement and a first-rate source of governmental and constitutional principles. In essence conciliarism was the application of the earlier canonistic corporation thesis,[2] of the Bartolist legislative sovereignty of the people,[3] and of the Marsilian standpoint,[4] to the government of the Church, the constitution of which had proved itself faulty. The events of 1378 had shown that the monarchic function of the papacy was in need of some drastic reform if the institution was to cope with contemporary contingencies.[5] Conciliarism as

---

[1] For some lit. see above, 182 n. 5; also W. Ullmann, 'The development of the medieval idea of sovereignty' in *EHR* (1949) 1ff; id., in forthcoming *Festschrift Nikolaus Grass* (1973).

[2] See above, 179 n. 3.   [3] Above, 109f.

[4] See M. J. Wilks, 'Corporation and representation in the Defensor Pacis' in *St. Grat.* XV (1972) 251ff. See also below, 282f.

[5] Cf. my *Origins of the Great Schism* (repr. 1972 with a new preface).

the practical application of the ascending theme of government to the ecclesiastical body, was therefore severely anti-monarchical in essence. Virtually all outstanding jurists, especially the canonists, attempted to explain the conciliarist thesis by a combination of juristic, historic and metajuristic considerations. It was perhaps the first time that history was intelligently and critically harnessed to the service of a constitutional programme. The views of the conciliarists were set forth not only in special *Consilia* and in Tracts, but also in the general lectures on the *Liber Extra* and the Sext.[1] Among the numerous sources the following deserve specific mention: the 'Speculator's' nephew Guilielmus Durantis, *De modo celebrandi concilium*,[2] Conrad of Gelnhausen's *Epistola Concordiae*,[3] Henry of Langenstein's *Epistola Pacis*,[4] and above all the *Consilia* of Franciscus Zabarella,[5] Antonius de Butrio,[6] Petrus de Ancharano,[7] Dominicus de san Geminiano,[8] Ludovicus Romanus Pontanus[9] and Paulus Castrensis.[10] One of the canonists who enjoyed—rightly—a great reputation was Nicholas de Tudeschis, popularly known as Panormitanus, whose output was quantitatively, but also qualitatively above that of his contemporaries.[11] Of an entirely different complexion was the very large

[1] It would only be tedious to give specific examples; every jurist expounded his views on the constitutional problem.

[2] Ed. Lyons 1534 (and other eds.). See below, 281.

[3] Ed. in E. Martène–U. Durand, *Thesaurus novus anecdotorum* (Paris 1717) II. 1200ff; written in May 1380.

[4] Ed. in H. v. d. Hardt, *Magnum oecumenicum Constantiense Concilium* (Frankfurt 1967) II, 3ff (written in 1381). He was vice-chancellor at Paris University but migrated to Vienna where he became rector of the university in 1384. Cf. also *LTK* V (1960) 190.

[5] Ed. Lyons 1552, here *Cons.* 150. Details in my *Origins* (above, 112 n. 3), 199ff; Tierney 220ff.

[6] Ed. Frankfurt 1587, here *Cons.* 420.

[7] Ed. Venice 1539, here *Cons.* 281.   [8] Ed. Lyons 1533, here *Cons.* 88.

[9] Ed. Frankfurt 1577, here *Cons.* 523.

[10] Ed. Frankfurt 1582, here *Cons.* 419.

[11] A pupil of Zabarella at Padua, taught at Siena, Parma, and Bologna. Main works: *Lectura* on *Lib. Extra* (ed. Lyons 1512); on the Sext (ed. Venice 1592); on the Clementines (ed. Venice 1591); his *Consilia* are esp. important (ed. Lyons 1534). A hitherto unknown, though unfinished Commentary on

work of Johannes de Turrecremata, who by combining theology and jurisprudence pointed to ways of upholding the traditional corporate character of Christian society and its monarchic government.[1]

Despite the very large output of canonistic studies in the fifteenth century, canonistic scholarship no longer manifested the same vigour, originality and earthiness which distinguished it in the antecedent periods. Part of the explanation may be that the ecclesiological substance of society was gradually being replaced by the new premises based on the revived Aristotle and naturalism; part of the explanation may be that a great deal of talent was siphoned off to humanistic pursuits of learning. In a word, canonistics had no longer the monopolistic relevance which it once had. Conditions had greatly changed in the preceding decades, and yet the law, here the canon law, was still the same in virtually all respects: and it was this law, in numerous regards not relevant to contemporary society, which the canonists had to interpret. The gulf between the *via moderna* and the legalized faith was beginning to affect the canonistic scholars whose output became little more than a diffuse regurgitation of stale, dead matter.

Yet on the very eve of the great revolution there were some canonists who realized the precarious if not perilous situation in which society found itself as a result of the monarchic position of the papacy. Some eminent canonists made valiant attempts to revive some kind of conciliarism. The early sixteenth-century efforts made by Cardinal Johannes Antonius de san Georgio,[2]

the *Decretum* discovered by A. Black, 'Panormitanus on the Decretum' in *Trad* 26 (1970) 440ff. His tract *De Concilio Basiliensi* (ed. Lyons 1520) is indispensable for understanding conciliarist thought. The papacy followed his opinion on the delicate question of the Bridgetine Order, see W. Ullmann, 'The recognition of St Bridget's Order by Martin V' in *RB* (1957) 190ff. In general see K. W. Nörr, *Kirche & Konzil bei Nicholaus de Tudeschis* (1964).

[1] He was raised to the cardinalate in 1439; died 26 Sept. 1468. His large *Summa de ecclesia* (ed. Venice 1561) and his *Commentaria super toto Decreto* (ed. Venice 1578) are sources of considerable importance both ecclesiologically and from the point of view of social structure. For some details see A. Black, *Monarchy & Community* (1970) 53ff, 135ff.

[2] In his commentaries on the *Decretum* (ed. Lyons 1522), esp. on *Dist.* 40.

Phillippus Decius[1] and others were intended to provide an evolution based on constitutionalism. This was perhaps the last attempt to show the relevance of canonistic jurisprudence as a social science in the literary meaning of the term, though these efforts have not yet attracted the attention they deserve. Part of the explanation why these canonistic (and civilian) efforts did not succeed was the traditional interlacing of law and theology—by the early sixteenth century a *damnosa haereditas*—which proved a virtually unsurpassable obstacle to the implementation of the ascending theme of government. In particular, the theologians were quite obviously less concerned with social reality than with abstract dogma: their rigidity prevailed against the flexibility of the canonistic lawyers.[2] For an assessment of the ideological forces displayed on the eve of the Reformation canonistic scholarship is an important source, even if no longer of governmental principles.

[1] Ed. of his important *Consilium* in M. Goldast, *Monarchia Romani imperii* (Frankfurt 1668) II, 1767ff. Cf. also Jason de Mayno, *Consilia* (Frankfurt 1609). Both were outstanding jurists of the 16th century.

[2] For some observations cf. W. Ullmann, 'Julius II and the schismatic cardinals' in *SCH* IX (1972) 177ff.

CHAPTER 6

Non-Roman Secular Law

Since society was overwhelmingly agrarian, customary law was of great importance throughout the medieval period. By definition customary law was based on mere usages which had been practised for some considerable time. It was therefore the outcome, not of any deliberate exercise of any law-creative will, but of actual concrete actions by a group of persons within regions or localities. The essential and material ingredient of the binding character of customary law was therefore the implicit consent of the populace. The importance of customary law began to decline when more and more topics became the subject of royally (or imperially) enacted written law. Nevertheless, customary law was prevalent and at all times a strong reminder of the binding force which the populace could impart to the law: the efficacy of customary law reflected the ascending theme of government in practice.[1]

The need to reduce customary law to writing was an infallible sign of an advanced state of society which for reasons of legal stability prompted the codification of unwritten, customary law. From the sixth century onwards this indeed was the case among the Germanic tribes and nations, once they had settled down in their surroundings. But even when customary law was committed to writing, it did not thereby change its substance, for the only effect of codification was that the law was more easily ascertainable. There were numerous Germanic codifications, but hardly any of them have been subjected to a rigorous analysis in regard to their constituent and governmental elements.[2] One of the reasons why their study is beset with very great difficulties is linguistic, and in so far their value as sources in the present context

[1] Cf. above, 62f and *MIL* ch. 4.
[2] For private substantive law see the instructive study by C. Bontems, 'Les dommages et intérêts dans les lois barbares' in *RHDFE* 47 (1969) 454ff. One could but wish that there were similar studies for public law.

is limited. For their language was almost exclusively Latin.[1] Only the Anglo-Saxon laws were written in the vernacular,[2] but even this began to give way in course of time to Latin, as Anglo-Saxon England gradually came to absorb Latin culture.

For the standard of the Latin varied greatly. There is, on the one hand the highly polished and refined language of the laws of the Visigoths of the seventh century,[3] the work of expert and highly trained jurists, and on the other hand there is the uncouth language of the so-called Folk-laws or less appropriately called *leges Barbarorum*.[4] The real difficulty for historical jurisprudence concerns the actual terminology. For in an overwhelming number of cases the Germanic codes were Latin translations from the vernacular, and the vernacular described ancient Germanic customs for which no exact Latin term was available. Yet it was precisely in an attempt to imitate Roman jurisprudence that the primitive law was rendered in the Latin tongue. Hence frequently enough the Latin term only approximated to the real meaning and sense of the original vernacular. Furthermore, since those who had to apply the law were rarely trained jurists familiar with Roman law, the text was re-translated into the vernacular for their bene-fit, thus producing further dangers of distortion.[5]

The codified customary law was overwhelmingly a *Weistum*, that is, the more or less formal declaration by the popular assembly (the Thing) of what was held to be the law: its was declaratory.

[1] For a good survey see *DDC* IV, 1495ff.

[2] Ed. F. Liebermann, *Die Gesetze der Angelsachsen*, 3 vols. (1906–13).

[3] Ed. K. Zeumer in *MGH. Leges Visigothorum*. For details see D. Claude, *Adel, Kirche und Königtum im Westgotenreich* (1971); and esp. the penetrating study by P. D. King, *Law and Society in the Visigothic Kingdom* (1972).

[4] For instance, *Lex Burgundionum*, ed. F. Beyerle in *Germanenrechte* (1936); *Lex Ribuaria* ed. K. A. Eckhardt, ibid., neue Folge (1959); *Leges Alemannorum*, 2 vols., by the same, ibid. (1958–62); *Lex Salica*, ed. by the same, ibid. 5 vols. (1953–6). The *MGH* ed. of these laws is still in progress. About the Roman law and its application in the codes and in the kingdoms themselves, see G. Astuti, 'Note critiche sul sistema delle fonti giuristiche nei regni romano-barbarici dell'occidente' in *Atti della Accademia Nazionale dei Lincei*, 8th series, 25 (1970) 319ff. See also below, 203 n. 3.

[5] For this see now G. Köbler, 'Amtsbezeichnungen in den frühmittelalter-lichen Übersetzungsgleichungen' in *HJb* 92 (1972) 334ff.

Yet in the very process of reducing unwritten to written law, there was plenty of margin for the display of the royal will, so that virtually all 'Folk-laws' were a mixture of customary and enacted law. After all, the king had the personnel which made possible the codification in his own chancery. The very nature of the vast material makes it necessary to give here only specific instances.

To begin with, the law-book of the Visigoths in Spain, the *Leges Visigothorum*,[1] contains as its kernel the oldest Germanic law code in existence. It is that of King Euric (466–85) which is preserved as a fragmentary palimpsest in the Paris Bibliothèque Nationale. Numerous questions still remain relating to the decipherment of the text.[2] This Eurician code experienced several recensions and additions. The final text shows a very high degree of Roman law influence, juristic sagacity and maturity, governmental perspicacity and concrete concern for the well-being of the subjects. There is also strong ecclesiastical influence exercised mainly by the archbishops of Toledo and Seville, though the individual laws were issued as royal laws. Amongst all the early medieval law codes the *Leges Visigothorum* reached the highest level of governmental juristic competence. The basic idea of the rule of law was here classically expressed in the memorable statement that 'the law was the soul of the whole body of the people'.[3] This Visigothic Code incorporated the descending theme of government, though there are some remnants of its ascending counterpart. This Code could well have become the model for medieval Europe, had not this civilized kingdom been raped by the Arab hordes in 711. It is only very recent research that has begun to see the influence of this Code on France and England.[4] For early medieval Europe it is an invaluable source for the reconstruction of governmental thought.

The other Germanic Code that deserves some remarks as a

---

[1] There is a partial ed. and GT by E. Wohlhaupter in *Germanenrechte* (1936).
[2] Cf. the Cambridge dissertation (unpublished) by P. D. King on the structure and genesis and scope of the Eurician Code. Cf. ed. as in n. 1.
[3] *Leges Visigoth*, I, 2, 2.
[4] See *CR* 69f, 81f (with further lit.).

source is the Lombard law-book which in contrast to the Visigothic Code was overwhelmingly Germanic in substance and structure. This is noteworthy in view of the geographical proximity of Rome and the survival of Roman institutions in Northern Italy.[1] The Lombard chancery must have disposed of first-rate personnel:[2] in regard to their substance, the Lombard laws constitute the most mature purely Germanic product of the early Middle Ages.[3] The first and oldest recension was issued by King Rothari in 643 who reduced to writing 'the ancient laws of our fathers, because they were not written down'.[4] He had, he declared at the end of his work, searched the records, had sifted the laws and issued them upon the counsel and agreement of the army and the principal judges. Further, Rothari also brought the old laws up to date so that they were not merely of antiquarian interest, but of direct relevance to his society. There were also fairly strong traces of Roman law influence and the impact of some Visigothic laws was also clear, but the essentially Germanic character was not thereby materially affected. There were also conspicuous borrowings from the Anglo-Saxon laws and Scandinavian sources.[5]

Although initially devoid of clerical influence, the *Leges Langobardorum* nevertheless hold that God was the source of law. Rothari's code exhibited strong theocratic traits. Further, the Ruler is here shown in his tutorial function—a conspicuously advanced theme based on the Germanic *Munt*. Rothari's successors greatly enlarged the code by appending new legal enactments which began to show more and more ecclesiastical influence. By the time of Liutprand (713–36) the king issued his own royal laws which no longer needed any co-operation or consent on the part

[1] For the general background cf. G. P. Bognetti, *L'età longobarda* (1966–8).

[2] See G. Astuti, *Lezioni di storia del diritto italiano: le fonti: età romano-barbarica.* (1953); F. Calasso *Medio evo* 311f.

[3] Ed. F. Beyerle, *Leges Langobardorum*, 2nd ed. (in *Germanenrechte* n. F. (1962).

[4] Ed. cit., cap. 386, p. 93.

[5] See esp. B. Paradisi, 'Il prologo e il epilogo dell'Editto di Rotari' *SDHI* 34 (1968) 1ff (which is a fine comparative and integrative study); also A. Cavanna, 'Nuovi problemi intorno alle fonti dell'Editto di Rotari' ibid., 269ff (an anatomical dissection of the sources of the Edict).

of a popular assembly.[1] The Lombard laws thus very clearly portray the development from the ascending to the descending theme of government, and few other Germanic codes are such excellent sources.[2] In the later Lombard laws the Ruler begins to detach himself from the people. While all other Germanic codes were relegated to legal antiquarianism as a result of the rapidly advancing Roman and ecclesiastic jurisprudence, the Lombard laws survived this onslaught and continued to be applied as well as studied at the law school of Pavia right down to the eleventh century, if not in part at least beyond. Part of the explanation lay in that the Lombards produced legal standards far superior to those of any of the other Germanic codes.[3] In the twelfth century there was even a revival of Lombard law in Southern Italy when on the model of Justinian's Code the subject-matter of the *Lombarda* was classified, divided and categorized according 'to the norm'.[4]

The Anglo-Saxon laws are noteworthy in that they were the only codes of law to be written down in the vernacular. They are indeed an embarrasingly rich quarry for the historian who wishes to construct the governmental principles which underlay Anglo-Saxon government. From the earliest codification right down to Cnut's masterly code they show certain common features which also reveal a continuity of legal and constitutional thought that is in every respect remarkable. Virtually each individual feature

[1] Ed. cit., 99ff.

[2] For some illustrative material relative to territorial conception of sovereignty see the documents of the Lombard dukes of Benevento in the eighth century: W. Deeters, 'Pro salvatione gentis nostrae' in *QFIAB* 49 (1970) 386ff.

[3] In the eleventh century the Lombard laws were collected in chronological order: this collection became known as the *Liber Papiensis* (1019–34), probably made by the Masters of the Pavia law school, ed. *MGH. Leges*, IV, 289ff. About this cf. also E. Genzmer, 'Die justinianische Kodifikation und die Glossatoren' in *ACDR* (1933) I, 345ff at 376ff. In general see *WH* I (1948) 314f. Karolus de Tocco collected the glosses on the *Lombarda* around 1200. They are now available in reprint of 1964 with an introduction by G. Astuti. For the glosses see also Savigny V, 174ff. About the Pavia school see B. Paradisi, *Storia del diritto italiano*, 2nd ed. (1967) I, 406ff.

[4] Ed. *MGH. Leges*, IV, 1ff. K. Lehmann, *Das langobardische Lehensrecht* (1896). See also preceding note.

as represented in the codes shows the continuing development very clearly: the status of the king was perhaps best reflected in the penal measures against breaches of the peace (beginning with the code of Aethelberht of 602–3);[1] the moralizing tone, conspicuous in Wihtred's code, was characteristic;[2] these laws can be spoken of as classic instances of vehicles which turned Christian precepts into an enforceable law by sometimes selective extracts from the Creed or from adjustments of biblical passages; their pronounced theocratic tone (together with an ever more increasing casuistry) was one more element that linked this great mass of sources together. These laws contain a very great deal of ideological-governmental matter which has attracted too little attention.[3]

In general the chief value of the Folk-laws as sources of governmental conceptions lies in their portraying quite faithfully the transition from a tribal to a civilized organization of public life and order. Even if the 'Barbarian' codes do not measure up to the quality and quantity of the Anglo-Saxon laws, they are nevertheless excellent testimonies for the attraction which Rome as a model had exercized: these codes potently cultivated the ground for the reception of essentially alien Roman and Christian elements which in the course of the ninth century were to achieve an amalgamation with the prevailing Germanic substance and thus yielded the ideological concept of Western-Latin Europe.

In order to understand this fairly rapidly proceeding 'Latinization' of Europe, it is necessary to draw attention to sources which are now studied only to a moderate extent, but appear extremely important in the present context. The problem which any government faces is, how to formulate what it wishes to be a binding rule: how to clothe and shape those ideas suitably which animate

---

[1] Ed. cit., I, 3ff.   [2] Ed. cit., I, 12ff.

[3] For penetrating observations see D. Whitelock, in *EHD* (1955) I, 327ff and for examples 357ff. Further, M. Wallace-Hadrill, *Early Germanic kingship in England and the Continent* (1971) 21ff; and H. R. Loyn, *Anglo-Saxon England and the Norman Conquest* (1962); further Hanna Vollrath-Reichelt, *Königsgedanke und Königtum bei den Angelsachsen bis zur Mitte des 9. Jahrhunderts* (1971) (esp. important for the changing character of kingship in 786–7 (at 33ff, 68ff)).

a given society or which the government desires to be instilled into the social and public body. This consideration should be kept in mind when one considers one of the most effective means of exercising government, that is, by the charter, a formal document by which the king conferred rights and duties on individuals, groups of persons, institutions, and so on. From the point of view of law, uniformity of charters was understandably always held to be a requirement, because in this was seen a guarantee for the validity and authenticity of the document itself, which thereby displayed greatly stabilizing effects on society. The problem was, how to express the king's will in a formal manner and one which would fit a great variety of contingencies. As law-creative instruments the charters were in all likelihood of more direct concern to the recipient than any general laws. And for the government the charter was an excellent means to make the royal will concrete and manifest. As a vehicle by which government was exercised within a firmly fixed framework, the charter as a source of governmental conceptions can hardly be overestimated. In the charter (mainly in the Arenga) the king was able to proclaim basic 'political' ideas for which, certainly in the early Middle Ages, no other outlet was available.[1]

The charter is therefore a very valuable source for recognizing governmental conceptions because in an unobtrusive manner it relates explicitly and implicitly to the status and function of the Ruler. Hence in the conferment of rights and duties the Ruler had ample opportunity to display governing authority. The charters were of considerable assistance to early medieval Rulers

[1] For the early medieval, mainly Frankish royal charters see esp. P. Classen, 'Kaiserreskript & Königsurkunde; Studien zum römisch-germanischen Kontinuitätsproblem' in *AD* 1 (1956) 1ff; 2 (1956) 1ff; here also a useful systematic survey of royal governmental acts (28ff). See further K. A. Debus, 'Studien zu merovingischen Urkunden und Briefen' ibid., 13 (1967) 1ff; 14 (1968) 1ff, ed. of documents 114ff. For the theme of royal grace see esp. F. L. Ganshof, 'La gratia des monarques francs' in *Anuario de estudios medievales* 3 (1966) 9ff; here also a most useful conspectus of the use of the term in the Theodosian Code (25f). For fine diplomatic observations on the Lombard charters see now C. R. Brühl, 'Chronologie und Urkunden der Herzöge von Spoleto' in *QFIAB* 51 (1971) 1ff, with copious examples.

in their attempts to apply the descending theme of government, and in this respect they formed a vital bridge from the Germanic ascending theme of government to its descending successor with its pronounced theocratic ingredients. Apart from the eighth-century Anglo-Saxon codes, the theocratic function of the Ruler had not much opportunity to come to the fore, but in the charters the theme of royal grace was familiar: it was the 'king by the grace of God' who 'graciously' conferred rights and duties, who 'conceded' rights to his subjects, and who threatened the withdrawal of his good will and grace. The Anglo-Saxon charters[1] and to a lesser extent contemporary Frankish charters[2] shows the essential elements of a quite well-developed descending theme of government and law.

The more the government became aware of the potential value of its charters, the greater care it lavished on them. The need for a properly equipped chancery personnel became therefore obvious. It consisted exclusively of clerics, and this composition makes understandable why theocratic Rulership made its effortless entry into a still basically Germanic system. In order to achieve uniformity of the charters and the necessary expertise of the personnel so-called Formulary Books came to be devised. They are important sources because they served as handbooks or guides or instructional books which reveal the formalized structure of a number of basic governmental ideas. These Formulary Books gave numerous instances of various kinds of charters which might concern all conceivable sorts and conditions of men in contemporary society. They are first-class mirrors of socially relevant matters. And since, precisely as a result of the law codes as well as of the charters, society became more and better organized, supplementations and additions to the Formulary Books proved neces-

[1] Ed. J. M. Kemble, *Codex diplomaticus aevi saconici* (1839–48); W. de G. Birch, *Cartularium saxonicum* (1885–93) (to 975); above all, P. Sawyer, *Anglo-Saxon Charters; an annotated guide and bibliography* (1968). For a rich selection of charters and good ET see D. Whitelock in *EHD* cit., 440ff.

[2] Ed. *MGH. Diplomata regum Francorum*, where the employment of the *Munt* by King Childeberth I in 528 can be witnessed: V.2. They as well as the Anglo-Saxon charters reflect the concession principle very well. See also C.R. Brühl, *Studien zu den langobardischen Königsurkunden* (1970).

sary. The most influential, comprehensive and elaborate Formulary Books came from the Frankish realms, the oldest being the so-called Formulae of Angers of late sixth-century origin.[1] The papal *Liber Diurnus* was for the papal chancery what the Formulary Books were for the royal chanceries.[2]

Here only two royal Formulary Books can be made the subject of a few remarks. The one is the very comprehensive Formulary Book of Marculf which contains 91 individual formulae.[3] Although the author names himself in the preface and dedicates his work to a Bishop Landeric, there is no certainty about the person or the author nor about the exact date of the composition. It was written in the latter half of the seventh century.[4] From the ideological standpoint the Marculf Formulae present themselves as respectably advanced applications of the descending theme of government and law, and by virtue of their comprehensiveness and ease of use they greatly contributed to the consolidation of the theocratic theme in Frankish lands. The instances cited above were in fact taken from these Formulae.[5] They can be called the fountainhead of Frankish chancery practices and therefore also of the descending theme of government. Because of their great usefulness they were augmented and supplemented in the eighth and ninth centuries, especially by Charlemagne himself.[6]

The other influential Formulary Book was that of Sens—the *Formulae Senonenses*[7]—which consists of an original part composed about 768–75 and additions made by Louis I. They as well as the

[1] Ed. in *MGH. Formulae*, 4ff.

[2] Ed. Th. Sickel, *Liber Diurnus* (1889). This is not the place to enter into a discussion concerning the thesis put forward by L. Santifaller, cf. *PG* 329 n. 2.

[3] Ed. cit., 36ff.

[4] See F. Beyerle, 'Das Formelbuch des westfränkischen Mönchs Markulf und Dagoberts Urkunde für Rebais in 635' in *DA* 9 (1952) 43ff. See further G. Tessier, *Diplomatique royale française* (1962) 7ff (excellent introduction to Merovingian and (39ff) Carolingian chanceries). Good survey in K. Kroeschell, *Deutsche Rechtsgesch.* I (1972) 56ff.

[5] See also *PGP* 119f. For a combination of diplomatic with interpretation see I. Heidrich, 'Titulatur und Urkunden der arnulfingischen Hausmeier' in *AD* 12 (1966) 71ff; see esp. 176ff for Marculf as a model. For the date see 180ff.

[6] See ed. cit. at 107, 113. [7] Ed. cit., 185ff.

Formulae imperiales, also from the same emperor's reign, containing 55 new formulae,[1] show what refinements and adjustments and classifications the Frankish chancery had managed to introduce into the charters. As sources they assume additional weight because they reveal the structural advance which the application of the descending theme of government had made in the shape of theocratic rulership. The opulent ideological material incorporated in these Formulary Books still awaits critical and historical analysis. They are among the most reliable witnesses of contemporary governmental practices and principles. Their mature, precise and succinct expressions and phraseology reveal a very great deal of governmental ideology.[2]

This kind of instructional book, in which collections of letters were also included,[3] was in fact produced throughout the medieval period. There is, to choose a few outstanding examples, the famous collection of Letters in the *Codex Udalrici* of the early twelfth century[4] which was quite strictly followed in Barbarossa's chancery, or the contemporary formulary book for notaries,[5] and in the late thirteenth century there was the instructional treatise by the Swiss Conrad of Mure (1275: *Summa de arte prosandi*), and as late as the mid-fourteenth century there was the Formulary Book for official prose composition (the so-called Baumgartner *Formularius de modo prosandi*).[6] The difference

[1] Ed. cit., 288ff.

[2] For instances of ideological reconstruction see, further, *PGP* 60 n. 2, 126 n. 2, and *IS* 17f. For the importance of the formulae as sources see W. Ullmann, in *Annali della Fondazione Italiana per la storia amministrativa* 1 (1964) 117ff.

[3] See C. Erdmann in *WH* I (1948) 415ff.

[4] Ph. Jaffé, *Bibliotheca Rerum Germanicarum* V (1869) 38ff. For details see C. Erdmann, loc. cit., 439ff.

[5] J. B. Palmieri, *Il formularium tabellionum di Irnerio* (1893).

[6] L. Rockinger, *Briefsteller und Formelbücher* (1863). For literature see F. Hausmann, 'Formularbehelfe der frühen Stauferkanzlei' in MIOG 58 (1950). for France, G. Tessier, *Diplomatique* (as 201 n. 4), 125ff and for later, id., 'L'activité de la chancellerie royale française au temps de Charles V' in *Moyen Age* 48 (1938) 14ff, 81ff; for further details of an unexpected kind see P. Cockshaw, 'Un rapport sur la chancellerie royale française du milieu du XIVe siècle' ibid., n.s. 24 (1969) 503ff. See also below, 211 n. 1.

between the later Books and the Frankish Books refers to their value as sources. The later Books, however important, did not possess the crucial significance which must be assigned to the earlier material, because by then many other forms of media had emerged which served as a platform for the dissemination of governmental ideas.

The charters and the Formulary Books played a vital part in the establishment of a smoothly working central government. Moreover, precisely because the charter was a vehicle of government, it played a most important part in providing historic continuity from late Roman to Frankish times.[1] The attempt, therefore, on the part of the Frankish monarchy, beginning with Charlemagne, to transfer a number of the principles underlying the charters to the generally applicable law is especially noteworthy.[2] The so-called *Capitularia* of the Frankish Rulers were royal enactments.[3] The name itself was derived from the division of certain kinds of royal enactments into *capitula*. In essence the Capitularies were royal laws, and as such they clearly exhibited the strengthening of royal power in the concrete law-creative process. The will of the king was the essential ingredient; they documented the *ius dicendi*, the power to lay down the law in a very conspicuous form. As regards the topics dealt with by the Capitularies, they ranged far and wide, but in their substance they constituted one of the most important vehicles by which the social programme of the Carolingian Renaissance was put into practice.[4] Although the division into mundane and ecclesiastical

---

[1] See P. Classen (as 199 n. 1).

[2] That the development was from the charter (notably the 'Privilege') to enacted law, has been convincingly shown by H. Krause, 'Königtum und Rechtsordnung in der Zeit der sächsischen und salischen Herrscher' in *SavZGA* 82 (1965) 1ff; see also id., 'Recht und Vergänglichkeit im ma. Recht' ibid. *GA* 75 (1958) 206ff; see further R. Sprandel, 'Ueber das Problem neuen Rechts im früheren MA', ibid. *KA* 48 (1962) 117ff.

[3] For Roman law and the Capitularies see F. L. Ganshof, 'Droit romain dans les capitulaires' in *IRMAE* I 2b cc α–β (1969). In general for the development of monarchic conceptions in Western Europe see E. Ewig, 'La monocratie dans l'Europe occidentale Ve–Xe siècles' in *Recueils Jean Bodin* 21 (1969) 57ff.

[4] Ed. *MGH. Capitularia* I–II. For some details see *CR* 30ff.

Capitularies is often made, it really is of little concern for the time, because no generally binding rule of action of whatever scope or subject could be issued by anyone but the king.

Of far greater significance from the governmental point of view was another division. Originally most of the laws incorporated in the various Germanic Folk-laws rested on the consent of the people or at least of the nobility (the *optimates*). That these laws were as often as not in need of adjustment to changing conditions goes without saying. Although the king had emerged as the fountain or source of the law, for large segments of public government he still could not unilaterally change the folk-law. In order to effect a change it was necessary to obtain the consent of the people or nobility, and these Capitularies were called *Capitularia legibus addenda*.[1] In principle they were modified folk-laws, though issued by the king's authority. The highly interesting point in the development of the king's law-creative power is that these Capitularies in course of time came to be replaced by the so-called *Capitularia per se scribenda*, that is, pure royal law, the material element of which was mainly the king's will. Perhaps nothing was more significant for the growth of royal power within the legal orbit than the view which was strictly upheld that no king could bind his successor—a demonstrable proof of the advance which the idea of personal sovereignty had made.

The increase of the Capitularies, already noticeable in Charlemagne's reign, had also another significance. Since they served as the instrument of the Carolingian Renaissance, and since its programme was the rebirth of Frankish society as a Christian society, the Capitularies became increasingly weighted towards the ecclesiastically inspired ideology. The result was that the ecclesiastics from Louis I's reign onwards began to have a correspondingly large part in the formulation of the Capitularies. This legislation not only increased in quantity and size and scope, but above all contained detailed guidelines for the actual execution of the Renaissance programme.[2] And from the thirties of the

---

[1] See *PGP* 123ff.   [2] See for details *CR* 24ff, 117ff, 174ff.

ninth century onwards the Capitularies frequently embodied decrees of the numerous councils either verbatim or in shortened form or, still a little later, under Charles the Bald, the doctrinal statements of some outstanding ecclesiastics, such as Hincmar of Rheims. The ecclesiastics emerged as the determinative segment of Frankish society and played a decisive role in legislation. The Capitularies were vital transmitters of the idea of law, of the idea that society rested upon the law incorporating fundamental Christian precepts. It is furthermore relevant to bear in mind that they primarily affected those parts of Europe which were henceforward to play a leading role, that is, the West-Frankish realms, later to emerge as France proper. Moreover, the Capitularies were also indispensable instruments for the unification of Europe as an ideologically identifiable entity. In assessing their value as historical sources one must not lose sight of the incontrovertible fact that Europe had little identity of its own before the ninth century, and that when it assumed its own identity it had a characteristic Latin ecclesiastical complexion relative to government. In the birth of the concept of Latin-Western Europe the law of the Frankish monarchy played a decisive role: it impregnated Europe with the basic elements of Rulership which were to remain structural ingredients.[1]

Despite the obvious absolutist inclination which theocratic Rulership harboured, the historical point deserves to be specially recorded that as soon as the ideological opulence of this kind of Rulership was realized, measures were initiated to curtail the range of governmental activity. And these measures were set forth in the Capitularies issued by the kings themselves, evidently upon ecclesiastical influence. The Capitularies of the ninth century conceived the king as a tutor of his kingdom, which signified a highly important confluence of Germanic and Roman elements: the Germanic *Munt* as supreme protecting authority combined with the Roman *tutela* yielded the all-important tutorial principle of Rulership, according to which the king was set up by divinity in order to govern the kingdom by protecting its interests. The

[1] Ibid., 135ff.

kingdom was viewed as a minor under age who needed a guardian, a protector, a tutor. It is hardly necessary to enlarge upon the nature of this principle which embodied as a necessary adjunct the principle of inalienability, that is, the prohibition against diminishing or reducing the public interests of the kingdom by alienating its rights or possessions. It seems clear that despite the ostensible proclivity of theocratic Rulership to absolutism the tendency was, at least on the level of governmental doctrine, rendered nugatory by the legal formulation of the king as *tutor regni*. This, however, is merely one instance of the role which the Capitularies played in amalgamating Roman and Germanic elements: seen from this angle, they were sound foundations for the European edifice to be built upon them.[1]

There is at least one more feature to which attention should be drawn in the present context, and that is that the idea of the role of law was applied to the Ruler himself—in the Capitularies. They as royal laws made it plain that though he was free to change the human (or what was later called 'positive') law, there was a basic law to which everyone, including the Ruler himself, was subjected. That was the divine law as interpreted by the ecclesiastics. The significance of this statement lay in the jurisprudential and ideological advance which the Capitularies had made in respect of the relations between the Ruler and the law: an advance that is far from being acknowledged by modern scholarship. As sources of the later (and modern) thesis that governments were restricted by the operation of a fundamental or basic law, the Capitularies assume their full historic significance. Yet, these same Capitularies of the ninth century also insisted on the sovereignty of the Ruler in his law-creative capacity; this sovereignty exempted him in his function as king from any human coercion.[2]

[1] For details see J. Gaudemet, 'Survivances romaines dans le droit de la monarchie franque du Ve au Xe siècles' in *RHD* 23 (1955) 160ff. See also G. Riché, 'Enseignment du droit au Gaule du VIe au XIe siècles' in *IRMAE* 5b, bb (1965).

[2] The Capitularies of Charles the Bald are here in the foreground: ed. cit., vol. II. For Italy see H. Keller, 'Zur Struktur der Königsherrschaft im karolingischen und nachkarolingischen Italien' in *QFIAB* 47 (1967) 123ff. For the tutorial principle in the 9th cent. see W. Ullmann, 'Schranken der Königsgewalt' in *HJb* 91 (1971) 1ff.

Another vital theme made its appearance in the Capitularies. It is the theme of the equality of all before the law of the Ruler. While he himself stood outside and above the law, there was no one in his kingdom who was not subjected to the law in equal measure. This was what the relevant Capitulary called a *parilis equalitas* of all before the law. Despite the social stratification into different layers, there was, as far as government was concerned, no difference in regard to the law. This all-important principle was laid down in a Capitulary of Charles the Bald whom Hincmar of Rheims made declare that the supreme vocation of the *regia maiestas* consisted in the equal dispensation of justice and equity: obedience to the law and equality before it now began to be correlative concepts.[1]

There is, however, one more aspect of the Capitularies to which at least a brief reference should be made. They were also transmitters of governmental ideology, not merely by way of expressing an abstract notion in the written word, but also by way of clothing symbolism in written language. That is to say, the skeleton of the later royal coronation orders can be found in the Frankish Capitularies of the ninth century. They contain the earliest prayer texts, the promises of the king, the use of emblems of ancient provenance but with a different meaning attached (e.g. the sceptre, armils, the throne, etc.) and a great deal concerning the anointing—the central feature of every royal inauguration ceremony. In assessing the value of the ritual, such as the coronation orders, as sources, one should bear in mind that allegory and its close relative, symbolism (and liturgy), were highly effective means of expressing abstract ideology by easily comprehensible concrete gestures, actions, symbols, the meaning of which could be grasped by the illiterate peasant as well as by the most learned contemporary. In overwhelmingly illiterate societies symbolism, allegory and the like, have always been necessary instruments for conveying ideas in the most suitable manner. But whereas the abstractly used word may be capable of different interpretations, the symbols used at particularly important public

---

[1] Capitulary of Pitres (862): *Cap* 272 p.t.

functions, such as the anointing and crowning of a king, the consecration of a bishop, etc., were to be chosen in such a way that they could not convey any other meaning but the one intended.

In a word, the use of symbolism as a means of transmitting an abstract idea presupposed the most careful handling and was based on a comprehensive intellectual process. The royal coronation orders as transmitted in the Capitularies[1] are in no wise inferior to the law itself as sources of governmental ideology, and in fact always stood, as regards authority, on a level with a law code. In this sense, the Capitularies constituted the firmest possible endorsement of theocratic Rulership and of the mediatory role assumed by the ecclesiastics in conferring the sacrament of unction on the king. Because they were quite obviously held to be juristic in contents and structure—hence were manifestations of juristic symbolism—they made their earliest appearance in the Capitularies. When they began to proliferate, they were no longer set forth in individual laws, but in books—the Pontificals—especially devoted to this genre of juristic symbolism.[2] Next to the abstract juristic notion symbolism is one of the most reliable sources which enables the historian to reconstruct governmental principles.[3] No

[1] The relevant Capitularies are: nos. 275, 276, 279, 281-3, 292, 296, 297, 300, 301, 302, 304. For the Anglo-Saxon sources see the *Ordines* ed. (and ET) by L. Wickham Legg, *English Coronation Records* (1901), 3ff, and 14ff. For the East-Frankish Orders, see C. Erdmann's ed. in his *Forschungen zur politischen Ideenwelt des Frühmittelalters* (1951) at 83f. For later sources see below, 264. For ed. of texts which show the development and commentary see P. E. Schramm, 'Die Krönung bei den Westfranken und Angelsachsen' in *SavZKA* 23 (1934) 117ff; id., 'Die Krönung in Deutschland bis zum Beginn des Salischen Hauses' ibid., 24 (1935) 184ff; id., 'Ordines Studien II' in *AUF* 15 (1938) 3ff; id., 'Die Krönung in England' ibid. 305ff; also his *Hist. of the English Coronation* (1937); id., *Der König von Frankreich*, new ed. (1960). Further details and sources (Hincmar) *CR* chs. 4 and 5, and the hitherto unpublished Cambridge dissertation by J. L. Nelson.

[2] The most important was the Roman pontifical; for its history see M. Andrieu, below, 263 n. 1. For pontificals in general see *DDC* VII, 28ff.

[3] As an example cf. V. Labhart, *Zur Rechtssymbolik des Bischofsrings* (1962); also I. Herwegen, *Germanische Rechtssymbolik in der römischen Liturgie* (repr. 1962).

other day counted so much in a king's life as the day of his coronation, or rather of his receiving unction: this sacrament[1] made him the Lord's anointed—the *Christus Domini*—a position which nobody else in his kingdom had achieved, and the importance of the day was acknowledged by the practice followed right down to the late thirteenth century of dating the regnal years from it.

When after the break-up of the Carolingian inheritance orderly conditions came to be re-established, it was once more the charter which served as the principal instrument of government. In both the Eastern portion of the inheritance—Germany—and the Western parts—France—the charter emerged as the incontrovertible assertion and acknowledgment of the rule of law by the kings, the Saxons in Germany, the later Carolingians and the Capetians in France.[2] Quantitatively the charter by far surpassed all other law-creative output which in comparison with that of the Frankish period was very small indeed. In regard to governmental principles the charters are a quarry that has not yet attracted sufficient attention.

Very great care was taken in the composition of the charter or the *diploma*. That the charters of the German Rulers in particular became qualitatively outstanding was due to the close connection of the German kings with Italy in the tenth century and the imperial status which from Otto I onwards they attained.[3] The contact of the chancery with the notariate in Italy resulted in the

[1] For unction as a sacrament see *CR* 73ff. It was still considered a sacrament in the thirteenth century.

[2] *Chartes et diplômes relatifs à l'histoire de France*, publ. by the 'Académie des inscriptions et belles-lettres' from 1908 onwards, comprise royal documents from the ninth century to the high M.A.; see esp. G. Tessier, *Diplomatique*, cit., 207ff.

[3] Here the prime sources are the *MGH Diplomata* from Conrad I (911) onwards: ed. of *DD. regum et imperatorum Germaniae* in progress. The preceding *DD. regum Germaniae ex stirpe Karolinorum* beginning with Louis the German are also in progress (1934–). They and their Arengae are overdue for an analysis in depth concerning governmental principles. For the government itself see H. Sproemberg, 'Die Alleinherrschaft im ma. Imperium' in *Recueils Jean Bodin* 21 (1969) 201ff.

refinement and better structuring of the charters (as well as of the Letters). The part which demands special attention is the Arenga. The Arenga was the preamble in which the king or for that matter any Ruler made known on the model of late Roman prototypes certain general or particular principles relative to public government. The Arengae[1] are of more direct concern to the historian of governmental ideas than the so-called dispositive parts of the document which conferred specific rights and duties on the recipient. For in the preambles the Ruler had ample opportunity of setting forth his aims, the means he intended to employ in order to achieve certain ends, the reasons which prompted him to take legislative measures, and the like. From the ideological standpoint the Arengae constituted the crux of the charter and formed a practically untapped source that allows the historian to fathom the reflexions, motivation, intentions, programme and outlook of the Ruler in his capacity as a dispenser of law and justice. Perhaps in no other field can the view be better demonstrated than in the charters that it was the Rulers themselves who propounded particular governmental themes and at the same time applied them in practice. It would however be misleading to think that the Arengae as heuristic instruments were confined to the charter. In fact, the development seems to have been from the charter to other official acts, including royal laws and the imperial constitutions.[2]

A comparison of the Arengae used in the imperial chancery in the tenth and in the twelfth centuries may be profitable, because they reveal a steady development that cannot be paralleled elsewhere. The comparison shows the advance made in linguistic precision, in juristic succinctness, in the thematic exposition of governmental doctrine and, above all, the width and scope of governmental duties. The governmental scheme of the Saxon and the Staufen emperors was most faithfully reflected in the Arengae

---

[1] Cf. the study by H. Fichtenau, *Arenga*, suppl. vol. of *MIOG* 18 (1957), For an analysis of private charters see H. Fichtenau, *Das Urkundenwesen in Oesterreich vom 8. bis zum frühen 13. Jahrh.*, ibid., 23 (1971).

[2] The Arenga had always been part of the papal letters which may indeed have exercised influence in this respect.

no less than in the body of their charters and other law-creative media.[1] Moreover, the official output, rapidly increasing as it did both in quantity and quality, not only contained the laws in the strict formal sense of the term,[2] but also the official acts concerning communications to other Rulers, treatises with other governments or princes, conferments of a special status on particular communities, proclamations and manifestos and encyclicals (especially during the imperial-papal conflicts), appeals for specific undertakings (such as crusades) as well as decrees concerning heretics,[3] their treatment and the procedure to be followed in prosecuting them, counterfeiting of coins, in a word anything that appertained to the (tutorial) function and sovereign status of the emperor came within the purview of the law.[4] Because they all constituted law, their Arengae are particularly valuable: they throw light upon an enormous variety of 'political', social, diplomatic, religious, constitutional contingencies. That these

[1] Throughout the medieval period the *Regesta* of imperial documents must be consulted: J. F. Böhmer's *Regesta imperii* (covering the period down to Maximilian I) by various editors (not yet completed) including the *Regesta* of popes (ed. H. Zimmermann, *Papstregesten 911–1024* (1969)); K. F. Stumpf, *Die Reichskanzler* (to 1197) (repr. 1960). The lit. on the imperial chancery is very large. See H. Bresslau, *Urkundenlehre*, 2nd ed. (repr. 1958); cf., e.g., D. v. Gladiss, *Die Kanzlei und Urkunden Kaiser Heinrichs IV.* (1938); H. Hirsch, 'Reichskanzlei und Reichspolitik im Zeitalter der salischen Kaiser' in his *Aufsätze zur mittelalterlichen Urkundenforschung* (1965); J. Fleckenstein, *Die Hofkapelle der deutschen Könige* (1959); H. M. Schaller, 'Die Kanzlei K. Friedrichs II' in *AD* 3 (1957) 207ff; 4 (1958) 264ff; for a later example see P. Moraw, 'Kanzlei und Kanzleipersonal König Ruprechts' ibid. 15 (1969) 428ff. For the Capetian training of the personnel especially the notaries see G. Tessier, *Diplomatique* cit. 137ff, 152f and 186ff.

[2] See H. Krause, *Kaiserrecht und Rezeption* (1952) 26ff.

[3] Special attention should be drawn to Frederick II's anti-heretical legislation in his coronation edicts which throw significant light on his governmental conceptions: *MGH Const* II, 85, pp. 107ff. For some details see G. de Vergottini, *Studi sulla legislazione imperiale di Federico II in Italia* (1952). Part of this legislation was re-enacted by the papacy (Gregory IX and Boniface VIII).

[4] Ed. *MGH Constitutiones et acta publica* (to 1348); J. F. Böhmer–J. Ficker *Acta imperii selecta* (1870) and for the period from 1198 onwards E. Winkelmann, *Acta imperii inedita* (1880–5). Ph. Jaffé, *Bibl. rerum germanicarum* (1864–73) is still indispensable, also for documentary evidence.

quite astonishingly rich official enactments required a trained professional personnel went without saying, and this personnel was overwhelmingly recruited from the graduates of the Law universities. And when the imperial declarations and laws became the subject of scholarly exegesis, a close relationship between the imperial chancery and the universities developed.

One of the probable reasons for the quantity and quality of the official imperial documents was that they served as a substitute for the rather poorly developed imperial literature: surprisingly enough, there was quite a dearth of literature that advocated the imperial cause during the Staufen period. However much the civilians were by and large adherents of the imperial scheme of things, their scholarly works did not (and were not meant to) reach wider circles. The imperial chancery, therefore, became the centre from which juristic-governmental principles and axioms emanated and were disseminated throughout the length and breadth of the empire. In this way wider sections of the populace were to some extent influenced. Theory and practice of government harmoniously blended and were directed by the same organ, the imperial chancery, and eventually the emperor himself.[1] With some qualifications similar observations can be made about the papal official output, the decretals. They also served as a substitute for the virtually absent polemical literature and for this reason assumed their great importance as sources. The advantage which the papal-hierocratic side had, became very clear in the numerous conflicts with secular powers: the papacy as an institution of government had a more or less efficient supervision of the ecclesiastical body throughout the Western hemisphere which was controlled by the canon law. The imperial side had nothing comparable to the institutional apparatus of the papacy, and hence had to rely almost exclusively on its own official output and law which was restricted to the empire, the enforcement of which was always a weak point of the imperial government.

[1] Cf. C. Erdmann, 'Die Anfänge der staatlichen Propaganda im Investiturstreit' in *HZ* 154 (1936) 491ff; E. Otto, 'Friedrich Barbarossa in seinen Briefen' in *DA* 5 (1942); O. Vehse, *Die amtliche Propaganda in den Staatsschriften Friedrichs II.* (1929).

Nevertheless, the imperial government had very much more opportunity for arguing a governmental case than other governments, such as the English or French, had. For the whole imperial edifice was based on certain ideological premisses of which none was more important than that the emperors were supposed to be the successors of the Roman Caesars. However much this successorship was contrived and artificial and however little it corresponded to reality, it nevertheless ensured that the German emperors governed within the grandiose Roman conception of the rule of law.[1] Consequently, the strife with the papacy could be, as indeed it was, conducted on the level of the law and concerned the scope of jurisdictional authority of the emperor and of the pope. Both institutions had 'inherited' this juristic complex which generated its own juristic ideology relative to government. Hence the importance of imperial and papal documents as sources of governmental principles. The imperial and papal official output assumes still greater importance, however, if due weight is given to their functioning as pieces of public propaganda. Some of the manifestos on both sides were propagandistic devices in the guise of juristic exercises[2] and yet for this very reason were especially valuable, because they embodied governmental programmes for which the existing law supplied only a tenuous basis.[3] Above all, this imperial legislative output from the twelfth to the fourteenth centuries reflects the rapidly accelerating process of secularization, in itself the result of the emperors' embracing of the Roman law as their 'own' law.[4]

[1] Cf. W. Ullmann, 'Über eine kanonistische Vorlage Friedrichs I.' in *SavZKA* 46 (1960) 430ff.

[2] A good instance is *Eger cui levia* (ed. E. Winkelmann (as 211 n. 4), II, 696ff) which has always been taken as an official manifesto. Its authenticity is now disputed, although it is still held to have emanated from Innocent IV's chancery. See P. Herde, 'Ein Pamphlet der päpstlichen Kurie gegen Friedrich II. von 1245–46' in *DA* 23 (1967) 468ff; here also a new and much improved ed. of the text.

[3] Most of the relevant sources are in *MGH Const* II–IV; and in *MGH Epp s. XIII e regestis pontificum romanorum selectae*; further in J. L. A. Huillard-Bréholles, *Hist. diplomatica Friderici II* (1852–61).

[4] See above, 77f, 85.

This consideration may furnish some explanation for the comparative paucity of governmental-doctrinal material in the English[1] and French[2] charters, laws and other official products of the respective chanceries. This is not to say that they were devoid of the relevant material. On the contrary, they presupposed, if they did not anticipate, a great deal of knowledge of governmental principles which are still in need of a much closer analysis than they have so far received, though this analysis is all the more difficult as these official acts contain far less argument and 'exposition' and far fewer general observations or reflexions than did their imperial (or for that matter, papal) counterparts. If they were not omitted altogether, the Arengae were very brief indeed and hardly allow insight into the mental workshop of the kings. The body of the documents is also much shorter than that of the imperial acts. These features were indubitably due to the smaller influence exercised by civilian jurisprudence, explicable in the English orbit by the feudal basis of government and in France by the absence of professional Roman law studies in the very university that was situated in the capital of the French kings.

By its very nature, ecclesiastically inspired as it was, theocratic Rulership stimulated law creative activity, and this mainly as a result of the duty imposed on the Ruler on the occasion of his becoming the 'King by the grace of God'. On this occasion the king swore to preserve peace in the kingdom, to punish evildoers and exterminate evil customs, and to render justice and equity in his verdicts. The breadth of these promises covered a very wide margin of royal law-creative activity, even if this was in the ninth century still largely within the framework of the charter

[1] For the Anglo-Saxon charters see above, 200. For the subsequent period see H. A. Cronne, et al. (eds.), *Regesta regum anglo-normannorum 1066–1154* (1913–1969); see also L. Delisle, *Recueil des actes de Henri II roi d'Angleterre concernant les provinces françaises* (1909). From 1216 there are the Calendars of the various kinds of rolls. Details in G. R. Elton, *England 1200–1640* (1969) 33ff. Cf. also *EHD* II, 39ff.

[2] Cf. *Chartes et diplômes* cit. (209 n. 2). The *Recueil des historiens des Gaules et de la France* (1896–1904) contains numerous relevant charters. Cf. also J. Flach, 'Le droit romain dans les chartes du IXe au XIe siècles en France' in *Mélanges Fitting* (1907) I, 390ff.

in the form of dispensation or privilege or by amending customary law. New royal law concerned itself mainly with the preservation of the public peace. Into the same category belonged the laws enforcing the Truce of God. This kind of legislation classically manifested the tutorial function of the king who in the exercise of this function stigmatized actions as criminal, because harmful to the interests of the kingdom, and thus greatly contributed to the growth of public criminal law. After all, the preservation of public peace was one of the foremost duties incumbent upon the king as the *tutor regni*. It was precisely in this context that the Roman principle of the *utilitas publica* came to assume its full significance: the custodian of the public interest and well-being was the king as the tutor of the kingdom.[1]

Unobtrusively and without much publicity, but with all the more enduring effect went a development which though chronologically parallel to the ascendancy of theocratic kingship, had nevertheless nothing to do with it. Feudalism had in the beginning emerged as an arrangement entirely on a private basis between lord and vassal. During the Frankish period this arrangement infiltrated into the sphere of public law and eventually became one of the pillars of public government throughout Western Europe. The common feature of all forms of the feudal arrangement was its consensual character, that is, the contract that bound lord and vassal together. As Sir Henry Maine said many years ago, 'feudal society was governed by the law of contract'. Every contract is a mutual affair: it contains rights and duties relating to each partner of the contract. In his capacity as feudal lord the king necessarily entered into contractual relations with his subjects, notably the tenants-in-chief.[2] Evidently, this affected the king as a law-creative organ, for by the working of the feudal contract

[1] The link between the tutorial function of the Ruler and the growth of criminal legislation (incl. procedure) and public law should long have been the subject of detailed analyses.

[2] Cf. J. Devisse, 'Essai sur l'histoire d'une expression qui fait fortune: Consilium et auxilium au IXe siècle' in *Moyen Age* 23 (1968) 179ff. For the essence of feudalism and its law see G. Astuti, 'Feudo' in *ED* XVII (1968) 292ff (with rich bibl).

severe limitations were placed upon the king's monarchic powers. For practical purposes the customs which had grown up within the feudal sphere were, after the tutorial function of the king, perhaps the most severe check on the exercise of any kind of unbridled royal absolutism.[1]

Once feudal kingship became operative, the unilateral royal creation of law became severely limited. Within the sphere of public law the feudal contract when once fully operational, contained many ingredients of the ascending theme of government and law precisely because the juristic element of consent predominated. In order to appreciate the resilience and strength of feudal practices, one ought to realize that they had grown slowly but naturally and had been woven into the texture of public law without any grand speculative argumentation. Effective feudal arrangements always presupposed team work based on mutual consent and trust. What needs stressing is that feudal arrangements were originally within the sphere of private law, but were in course of time transferred to the realm of public law. By the eleventh century this transfer had been completed in the Western parts of Europe. By that time there had developed what one may well call a system of feudal law which was, however, in form, substance and structure customary law. Royal or imperial legislation endorsed and supplemented it, as classically instanced by the measure of the Emperor Conrad II of 1037.[2] No satisfactory systematic explanation or interpretation of feudal law was possible until it was made available in a form capable of being handled in a scholarly manner. Civilian jurisprudence at Bologna encouraged the reduction of all feudal customary law to writing

---

[1] In this context the influence of the ancient concept of equity especially on the English legal system should be borne in mind. Cf., e.g. E. Wohlhaupter, 'Der Einfluss naturrechtlicher und kanonistischer Gedanken auf die Entwicklung der englischen equity' in *ACII* (1935) II, 437ff, esp. 445ff; H. Coing, 'English equity and the denunciatio evangelica of canon law' in *LQR* 71 (1955) 223ff; see also E. M. Meijers, 'Le conflit entre l'équité et la loi chez les premiers glossateurs' in *Études* IV (1966) 142ff. For the general background see P. G. Caron, *Aequitas romana, misericordia patristica ed epiekeia aristotelica nella dottrina dell'aequitas canonica* (1968); also P. Fedele in *Études Le Bras* 73ff.

[2] Ed. in *MGH. Const* I, 45, p. 90 (for Italy).

as well as the compilation of the enacted feudal laws. The Milanese
Consul Obertus de Orto finished his compilation at Bologna in
the fifties of the twelfth century. The work entitled *Consuetudines
Feudorum* (shortly afterwards called *Libri Feudorum*)[1] though once
more a purely private effort, nevertheless remained the basis of
all subsequent feudal expositions. It underwent augmentation and
supplementation, and was also the subject of lectures and commentaries in the universities.[2] The final version was reached in
about 1220 and styled the Vulgate: it was added as the tenth
Collation to Justinian's nine Collations of his Novels by the
famous civilian Hugolinus (d. 1235). Some of the most outstanding commentators were the just-mentioned Hugolinus whose
Summa is not printed, Andreas de Isernia (d. 1350)[3] and Baldus
de Ubaldis.[4] What is hardly ever noticed—and it is especially
important in the context of government—is that the scientific
investigation of the feudal law made contemporaries aware of
the intrinsic differences between the feudal concept of law and the
traditional Roman-inspired concept, differences which in the final
resort went back to the different meanings attributed to justice.[5]

[1] Ed. as an appendix to most of the old editions of the *Corpus Iuris Civilis*.
See K. Lehmann, *Das langobardische Lehensrecht* (1896).

[2] Jacobus de Ardizone's *Summa sive Epitome iuris feudorum* (ed. Cologne
1562) led to a second recension of the *Libri Feudorum* (so-called *Ardizionata*)
and this gave rise to the Accursiana (Vulgate) recension (which is the one usually
printed in the old editions of the *CIC*). About these stages see K. Lehmann,
op. cit. 44ff, 58ff (*Ardizionata*) and 83ff (modern ed. based on many MSS).
For the part played by Accursius in the gloss on the *Libri* see U. Gualazzini,
'I Libri Feudorum e il contributo di Accursio alle lore sistemazione e alla
Glossa' in *AA* 577ff. For early glossators, esp. Johannes Bassianus, see E. M.
Meijers, 'Les glossateurs et le droit féodal' in *Études* III (1959) 261ff.

[3] Andreas de Isernia, *Super usibus feudorum* (ed. Venice 1514). Jacobus de
Ravanis also wrote on feudal law, see R. Feenstra, 'Quaestiones de materia
feudorum de Jacques de Revigny' in *Studi Senesi* 21 (1972) 379ff, ed. 391ff.

[4] Baldus, *Commentaria ad libros feudorum* (ed. Lyons 1585).

[5] Cf. here the fine semantic analyses by K. Kroeschell, 'Recht und Rechts
begriff im 12. Jahrh.' in *Vorträge und Forschungen*, XII (1968) 309ff, esp. 316,
318ff; now id. 'Rechtsfindung: die ma. Grundlagen einer modernen Vorstellung' in *Festschrift H. Heimpel* III (1972) 498ff which is a most important study
concerning the nature of the law in the MA. Cf. in this context also R. van
Caenegem, *The Birth of the English Common Law* (1973), esp. 85ff.

Every medieval king was a theocratic as well as feudal Ruler. Yet the two functions were irreconcilable. Whether the one or the other prevailed depended not on theory, but on the actual situation and factual circumstances of the time. For reasons irrelevant in this context, the theocratic component part of Rulership prevailed in France under Philip II Augustus.[1] In England[2] his contemporary John governed in so clumsy and ham-fisted a manner that in order to avoid a collapse of public order and peace the baronage was left with only one course, namely to turn the potentiality of the feudal component part of his Rulership into a governmental reality. There was a thoroughly feudal instrument at hand: the threat of repudiating the feudal contract (*diffidatio*) which signified the withdrawal of trust from the king.[3] John's wings as a theocratic Ruler were severely clipped, and clipped they were also in the resulting document, the Great Charter of June 1215, which in form was theocratic-royal, in substance thoroughly feudal.[4] Within an entirely feudal framework the Charter gave

[1] For the development in France see P. Pétot, 'La royauté française au M.A.' in *Recueils Jean Bodin* 21 (1969) 389ff; also F. Lot et R. Fawtier *Hist. des institutions françaises au Moyen Age*, esp. I (1958) and II (1959).

[2] For an instructive survey see R. Foreville, 'Le régime monocratique en Angleterre au Moyen Age des origines anglo-saxonnes à la mort d'Edouard I' in *Recueils Jean Bodin* 21 (1969) 119ff. The continued threat to make the universality of the Roman emperor a reality acted as an accelerating stimulus to erect the feudal law as a bulwark against imperial encroachments. For the threat see the indiscrete speech by Siegfried of Mainz, above, 104 n. 1. There was a fairly strong Roman law influence in the Dialogue of the Exchequer (cf. Ch. Johnson's observations in the ed. of the *Dialogus de Scaccario* (Nelson Medieval Classics 1950), pp. XIff) and also in Glanvill's book, see *P & M* I, 162ff. Further R. van Caenegem, *Royal Writs . . . to Glanvill* (Selden Soc. 77 1959), esp. 379.

[3] It was the renuntiation of *fides* owed to the lord. About the double meaning of *fides* (i.e. faith and faithfulness (loyalty)) cf. H. Helbig, 'Fideles Dei et regis' in *AKG* 33 (1951) 175ff.

[4] Numerous eds. ET by J. C. Dickinson in Hist. Association pamphlets (1953). For details cf. J. C. Holt, *Magna Carta* (1965) (here also ET); *PGP* 159ff; *IS* 70ff. H. Mitteis, *Der Staat des hohen Mittelalters* (1944) 367; W. Ullmann, 'On the influence of Geoffrey of Monmouth in English history' in *Speculum Historiale* (=*Festschrift J. Spörl*) (1966) 257ff, at 264ff; for valuable insights into the 'common counsel of the realm' (arts 12, 14) see G. Langmuir, 'Per commune consilium regni' in *St. Grat.* XV (1972) 467ff.

the clearest possible expression to the idea of the rule of law and at the same time also showed that there were certain basic interests which every freeman enjoyed as of right without any specific concession or grant by the king; the interests specifically mentioned and protected by the (feudal) law were (art. 39) life, property and freedom. No other system of law could have yielded this result, achieved as it was with the virtual absence of all speculation and argumentation. Feudal law was always a law born out of practical exigencies—and the result was similarly practical. Its ideological significance can hardly be exaggerated. It is nevertheless of some moment to bear in mind that the basic text of the relevant clause of the Great Charter went back to the feudal law of Conrad II with which the draftsman of the clause was indubitably familiar.[1] In this context the early thirteenth-century so-called *Leges Anglorum* assume great importance as a source because their author pointed to the need for a 'common' law and drastic legal-constitutional changes.[2]

Feudal law was the source of the English common law which originally was the law common to the king and the baronage (his tenants-in-chief) and therefore, by construction, of the country as a whole. It became the third great European system of law (next to Roman and Canon law). The Great Charter was the formal source, while its material ingredient was the contractual relation between the king as feudal lord and the barons as vassals. The truism that law is a great educator and a formative organ of society, finds its confirmation in the application of common law in the thirteenth and fourteenth centuries. It potently assisted not only the constitutional development of England, but also, and perhaps more so, helped to shape society in a manner which no descending theme of government and law could have done, because it was a law that had grown on native soil and was the legal response to social needs. The release of the individual from the status of a subject and his assumption of the status of a citizen were greatly stimulated, if indeed not made possible, by the

[1] For this see above, 216.
[2] Ed. in F. Liebermann, *Gesetze der Angelsachsen* cit. I, 635f; some details in *Speculum Historiale* cit., 260ff.

common law which, precisely because it incorporated the element of consent, presupposed and demanded the exercise of the individual's own judgment and evaluation of a situation.[1] The lectures and commentaries of the jurists in the universities clearly reflected the penetration by the scholars into the matrix of feudal law: they are a hitherto almost unacknowledged source.[2]

Common law gave rise to a special kind of native literature, especially when it began to spread its wings: its systematization and analysis became necessary in the interests of a controlled legal development. Himself a practitioner of renown, Henry Bracton wrote a lengthy book (*De legibus et consuetudinibus Angliae*) which was the first attempt at clarification and classification of this new body of law. It was 'the crown and flower of English medieval jurisprudence' (Maitland). It had quite evidently far-reaching implications in regard to governmental principles, and quite specifically the creation of law, the relationship of the king to the law, the role which the community of the realm played in the law-creative process, and similar topics. From the technical and also partly from the substantive point of view Roman law had a greater influence on the work than was at one time held by Maitland:[3] 'the uninstructed Romanist disappears'. Bracton's statements that the king could not change the law unilaterally (nor for that matter the baronage), or that the king was under the law, had not only profound jurisprudential significance, but also ideological and governmental import: they amounted in their totality to the reiterated expression of the rule of law. That the descending theme of government thereby suffered severe inroads went without saying.[4]

[1] For details cf. *IS* 75ff.

[2] Cf., e.g., the mature works on feudal law by Andreas de Isernia or Baldus (above, 217 nn. 3, 4).

[3] See F. W. Maitland, *Select passages from the works of Bracton and Azo* (Selden Soc., 8 (1895)); and now S. E. Thorne, *Bracton on the laws and customs of England* (ET 1968) I, pp. XXXIIff: almost 500 different sections of the Digest and Code are quoted, though the transmitted work was never seen by Bracton himself; but cf. already Savigny IV, 584ff.

[4] Ed. G. E. Woodbine, *De legibus et consuetudinibus Angliae*, 4 vols. (1915–42). ET by S. E. Thorne, cit. (1968– in progress). For some details cf. B. Tierney, 'Bracton on government' in *Speculum* 38 (1963) 295ff; also *PGP* 176ff.

Bracton's example was followed by lesser lights. While he himself used Latin, the custom grew to set forth the principles of the English common law in French, the language used by the professional lawyers. One such example was the work called *Britton* which purported to be a code of law issued by royal authority. Most probably it was made in the middle of Edward I's reign (in the 1290s). It always enjoyed great popularity, though its principles of government were often implied rather than explicit. Its study from the purely governmental standpoint would be rewarding, notably the Prologue and early chapters which deal with the authority of the king and royal officers. Governmental doctrine is here set forth in the guise of a royal constitution (which it certainly was not) and differed markedly from Bracton's exposition of related themes.[1] Very little information concerning governmental principles can be gathered from the later thirteenth-century *Mirror of Justices*[2] which is a rather inept and curious source of contemporary English law and has been called 'the most fantastic work in our legal literature' (Plucknett). It did not apparently circulate in the Middle Ages, but was revived by the antiquarians of the early seventeenth century. The contemporary (Latin) compendium called *Fleta* was Bracton brought up to date, though governmental problems did not greatly excite the author.[3]

An aim similar to that of *Britton* could be witnessed in both France and Germany. There were the *Etablissements de s. Louis*[4] which is also a code of law though certainly not made by royal authority. There was also, on a different plane, the work by Philippe Beaumanoir on the *Coutumes de Beauvaisis*.[5] For the actual application of law there was the singularly important

[1] Ed. F. M. Nichols, *Britton*, 2 vols. (1855), with a welcome ET of the lawyers' French.

[2] Ed. F. W. Maitland, *The Mirror of Justices* (Selden Soc., 7 (1895)).

[3] Ed. H. G. Richardson and G. Sayles in Selden Soc. 72 (1955) which is vol. II (I has still to appear).

[4] Ed. P. Viollet, *Établissements de s. Louis*, 4 vols. (1885–6). Vol. I contains an excellent introduction.

[5] Ed. A. Salmon, *Coutumes de Beauvaisis*, 2 vols. (1899–1900). Beaumanoir was also a poet of standing.

collection of *Les Olim* which contained the 'inquests' and decisions of the parlement of Paris, and consists of four large parts belonging to the thirteenth and fourteenth centuries, begun by a member of the royal curia, Jean de Montluçon. They together with Beaumanoir offer an excellent basis for the reconstruction of certain governmental ideas and France's constitutional development.[1] Of probably more theoretical value was the work by Philippe de Rémy (the father of Philippe Beaumanoir) known as *Livre de Jostice et de Plet* written in the fifties of the thirteenth century: it was a very subtle combination of Roman law (195 titles), of canon law (31 titles) and 96 titles dealing with the customs of Orléans.[2]

In Germany there was the *Mirror of the Saxons* by Eike of Repgow who finished the final version in the early thirties of the thirteenth century. Its original was written in Latin which the author himself translated into the vernacular. The *Mirror* was therefore the first legal work transmitted in the vernacular language. It codified the customary law—the work was private and the author made it clear that his intention was to record the law which he knew from first-hand experience and practice—and contained many governmental principles which in this case are particularly important as they throw light on the papal-imperial relations, just then at a difficult stage; the work is also revealing for the contemporary concept of freedom.[3] In so far as the work reflected practice, it was the German counterpart of Bracton, though it was not so much a scholarly exposition of the law as its 'mirror': the author clothed legal customs and practices in the polished language of the law. It was made the subject of many glosses and

---

[1] Ed. Count Beugnot, *Les Olim ou régistres des arrêts rendues par la court du roi* (1839–48).

[2] Ed. G. Rapetti, *Le livre de jostice et de plet* (1850); for details see E. M. Meijers, *Études* III (1959) 56ff (also on the *Établissements*; also *PGP* 198ff). Cf. further R. Feenstra, 'Jean de Blanot et la formule "Rex Franciae in regno suo princeps"' in *Études Le Bras* 885ff; also M. Boulet Sautel, 'Le "princeps" de Guillaume Durand' ibid. 803ff. Cf. also F. L. Cheyette, 'The sovereign and the pirates' in *Speculum* 45 (1970) 41ff.

[3] Cf. F. Merzbacher, 'Die Bedeutung von Freiheit und Unfreiheit' in *HJb* 90 (1970) 257ff.

commentaries down to the fourteenth century.[1] In importance the other thirteenth-century work, the *Mirror of the Germans*[2] and related to it the *Mirror of the Swabians*,[3] cannot compete with the work of Eike. Nevertheless, they command respect as sources in the present context, because they reflect in a somewhat inarticulate manner what less well trained jurists (or even laymen) considered to be basic to the government of society. All these sources were written in the vernacular which was a noticeable feature in most European countries in the second half of the thirteenth century and of great symptomatic significance. The days of the descending theme of government and law began to grow visibly shorter. Clearly, the view had become dominant that since law was a living social phenomenon it could only be adequately expressed in a living language. This development signified the dawn of the modern era.[4]

[1] Ed. Cl. v. Schwerin (1937) and with a new introduction ed. by H. Thieme (1956). Johann von Buch glossed the book in the 14th century. The work was translated into a number of European languages.

[2] Ed. K. A. Eckhardt in *MGH. Fontes iuris germanici antiqui* (1933).

[3] Ed. ibid. (1964).

[4] The use of medieval (legal) French in England down to the 16th century was no exception, because 'it was the ordinary dialect of the court and of the governing class of the community,' F. M. Nichols ed. cit. (as 221 n. 1), p. XLV.

CHAPTER 7

Governmental Doctrines in
Literary Sources

A large, though extremely variegated fund of source material relative to governmental doctrines and the law is to be found in the vast number of writings which partake of a number of different branches of learning, if present-day categories were to be employed. One of the common features of this huge output from the fifth century onwards was the christocentric theme. Christocentric cosmology, all-embracing as it was and affecting every segment of public life, accounted for the exposition of many governmental themes which a later age would have assigned to 'political theory' proper, but which by virtue of the very nature of the Christian theme itself were as yet quite undifferentiated and dealt with in theological tracts, in epistolary communications, in devotional sermons, in dogmatic treatises, in encyclopaedic dictionaries, in liturgical arrangements and in instructional monographs—in short, any conceivable literary genre served as a platform from which to propagate the one or the other governmental item. The very nature of this variegated source material makes it imperative to limit the topic to typical examples in chronological sequence, if the subject is to be kept within manageable terms.

Since society was to be shaped by Christian ideas capable of being moulded into the law, the concept of justice evidently stood in the foreground either explicitly or implicitly. A whole cluster of ancillary ideas surrounded this concept especially when its biblical substance was merged with its Roman counterpart. In one way or another the relevant literature concerned itself with an analysis of justice within the Christian framework. This was the core of all the varied intellectual efforts which tried to apply Christian principles to public government. Nevertheless the number of writers and the public to which they addressed themselves was quite small, since both the composition and consumption of the writings presupposed a certain educational attainment. Part of the explanation why despite the smallness in numbers some

writers exercised great and enduring influence lay in their participation in government, either in a ruling capacity or in their
function near the centre of government. Another point worth mentioning in this context is that before the late eleventh century the
necessary educational standards were confined to clerics. The
literature relative to governmental themes is therefore strongly
flavoured by the ecclesiastical-religious complexion.

It was assuredly a unique feature that the Ruler himself became
a scholarly expositor of the very themes which formed the backbone of his law and government. Theory and practice were thus
indissolubly linked. And this was particularly clearly demonstrated by the papacy which from the late fourth century onwards had begun to monopolize the Matthean passage (Mat. 16,
18f) for its monarchic theme. It was during the all-important
pontificate of Damasus that not only the conciliar decision was
taken in 381 according to which the papacy was founded by two
apostles,[1] but also at least one literary source emerged which
played a great role in the development of the monarchic function
of the papacy. This was the so-called *Ambrosiaster*, the author of
which may have been the Jew Isaac.[2] The work was a commentary on the Pauline epistles (except Hebrews) and in a severely
scholarly manner without any recourse to allegory endorsed the
double primacy of Peter and Paul and thus the synodal decision.
And only a few years later the spurious letter which Clement I
was supposed to have written to St James in Jerusalem was
translated from Greek into Latin: in a vividly concrete manner
the source described how St Peter, feeling the proximity of his
death, had handed over in front of the assembled Christian community in Rome all the powers which Christ had given him
personally: this was the institution of an heir in a thoroughly
legal manner, and the whole transaction was presented as a purely

[1] For details of this Roman synod and its background see *PG* 4ff and *SHP*
10ff.

[2] Ed. in *PL* 17, 45ff; new ed. in *CSEL* 81 (3 parts 1961–9). Details in H.
Vogels, *Das Corpus Paulinum des Ambrosiaster* (1957); O. Heggelbacher, *Vom
römischen zum christlichen Recht: Juristische Elemente in den Schriften des sog.
Ambrosiaster* (1959) and L. Voelkl in *RQ* 60 (1965) 120ff.

legal transmission of powers from one person to another. As a source of governmental ideas within the ecclesiastical-papal orbit this letter commands the same attention as the original Matthean passage.[1]

Indeed, a good example of the close connection of theory and practice in the Ruler himself was Leo I in the mid-fifth century. Apart from his official decretal output he merits attention in the present context because of the numerous sermons which he preached and which are preserved.[2] They were not merely exemplary from a linguistic standpoint, but especially because of their rich ideological contents: in them the primatial-monarchic position of the pope was one of the chief topics. In working out the function of the pope Leo displayed a mastery of Roman law as well as of biblical exegesis which was second to none. And this governmental edifice was to remain the basic structure of the papal government or of government in a Christian setting. But the sermons also gave ample opportunity of setting forth a great many subordinate themes, notably the crucial distinction between the (objective) office and the (subjective) person of the office-holder.[3] Another example of the same kind towards the end of the same fifth century was Gelasius I, whose influence was no less than that of his great predecessor. He propounded basic governmental themes in specially written Tracts[4] and thereby completed what Leo had begun. He too was an expert in both Roman law and biblical exegesis.[5] The Gelasian argumentation relative to the papal government had added significance as it was set forth in the middle of the first serious schism between East and West, that is, between the Roman *Church* and the Roman *empire*, between the

---

[1] Ed. in B. Rehm, *Die Pseudo-Klementinen* (1953), 3ff; on this see W. Ullmann, 'The significance of the Ep. Clementis in the Pseudo-Clementines' in *JTS* 11 (1960) 295ff.

[2] Ed. in *PL* 54, 593ff (Ballerini); modern ed. by E. Schwartz, *Acta Conciliorum Oecumenicorum* II, 4 (1932).

[3] Some details in 'Leo I and the theme of papal primacy' in *JTS* 11 (1960) 25ff.

[4] Ed. in A. Thiel, *Epistolae romanorum pontificum genuinae* (1862) 295ff.

[5] See above, 123.

papacy and the imperial government in Constantinople.[1] The Gelasian sources reveal the exposition of the all-important principle of division of labour, the function allocated to secular power located as it was *within* the Church, the determinative role assigned to the papacy as a governing institution, and the insistence on the corporational character of the universal Church, thereby accommodating the Pauline concept of the *corpus* within the governmental scheme.[2]

Two literary products of the second half of the fifth century deserve some attention. Neither author is known. The one is the so-called Pseudo-Denys. He pretended to be Denys, the pupil of St Paul, and wrote two small tracts in Greek which exercised an enormous influence throughout the subsequent ages. They were called *On the celestial hierarchy* and *On the ecclesiastical hierarchy*.[3] It was this author who coined the very terms *hierarch* and *hierarchy* (neither known to classical Greek). The backbone of these two tracts was the descending theme of government and law which became an essential attribute of all theocratic forms of government in the Middle Ages. The stern hierarchical ordering of society—in any case foreshadowed by St Paul and the earliest official papal communication[4]—found in Pseudo-Denys its most influential expositor.[5] The other product, probably made during

[1] The collection of Letters in the *Avellana* (ed. *CSEL* 35) is most important, and so are the documents ed. by E. Schwartz, 'Publizistische Aktenstücke zum akazianischen Schisma' in *Abhandlungen der Bayr. Akad.* 10 (1934).

[2] The so-called *Decretum Gelasianum* was not his, but was of near-contemporary southern French origin; its 'decrees' shed light on many currently held views of government: ed. E. Dobschütz in *TU* 38, 3 (1912); cf. also H. Leclercq in *DAC* VI, 722ff.

[3] Ed. in *PGr* 3, 119ff. (*De coelesti hierarchia*) and 369ff (*De ecclesiastica hierarchia*) both with LT; ET: J. Parker (1899); FT: M. de Gandillac (1943); GT: W. Trisch (1955); authorship is still uncertain: U. Riedinger, 'Der Verfasser der ps.-dionysischen Schriften' in *ZKG* 75 (1964) 146ff.

[4] W. Ullmann, 'The cosmic theme of the Ia Clementis and its significance for the concept of Roman Rulership' in *Studia Patristica* XI (1972) 85ff.

[5] For a detailed examination of his influence see now W. Maurer, 'Luthers Lehre von den drei Hierarchieen und ihr mittelalterlicher Hintergrund' in *SB Munich* (1970) fasc. 4, at 45ff (with full bibl.).

the Acacian schism, was the so-called *Legenda sancti Silvestri*[1] which purported to deal with Constantine's conversion and in so doing allocated to the papacy a role in the decision of Constantine to transfer his capital to the city which bore his name. The background to this tendentious novel was the clash between imperial government and papacy when the former claimed universal monarchic power in all matters of concern to Christian society: the basis of this claim was that the civil status of a city also determined its ecclesiastical status, with the consequence that Rome was accorded an inferior rank (being no longer the capital) and the papacy was thus relegated to a mere patriarchate. The primatial-monarchic function of the institution was denied by New Rome, and part of the design of the author of this novel was to show that in actual fact the papacy played an important role in raising Constantinople to the status of the capital of the empire. The full implications of this novel were not drawn until the forger in the mid-eighth century concocted the Donation of Constantine.[2]

It is not possible to leave the literary scene of the fifth century without specifically drawing attention to one of the greatest literary figures in the century. Although the writings of St Augustine mainly imprinted their seal on theology (especially concerning the trinity, grace and soteriology), they nevertheless also left their mark on ideas of government. Yet in this respect their influence was not as overwhelming as had once been thought. The doctrines which were influential were (1) the ecclesiology set forth in a number of his works, but especially in his sermons and epistles;[3] (2) the prominence he gave to the idea of Christian justice in one of his main works, the *City of God*; and (3) the view concerning the universal character of the Church that was to him

---

[1] Ed. in B. Mombritius (ed. H. Quentin and A. Brunet), *Sanctuarium seu vitae sanctorum* (1910) II, 508ff. Interpretative details in *PG* 75ff.

[2] See also C. B. Coleman, *Constantine the Great and Christianity* (1914) 217ff; W. Levison, 'Konstantinische Schenkung und Silvesterlegende' in *Misc. F. Ehrle* (1924) II, 181ff is fundamental.

[3] Y. Congar, *L'église: de saint Augustin à l'époque moderne* (1970) 12–67; 90ff.

a body corporate within which there was no room for an independent, self-sufficient State.[1] St Augustine was also one of the first literary exponents of the idea of the just war[2] and powerfully contributed to the medieval teleological thesis in regard to governmental actions.

In proximity to this Augustinian material there were fifth-century sources elaborating some of his ideas which gained wide acceptance in later ages. One of these was the *History against the Pagans* by Orosius who applied teleology to history and held that because the birth of Christ and the evangelization of the world had taken place within the confines of the Roman empire, they were providentially willed.[3] Into the same category of 'political teleology' came the mid-fifth century anonymous tract *De vocatione omnium gentium*[4] which alluded to the providential establishment of the Roman *empire* and thus quite in consonance with the Western reaction to the Council of Chalcedon aired the problem of the relations between Rome and Constantinople.

[1] Ed. of *Civitas Dei* in *CSEL* 40; often translated, cf. R. H. Barrow (1950); B. Zema and B. C. Walsh in *Fathers of the Church* (1950). Ed. of Letters in *CSEL* 34, 44, 57–8 (esp. *Epp* 93, 155, 185); his *Enarrationes in Psalmos* (*PL* 36 p.t.) are rich in obiter concerning governmental ideas. The literature on him is profuse. Some guidance can be had from G. Combès, *La doctrine politique de s. Augustin* (1927); N. Baynes, *The political ideas of St Augustine* (1936); R. Schneider, *Welt & Kirche bei Augustinus* (1949); G. Burleigh, *The City of God: a study of St Augustine's philosophy* (1950); V. Giorgianni, *Il concetto del diritto dello stato in s. Agostino* (1951); H. X. Arquillière, *L'augustinisme politique*, 2nd ed. (1955); J. S. Grabowski, *The Church: an introduction to the theology of St Augustine* (1957); H. A. Deane, *The political and social ideas of St Augustine* (1963); M. J. Wilks, 'St Augustine and the general will' in *Studia Patristica* IX (1966) 487ff; id., 'Roman empire and christian state in the "De civitate Dei"' in *Augustinus* (1967); R. Markus, *Saeculum* (1971); for his and Jerome's views on the people and its role in society see J. D. Adams, *The populus of Augustine and Jerome* (1971) 46ff, 113ff.

[2] C. Erdmann, *Die Entstehung des Kreuzzugsgedankens* (repr. 1964) ch. 1; R. Regout, *La doctrine de la guerre juste de s. Augustin à nos jours* (1935).

[3] Ed. in *CSEL* 5; ET by I.-W. Raymond, *The seven books of history against the pagans* (1936). For the influence of Orosius on King Alfred see J. M. Wallace-Hadrill, *Early Germanic Kingship* cit. 145ff.

[4] Ed. in *PL* 51, 634ff. ET by P. De Letter: Prosper, *The Call of all nations* in *Ancient Christian Writers* XIV (1952).

The author of this tract was in all likelihood Prosper of Aquitaine who exercised very great influence down to and including the Frankish age.

The exhausting christological disputes in the sixth century were not conducive to the production of works relative to public government. The possible exception was Ennodius of Pavia who as bishop wrote a number of influential letters and so-called *opuscula* which in a scholarly manner propounded the unaccountability of the pope, and thus followed the lines laid down by Gelasius I.[1] Ennodius was also one of the first who reserved the title of 'papa' solely for the Roman bishop. The concept of the personal sovereignty of the pope had reached the point of crystallization.[2]

Partly because of their influence and partly because of their contents, the writings of Gregory I as author (and not as pope) deserve some remarks in the present context. Of particular interest are his sermons, homilies and individual small treatises which were written for consumption by a large public and therefore, though not masterpieces of Latin and style (in contrast to his official correspondence with Constantinople), are at any rate easily comprehensible literary products.[3] Despite their unsystematic exposition, there is a great deal that relates to public law and government, such as the idea of obedience by the inferior to the superior,[4] the idea of inequality in the members of society,[5] the consistent emphasis on strict hierarchical ordering if peace and order were to be established and maintained, and capping it all the insistence on the primatial-monarchic functions of the pope.

In Isidore, the bishop of the lively Visigothic see of Seville, Gregory I had a contemporary who in many respects was a perfect complement to him. For Isidore provided the theoretical material with which to erect that European edifice which

---

[1] Ed. *MGH. AA.* VII, 48ff (*Libellus pro synodo*, anno 503); his letters, ibid.

[2] For some details cf. W. Ullmann, 'Romanus pontifex indubitanter effcitur sanctus: DP 23 in retrospect and prospect' in *St. Greg.* VI (1961) 229ff.

[3] His Homilies and interpretations of biblical literature ed. *PL* 79, 9ff; his *Moralia* ed. ibid. 75 and 76, 9–782. The ed. in the *CC* is in progress.

[4] *PGP* 107; *IS* 13, 31f.   [5] *IS* 14f.

Gregory's prophetic vision had delineated. Isidore's output was a source of major dimensions: it supplied the bridge between the Roman and Germanic worlds, and this applied with particular force to governmental principles. Isidore was not only a man of encyclopedic knowledge but also a writer with the requisite power of succinct and orderly expression, and one who was familiar with patristic lore as well as papal and secular history. In regard to influence his *Etymologies* take pride of place[1] together with his *Sentences*[2] and *Allegories*.[3] The latter furthered the understanding of complicated thought-processes by explaining them in an allegorical manner. In one way or another every one of his works touches on the question of Rulership and its purpose in a Christian society, with the consequence that the problem of coercion necessitated his anatomy of the idea of justice. In pursuit of his interpretation he came to consider the king who set aside justice: the tyrant now began to have contours and profile. His insistence on the application of the Pauline idea of *ministerium* to the king as a minister of God was to have far-reaching implications for medieval Rulership. No one single author can be said to have exercised such an overwhelming influence on the science of government as Isidore.[4]

Probably still belonging to the seventh century is an Irish source which exercised an unobtrusive but all the stronger influence, very likely owing to the authorship that was ascribed at one time to St Patrick, another time to St Augustine, yet another time to Isidore, and since the ninth century to Cyprian. None of

---

[1] Ed. W. M. Lindsay (1911). About the alleged Old High-German translation of Isidore cf. F. Delbono, 'Osservazioni sull'Isidoro in antico alto tedesco' in *Studi Medievali* 7 (1966) 277ff.

[2] Ed. in *PL* 83, 537ff. For his views relative to the role of the Christian people in society cf. J. D. Adams, op. cit. (as 232 n. 1) at 120f.

[3] *PL* cit., 97ff.

[4] The literature is too large to be cited in full. Cf., e.g., *Isidoriana* (1961) containing excellent contributions (notably by B. Bischoff); H. Löwe in *DA* 9 (1952) 361ff; E. Ewig, 'Zum christlichen Königsgedanken im Frühmittelalter' in *Das Königtum* (=*Vorträge & Forschungen* III (1956)) 29ff; *PG* 28ff; H. H. Anton, *Die Fürstenspiegel und Herrscherethos in der Karolingerzeit* (1969) 55ff; P. D. King, *Law & Society in the Visigothic kingdom* (1972) 25, 30, 33, 38, 47f.

these composed the work *De XII abusivis saeculi*. The now commonly adopted designation of the author is Pseudo-Cyprian.[1] In actual fact, this tract proves the influence of Isidore.[2] The author focused attention on the idea of justice, thereby also developing Isidore's basic axiom of the Ruler as the *terror disciplinae* within a Christian commonwealth. Two notions make their appearance in this tract: the *negotia regni* (which were to have a great future, especially in English constitutional history) and the exercise of the king's *tutamen patriae* (the protection of the fatherland) which became one of the roots of the later tutorial principle. In his analysis of justice the author was necessarily led to the concept of the king as a *rex iniquus* which too had a very great future before it.[3] Altogether the tract is suffused with the hierarchical order of society and the relations of the superior to the inferior members.

The literary poverty of the Frankish period down to the late eighth century unequivocally indicates the low educational standards in the Merovingian age. Such literary productions as there were came from ecclesiastics who were not Franks, as for instance the Anglo-Saxons Boniface and Cathwulf.[4] It was partly the result of the close association forged between the Franks and the papacy in the earlier part of the eighth century that Charlemagne later conceived of the idea of a social Renaissance of the vast empire he had created. The implementation of this social rebirth needed however an adequately trained personnel. The cultivation of an intellectual élite that consisted of the higher ecclesiastics was one of the devices adopted. Its aim was to have the right men available for the gigantic task of reshaping or re-forming or

---

[1] Ed. S. Hellmann, *Pseudo-Cypriani de XII abusivis saeculi* (in *TU* 1929) with a valuable introd., 3ff, ed. 32ff. The work was still copied in the 15th century: ULC. MS Ii, 1, 29, fo. 96ff and ascribed to Augustine.

[2] P. D. King, op. cit., 195-6, here further lit., esp. R. Hillgarth; for his influence on Frankish writers cf. H. Anton, op. cit. s.v.; also *CR* 84f, 105f.

[3] Cf. E. Peters, *The Shadow King: Rex inutilis in medieval law and literature* (1970) who pays no attention to this source; cf. my review in *Cath. Hist. Rev.* 57 (1972) 264ff.

[4] Ed. of Boniface's Letters in *MGH. Epp* III, esp. nos. 16, 33-5, 48, 50, 63, 69, 73, 91, 93, 107-9; Cathwulf, ibid., IV, 501ff. Some details in *PG* 43, 48f, 50, 53, 61; *CR* 49f; H. Anton, op. cit. 75f.

regenerating Frankish society on exclusively Christian lines. Among the king's most dedicated servants was another Anglo-Saxon, Alcuin. In his responsible position as a 'chief minister' to Charlemagne Alcuin had ample opportunity of composing, not a tract, but numerous Letters on behalf of the king as well as in his own name. In them he touched upon very many governmental questions as they affected the actual exercise of royal power.[1] In none of the Letters is there any systematic or methodical treatment of problems of government: by and large the voluminous output of Alcuin was prompted by the actuality of the situation to which he was responding. Hence problems of government were firmly set within Christian morality, current theological views and the transmitted Roman aretology. In a word governmental questions were treated as ancillary to the theological-moral framework which explains his dependence on 'authorities' to such an extent that the substance of his own thought was in danger of being suffocated by them.

The more the Carolines succeeded in transforming Frankish society, the more the problem of Rulership demanded attention. The essential point is that this problem came perhaps first to be seen by the Franks in a concrete manner and in all its dimensions and ramifications. Hence it could no longer be effectively treated as merely incidental to religious or theological issues. It became, so to speak, a topos of its own, but was understandably still embedded in the Christian substance from which it evidently derived its sustenance and structural elements. Nevertheless, there was no explicit model for this treatment of the problem; there was no previous blue-print that could serve as a pattern; there were plenty of detailed views relative to this or that governmental topic but no analytical examination nor a synthesis. The numerous papal statements relative to government referred to the imperial government and had little relevance to the Carolingians. There was therefore a need for an analysis of governmental problems *ex professo*. Moreover, what was dispersed in all sorts of sources had now to be channelled into the specific Frank-

---

[1] Ed. in *MGH. Epp* IV, 1–481; details in H. Anton, op. cit. 85ff.

ish mould and adapted to the needs of this 'reborn' society. But this could no longer be done within the confines of a topical Letter, however lengthy, or even of a homily. It needed a special tract or treatise devoted to the problem of Rulership in a Christian society. The answer was the new literary genre of the tract on government.

The tract as a specific literary genre within the precincts of governmental ideas came into being in the ninth century and was closely linked with the implementation of the Carolingian Renaissance. The authors were the educated ecclesiastics. The tract was a systematic exposition of topics relative to government within contemporary society and therefore of christocentric themes and their immediate relevance to matters of public interest—a distillation of general Christian ideas which were held applicable to Rulership and attendant questions. This explains the adoption of the wholeness standpoint according to which no conceptual differentiation was made between religious, political, moral etc. norms. Hence there was no distinction between a Church and a State[1] nor was there a pluralist society: matters falling within the precincts of government were classed as ecclesiological and dealt with by ecclesiastics. Some of the tracts frequently appeared as *Specula regum*, that is, instructional books for kings (or princes) on the fundamentals of public government. They were primarily educational and had a restricted circulation. Nevertheless, they were vehicles which disseminated basic governmental principles in the most influential circles.

One of the earliest Frankish tracts was that by Smaragdus, characteristically called *Via regia*, written for Louis I between 811 and 814 when still king of Aquitaine.[2] The tract constitutes the beginning of a specific Frankish literature on theocratic Rulership. Dependent as he was on the Old Testament and possibly also influenced by Visigothic models, Smaragdus introduced royal

---

[1] *CR* 16ff.

[2] Ed. *PL* 102, 931ff. Biographical data in H. Anton, op. cit. 132ff; here also further lit.; on the *Via* itself ibid. 172ff, and M. Wallace-Hadrill, 'The via regia of the Carolingian age' in *Trends in medieval political thought*, ed. B. Smalley (1965) 5ff.

unction as the essential element of Christian kingship: it effected a rebirth of the king.[1] Further, the office of the king was seen as having been conceded by divinity so that the concession principle now began to have sharply defined contours. Hence, God had conferred on the Ruler the *ministerium regale* so that he could be said to function on behalf of Christ on earth.[2] The bishop of Orléans, Jonas, wrote two tracts, one entitled *De institutione laicali*[3] written in the twenties of the ninth century, and the other under the title *De institutione regia*.[4] The very subject of the first work is revealing: no author had hitherto considered the standing of the layman important enough to devote a whole tract (consisting of three books) to this subject. But Jonas examined the special role allotted to the layman in a Christian society and delineated on an ecclesiological basis the relations between the lay and clerical members of the Church. The large and important Council of Paris (829) was greatly influenced by the theses of Jonas. The other tract was thoroughly ecclesiological in substance. It wove biblical and patristic material into the themes, but was interspersed with excerpts from Isidore, Alcuin, Smaragdus and, above all, papal law, notably Gelasius I. The notion of the *persona regalis* made its début and herewith the concept of the office (*ministerium*) became accessible to analysis and definition. Quite in keeping with the ecclesiological basis the ecclesiastics assumed a determinative role in the tract, so that the hierocratic theme here emerged in the episcopalist shape which was also the predominant tenor of the decrees of the Council of Paris.[5]

An exact contemporary of Jonas was the abbot of Corbie,

---

[1] On this see *CR* 101ff.

[2] H. X. Arquillière, *L'augustinisme politique* (as 232 n. 1) is fundamental.

[3] Ed. in *PL* 106, 121ff; details in H. Anton 213; *PG* 129f, 134 and *CR* 35, 51ff, 60f, 67f, 122n, 176.

[4] Ed. J. Réviron, *Les idées religieuses d'un évêque du IXᵉ siècle: Jonas d'Orléans et son De institutione regia* (1930) 119–94; cf. H. Anton, op. cit. 214f; *PG* loc. citt.; E. Delaruelle, 'Jonas d'Orléans et le moralisme carolingien' in *Bull. de la littérature ecclésiastique* 55 (1955) 129ff, 221ff.

[5] Cf. *PG* 129f, 134; *CR* 24ff, 123ff, and H. Anton op. cit. 212 notes 373–5. The book merely re-states the decrees of the Council of which he was the draftsman.

Wala, a cousin of Charlemagne. His tract was a well thought out plan of reform and conceived entirely on ecclesiological premisses; it contains one of the earliest attacks on the by then exuberant proprietary church system.[1] Clearly this system was based upon a number of basic governmental assumptions which, according to Wala, were irreconcilable with the premisses of a Christian society. He advocated the adoption of the principle of division of labour, and on its basis the secular power had no right to intervene in specifically ecclesiastical matters. Wala went even further and clothed his attack in a juristic garb, declaring that ecclesiastical property was immune from any royal interference. He concluded that if disorder were to be prevented, the juristic spheres of ecclesiastical and royal jurisdiction should be kept apart. They represented the two orders of the Church which was able to function properly only if each adhered to its competent spheres of jurisdiction.[2] As a source Wala's tract was an important milestone on the road to Canossa. Exactly the same opposition to the proprietary church was voiced by Archbishop Agobard of Lyons (d. 840) who, demonstrating great agility of mind, expressed himself on most contemporary problems of public government. By exercising control over property that included churches, laymen infringed upon one of the oldest principles laid down in canon law: lands and goods assigned to ecclesiastical use were to be removed from lay control altogether. The system as practised was dubbed a continuing sacrilege.[3] Agobard was one of the first who showed himself aware of the need for a common law for the whole of the Frankish realms: for the sake of maintaining the common faith a common law was necessary. Just as the common faith established a cementing bond, in the same way a common law guaranteed public security.[4]

---

[1] Transmitted by Paschasius Radbertus, *Epitaphium Arsenii*, ed. E. Dümmler in *Abhandlungen Preuss. Akad.* (1900) fasc. 2, 18ff; *PG* 135 n. 1; H. Anton 202f.

[2] See ed. cit. 62f; correctly interpreted by H. Anton 203 n. 328 at end.

[3] Ed. *MGH. Epp* V no. 5 and 11, pp. 167ff, 203ff; *PG* 134ff.

[4] In his *Adversus legem Gundobadi*, ed. in *MGH Epp* V, 158ff. His literary agitation against the Jews (cf. *MGH Epp* V, nos. 4, 5–9, pp. 164ff) seems to have been motivated by the same fervour for a common law: to him the Jews were

Yet another topic in the astonishingly rich literature of the ninth century concerned the very idea of Europe as a Roman-Latin unit held together by the bond of a common faith nurtured by the Church of Rome. There are literary sources which were symptomatic of their authors' awareness that Western Europe had assumed an ideological entity and individuality and in its structure, ideology and outlook was therefore different from the Greek-dominated Eastern half. Ratramnus of Corbie in his *Contra Graecorum Opposita*[1] as well as the bishop of Paris, Aeneas, in his *Adversus Graecos*[2] (both written in 867–8), show how much the West had become a unit with a common outlook, common basis and common front against what it held to be the arrogant pretensions of the Eastern empire which called itself Roman but in which hardly anyone spoke Latin. Into the same segment of public government fell the synodal expressions on this topic: as sources revealing an extraordinarily uniform viewpoint they were especially important for the assessment of the forces which contributed to the making of the Occident.[3]

The three *Specula regum* by Servatus Lupus (he died as abbot of Ferrières in 862),[4] while not overwhelming in new perspectives, nevertheless show how stimulating the Carolingian Renaissance had been in the revival of Roman conceptions and their adaptations to contemporary Frankish society. Here it was the concept of the *utilitas publica* which Servatus linked with the traditional Christian theme of justice and the Pauline principle of a division of labour in its Gelasian form. The lay power should implement what the sacerdotal authority had taught. His contemporary

---

an alien element in Christian society with whom no contact should be maintained. For all facets of this prince see E. Boshof, *Erzbischof Agobard von Lyon: Leben und Werk* (1969).

[1] Ed. in *PL* 121, 225ff; details in *CR* 157ff.

[2] Ed. in *PL* cit., 691ff; details in *CR* 154ff.

[3] Synod of Worms (May 868), ed. T. Neugart, *Episcopatus Constantiensis Alemanniae* (St. Blasien 1803) 520ff; details *CR* 160ff.

[4] Ed. *MGH Epp.* VI, no. 33, 37, 83, 93; also no. 81; details L. Levillain, *Les classiques de l'histoire de France au Moyen Age* 10 (1926); 16 (1935). See esp. H. Anton, op. cit. 148ff.

Sedulius Scotus, a member of the Irish colony at Liège, expressed similar views in his tract significantly entitled *De rectoribus christianis*. He denied any autonomous standing to the Christian Ruler who had become what he was solely through the working of divine grace and whose function was to govern *ad utilitatem reipublicae*.[1]

Of the ninth-century authors none exercised greater influence than the towering figure of Hincmar, archbishop of Rheims, who was unsurpassed in intellectual brilliance, acumen and mental flexibility. His very large output on public government revealed a depth the like of which was not to be witnessed again until very much later. Though many of his writings are still accessible only in deficient editions, they have a width which assured them of longevity. He was at home as much in theology proper as in applied theology as well as in law, history and hagiography. His contribution to medieval governmental principles can be classified under these headings: the supremacy of law also to be observed by the king; autonomy of ecclesiastical jurisdiction in all matters basic to the well-being of Christian society; the determinative role of the ecclesiastics; the creation of the specific royal coronation Orders which in symbolic, liturgical and doxological language expressed some very profound themes relative to Rulership, and here especially the theme relating to the rebirth of the king through unction (establishing a vital element that enabled the hierarchy to exercise control over the king's government). The decrees of the synod of Fismes shortly before his death testify to his influence.[2]

[1] Sedulius Scotus, *De rectoribus christianis*, ed. S. Hellmann in *Quellen und Untersuchungen zur lateinischen Philologie des MA* (1916) 19–91. Some details in R. Buchner, Beiheft to *WL: Die Rechtsquellen* (1953) 59 (with the older lit.); CR 61.

[2] Of Hincmar's tracts only the most important can here be mentioned. *De divortio Lotharii regis* in *PL* 125, 619ff; *De officio episcoporum*, ibid. 1087ff; *De regis persona et regis ministerio*, ibid. 833ff; *Ad episcopos regni* ibid. 1007ff; *Iuramentum quod Hincmarus edere iussus est*, ibid. 1125ff; *Pro ecclesiae libertatum defensione quaterniones* ibid., 1035ff; *De ordine palatii* in *MGH. Capit.* II, 517ff; his Letters ed. in *PL* 126, 9ff; and in *MGH Epp* VIII, fasc. 1 (1939) (no more appeared). For the *Speculum* preparatory to his *De regis persona* see the discovery

Understandably, many ninth-century writers busied themselves with the application of certain biblical themes to public goverment. The essence of the Carolingian Renaissance demanded this. Their views were set forth in a variety of media, such as Sermons, Letters, Tracts. The theme of Rom. 13, 1–7 attracted special attention[1] although hardly any relevant biblical passage remained untouched. As good specimens of this kind of source mention may be made of the biblical commentaries of Claudius of Turin written in the second and third decades of the ninth century. These had a number of pertinent things to say on obedience and the ministerial function of the Ruler, and attendant problems.[2] Hrabanus Maurus (d. 856), abbot of Fulda in the Eastern portion of the Frankish realms, touched on questions of government in his Sermons and in his biblical commentaries. Although not highly original, he nevertheless was a diligent collector of excerpts from patristic writers and applied them to his themes on government in a Christian society.[3] One of his tracts shows what part he expected the clergy to play in the process of implementing the Renaissance.[4] A third specimen of this literary genre is Haimo of Auxerre who in his commentary on Romans evidently had to treat of obedience and the character of the law issued by the Ruler.[5] Florus of Lyons (d. ca 860) may serve as an example of how much biblical study had sharpened the

by G. Laehr in *NA* 50 (1935) 410ff. Details in *CR* 83ff, 99ff, 115ff; Anton op. cit. 281ff (a very good analysis of Hincmarian ideas, though the coronation Orders might well have been accorded some prominence; here also further lit.). The standard work on Hincmar is still H. Schrörs, *Hinkmar von Reims* (repr. 1969); cf. now the instructive pages in M. Wallace-Hadrill, *Early Germanic Kingship* cit. 131ff (Hincmar's ideas on royal power).

[1] For the commentaries on this Pauline passage see the admirable analyses by W. Affeldt, *Die weltliche Gewalt in der Paulus Exegese* cit. (above, 35 n. 3).

[2] For eds. and lit., see W. Affeldt, op. cit. 263, and for the full text his own ed., 286ff.

[3] Esp. *Commentaria in Genesim* in *PL* 107, 443–670; and *Enarrationes in Epistolas b. Pauli: expositio in Ep. ad Romanos*, in *PL* 111, 1275ff.

[4] Ed. of his tract *De ecclesiastica disciplina* in *PL* 112, 1191ff.

[5] Ed. in *PL* 117, 362ff; details in W. Affeldt, op. cit., 121ff, 134ff, 266.

scholar's awareness of certain contemporary practices which appeared irreconcilable with Christian or ecclesiastical propositions. According to Florus the contemporary creation of bishops was a malpractice: it was solely divine grace which constituted a bishop, and not royal appointment, with the consequence that he relegated the king's role to one of consent to a canonically performed election.[1] Florus of Lyons also castigated the practice whereby clerics were tried by royal courts, which was nothing but a challenge to established royal practice on the grounds of the claim to the *privilegium fori*.[2]

Law is a mirror of society, and so is its literature. This truism can be applied to the age succeeding the demise of the Carolingian empire. The subsequent decades produced very few literary sources which materially contributed to the advancement of the science of government and law. The stimulus provided by the Carolingian Renaissance had lapsed, hence the dearth of pertinent literature. With the removal of the external threats from tenth-century society more orderly conditions began to prevail again, and questions of government and law came again more and more to the foreground. The turn of the tenth and eleventh centuries witnessed many foundations of new schools, especially in Northern Italy and the Western parts of the empire. The quantitative increase in schools augured well for advanced studies, because they certainly were a response to the needs for greater educational facilities. But it was still to be a long time before literature attained the high standards of the Carolingians. An example of tenth-century literature is the work of Rather of Verona, bishop of Liège (d. 974), who was reflective and reproductive, but by no means original or familiar with basic questions of government.[3] There was also Atto of Vercelli, imperial chancellor in Italy in the second half of the tenth century whose literary output was a

---

[1] Ed. of his *De electione episcoporum* in *PL* 119, 11ff. On this point see W. Ullmann, 'The elections of bishops and the kings of France in the 9th and 10th centuries' in *Concilium* 7 (1972) 79ff.

[2] See C. Nissl, *Der Gerichtsstand des Clerus im fränkischen Reich* (1888) (still fundamental).

[3] See his *Praeloquia*, esp. Bk. I, 7, 9, 10; Bks. II and IV in *PL* 136, 145ff.

mirror of the time, though its yield in the sphere of governmental ideas should not be overestimated.[1]

It is against the contemporary religious, social and governmental background that the Cluniac movement should be seen. It was merely reformatory and did not aim at a rebirth or renaissance of society in the same sense that the Carolingian movement did. The Cluniacs aimed at revivifying the substance of Christian society which indubitably was in need of readjustment and resuscitation. They attempted to cleanse contemporary society of its excrescences and abuses. The movement was strongly represented in Lorraine where it captured the intellectual circles which eventually gave a strong impetus to the literary exposition of topics fundamental to society. Nevertheless, the Cluniacs themselves took little part in discussions directly affecting public law and government, although they had greatly fertilized the ground for the dissemination of ideas held to be germane to a Christian society.[2] For it was due to their teachings and preachings that the soil was made receptive for the acceptance of hierocratic-descending themes of government.

Extraneous stimuli sparked off a spate of literary productions from the mid-eleventh century onwards. This only goes to show once again how closely governmental theories were linked with the actuality of the situation. The Emperor Henry III had provided the Roman Church with excellent personalities who were learned and versed in literature and had been under the strong influence of the Cluniacs: from their ranks rose popes and counsellors and advisers, all animated with a burning zeal for re-shaping and reorganizing society according to what they held to be Christian tenets. The early and unexpected death of Henry III

---

[1] His *Perpendiculum* (or *Polipticum*) was a criticism of the existing restless political conditions, ed. G. Goetz in *Abhandlungen sächs. Akad.* 37, fasc. 2 (1922), ed. at 14ff; GT 55ff.

[2] For the background cf. H. E. J. Cowdrey, *The Cluniacs and the Gregorian reform* (1970); documents in N. Hunt, *Cluniac monasticism in the central M.A.* (1972). But cf. also K. Hallinger, *Gorze-Kluny* (1950–1). The standard work is still E. Sackur, *Die Cluniazenser* (1892–4); cf. also H. Hoffmann, 'Von Cluny zum Investiturstreit' in *AKG* 45 (1963) 165ff.

was a circumstance as favourable as any could be, because the regency was in the flabby hands of the widow who acted on behalf of her six year old son, the future Henry IV. The Normans in Sicily had begun to settle but lacked proper recognition by the European powers, a state of affairs which the papacy was soon to remedy. The formal break with Constantinople in 1054 cleared the air considerably and provided the opportunity for deploying arguments in the purely ecclesiastical sphere.[1]

Some general observations on the literature of the eleventh century are called for.[2] It was not a revival of the ninth-century kind of literature but a deliberate attempt to create, shape and influence public opinion. 'Political' literature as such became part of public life; it was an instrument by which the warring parties appealed to larger sections of the populace. It was the first time in European history that literature had been put to this use, and it has never lost this function, which indeed is peculiar to Western Europe because nothing comparable has ever existed in the Eastern half. This literature, aiming as it did at broad sections of the public, is rightly called publicistic—in pamphlets, tracts and monographs it pursued the intention of moulding public opinion by a severe scholarly analysis of governmental matters. These literary products were scholarly efforts which began to utilize earlier literature as well as the Bible and the law for their own purposes: yet every statement and assertion had to be supported by 'authority'. The more ancient the 'authority', the greater its weight. The tracts contain no glib expositions of partisan standpoints.

The question how they could influence public opinion, since they were written in Latin and employed the whole arsenal of theological, patristic, Roman, canonical and historical arguments, can easily be answered. The issues of the Investiture Contest had brought into the open problems which had not been perceived before. All the hitherto unquestioned assumptions upon which

---

[1] For details of the situation cf. *SHP* 126ff.

[2] For general characterization see the classic work by C. Mirbt, *Die Publizistik im Zeitalter Gregors VII.* (repr. 1965). For details about a great many writers to be mentioned see *WH* I (1948).

society and government rested came to be questioned and scrutinized. Although both authors and readers were clerics, it was their very number which facilitated the dissemination of the ideas contained in the tracts, for in every household of any standing there was at least one cleric who had administrative or educational or cancellarial or managerial duties and thereby had intimate contact with the lay population. Obviously, what reached the latter was attuned to their capabilities and consequently represented a diluted version of some difficult abstract exposition. In this way larger and larger circles obtained a greater share of information and knowledge and began to take part in the debates. The increase in literary productions reflected the demand for them. From now onwards public opinion shaped as it was by this literature became a force which no government could disregard with impunity. Seen from a wider perspective, the public itself began to enter the arena of 'political' discussion, with the consequence that the foundations of the descending theme of government and law came in course of time to be slowly, imperceptibly, but steadily eroded and the ascending theme gained ground proportionately.

Some features were common to all writers of whatever persuasion they were. Methodologically it was the deductive mode of enquiry which predominated: the last ounce was squeezed out of a general principle or axiom by a logically flawless process of reasoning. This was a method germane to theocentric cosmology. Similarly, the descending theme of government was the one which was overwhelmingly if not exclusively advocated. Differences of opinion did not concern the character of society, but solely its government. In the opinion of one side it was the king who by tradition and history was entitled to govern it. Moreover, this entitlement was shown by his having been distinguished by divinity as the recipient of divine grace that conferred governmental powers on him. In the opinion of the other side, it was the papacy (and not necessarily an individual pope) that alone was entitled to govern this Christian society which was only another name for the Church universal. The very sacrament of unction now served as a gratuitous gift to the ecclesiastical side, for who else but the ecclesiastics were qualified to pronounce on sacramental matters? Unwittingly, unction provided the ecclesiastics with a juristic handle with which to control the exercise of royal power. Further, the governmental principle of division of labour was one more principle that was agreed upon by all shades of opinion, though its application to the concrete situation differed widely and in fundamental respects. It was mainly in pursuit of this principle that each side was forced to express itself on the very substance of authority, its origin, scope, purpose and the numerous other attendant questions. And since this society was professedly a religious and ecclesiological unit, the scales were heavily loaded against the royal side. The intellectual lead indubitably belonged to the papal-hierocratic side. What the royal or lay or imperial opponents groped for but with the means at their disposal were unable to find, was the concept of the State as an entity that was autonomous, independent, self-sufficient and lived on its own norms. As long as the ecclesiological presuppositions prevailed the concept of the State could not emerge: to bring it about needed a force that had nothing to do with the Bible or with Christianity. And when that situation emerged as a result of the overpowering influence of Aristotle, the science of government was to turn into the science of politics.

Even before the great conflict had broken out, some authors raised serious doubts about the right of the lay Rulers to install and depose popes, the very measure which had been the constitutional principle since 962.[1] The anonymous author of the tract *De ordinando pontifice*—probably originating from Lorraine —flatly denied the right practised by Henry III at Sutri and afterwards.[2] The noted Cardinal Peter Damian (d. 1072) in his *Liber gratissimus*, of which the first recension dated from 1052–3 and the second some nine years later, dealt with the constitutional position of those who had been ordained by simoniacs:[3] this was a crucial

---

[1] On the *Ottonianum* cf. W. Ullmann, 'The origins of the Ottonianum' in *Cambridge Hist. J.* II (1953) 110ff.

[2] Ed. in *LdL* I, 8ff; details in *PG* 263ff.

[3] Ed. *LdL* I, 17ff. Further *opuscula* ed. by P. Brezzi in *Edizione nazionale dei classici del pensiero italiano* V (1943); IT B. Nardi ibid.

problem once the demand was made that the ecclesiastics should play not merely a determinative role, but should in actual fact themselves lay down the (basic) norm of living in a Christian society. And simony—that is, the selling and buying of ecclesiastical offices—was considered to run counter to the very structure of a Christian society.[1] The same cardinal also wrote a shorter tract which was a semi-official commentary on the papal election decree of 1059. This was the *Disceptatio synodalis* which explained the legislative measure and showed why complete freedom of papal elections was a necessary prerequisite for the 'proper' government of Christian society. In some ways this tract can be considered one of the first effective steps towards translating the thesis of papal monarchy into practice.[2] The evil which many contemporaries viewed as fundamental was the proprietary church system. It was Cardinal Humbert of Silva Candida (d. 1061), another member of the Lorraine circle, who in his book *Adversus simoniacos* (1058-9)[3] with passionate zeal trenchantly attacked the system which to him was a violation of the right order that should prevail in a Christian society. His demands culminated in the establishment of order and harmony—or as he called it: *una concordia ex diversitate*—which, however, could not come about if the laity were allowed to play their accustomed role in laying down the norms of a Christian society. Hence his aim was the reduction of the laity to a purely passive role, and hence the full insistence on obedience to hierarchical orders. The descending theme of government with its corollary of the concession principle found in Humbert one of its most effective exponents. The work underpinned the hierocratic form of government and gave it conceptual width by harnessing the complex allegory of the

---

[1] L. Saltet, *Les réordinations* (1907) (fundamental); A. Schebler, *Die Reordinationen in der 'altkatholischen' Kirche* (1936); J. J. Ryan, *St Peter Damian and his canonical sources* (1956); J. Gilchrist, 'Simoniaca haeresis' in *PICL* II (1965) 209ff.

[2] Ed. in *LdL* I, 77ff.

[3] Ed. *LdL* I, 205ff; details in *PG* 265ff; cf. also W. Ullmann, 'Cardinal Humbert and the ecclesia Romana' in *St. Greg.* IV (1954) 111ff; also H. Hoesch, *Die kanonischen Quellen im Werk Humberts von Moyenmoutier* (1970).

soul and body to jurisprudential issues. The tract was no less remarkable for its emphasis on the tutorial function of the Ruler.

Although a mere practitioner, the bishop of Metz, Hermann, was the addressee of several most important expositions of governmental doctrines by Gregory VII himself. In two lengthy letters (amounting to tracts) the pope himself, as the chief exponent of the hierocratic theme in theory and practice, presented his mature views. In diction, forcefulness of argumentation and dexterous manner of using antecedent literature they exercised very great influence, because they set forth the hierocratic theme in an official manner. Many excerpts found their way into canon law collections.[1] The communication sent by Gebhard of Salzburg to Hermann of Metz[2] approached the problem of the binding nature of the oath taken to the king by his subjects—a most delicate problem then as in more recent history—and concluded that an oath to an excommunicated king was no longer binding; contact with excommunicate persons was in any case illicit.[3] These were understandably serious social and 'political' problems. A little later, probably about 1084, Gebhard was the recipient of a tract written by Manegold of Lautenbach (died 1103), entitled *Ad Gebehardum Liber*,[4] which despite an unscrupulous adherence to and defence of the hierocratic party nevertheless contained some constructive arguments: he based himself on the tutorial principle and argued for the existence of a contractual arrangement between Ruler and subjects;[5] and he also made use of the Roman law and notably of the *Lex regia* which he declared was a merely revocable grant made by the Roman people to the Roman

[1] *Reg* IV, 2 and VIII, 21 (ed. E. Caspar (repr. 1955) 292ff, 546ff). Details in *PG* 276ff.

[2] Ed. *LdL* I, 263ff.

[3] The pope himself mitigated the rule which then became the law: see Gregory VII's *Reg* V, 14a, cap. 16 ed. cit. 373; also *Reg* IX, 24, ed. cit. 605f.

[4] Ed. *LdL* 308ff. Cf. also *PL* 155, 149ff attacking Wenrich of Trier and all scholarship hostile to the 'faith'.

[5] His importance for the early phases of scholasticism has been thoroughly examined by W. Hartmann, 'Manegold von Lautenbach und die Anfänge der Frühscholastik' in *DA* 26 (1970) 47ff (this study also important for the philosophic background of some publicists).

emperor.[1] Guido of Ferrara revealed a more practical bent in his tract *De schismate*,[2] written in 1086. He focused attention on the so-called *Regalia*, that is, rights which by virtue of his office belonged to the king, were issues of public law, and upon which the king himself could therefore not encroach in his function as a tutor: it was this view which formed the essential basis of the various settlements that ended the conflict. An exact contemporary tract was that by Bonizo of Sutri who in 1085-6 composed his *Liber ad Amicum*[3] which is remarkable for employing history to support hierocratic ideology. He concluded that 'royal power was subjected to that of the pontiffs'. An interesting and quite original combination of juristic and theological thinking and methods of enquiry concerning specific topics, which he treated in a manner approaching monographic character, can be detected in the strongly papal writings of Bernold of Constance who pointed to new approaches, precisely because he associated the two branches.[4] The attempt to reconcile the opposing standpoint was made by the anonymous author of the *De unitate ecclesiae conservanda* written in the last years of the eleventh century.[5] He proposed that the principle of division of labour should be raised to an autonomous principle and concluded that in the final resort royal authority alone had jurisdictional power, while its sacerdotal

[1] Ed. cit. 365, 391 (caps 30 and 67). For his familiarity with Macrobius' *virtus politica* which led him to the ascending theme in regard to the secular prince see *PGP* 113 n. 1.

[2] Ed. *LdL* I, 532ff; details in *PG* 407ff.   [3] Ed. *LdL* I, 571ff.

[4] Ed. *LdL* II, 7ff; of special significance is his *De damnatione schismaticorum* ibid. 27ff; *Apologeticus* ibid. 60ff; and *De excommunicatis vitandis* ibid. 113ff. For details cf. H. Weisweiler, 'Die päpstliche Gewalt in den Schriften Bernolds von St Blasien' in *St. Greg.* IV (1952) 129ff; J. Authenrieth, *Die Domschule zu Konstanz* (1956).

[5] Ed. *LdL* II, 173ff; details in *PG* 404ff. Further lit. in *WH* I, 406f. In the late 16th century Francois Hotman was to all seeming quite familiar with this tract, cf. *Francogallia* ed. cit. (below, 292 n. 4), 352, 358, 362 which in view of its tendency is not surprising. Cf. Z. Zafarano, 'Ricerche sul Lib. de unitate ecclesiae conservanda' in *Studi Medievali* 7 (1966) 617ff whose diligence is not always matched by understanding; see also W. Affeldt, 'Königserhebung und Unlösbarkeit des Eides im Lib. de unitate ecclesiae conservanda' in *DA* 25 (1969) 313ff.

counterpart should spread the 'verbum Dei'. The tract had no influence: the situation was not ripe for such compromising views.

On the royal (or imperial) side, which was overwhelmingly on the defence, prime importance must be attached to Peter Crassus and his tract which has already been the subject of comment.[1] Attention should be drawn to two further significant products. The one is French, the other Anglo-Norman. Hugh of Fleury's tract *De regia potestate et sacerdotali dignitate*, dedicated to King Henry I of England and written ca. 1103,[2] defended the royal position by recourse to history, tradition and the ancient law. He quite vigorously assailed the Gregorian (Augustinian) view that royal power owed its existence to evil. He was one of the few who realized the need to divest royal power of its ecclesiological encumbrances, and in this respect dimly also reflected the Anglo-Norman view that the king did not directly owe his power to the grace of God. The small anonymous tract *De investitura episcoporum*, written ca. 1109,[3] probably in the diocese of Liège, firmly supported the royal side mainly on the ground that in view of the wealth and prosperity of ecclesiastical possessions the secular Ruler could hardly show himself indifferent to the making of ecclesiastical princes. The 35 tracts of undoubted Anglo-Norman origin (variously ascribed to Gerard of York, Archbishop William Bona Anima of Rouen, etc.) most vigorously advocated the royal cause in a rather unusual manner. They are distinguished by (1) the extraordinary learning of their author and (2) the argumentation which in contrast to other anti-hierocratic writings was based on pure theological doctrine and biblical exegesis and above all on an involved christological thesis according to which the king was intended by divinity to be the vicar of God and thereby was endowed with sacerdotal and charismatic functions.[4]

[1] See above, 77f.

[2] Ed. *LdL* I, 466ff. The author died as a monk at Fleury in 1120.

[3] Ed. *LdL* II, 498ff.

[4] Ed. *LdL* III, 642ff. Additional tracts in H. Böhmer, *Kirche & Staat in England* (1899) and in G. H. Williams, *The Norman Anonymous of 1100 A.D.* (1951). About the unfortunate attempt by K. Pellens, *Die Texte des normannischen Anonymus* (1966) cf. my review in *HZ* 206 (1968) 696ff. Details of doctrine in *PG* 394ff; also N. Cantor, *Church, Kingship and Investiture in England* (1958).

However learned and penetrating the author, however closely argued the thesis, no interpretation of the Bible had hope of success at that time if its premisses were at variance with the traditional interpretation. And from the point of view of the science of government the tracts were too idiosyncratic and too little attuned to reality to make a significant contribution. Only one manuscript is known to exist. On the German side the outstanding writer was Wenrich of Trier who in a calm and detached way criticized the hierocratic arguments of Gregory.[1]

It was also at the height of the great conflict that some adherents of the royal cause (possibly belonging to the Ravenna school) embarked upon the production of forgeries in order to buttress their point of view. Although pretending to be official papal documents, these spurious pieces can be classed as publicistic or polemical literature. Apart from the papal election decree of 1059 which may possibly have been tampered with by the royal side,[2] there were in the main four forgeries. None of them showed the dexterity and versatility which distinguished the great royal opposition party. The tenor of all of them was to prove that 'the right order of things' was the exact reverse of what the papal hierocrats asserted.[3] Above all, the secular Ruler had been given the right to nominate the pope by a formal papal *Privilegium* and this concession was in fact buttressed by both the Old Testament and the Roman law. The other significant point of these pieces was that they tried to harness history to the royal cause. Their weakness was not at all dissimilar to the weakness which characterized the Donation of Constantine, only of course in the reverse order, that is that the alleged supreme position of the emperor was based on a papal grant and concession. It is also worth remarking

[1] Ed. *LdL* I, 280ff.

[2] Ed. *MGH. Const* I, 383, pp. 541ff. Details H. G. Krause, *Das Papstwahldekret von 1059 und seine Rolle im Investiturstreit* (= *St. Greg.* VII (1960)); W. Stürner, 'Salvo debito honore et reverentia' in *SavZKA* 54 (1968) 1ff; D. Hägermann, 'Untersuchungen zum Papstwahldekret von 1059' ibid., 56 (1970) 157ff.

[3] They are: (1) the *Hadrianum*, purporting to originate with Adrian I; (2) the *Privilegium minus* and (3) the *Privilegium maius* of Leo VIII and (4) the *Cessatio donationum*, all ed. in *MGH Const* I nos. 446ff, pp. 659ff. Details and lit. in *PG* 352ff.

that the *Lex regia* was somewhat clumsily adduced here to show that ecclesiastical authority had nothing to do with the making of a Ruler.

It is evident that in the publicistic literature of the eleventh and early twelfth centuries specific problems were not always consistently integrated into the general framework of Christian-governmental themes: the legality of investiture, the nature of an oath, deposition and excommunication of Rulers, suspension of bishops, concubinage, simony, and similar topics were frequently treated in isolation and unrelated to an overall basic standpoint. Nevertheless, the literature of the first half of the twelfth century shows that details began to be relegated to a second place and seen as issues and specific manifestations of the comprehensive pattern on which Christian society was considered to rest. This progress is understandable in view of the quite unparalleled impetus the conflict had given to scholarship: there was now available a far greater reservoir of trained writers than in the preceding period. More material, too, was now accessible.

Honorius Augustodunensis, probably of English origin, certainly a pupil of St Anselm of Canterbury, and from 1126 onwards at Regensburg,[1] was one such author in the twenties and thirties of the twelfth century who saw matters from a higher vantage point. In his so-called *Elucidarium*[2] he intended to present 'the sum-total of all Christian theology' ('summa totius christianae theologiae'). He subordinated problems of government to theological speculation, as can be seen from the three books of the work: God and Christ; the Church as the congregation of all the faithful; eschatological questions. Within this scheme he 'elucidates' general problems relative to government in a Christian society. Hence he has recourse to all sorts of sources, including the Donation of Constantine, to show how the individual item fitted into the general pattern.[3] This work was translated into the

---

[1] See how V. L. Flint, 'The career of Honorius Augustodunensis: some fresh evidence' in *RB* 82 (1972) 63ff.

[2] Ed. in *PL* 172, 1109ff. Further, Y. Lefeuvre, *L'élucidarium et les élucidaires* (1954) 361ff.

[3] I, 28–33 in *PL* cit. 1129ff.

vernacular and frequently copied.[1] It was the background of his very influential *Summa gloria* which was much more specifically governmental, as is indicated in the first lines depicting Christ as true king and priest.[2] His main principle in the work was unity of Christian society and therefore of government. The strong biblical-exegetical flavour was neatly balanced by the historical approach to governmental questions. Its strength lay in the integrative power of this writer.

An author endowed with considerable intellectual gifts and a large literary output to his credit was Gerhoch of Reichersberg who approached virtually all relevant governmental questions of the day and analysed practices in the light of pure theory. He was primarily a theologian, and hence questions of government were to him essentially questions to be answered by theology. He bitterly attacked curial practices as irreconcilable with the vocation of the papacy. It would be an exaggeration to claim that there was consistency in his output. The picture presented in his *De edificio Dei* (written 1128–30)[3] of an idealized form of government and that shown in his later *De investigatione Antichristi* (written in the early sixties) reflect the development of the author.[4]

Gerhoch may usefully be contrasted with his exact contemporary Hugh of St Victor, one of the very great and independent thinkers and writers. His main work *De sacramentis* set forth a comprehensive exposition of theology with particular reference to governmental questions.[5] This is a source of first rate importance. It was a highly successful integration of theology and jurisprudence and presented all the structural elements of the papal hierocratic system in their maturity. His ecclesiological basis

[1] Cf. J. A. Endres, *Honorius Augustodunensis* (1906) at 25.

[2] Ed. *LdL* III, 63ff; details in *PG* 414ff.

[3] Ed. *LdL* III, 126ff.

[4] *LdL* III, 305ff; further *De quarta vigilia noctis* ibid. 503ff; and the latest of his works ibid. 288ff. Details in D. van den Eynde, *L'oeuvre littéraire de Geroch de Reichersberg* (1957); E. Meuthen, *Kirche & Heilsgeschichte bei Gerhoh von Reichersberg* (1959); also P. Classen, *Gerhoch von Reichersberg* (1960).

[5] Hugh of St Victor's works ed. in *PL* 176, 183ff; details in *PG* 437ff (also influence). Selected passages in ET in *LCC* X (1956) 300ff.

made him state that 'spiritual power had to institute the secular power: if the latter failed to fulfil its obligations, it had to be judged by the former'. The idea of the rule of law re-appeared here in the allegory of soul and body. Some statements of Hugh were borrowed literally (though without acknowledgment) in Boniface VIII's *Unam sanctam*.[1]

Exceptional importance must be attributed to the tract (as well as the letters) of St Bernard of Clairvaux, *De consideratione*.[2] The election of his former pupil as pope (Eugenius III) was the occasion of Bernard's writing this tract which can be classed as a *speculum paparum*. What Hugh did from the purely theoretical angle, Bernard did on a practical basis. His was perhaps the best illustration of how ecclesiological ideas were to be applied to the centralization of government. Hence the development of the papal vicariate of Christ in the tract which expressed the pope's successorship to St Peter in easily comprehensible form. The principle of division of labour made its appearance here in the allegorical form of the two swords which in any case had a distinguished ancestry in the coronation ordines. The tract served as a handbook in the papal chancery, as the numerous papal acts in the subsequent period testified,[3] and it was also cited (again without mentioning the author) in *Unam sanctam*.

John of Salisbury's tract, *Policraticus*, indubitably presents the culmination of that literature which dealt monographically with problems of government applicable to a Christian society. Finished in 1159 and dedicated to Thomas Becket, the royal chancellor, it is far more than a mere *speculum regis*: it is a comprehensive synthesis and exposition of those basic ideas upon which any Christian government should rest. In the work itself, which

---

[1] For this analysis cf. *HPT* 114f.

[2] Ed. in *S. Bernardi Opera*, ed. J. Lerclercq et al. III (1963) 393ff; further *Ad milites templi* ibid. 213ff; some of his Sermons are very important in the present context, ed. cit. I (1957) 3ff. (*Super Cantica Canticorum*); and IV (1966) 69ff. For some details and further lit. cf. *PG* 426ff; S. Chodorow, *Christian Political Theory and Church Politics in the mid-twelfth century* (1972) 46f, 114ff, 260ff.

[3] For examples cf. *PG* 431 n. 1, 432 n. 3, 433 nn. 2, 3; 434, 436 n. 4, 437 n. 4. Some of his letters were blatantly propagandistic.

surpasses all other similar tracts in size, John combines philosophy with history, and jurisprudence with theology.[1] Above all the work is suffused with a wholesome sense of realism gained by practical experience. Of specific value are the fourth, sixth and eighth books which treat of the Ruler's duties and obligations who as a prince with ministerial functions and as a member of the Church was subjected to sacerdotal rulings. John injected teleological considerations into his notion of law and applied the allegory of soul and body to the law in an original way. No less important was his insistence upon the higher rank of *utilitas publica* if there was a conflict with private interests. His thesis of the Ruler's tutorial function made him advocate regicide, if all other means, including prayer, should have failed to remove the tyrant. The *Policraticus* represented indeed the high-water mark of monographic literature on government.[2]

The appearance of John of Salisbury's book coincided with the papacy's rapid ascent to the dizzy heights of its medieval position; the book appeared moreover at the time when the kingdoms of England and France began to develop their own organization, not to mention the concomitant consolidation of Aragon, Castile and Navarre on independent lines. It was also in these decades that the empire reached its apogee. Above all, the appearance of the *Policraticus* coincided with the unparalleled upsurge of jurisprudential scholarship in all contemporary seats of learning. The

[1] See also H. Liebeschütz, 'Chartres und Bologna: Naturbegriff und Staatsidee bei Johannes von Salisbury' in *AKG* 50 (1968) 3ff.

[2] Ed. C. C. J. Webb (1909); ET of Bks. 4–6 by J. Dickinson (1927). Ed. of his Letters in Nelson's Medieval Texts I (1955); in *PL* 199. Lit.: W. Berges, *Die Fürstenspiegel* cit. 131ff; *PG* 420ff and *PGP* s.v.; G. Miczka, *Das Bild der Kirche bei Johannes Sarisberiensis* (1970). Influence: Berges 291ff, and W. Ullmann, 'The influence of John of Salisbury' in *EHR* 59 (1944) 384ff. About Helinand of Froidmont who wrote a *Speculum regis* by the order of Philip II (about 1200) and heavily relied on John of Salisbury, cf. Berges 295f (*PL* 212, 735ff). That John's *Policraticus* exercised influence on Chaucer, has been shown by M. J. Wilks, 'Chaucer and the mystical marriage in medieval political thought' in *Bull. John Rylands Library* 44 (1962) 489ff, esp. 502ff (this study is also important for assessing the canonistic and publicistic background of Chaucer's political views. The 'wife' symbolized the country (or Church) and was thus a means to bring the tutorial principle into clear relief).

remarkable point must be borne in mind that for about a century afterwards there was no tract or scholarly monograph that resembled the kind of work just surveyed. The explanation seems to be that most of the intellectual and academic energy was spent on the interpretation of the two laws—the Roman and canon laws—and in this way jurisprudence monopolized the scholarly handling of governmental issues which were now seen mainly, if not exclusively, as issues of jurisdiction. Although jurisprudence kept its links with theology and ecclesiology, there was nevertheless a very marked accentuation on secularism fostered especially by the civilians.[1] This secularist complexion of juristic and hence governmental thought was of invaluable assistance to the progress of the 'new' forces in the thirteenth century. The wide scope of theoretical and also practical jurisprudence accounts for the total absorption of applied ecclesiology or theology by jurisprudence.[2] In the course of the thirteenth century this governmental jurisprudence was to separate from the main body of jurisprudence and was to emerge as a science of its own and become political science or politics.

The non-juristic literature between the mid-twelfth and mid-thirteenth centuries, while in no wise approaching the scholarly quality or indeed width of conception or quantity of the preceding age, nevertheless has certain features which raise it to the level of an important source of governmental ideas. To begin with there are the Sermons, of which those given by Innocent III were a particularly good example because they were first-rate witnesses of the advance which papal governmental thought had made in the decades since Bernard or John of Salisbury. These Sermons handled the Bible with consummate juristic skill and revealed the full maturity of hierocratic ideology, especially the monarchic function of the pope, to which a number of biblical passages were made to apply directly.[3] Above all this period was rich in instructional books for young princes—the *Specula regum* —of which some notable examples were Peter of Blois' so-called *Dialogus cum Henrico* (written before 1189) which was a gentle

---

[1] See on this process of secularization of ideas and government above, 77f.
[2] For this development see *PG* 359ff.   [3] *PL* 217, 313ff.

criticism of Henry II's governmental principles,[1] and Gerald of Wales' *De principis instructione* (probably written in the early years of Henry III's reign) which despite its title does not excel in substantial contribution to governmental thought.[2] In France two important 'Mirrors' were written in the middle of the thirteenth century, both by the famous historian Vincent of Beauvais. His *De eruditione filiorum regalium* (ca. 1250) was envisaged as a prologue to a large 'political' work of which the first book was *De morali principis institutione* written about 1260. It was strongly theocratic and therefore conceived on the descending theme of government; it also showed the influence of John of Salisbury. The author tended to be diffuse, and long-winded, and cannot be said to have been familiar with basic juristic ideas concerning government. The moral tone was predominant.[3] Within the empire a notable 'Mirror' was that composed by Henry VI's tutor and chaplain, Godfrey of Viterbo: his *Speculum*, supplemented by his *Liber memorialis* and the *Pantheon*,[4] constituted a somewhat poetic transfiguration of the emperor who was successor of Jupiter as well as of the Roman Caesars, and moreover *divus Heinricus*, and in any case the only legitimate heir of Charlemagne (the sting directed against France was not to be missed).[5] Scandinavia is represented by the mid-thirteenth century *Konungs-Skuggsjá* or *Speculum regale* which is a unique source of greatest value, because its author has preserved for us a great many old-Germanic ideas of kingship which the historical development had obliterated in other regions: in fact, this most interesting 'Mirror' tries to combine old-Germanic governmental conceptions with the new, that is, Christian principles, and yet specifically admonishes the Ruler to pay heed to the Old Testa-

[1] Ed. J. A. Giles, *Petri Blesensis Opera Omnia* (1846) III, 289ff. W. Berges, *Fürstenspiegel* cit. 294.

[2] Ed. *RS* (1891); Berges 294.

[3] Ed. Basle 1481, see Berges 304, 307.

[4] Ed. *MGH. SS XXII*, 21ff; 94ff; 107ff. The *Pantheon* apparently impressed François Hotman some 400 years later as can be seen by the frequent references, ed. cit. (below, 292 n. 4), 184, 188, 238ff, 264, 486.

[5] For Henry VI's intentions of translating the idea of universal lordship into practice see Roger of Hovedon's report, above, 103 n. 1.

ment.[1] As an example of a later kind of *Speculum* may be cited
the *Speculum regis Edwardi III* (1331) which was composed by
William of Pagula writing at Windsor.[2]

The ferocious Staufen conflict with the papacy from the thirties
of the thirteenth century onwards gave rise to a great many
manifestoes, encyclicals, and appeals on both sides. Some of these
were specimens of stylistic beauty. And some others were examples of significant gifts of exposition which blended the rational
with the emotional and played upon the susceptibilities of the
public addressed by purporting to act in their interest alone, but
the contribution of these to governmental ideas should not be
overestimated. They are important sources from another point
of view: they were largely propaganda pieces of a very high
calibre, composed by the respective chanceries, and they therefore
constituted one of the earliest instances of a centrally directed
propaganda aiming to influence public opinion. The publicistic
literature of the eleventh and twelfth centuries was the work of
private scholars and was on the whole severely scholarly, but by
the mid-thirteenth century the creation of public opinion had
become a matter of direct concern to the Rulers themselves.[3]
This kind of production employed all the relevant branches of
learning and reached a high-water mark in early fourteenth
century France when the king was locked in combat with the
papacy. The royal chancery now also issued forged papal letters

[1] Ed. F. Jónsson, *Speculum regale* (1920); details in Berges 159ff, 314ff. For
Spanish, Aragonese and further French 'Mirrors' cf. ibid. 299f, 308ff, 328ff
(Castile, 335ff (Raimundus Lullus), 340ff (Arnald of Villanova, Juan Manual
and Alvarus Pelagius (for King Alphonse XI).

[2] Ed. J. Moisant, *De speculo regis Edwardi III* (1891). That William of Pagula
was its author has been convincingly shown by L. Boyle, 'William of Pagula
and the Speculum regis' in *Med. Studies* 32 (1970) 329ff.

[3] The imperial documents are ed. in *MGH. Const* II nos. 119, 122, 124, 126–
149; 214–17; 224–34, 236–8; 262, 265. See further Winkelmann, Böhmer-
Ficker, above, 211., also J. L. A. Huillard-Bréholles and *MGH. Epp sell XIII s.*
above, 211 n. 4. For characteristics of this kind of literature see, e.g. F. Graefe,
Publizistik in der letzten Epoche Kaiser Friedrichs II. (1909); O. Vehse, *Die
amtliche Propaganda in der Staatskunst Kaiser Friedrichs II.* (1929); H. Wieruszow-
ski, *Vom Kaisertum zum nationalen Königtum* (1933). Cf. also above, 212 and for
Eger cui levia above, 213 n. 3.

to whip up French emotions, and moreover manufactured royal replies to these forgeries which contained highly charged vituperations and outbursts against the pope. There can be no doubt about the efficacy of these propagandistic devices, especially when coupled with the scholarly efforts by the academics who, like the personnel serving the king, came from social strata which were not burdened by tradition or other impediments as a bar to the free deployment of their political talents.[1] The important point is that these lay authors put their services as university teachers at the disposal of the king—two generations later it was to be the universities themselves which engaged themselves in their corporative capacity in efforts to shape public opinion.

The tracts written by the French academics—almost wholly anonymous—were *pièces d'occasion*, short, pithy, without learned apparatus but very hard-hitting, concise and highly perspicacious. These tracts were mainly juristic and on the whole show few traces of the new Aristotelian-Thomist influence. Their value as sources lies in their being essentially learned propaganda pieces designed to sway public opinion in favour of the king. The chief target was papal jurisdiction the comprehensiveness of which was denied on juristic grounds,[2] or on economic-financial grounds,[3] or on principles derived from natural law.[4] The intellectual milieu of these tracts was really the Roman law in its

[1] It was from the reign of Louis IX onwards that laymen came to be in charge of the royal chancery, cf. Q. Griffiths, 'Origines et carrière de Pierre de Fontaines' in *RHDFE* 48 (1970) 544ff (he was one of the first laymen). See further F. J. Pegues, *The lawyers of the last Capetians* (1962).

[2] By the author of *Rex pacificus*, ed. P. Dupuy, *Hist. du différend entre le pape Boniface VIII et Philippe le Bel* (repr. 1956) 663ff; or that of the *Quaestio in utramque partem*, ed. M. Goldast, *Monarchia* (ed. Frankfurt 1668) II, 96ff; for this literature see esp. J. Rivière, *Le problème de l'église et de l'état au temps de Philippe le Bel* (1926); about the first-mentioned tract cf. W. Ullmann, 'A medieval document on papal theories of government' in *EHR* 61 (1946) 180ff; about the second see J. A. Watt, 'The Quaestio in utramque partem reconsidered' in *St. Grat.* XIII (1967) 411ff (important for its sources and conclusions).

[3] By the author of the *Disputatio inter clericum et militem*, ed. in M. Goldast, *Monarchia* cit., I, 13ff; details in J. Rivière, op. cit. 128ff, 137f, 253ff.

[4] *Antequam essent clerici* ed. P. Dupuy, *Histoire* cit. 21ff; details in Rivière 99ff, 258.

specific French interpretation, hence the strong insistence on the lay element in the kingdom. From the purely ideological standpoint these tracts cannot be said to have advanced governmental science much, for the simple reason that on the basis on which they (and their papal opponents) operated no material advance would have seemed possible. But as sources of a 'political' propaganda in the hands of the newly arisen third estate, they are very valuable indeed.

Whereas these French products exhibited all the subtleties of a merciless, cold rationalism characteristic of the French school, a source from across the Rhine and written a few years earlier deserves a passing remark. This is the tract by Alexander of Roes, the canon of Cologne cathedral, written in the late eighties of the thirteenth century, which is of interest on two counts. First, there is the intrusion of what may be called the national element into governmental literature, and associated with this the attempt to utilize national sentiments in the service of a constructive programme. The author[1] rested the unity of the (Latin) West on the three nations—the Germans, Frenchmen and Italians. The Germans were destined by divinity to be the leaders and were therefore rightly in possession of the empire, whereas the role of the French was the pursuit of scholarship as demonstrated by the University of Paris; the Italians were singled out as the leaders of religion and therefore rightly in possession of the papacy. It was on these three—*imperium, sacerdotium* and *studium*—that the whole edifice of the Church should rest. The very high number of extant manuscripts as well as of later translations indicates the great appeal of this tract.

This chapter may profitably be concluded by drawing attention to sources which though non-juristic, nevertheless contain a very great deal of material that is of direct concern to governmental ideas. These are the so-called Pontificals and other liturgical books, as they came to be transmitted from the eighth century onwards.

[1] Alexander of Roes, *Memoriale*, ed. H. Grundmann and H. Heimpel (in *Kritische Studientexte der MGH* (IV (1949)); and critical ed. in *Staatsschriften des späteren MA* (1958). For some details and the occasion which prompted the tract cf. *HPT* 187ff.

As already indicated, their substance consists of instructions in regard to the actions, gestures, prayers, etc., to be followed on specific occasions.[1] And one of the most immediately relevant subjects touched the coronation of kings and emperors, and the consecration and later the coronation of the popes. The chief importance of these *ordines* lies in their expression of abstract thought in the language of commonly understood symbols. Apart from allegory, symbolism was the most favoured means of conveying difficult abstract thought processes by easily comprehensible, unambiguous, concrete actions, gestures, insignia, emblems, specially selected biblical texts or texts prepared for the occasion, the position and rank of the acting persons, and similar devices. These had to be chosen in such a manner as to preclude any misinterpretation or misconstruction. Broadly speaking the *ordines* came under the heading of liturgy: that is why they were also called *officia*, the very name of 'liturgy' being unknown in the Middle Ages. Within their realm there is still vast room for research. In numerous respects the symbolism employed in the *ordines*, though clad in liturgical garb, is at least as important and illuminating as the literary exposition of a governmental topic. As a source, symbolism is on a par with the governmental decree or the literary exposition of governmental topics.[2]

Evidently, these manuals first came into use within the precincts of the Roman Church, and here they concerned the consecration of the elected pope and from the eleventh century onwards his coronation. Virtually all the details are significant— from the physical taking possession of the Lateran, the sitting on the two curule chairs (symbolizing the position of the pope as successor to two apostles) and his being raised from the *sedes stercoraria* (the night commode: a symbolic enactment of I Kgs. [I Sam.] 2, 8) in front of the Lateran to the so-called investiture

[1] See above, 207ff.
[2] See esp. P. E. Schramm, *Herrschaftszeichen und Staatssymbolik*, 3 vols. (1954–6); id., *Sphaira, Globus, Reichsapfel: Wanderung und Wandlung eines Herrschaftszeichens von Caesar bis Elisabeth II.* (1958); id., 'Der Schirm' in *Festschrift f. H. Heimpel* III (1972) 567ff; and E. Baldwin Smith, *Architectural Symbolism of imperial Rome and the Middle Ages* (1956).

by the deacon of the Roman Church (to exclude all possibility of an assertion that bishops or cardinals had conferred papal power), the conferment of the pallium taken from St Peter's altar, the kissing of the papal feet, and so on—and bore an unambiguous meaning which contemporaries at once understood. That the Donation of Constantine served as a basis for much that was used in the ritual is obvious: the colour of the pope's clothing (white), the scarlet of the cope (the *cappa rubea*), the sceptre, and so on, were intended to stress the monarchic function of the pope.[1] It should not, however, be assumed that councils, particularly the general councils did not provide ample opportunity for expressing abstract governmental ideas by symbolic means, especially in regard to the seating order, precedence. and similar matters.[2]

Because the Western emperor was the ideological offspring of the papacy, the ritual to be applied to his solemn inauguration was devised by the papacy. The imperial coronation orders are particularly rich in their symbolic contents which compellingly focalized the essential structural elements of Western emperorship.

[1] For the early ed. of the *Ordines Romani* see *PL* 78, 937ff (*Ordo Romanus* I and IX (at 1003ff) and XIII and XIV (at 1105ff), and the modern ed. by M. Andrieu, *Le pontifical romain au Moyen Age*, 4 vols. (1938-41); id., *Les ordines romani du haut Moyen Age*, 3 vols. (1931-51); E. Eichmann, *Weihe und Krönung des Papstes* (1952); B. Schimmelpfennig, 'Ein bisher unbekannter Text zur Wahl und Krönung des Papstes im 12.Jh.' in *AHP* 6 (1968) 43ff; id., 'Ein Fragment zur Wahl, Konsekration und Krönung des Papstes im 12. Jh.' ibid., 9 (1970) 323ff. In general see F. Wasner, 'De consecratione, inthronizatione, coronatione summi pontificis' in *Apollinaris* 8 (1935) 86ff; 249ff; P. E. Schramm, 'Zur Geschichte der päpstlichen Tiara' in *HZ* 152 (1935) 307ff. See also F. Tamburini, *Le cérémonial apostolique avant Innocent VIII* (1966); M. Dykmans, 'Le cérémonial de Nicolas V' in *RHE* 63 (1968) 365ff; 785ff with new important texts; id., 'Le cérémonial de Grégoire X' in *Gregorianum* 53 (1972) 535ff (about 1273) (here further lit. referring to the forthcoming ed.). For basic considerations see F. Wasner, 'Tor der Geschichte: Beiträge zum päpstlichen Zeremonienwesen im 15. Jh.' in *AHP* 6 (1968) 113ff; and B. Schimmelpfennig, *Die Zeremonienbücher der römischen Kurie im Mittelalter* (1973).

[2] See M. Andrieu, *Ordines Romani* cit., s.v.; W. Ullmann in *Studies A. Gwynn*, ed. J. A. Watt et al., 359ff, at 379f; and now esp. B. Schimmelpfennig, 'Zum Zeremoniell auf den Konzilien von Konstanz u. Basel' in *QFIAB* 49 (1970) 273ff.

The symbolic pregnancy of the numerous imperial coronation *ordines*[1] reveals the great intellectual efforts which went into their making. They are nothing but the symbolic translation of abstract governmental ideology. From the beginning of the rite down to the last action at the end of the long service there is an almost embarrassing richness of illuminating symbolism. The reception of the future emperor who approaches the seated pope and kisses his feet, the subsequent scrutiny, that is, the public examination of the imperial candidate, his oath, and the specific kind of unction administered not by the pope, but by the senior cardinal, the conferment of the insignia, notably the sword taken from St Peter's altar with which the pope personally girded the emperor, the well thought-out assignment of different roles to the acting persons, and so on—they all unambiguously portrayed the essential function attributed to the Roman emperor: they left no doubt about the auxiliary place that was allocated to him within the Church.[2] The symbolic means of showing this subordinate role of the emperor as an officer of the Church was the absence of a throne or anything even faintly suggesting an enthronement.

In no wise less illuminating are the royal coronation *ordines* which began in the ninth century and, for evident reasons, were composed by ecclesiastics:[3] in contrast to the Germanic king

[1] Ed. R. Elze, *Ordines coronationis imperialis* in *MGH. Fontes iuris germanici antiqui* (1960).

[2] Details in E. Eichmann, *Die Kaiserkrönung im Abendlande* (1942) (fundamental); *PG* 143ff, 253ff; addit. lit. 471, 479. See also H. Hirsch, 'Der mittelalterliche Kaisergedanke in den liturgischen Gebeten' in his *Aufsätze zur mittelalterlichen Urkundenforschung* (1965) 1ff.

[3] For early sources see above, 207f; further R. Elze and C. Vogel, *Pontificale Romano-Germanicum* (in *Studi e Testi* 226-7 (1963) and 269 (1972)); for France see U. Chevalier, *Sacramentaire et martyrologe de l'abbaye de Saint-Rémy* (1900) 224ff (*Ordo* of 1270); E. Martène, *De antiquis ecclesiae ritibus* (1702) II, 196ff; the famous *Ordo* of Senlis ibid. 222ff; E. S. Dewick (ed.), *The Coronation Book of Charles V of France* (HBS 16, 1898) contains the text composed by the order of Charles V in 1365. For England cf. L. Wickham Legg, *English Coronation Records* (1901), 30ff, and 81ff (also ET); P. L. Ward, 'The coronation ceremony in medieval England' in *Speculum* 14 (1939) 161ff; W. Ullmann (ed.), *Liber regiae capellae* (HBS 92 (1961), ed. 74ff (*Liber regalis* with the additions of the

chosen by the people—the essence of the ascending theme—the theocratic king needed a solemn ritual to show publicly that God's grace had conferred power on him—the essence of the descending theme of government. These *ordines* too were liturgical manuals in which the symbolic element was similarly conspicuous. What they aimed at was the ritual presentation of the king's (personal) sovereignty by well-chosen symbolic and doxological devices.[1] Here the prayer texts as well as the ritual instructions for the conferment of the emblems are especially revealing, and so are the selected biblical texts. The redactors took great care to show that the Recognition was given due prominence because it replaced the formerly practised elections by the princes.[2] Now that the theocratic king was elected by the officiating ecclesiastics and within the framework of the divine service the 'election' by the princes was no more than a designation.[3] The French *ordines* serve as classic sources of the monarchy's theocratic designs: even the last pale remnant of an 'election'—the Recognition—was eliminated from the order composed in 1270.[4] All the more prominent and in actual fact the centre-piece of the service was in all West-European *ordines* the unction by the metropolitan with chrism. The kind of oil used, the part of the body (the vertex) anointed, and the place which was accorded to unction within the rite itself sharply brought into focus the differences between a king and an emperor: the latter was not anointed by the pope nor with chrism, but with an inferior oil, and this was administered at a side altar and only on the right arm and

fifteenth century); for the other relevant English texts see P. E. Schramm above, 208 n. 1; see further J. Brückmann, 'The ordines of the third recension of the medieval English coronation Order' in *Essays Bertie Wilkinson* (1969) 99ff. For Spain see B. P. Martin 'La bulla de Innozencio III y la coronación de los reges de Aragón' in *Hispania* 29 (1969) 485ff.

[1] For some details cf. W. Ullmann, 'Der Souveränitätsgedanke in den Krönungsordines' in *Festschrift P. E. Schramm* (1964) I, 72ff.

[2] Cf. *PGP* 145ff, 202f; introduction to *Lib. reg. cap.* cit., 33ff.

[3] H. Mitteis, *Die deutsche Königswahl*, 2nd ed. (1943) and *SB. Munich* (1950) 40ff; W. Schlesinger, 'Die Anfänge der deutschen Königswahl' in *Die Entstehung des deutschen Reiches* (ed. H. Kämpf) (1956) 313ff, esp. 348ff; *PGP* 145f.

[4] Text of the *Ordo* of Rheims in U. Chevalier, *Sacramentaire* cit. at 223f.

between the shoulder blades. The crowning of the king, quite in agreement with the theocratic theme, failed to occupy the prominence it had at an imperial coronation. On the other hand, enthronement and the relevant doxology conspicuously highlighted the territorial power of the king, once more a feature that sharply distinguished king and emperor, and one that no literary exposition, no legal enactment, no tract could have demonstrated so persuasively. The Orders reflect the constitutional development in a singularly convincing way, as the changes—either merely intended or actually introduced—in the late medieval English *ordines* from Henry IV onwards prove.[1]

[1] Cf. W. Ullmann, 'Thomas Becket's miraculous oil' in *JTS* n.s. 8 (1957) 129ff and *Lib. reg. cap.*, cit. 37ff, 89f; J. W. McKenna, 'The coronation oil of the Yorkist kings' in *EHR* 82 (1967) 96ff; T. A. Sandquist, 'The holy oil of Thomas of Canterbury' in *Essays Wilkinson* (above, 264 n. 3), 330ff.

CHAPTER 8

The New Science of Politics

The cosmological revolution which the absorption of Aristotle wrought in the 13th century, displayed its greatest effects in the sphere of governmental science.[1] What secular governments, writers, jurists, polemicists, had been groping for, especially in the period since the Investiture Contest, was now presented by Aristotle in the form of a natural unit that had grown entirely in accordance with the laws of nature, wholly independent of divine intervention and grace or theological or other speculative reflexions. Asistotle's concept of the State as 'a body of citizens sufficing for the purposes of life' seems innocuous enough, but nevertheless introduced new dimensions into thought concerning society and its government. It led to the abandonment of the hitherto predominant wholeness point of view. By introducing the concept of the State as a viable notion, the complementary concept of the citizen also made its début. In a more accurate sense, both concepts were not so much introduced as reborn and raised to major proportions within the new orientation. Both the State and the citizen were to prove concepts detrimental to the structure of medieval Christian society and government.

For what the Aristotelian revolution effected in the thirteenth century was a rebirth of the very creature that had been hibernating for many a century, that is, natural man or the man of flesh who, as St Paul had taught, was successfully washed away by baptismal water which infused divine grace into the recipient and turned

---

[1] Aristotle's works on logic had long been known to theologians and philosophers. Some civilians also had a smattering of knowledge of some of his works on logic, as can be seen from Accursius' *glossa ordinaria*: there were at least seven references altogether, cf. G. Otte, 'Die Aristoteleszitate in der Glosse' in *SavZRA* 85 (1968) 368ff (no reference to the *Politics* or *Ethics*). For the background see F. van Steenberghen, *Aristotle in the West* (1955); id., *La philosophie au XIIIᵉ siècle* (1966). For the intellectual revolution see esp. H. Mitteis in *HZ* as cit. in *PGP* 231.

him into 'a new creature'.[1] The effect was that man as a Christian was incorporated into the Church and had to follow the rules laid down for its members. This incorporation meant that the Christian norm of living (in the making of which he had no share) had become decisive, with the result that in all matters appertaining to Christian life—and they after all covered every contingency from the cradle to the grave—he had lost that autonomous status which he had possessed as a mere natural man before baptism. Now, however, this natural man came so to speak into his own again and took his place next to the Christian: he was restored to his earlier autonomous position. In abstract terms the *homo* (man as such) had a standing next to the *christianus*. The unipolarity or totality of the individual as a Christian gave way to a bipolarity of the individual as a natural man and as a Christian. Integration began to yield to departmentalisation or specialization. Aristotle himself had shattered the (Platonic) wholeness standpoint by stating that man and citizen corresponded to two different categories of thought: the good citizen need not be a good man, and vice-versa. This statement expressed a profound new dimension—it expressed the difference between politics and ethics. For each category different norms prevailed, although in an ideal community they would be identical. The moral code laid down what made a good man, while the political-legal code formulated the demands to be made on a good citizen. This was the beginning of the process of atomization of human activities into moral, political, religious and other categories.

The very terminology of Aristotle's *Politics*[2] caused difficulties to the translator of Aristotle's works. Language is always a reliable guide to thought-processes, and if the mind is not aware of a concept, no term is available. The translator, the Dominican William of Moerbeke (d. 1285)[3] had to coin a new word for the Aristotelian term *politeuesthai*: the new coinage was *politizare*

---

[1] See St Paul, I Cor. 2, 14; 3, 3; II Cor. 5, 17; Gal. 5, 17 and 24; Col. 2, 12; etc. See also St John, 3, 3–5.

[2] ET of the *Politics* by B. Jowett, ed. H. W. C. Davis (1905 and many reprs.),

[3] Ed. F. Susemihl, *Aristotelis Politicorum Libri Octo* (1872). Cf. G. Lacombe. *Aristoteles Latinus* (1939) (here good extracts from MSS).

which designated acting as a citizen and in a political manner. Evidently, the new concept corresponded to new mental categories and therefore to their needs, and so did the other terms which now began their triumphant careers, such as *politia* for government or *politicum* (for political). The individual came to be viewed in the political sphere as a citizen, endowed with full autonomous powers capable of fashioning his own fate by *politizare*. To the individual's *humanitas* (being a mere *homo* in the ethical field) corresponded his status as a citizen in the public field, and from both must be clearly distinguished his *christianitas*. The former concept was of the natural, the latter of a supernatural, order. Bipolarity or a double ordering of things took the place of unipolarity.

The citizen was to replace the *sub/ditus*, the individual as a subject of higher authority. Once the citizen took part in the shaping of his own community, the State, by creating the law, the ascending theme of government and law made its re-appearance after centuries of hibernation. It is not therefore surprising that as a result of the Aristotelian absorption there emerged the *scientia naturalis*, of which the (newly coined) *scientia politica* was its counterpart in the political field. It is evident that the introduction of Aristotelian theses was a serious challenge to the accepted premisses of public and social life.[1] The axiom of Aristotle that man was a political animal epitomized the challenge, because at once the Pauline 'natural man' sprang to mind, the very being that was supposed to have been washed away by baptismal waters.

The gigantic task of creating a synthesis of the apparently irreconcilable differences was nevertheless successfully accomplished by the great Dominican scholar, Thomas Aquinas, who, as has been said (Grabmann), mastered the intricate Aristotelian corpus as nobody else has before or since. Some of his chief points have in fact just been mentioned, notably the crucial distinction

---

[1] That the soil had been prepared in the 12th century, mainly by civilians is evident. Cf. *IS* 81, 101ff; for other preparatory agencies see F.-J. Schmale, 'Das Bürgertum in der Literatur des 12. Jh.'s' in *Vorträge & Forschungen* XX (1968) 409ff, esp. 418ff (concerning the institutional role of the universities in this process of preparation).

between *humanitas* and *christianitas* and the double ordering of things. But the great breakthrough in his doctrine lay in his operating with the concept of nature as a fundamental notion: he considered nature a divine creation and for this reason credited it with autonomous standing. Yet, in order to attain his full ends, man was in need of faith and grace. 'Grace does not do away with nature, but perfects it.' The natural product, the State, had nothing to do with faith or grace in regard to its origin or operation, but for its better working, grace and faith were necessary complements. This was the result of the double ordering of things— the natural and supernatural order—or seen from a different angle, it was the beginning of the process of atomization. The laws of the human State were valid in their own right, but in order to be perfect, and adequate for Christian society, they still were in need of ecclesiastical approval. Thomas's thesis was one of two tiers which complemented, but did not exclude, each other. It was in fact he who coined the term *scientia politica*. And Thomas materially contributed to the release of the individual as a mere subject from the fetters of 'superior authority' and to his re-formation as a fully-fledged citizen.[1]

Thomas set forth what in the end approached political philosophy proper. He never expressed his thought in a systematic manner; his theories must be gathered and reconstructed from a conspectus of all the relevant utterances he made in a great variety of his writings. His own commentary on the *Politics* is most important, but he left the work unfinished (he appears to have been at work on it between 1268 and 1272), having reached only an early stage in the third book.[2] The rest was finished by Peter of Auvergne.[3] His *De regimine principum* was likewise not

[1] Cf. L. Lachance, cit. below, 273 n. 5.

[2] Ed. *Opera omnia* (Parma 1867) XXI, 364ff. Other works in the so-called Leonine ed. of the *Opera omnia* (1882–1948). For a complete list of works see M. Grabmann, *Die Werke des hl. Thomas*, 3rd ed. (1949).

[3] For details see M. Grabmann, 'Die mittelalterlichen Kommentare zur Politik des Aristoteles' in *SB Munich* (1941) fasc. 10 (fundamental). Selected passages in ET in A. P. d'Entrèves and J. G. Dawson, *Selected political writings* (1948); A. C. Pegis, *Basic writings of Thomas Aquinas* (1946), esp. vol. I; and R. Lerner & M. Mahdi (eds.), *Medieval political philosophy; a source book* (1963)

finished: it ended at the beginning of the second book. The tract, completed by his pupil Ptolemy of Lucca, enjoyed great popularity in the fourteenth century.[1] But Thomist principles in all their maturity were best expounded in the comprehensive *Summa Theologiae* which is a model of clarity and conciseness.[2] In it Thomas attempted the integration of Christian and Aristotelian elements, notably the ideas of justice. His exposition can indubitably be classed as a mature legal philosophy. He set forth the various kinds of law and their mutual relationships, and even if his scholastic distinctions may sometimes appear a shade artificial, they nevertheless greatly clarified basic jurisprudential notions. Thomas' knowledge of Roman law was considerable.[3] In a number of his other writings he addressed himself to problems of political science, as in his Commentary on the Sentences of Peter Lombard[4] and on the various books of the New Testament, and in his very large *Summa contra gentiles* (1258–64) which was apparently intended for use by Dominican missionaries.[5]

297ff. For a full list of Latin commentaries on Aristotle's works with admirable detailed literature, see C. H. Lohr in *Trad* 23 (1967) 313ff; 24 (1968) 149ff; 26 (1970) 135ff; 27 (1971) 251ff; 28 (1972) 281ff (continuing). The commentaries on the *Politics* are rather rare.

[1] Ed Parma (1964) XVI, 225ff. ET by G. Phelan and I. T. Eschmann (1949). Details in M. Grabmann, 'Studien über den Einfluss der aristotelischen Philosophie auf die ma. Theorien über das Verhältnis von Kirche und Staat' in *SB Munich* (1934) fasc. 2, with ed. of new texts 134ff; id., *Die Werke* (above 272 n. 2) esp. 330ff.

[2] New ed. with ET in 60 vols in progress since 1964.

[3] See J. M. Aubert, *Le droit romain dans l'oeuvre de s. Thomas* (1955). The immediately relevant parts in the *Summa theologiae* are Pars I, qu. 92ff, I–ii, qu. 90ff and II, ii, qu, 10–12, 39f, 57ff, 104; best ed. in Leonine ed., vols. IV–XII.

[4] Ed. Parma VI (1856), VII (1858).

[5] Best ed. Leonine XIIIf (ET 1922). In parenthesis it should be noted that in his earlier writings there were very strong hierocratic strains, such as in the work commissioned by Urban IV, *Contra errores Graecorum*. Cf. *PG* 444 n. 1; *HPT* 185 for the literal borrowing from this work by Boniface VIII in his *Unam sanctam*. For modern expositions of Thomist 'political' ideas cf., e.g., A. P. d'Entrèves, *The medieval contribution to political thought* (1939); G. Manser, *Das Naturrecht in thomistischer Beleuchtung* (1944); F. Flückiger, *Geschichte des Naturrechts* (1955) 436ff; G. Bullet, *Vertus morales infuses et vertus morales acquises*

Of the numerous pupils and followers[1] of Thomas Aquinas
three deserve specific mention. Their writings were important
sources because they show how difficult it was for the exponents
of the new political thought to detach themselves from the traditional governmental doctrine. Aristotle, one suspects, furnished
the trappings rather than the substance of their ideas. There is
Remigio di Girolami, a Dominican and teacher of Dante who
in his three tracts touched on topics which can justifiably be said
to belong to political science proper.[2] Despite his Aristotelian and
Thomist background he constructed the old descending theme of
government in the shape of the hierocratic system; he even adduced Pseudo-Denys in support of his argumentation in proximity to Aristotle's *Physics* and *Nichomachean Ethics*. The other pupil
was the already mentioned Ptolemy of Lucca. To him almost the
same observations apply as to Remigio. His tract *Determinatio
compendiosa de jurisdictione imperii*, written in the very first year of
the fourteenth century, is one of the most extreme hierocratic
writings. He employs the *anima-corpus* allegory as well as Pseudo-
Denys and the two-sword thesis to justify his uncompromising
presentation of the by now stale hierocratic ideology.[3] The last
pupil to be mentioned is the gifted, versatile and volatile Aegidius
Romanus (Giles of Rome). His instructional book for the young
Philip IV of France, *De regimine principum*, revealed him to be an
apparently thorough-going Aristotelian, whereas in his later work
De ecclesiastica potestate (1302) he showed himself as thoroughly

selon s. *Thomas* (1958); M. J. Wilks *Sovereignty* (below following n.) 124ff;
210ff; W. Ullmann, *The medieval papacy, St. Thomas and beyond* (Aquinas Lecture 1960); *PGP* 243ff addit. lit 312f; *IS* 124ff; L. Lachance, *L'humanisme de
s. Thomas* (1965). The *Rev. Thomiste* has regular bibl. bulletins.

[1] For very useful biographical notes on some of the authors to be mentioned
in the following pages see M. J. Wilks, *The Problem of Sovereignty in the later
Middle Ages* (1963), App. 3: 'Notes on the publicists and anonymous works'
(548ff).

[2] Details in M. Grabmann *SB Munich* (1934) cit. at 18ff.

[3] Ed. Mario Kramer in *Fontes iuris germanici antiqui* (1909) 1ff; here also the
unrewarding tract *De origine ac translatione et statu romani imperii* 66ff. He also
wrote a little tract *De iurisdictione ecclesiae super regnum Siciliae et Apuliae* ed.
S. Baluzius- J. D. Mansi, *Miscellaneorum liber primus* (ed. Paris 1761) 468ff. He
was a notable historian.

un-Aristotelian: the unwary reader might well suspect that the two works were not written by the same man.[1] In the first-mentioned work he certainly attempted some accommodation of Aristotelian principles to contemporary conditions and also outlined a political doctrine which went into considerable detail concerning individual topics relative to the management of the State.[2] Yet the second tract in which he trenchantly restated the hierocratic ideology shows not a trace of Aristotelian influence.[3] It adhered as strongly to the descending theme as the first tract did to a somewhat superficial exposition of the ascending theme.

The early fourteenth century is also rich in other sources which indicate that the one-time unquestioned unipolarity of political ideology was slowly giving way to bipolarity. Although there were still the old papal hierocrats represented by the official papal output which was untouched by the new ideas, there were nevertheless writings which attempted an accommodation of Aristotelian-Thomist thought within the theocratic framework, with drastic restrictions however on the jurisdictional power of the ecclesiastical authorities. There were furthermore writings which took their stand on the new principles with a view to counteracting the ominously rapidly rising doctrine of territorial sovereignty. The same age witnessed the initiation of what later became known as the Conciliar Movement, which was nothing less than the direct application of the ascending theme to the purely ecclesiastical government and the whole Church. And lastly

---

[1] *De regimine principum*, ed. Venice 1502. The work was translated into many languages in the 14th century, incl. Italian, Swedish, Portuguese and Hebrew (the English translation was by John of Trevisa). For all relevant details W. Berges, *Fürstenspiegel* cit. 320–2, where all extant MSS are cited. The *De ecclesiastica potestate* ed. by R. Scholz (1929). His tract which is only peripheral to political ideas proper, *De renuntiatione papae*, is in J. T. Roccaberti, *Biblioteca maxima pontificia* (ed. Rome 1698) II, 1, 1ff. Selections in ET in R. Lerner & M. Mahdi, *Medieval political philosophy* cit. (above, 272 n. 3), 391ff.

[2] The most satisfactory summary is still that by R. Scholz, *Die Publizistik zur Zeit Philipps d. Schönen und Bonifaz' VIII.* (1903 and repr. 1969), 98ff.

[3] As a curiosity it may be remarked that of the three invocations of the *Politics* one serves him as a prop for the view, that the pope was the *imitator Dei* and hence above the law (III, 9, at 194ff).

there is the radical orientation in writings that abandoned the vital Thomist principle which had in fact made possible the reconciliation of naturalism with Christian axioms. This group of sources severed the ingeniously conceived link of nature with divinity, so that the 'natural' and the 'supernatural' fell apart. It is a very variegated picture which the early decades of the fourteenth century shows.

Among the sources of the first-mentioned kind of writings are the official declarations of the Bonifacian papacy during its conflict with France. These are the decrees *Clericis laicos* (1296), *Apostolica sedes* (1300), and *Unam sanctam* (1302).[1] Their main points were comprehensive papal jurisdiction and the papal right to establish empires and kingdoms, to depose Rulers and demand obedience from everyone. Ideologically they contained nothing new except the pithy, succinct and concise formulation of mature hierocratic ideas. Moreover, some of them did not merely regurgitate, but set their face against the newly advancing ideologies. This indeed was the vital importance of *Unam sanctam* (one that has hardly been recognized). It contained an apotheosis of the *homo spiritualis* as the measure and judge of all things: this was a very well-aimed attack on the new Aristotelian-Thomist movement with its emphatic insistence on 'natural man'. The purpose of this solemnly broadcast statement was to warn contemporaries against the 'pernicious' naturalist ideas which constituted a danger to the whole foundation of the Christian framework.[2]

A source that combines a realistic outlook with a critical detachment from the traditional hierocratic standpoint and that rested on a very intelligent adaptation of Thomism was the tract written in the first years of the fourteenth century by John Quidort (John of Paris): *De potestate regia et papali*.[3] The author

[1] All conveniently available in C. Mirbt, 208ff; ET in B. Tierney, *The crisis of Church & State 1050–1300* (1964) 188f.

[2] For this cf. *IS* 129f, and 'Die Bulle Unam sanctam' in *Röm. Hist. Mitt.* (forthcoming).

[3] Ed. F. Bleienstein (1969) which supersedes the ed. by J. Leclercq (1942). ET J. A. Watt (1972). Details in R. Scholz, *Publizistik* (275 n. 2), 275ff; J. Rivière op. cit. (above, 260 n. 2), 281ff; Wilks, *Sovereignty* s.v.; *PGP* 263ff.

was a man of formidable calibre who presented a closely argued and firmly knit political treatise which has commanded increasingly high respect. The replacement of the old doctrine by a political doctrine based on naturalism was one of the purposes of his writing. It was a highly efficient surgical operation which John performed with the help of a Thomism that he himself quite skilfully developed. On Thomist lines he dealt with man in the State and postulated elective kingship; the king could be deposed by the people. The ascending theme was applicable both to the secular State and the Church. This tract marked the entry of the concept of the State as an independent, autonomous entity into the arena of scholarly political discussion. Intellectual superiority of quite remarkable dimensions enabled John partly to ridicule, partly to destroy, hierocratic arguments. He had been one of the outstanding masters at the University of Paris (d. 1306).

An example of publicistic rather than scholarly writing that stood between the succinct exposition of John of Paris and the apotheosis of medieval universalism represented by Dante was the stimulating but largely eclectic work by Pierre Dubois, an extremely gifted layman and excellent observer of contemporary conditions. He had attended the lectures of Siger of Brabant and of Thomas Aquinas. His tract *De recuperatione terrae sanctae*[1] (dedicated to Edward I) is a characteristic example of contemporary publicistic literature. Despite the sometimes quite startling confusion which the reader meets, there are three points specially worthy of attention: the emphatic insistence on the layman as a citizen and hence as a full bearer of public power;[2] the equally strong chauvinistic tone and eloquent advocacy of territorial sovereignty with the concomitant rejection of any sort of universalism;[3] and thirdly, the detailed treatment of questions relative to

[1] Ed. C.-V. Langlois (1891); ET by W. I. Brandt (1956); the tract was written 1305–6; for important corrections of the text see L. Boyle in *Med. Studies* 34 (1972) 468ff. Details in R. Scholz 391ff; Wilks, *Sovereignty*, s.v.

[2] For laymen in the royal chancery see above, 260 n. 1.

[3] Cf. esp. *De recuperatione*, ed. cit. at 54. And yet in a special memorandum to Philip IV (1308) Pierre craftily suggested that the king should propose to Clement V to make him emperor by depriving the German electors of their papally granted (!) electoral rights on the ground that they had misused this

education, judiciary, defence, taxation and similar problems, including population policy, stabilization of prices, value of money, colonization, and attendant topics. This tract gives a good picture of intellectual and ideological trends in early fourteenth-century France.

Dante's tract *Monarchia*[1] mirrored another and most significant trend of political thought. In some respects it was the contemporary answer to the malaise observed by one of the most sensitive and perceptive minds medieval Europe had produced. The tract constituted the earliest explicit rejection of the idea of territorial sovereignty which indeed had made quite rapid headway by that time. Written in the second decade of the fourteenth century it took its stand against the fragmentation and atomization of what was once a consistent and united whole, and it did so with concepts which belonged exclusively to political categories. In every respect Dante was a faithful follower of Thomas Aquinas, even if he went much further in his refusing to attribute jurisdictional powers to ecclesiastical institutions. His basic concept was that of *civilitas*. It designated the corporate union of all mankind which included not only Christians, but also Jews, pagans and infidels, in short all men who qualified as citizens. It was precisely in order to combat the incipient decomposition of European unity that he advocated a world-state within which alone the individual States and nations were guaranteed freedom of deployment, just as within the State alone the citizen had the possibility of developing all his faculties and abilities. Freedom of the citizen was to Dante 'the greatest gift conferred by God on man'.[2]

right by electing papal opponents (!); Pierre even fixed the amount of the bribe; see E. Boutaric (ed.), *Notices et extraits* XX (1865) part 2, no. 30, at 186ff.

[1] Best and most recent ed. by P. G. Ricci, *Dante Alighieri: Monarchia* (1965). ET by Ph. Wicksteed (1892 and numerous reprints) and R. W. Church (1898 also repr.).

[2] Details in F. Baethgen, 'Die Entstehungszeit von Dantes Monarchia' in *SB Munich* (1967) fasc. 5; *PGP* 258ff; *IS* 133ff; P. Fedele, 'Dante e il diritto canonico' in *Ephem. iuris can.* 21 (1965) 213ff, esp. 285ff (superseding M. Maccarrone's and G. Vinay's studies); cf. also J. A. Watt, 'Dante, Boniface VIII and the Pharisees' in *St. Grat.* XV (1972) 201ff.

The assumptions and aims revealed in Dante's *Monarchy*
provoked challenges almost immediately, and one of these was a
tract called in the traditional manner 'On the power of the supreme pontiff' by a Franciscan written between 1316 and 1322 and
dedicated to John XXII. This tract has only very recently been
discovered and edited. It shows that its author could do nothing
but employ very stale hierocratic material without even attempting to answer some of the tacit assumptions or presuppositions
upon which Dante's edifice rested. The author had only a very
vague knowledge of Aristotle, and his occasional reference to the
Philosopher never included his *Politics*.[1]

In proximity to Dante's tract, both in time and substance, was
another writing on world monarchy, though its author was not a
layman but a very learned and retiring abbot, Engelbert of Admont (d. 1331). In his *On the origin and purpose of the Roman
Empire*[2] he advocated the resurrection of the Roman empire in
order to re-establish peace and justice, for which the presupposition was concord between papacy and Western empire. His prime
aim was to construct a programme that would prove itself as a
bulwark against Anti-Christ. For the growth of sovereign national
States in his time appeared to him to herald the reign of Anti-
Christ. As a student at Prag he had become familiar with the
Thomist-Aristotelian doctrines and he attempted to wed them to
the traditional ideological material. The work had a strong
teleological tinge. The result was not free from inconsistencies.
The tract had none of the vision that characterized Dante's.
Engelbert's *De regimine principum*[3] stood on a far higher plane.
It was a penetrating political tract in every sense of the term. He
had intelligently absorbed and applied Aristotle's *Politics*. The

---

[1] See R. de Ponte, 'Il tractatus de potestate pontificis di Gugliemo da Sarzano'
in *Studi Medievali* 12 (1971) 997ff, first ed. at 1020ff. There is a good and
informative introduction by O. Capitani. For Guido Vernani's attack on Dante's
bipolarity see ed. by T. Kaeppeli in *QFIAB* 28 (1938) 123ff.

[2] *De ortu et fine romani imperii*, ed. M. Goldast, *Politica imperialia sive discursus
politici* (ed. Frankfurt 1614) pars. 18, pp. 754ff.

[3] Ed. I. G. Hufnagel (Ratisbon 1725); cf. A. Posch, *Die staats- und kirchenpolitische Tätigkeit Engelberts von Admont* (1920); G. B. Fowler, *Intellectual
interests of Engelbert of Admont* (1947).

concept of the State as a self-sufficient entity and the corresponding notion of the citizen as the integral structural part of the State form the backbone in this tract which has not yet been accorded the recognition that it clearly deserves as a contemporary source.

Although written in the decade before both Dante and Engelbert composed their works, the tract by James of Viterbo, *De regimine christiano*[1] demands some observations since it is a very illuminating source. Its importance lies in that it was in actual fact the first medieval tract or writing that explicitly and *ex professo* dealt with ecclesiology, especially the concept of the Church. That this topic had not been made the subject of specific scholarly enquiry before is certainly a remarkable feature. But it is precisely this which makes the tract particularly important. Considering the time (the very first years of the fourteenth century) and the argument adopted, one can without fear of contradiction assign this tract a place next to Dante's, at least in ideological respects. A careful study of the work shows that the author was fully aware of the potentialities of the Aristotelian-Thomist thought-patterns and the latent deleterious impact which this new category of thought could have upon the traditional descending theme of government. In a word, James realized the danger presented by the (Thomist) doctrine of bipolarity to the accepted christocentric scheme of things. But he also saw the danger of fragmentation and atomization of what was once a consistent whole. In this latter respect he was of the same mind as Dante and Engelbert. Where they differed was about the means: the first adopted a political solution, whereas James opted for an ecclesiological project. This served him, additionally, as a handle with which to render harmless the implications and applications of Aristotelian-Thomist ideas. He used these arguments to construct a universal State in the shape of the Church: the only entity deserving the name State was the Church which, moreover, was seen in an Aristotelian garb. In a word, James appropriated

[1] Ed. H. X. Arquillière, *Le plus ancien traité de l'église: Jacques de Viterbe, De regimine christiano* (1926) with an excellent introd., 13ff, esp. 54ff; further Wilks, *Sovereignty* s.v.

the new political thought—in order to buttress the descending theme of government. The Augustinian 'City of God' was to be transformed—or reborn—with the means provided by Aristotle's theses. Indeed, to harness this kind of armoury to a system of thought to which it was ostensibly inimical, was no mean intellectual feat. The ideological result was that the Church as the one and only universal State became a political entity. This tract is a most important source of political ideas. Indubitably it had grave flaws, but intellectually it was an achievement of considerable dimensions. It was a complement to *Unam sanctam* which attempted the same end, though with blunted and stale arguments.

For submission to the impending Council of Vienne (1311) Clement V commissioned a tract by Guilielmus Durantis[1] which was a badly organized and structured work. But what gives this piece its importance as a source is that its author—a member of the French aristocracy and opponent of the Bonifacian kind of hierocratic government—was not only one of the most learned and versatile writers of the time but also a man with a scintillating mind that was able to combine ideas and thus construct something new where previously there had been a vacuum: hitherto unrelated ideas were associated to form a new pattern of thought. With Durantis, one can safely say the conciliarist theme began to assume concrete shape. To an equal degree he mastered canonistic and civilian jurisprudence as well as Aristotle, and he linked divergent strains of thought together to construct a firm foundation on which he built an imposing edifice. The canonistic theory relative to corporations (assigning specific functions to the head and members of the corporation) could without difficulty be applied to the government of the whole Church, with the result that the alleged omnipotent monarchy of the pope was severely curtailed.[2] And in its section on 'The maxims of law' the recently published *Liber Sextus* contained a saying culled from the ancient

---

[1] Ed. of *De modo concilii generalis celebrandi et corruptelis in ecclesiis reformandis* (Lyons 1534). He is not to be confused with his uncle, the great 'Speculator'.

[2] B. Tierney, *Foundations of conciliar thought* (repr. 1969) (basic), here 190ff; also Wilks, s.v.

Roman law: 'What touches all must be approved by all',[1] a maxim which supplied Durantis with the key to the construction of the representative character of a general council. Thereby he opened the gates to the influx of Aristotelian themes as well as to the (correctly understood) idea of representation. Original power in the Church was seen to be located in the totality of all Christians whose representative organ was the general council. Since matters of faith concerned all, they must be decided by all.[2] Evidently, a serious breach in the papal fortifications was effected which, at the time, was purely theoretical, but of which practical use was made less than two generations later.

A new phase opened with the appearance of Marsilius of Padua's *Defender of the Peace* which was finished in June 1324.[3] The work attracted attention almost at once. In 1327 the papacy formally condemned a number of its propositions and declared Marsilius and his associate Jean of Jandun heretics.[4] The tenor of the book was in some respects the logical extension of the Thomist thesis. Marsilius knew that both the strength and weakness of Thomas was the thesis that God was the author of nature, but according to Marsilius this link was an axiom of faith and hence outside the

[1] VI: V *de regulis iuris, reg.* 29. About the origin of this Roman view see H. F. Jolowicz, 'The stone that the builders rejected' in *Seminar* 12 (1954) 34ff.

[2] A very similar idea had been put forward by Richard de Mores, the noted English canonist, see *MP* 21f, and 213ff.

[3] Ed. C. Previté-Orton (1928) and R. Scholz (1932–3); ET by Alan Gewirth, *Marsilius of Padua: The Defender of the Peace* (1956). For the exact date cf. J. Haller in his *Abhandlungen zur Geschichte des M.A.s* (1944) 335ff, at 354ff. Details: A. Gewirth, *Marsilius of Padua and medieval political philosophy* (1951); G. de Lagarde, *Le Defensor Pacis* (1970); *PGP* 268ff; J. Quillet, *La philosophie politique de Marsile de Padoue* (1970) with good bibl.; M. Wilks, *Sovereignty* s.v.; and id., 'Corporation and representation in the Defensor Pacis' in *St. Grat.* XV (1972) 251ff. On the question of Augustinian influence see D. G. Mulcahy, 'The hands of St Augustine but the voice of Marsilius' in *Augustiniana* 21 (1971) 457ff; id., 'Marsilius's use of St Augustine' in *Rev. des Études Augustiniennes* 18 (1972) 180ff. On Marsilius and his contemporary Ockham see G. de Lagarde in *Études Le Bras* 593ff.

[4] See O. Raynaldus, *Annales ecclesiastici* ed. Bar-le-Duc, XXIV (1872) 322ff. The two were always referred to as 'perditionis filios et maledictionis alumpnos', cf. *MGH. Const* VI no. 361, at 265f and in many other places.

purview of political science proper. He cut this essential link and made nature rest on its own basis. He therefore with one stroke achieved a tidy dichotomy of the natural and the supernatural. In matters of the human State only natural things counted. Hence only human jurisdiction and human law were valid and determinative norms. Law was enforceable precisely because it embodied the will of the citizens. The idea of hierarchy has vanished.[1] To Marsilius the State was the corporation of all citizens (*universitas civium*) who had full autonomy. Rationalism was the hallmark of political science; what was irrational lay outside its realm and belonged to religion. The voluntarism of Marsilius's system marked indeed the breakthrough to a fully-fledged political science that rested on its own norms and axioms and the insight and judgment of the citizens. The book appeared at exactly the right time when contemporaries had become more and more disenchanted with the accepted ways of thinking and government. The Thomist synthesis no longer seemed to make the ready appeal it once commanded. That Marsilius's doctrine later had success in unexpected quarters, as in the conciliar movement and in the feudally soaked English soil, is easily comprehensible: both conciliarism and English constitutional reality had been decisively prepared for the receptivity of Marsilian ideas by antecedent doctrines and practice.[2]

The sources of the fourteenth century unmistakably reveal the emergence of 'politics' as an autonomous science that took its place next to professional jurisprudence. The two still had a very great deal in common, but their basic assumptions began to change perceptibly. Nevertheless, one of the main ideas common to both was that of justice: jurisprudence worked backwards from the law to fix the contents of justice, whereas politics operated

[1] See W. Maurer in *SB Munich* (1970) (above, 230 n. 5) who remarks (94f) concerning Marsilius' advance: 'Der Areopagite entmachtet; eine Entwicklung von beinahe 600 Jahren aufgehoben; Aristoteles triumphiert.' The 'hierarch' was replaced by the *yconomus* (the steward) and the citizen.

[2] See *PGP* 190ff; *PK* 71ff; Wilks, *Sovereignty* 190 n. 2, referring to the medal with the inscription: 'Populi dat iura voluntas' commemorating Edward III's accession.

with the a-legal idea of justice and therefore looked forward to the future law. Hence the expositions by writers on politics were considerably freer and were able to develop the thought-processes without regard to the existing law—hence also the greater importance which the University of Paris assumed in the fourteenth century. The loosening of the jurists' monopolistic position was the conspicuous result of the establishment of politics as a science on its own. It was perhaps symptomatic of this state of affairs that there was now also a stagnation in the official output which in the antecedent periods fed the two legal systems. For from the thirteenth century onwards no imperial laws or decrees were added to the *Corpus Iuris Civilis* and in canon law a very similar situation came about as a result of the publication of the *Clementines* in 1317: no further canon laws were added to the *Corpus*. All the greater importance came to be attached to the regional, royal legislation which as a rule no longer served as a medium for the fixation and dissemination of governmental principles, because these were in any case implicitly assumed by the law-creative organs.

There was, however, a genre of sources which deserves some remark: the professional commentary on Aristotle's *Politics*. This new genre had emerged in the second half of the thirteenth century and established itself fully in the fourteenth. As an important source of political ideas the commentaries cannot be eclipsed, and yet hardly any of them are available in modern editions, and considerable spade work has still to be done. Only some specimens can be given here.[1] Walter Burleigh, the great Oxonian (d. 1343), wrote a commentary which survives in numerous manuscripts in England, France, Germany and Italy, a feature which in itself would indicate the wide dissemination, appeal and usefulness of the work. Its level of scholarship was higher than that of Albert the Great or Thomas.[2] Of particular concern was the detailed analysis of the structure of the State

---

[1] For the basic work on the commentaries on the *Politics* see M. Grabmann (above, 272 n. 3).

[2] Grabmann 33; L. J. Daly, 'Some notes on Walter Burley's Commentary on the Politics' in *Essays Bertie Wilkinson* (1969) 270ff.

which shows his highly developed integrative faculties. He was thoroughly conversant also with the substance of other Aristotelian works which he managed to weave into his exposition. Similar observations can be made about Ockham's pupil John Buridan (d. 1358)[1] who was one of the most fertile exponents of Aristotle in Paris, where he was rector several times; his influence on the nascent German universities was outstanding. He attempted to adduce the *Politics* for the solution of a number of topical problems, such as universal monarchy, or the relevance of 'theological truth' to political science, or the legitimacy of modifying the exchange rate of money, and so on. One of his main points was his insistence on the rule of law. Of particular significance was Nicholas d'Oresmes (d. 1382 as bishop of Lisieux) who appears to have come near Newton's concept of natural forces in his thesis on *impetus*.[2] On royal command he translated the *Politics* into French and added his own glosses which take up more space than the text itself.[3] He also made use of civilian and canonistic jurisprudence as well as of Marsilius of Padua. The German Aristotelian Henry Totting of Oyta, at one time professor at Prag and later at Paris and Vienna (d. 1397),[4] appeared as an independent thinker in his Commentary, in which he called the State the *germinatio politica* being the *principalissima communitas et communissima*. According to him the function of the law necessitated a distinction between a royal and a political government, anticipating the not dissimilar view of Sir John Fortescue. This source has never been printed.

[1] Grabmann 36ff; *DHGE* X, 1370ff (rich bibl.). Most of his works were printed very early, cf. his *Quaestiones super octo libros politicorum* (ed. Paris 1513). There are no modern eds. except his commentary on the *De coelo et mundo* by E. A. Moody in *Publications of the Medieval Academy of America* XL (1942).

[2] Grabmann 43ff, esp. 45f. His *De origine, natura, iure et mutatione monetarum* was very important, see Ch. Johnson's introduction and ET of *The De moneta of Nicholas d'Oresme and English Mint Documents* (in Nelson's Medieval Texts 1956); IT by G. Barbieri in *Fonti per la storia delle dottrine economiche* (1958).

[3] Printed Paris 1498, see Grabmann 47.

[4] Grabmann 57ff with further lit. For the quotation in the text see Grabmann 61. He was also a jurist of calibre, cf. his *De contractibus* (ed. Paris 1506).

The bitter conflict between John XXII and Louis the Bavarian[1] occasioned a brisk literary activity of varying standards. Some of the writings were frankly partisan, notably on the papal-hierocratic side. The great majority down to the mid-fourteenth century were *pièces d'occasion* lacking originality and width of perception. Some were Thomists who yet refused to accept Thomas' principles. Such was, for instance Hervaeus Natalis (Hervé Nédellec) (d. 1323) in his *De potestate ecclesiastica papali*.[2] The tract by Petrus de Palude[3] is a good example to show how difficult an indubitably gifted writer found it to detach himself from the traditional ways of thinking. He realized the starkness of the essential problem which the clash of the ascending and descending themes of government revealed, and yet his tract is wholly inconclusive.[4]

One of the most prolix, discursive yet nevertheless quite original writers was Augustinus Triumphus whose literary career started in actual fact before the great imperial-papal conflict. His main work, the *Summa de potestate ecclesiastica* (finished 1326) is a very characteristic product of the time. This huge source can serve as an example of how the new political science was utilized in the service of the descending theme of government. One cannot deny that Augustinus exercises a certain attraction on this count alone. His work has only recently found adequate apprecia-

[1] For the background see H. S. Offler, 'Empire and papacy: the last struggle' in *TRHS* 6 (1956) 21ff; for the manifestos and declarations before 1330 see *MHG Const* VI (imperial coronation at 285ff) (vol. VII not yet publ).

[2] Ed. Paris 1506, here also the tract by Guilielmus Durandus de s. Porciano, *De iurisdictione ecclesiastica* (about which see *MP* 85ff, 125) and of Petrus Paludanus, *De causa immediata ecclesiasticae potestatis*. This ed. has no foliation or pagination. His tract *De paupertate Christi et apostolorum* ed. with a very valuable introd. by J. G. Sikes in *Archives d'hist. doctrinale et littéraire* 9 (1938) 209ff. For the tract *De iurisdictione* see L. Hödl in *Mitt. Grabmann Institut* II (1959).

[3] Title and ed. in preceding note.

[4] See J. G. Sikes, 'John de Poulli and Peter de la Palu' in *EHR* 49 (1934) 219ff (important for showing the interdependence of theology, canon law and politics in the first half of the 14th century). For their view on papal inerrancy see B. Tierney, *Origins of papal infallibility* (1972) 146ff.

tion.[1] By dexterous handling of the sources, notably St Augustine and papal statements, even Aristotle himself could be made to support the hierocratic ideology. There is a good deal of sound criticism of individual features of the contemporary papacy, and this very criticism prompted Augustinus to present the hierocratic theme in a very accentuated form: only in the observance of its axioms did he believe that further evils would be prevented.

His contemporary, Alvarus Pelagius, a Spaniard trained as a jurist at Bologna, was also a theologian of calibre and very expert in Thomist thought. His large work *De planctu ecclesiae*[2] (1330–2) appeared in several recensions, the last in 1340.[3] He was a sharp critic of the papacy and contemporary ecclesiastical conditions generally: again, it was his criticism which stimulated him to propose radical solutions. In general, his aim was not at all unlike that of Boniface VIII or James of Viterbo (or for that matter of Dante and Engelbert), that is, to make the Church the one universal State. In order to put his programme on firm foundations, he geared up the supreme monarchic function of the pope to such dimensions which, in any realistic assessment, removed the pope from the arena of government and politics altogether. By that time it was wishful thinking to hope that the fragmentation of Europe could be halted by a full-scale resuscitation of the descending-hierocratic theme, especially as the papacy had endorsed the concept of territorial sovereignty.[4]

A special place in the literature provoked by the conflict of the papacy with Louis IV and the Minorities (on the poverty question) must be accorded to William Ockham (d. 1349). His enormous output is, however, a source of the history of philosophy

---

[1] Ed. Rome 1582. For all details see Wilks, *Sovereignty* which gives also an excellent insight into the checkered fate of Aristotelian-Thomist ideas in the 14th century. Here also MSS of the main works, 560, 562.

[2] Ed. Venice 1506. Full monographic treatment by N. Iung, *Alvaro Pelayo* (1931). His *Speculum regum* does not seem to be printed, cf. Iung 56ff.

[3] *De planctu ecclesiae*, I. 61. Cf. Wilks 21f, 41, 63 n. 3, 68, 477 n. 1.

[4] About this process of fragmentation stimulated by *Pastoralis cura* see above, 186, and also W. Ullmann, 'Zur Entwicklung des Souveränitätsbegriffs im Spätmittelalter' in *Festschrift Nikolaus Grass* (forthcoming). For the *Somnium viridarii* see below, 291.

and theology rather than of political ideas. Nevertheless, his standing, training and involvement in contemporary affairs eminently qualified him to put forward his views on questions of a political nature, though even here it is still difficult to draw a neat conceptual line between theology and politics. His political theses were in actual fact integral and constituent parts of his philosophy and theology and can be understood only in this framework. Those of his works which primarily come into question in the present context are the *Opus nonaginta dierum*, so-called because it was written in 90 days and directed against John XXII;[1] the huge *Dialogus*,[2] and the *Octo quaestiones de potestate papae*,[3] as well as the *De imperatorum et pontificum potestate*,[4] and smaller works now collected and edited in the *Opera Politica*[5] which contain violent attacks on contemporary popes and also lengthy analytical tracts on abstract problems, such as the basis of papal power, the *raison d'être* of the papacy as an institution, and especially his concept of the Church.[6] The tract on tyranny[7] belongs

[1] Ed. in *Opera politica*, ed. J. G. Sikes, R. F. Bennett, H. S. Offler I (1940) 287ff; II (1963) p.t. (here valuable introduction by the ed., H. S. Offler). Lit.: J. Miethke, *Ockhams Weg zur Sozialphilosophie* (1969) and A. S. McGrade, *The political philosophy of Ockham* (forthcoming).

[2] Ed. M. Goldast, *Monarchia* (Frankfurt 1668) II, 393–957.

[3] Ed. in *Opp. poll.* I (1940) 13ff. Some passages in ET in *LCC* X (1956) 437ff.

[4] Ed. by R. Scholz, *Unbekannte kirchenpolitische Streitschriften aus der Zeit Ludwigs d. Bayern* (1914) II, 453ff; also K. C. Brampton (1927).

[5] As above n. 1 in progress.

[6] Numerous examples could be cited to show how much his 'politics' was interlaced with ecclesiology. Cf,. e.g., Miethke op. cit. 502ff, and id., 'Repräsentation und Delegation in den politischen Schriften Wilh. v. Ockham' in *Misc. Med.* VIII (1971) 163ff, at 171ff. Cf. also B. Tierney, 'Ockham, the conciliar theory and the canonists' in *J. Hist. of Ideas* 15 (1954) 40ff. For the original way in which Ockham used Aristotle's *Politics* see M. Grignaschi, 'L'interprétation de la "Politique" dans le Dialogue de Guillaume d'Ockham' in *Liber memorialis Georges de Lagarde* (1970) 57ff. For general accounts cf. L. Baudry, *Guillaume d'Ockham; sa vie, ses oeuvres, ses idées sociales et politiques* (1949); W. Kölmel, *Wilhelm Ockham und seine kirchenpolitischen Schriften* (1962). For his denial of papal infallibility see now B. Tierney, *Infallibility* cit. 205ff (best recent explanation).

[7] Ed. R. Scholz, *Wilh. v. Ockham als politischer Denker und sein Breviloquium de principatu tyrannico* (repr. 1952).

to the same category. The influence of Ockham on the development of political ideas was less marked than on philosophical discussion in the subsequent age.

Some remarks must be made about a source quite obviously provoked by the quarrel between Louis IV and the papacy which put forward a programme that reflected the very deep concern if not apprehension of contemporary thinkers in regard to the role which the national kingdoms were to play in the future. For, despite its name, by the thirties the empire had shrunk to a mere German principality. The work was the *Planctus ecclesiae in Germaniam* by Conrad of Megenberg (d. 1379), written in the same year 1338 in which Louis IV issued the decree *Licet iuris*.[1] The work was composed in the form of a poem.[2] By escalating, if not resuscitating, the significance of the imperial idea, Conrad attempted to recreate the concept of a universal State but—in contrast to Dante and also Alvarus—the main instrument in achieving this result was to be the papacy. Realism was certainly not the strength of Conrad, although his criticisms of the conditions in the papal curia were penetrating, biting and sarcastic. According to Conrad, the implementation of his scheme would reduce the role which the national states were beginning to play.[3] This piece was symptomatic of the outlook of an educated secular cleric who also wrote a tract on the translation of the empire in which he once more set forth his universalist views,[4] as well as a tract entitled *Economica* which despite its name has little to do with

---

[1] According to this decree the elected German king became automatically Roman emperor so that the papal coronation was now really only a formality. It foreshadowed the Golden Bull of Charles IV (1356). Ed. in K. Zeumer, *Quellensammlung zur Gesch. der deutschen Reichsverfassung* (1913) I, 184. For the problem itself W. Ullmann, 'Dies ortus imperii' in *AA* 661ff. For an interesting new view of this source see A. Wolf, 'Das kaiserliche Rechtsbuch Karls IV (sog. Goldene Bulle) in *Ius commune* 2 (1969) 1ff. The Golden Bull remained constitutional law until 1806.

[2] Ed. by R. Scholz in *MGH. Staatsschriften des späteren M. A.s* (1941); further H. Kusch, *Leipziger Uebersetzungen u. Abhandlungen zum M.A.* (1956) in GT.

[3] Commentary in R. Scholz, *Unbekannte* (above, 288 n. 4), I, 79ff.

[4] *Tractatus de translatione imperii*, ed. R. Scholz, *Unbekannte* II, 249ff; his attack on Ockham ibid. 346ff; commentary ibid. I, 95ff, 127ff.

economic matters but dealt rather with the management and organization of estates.[1]

The work of Lupold of Bebenburg, bishop of Bamberg, was remarkable in at least two important respects.[2] In the fourteenth century the historical method began to be employed according to which assistance from historical precedents was sought in order to underpin theoretical propositions. This recourse to history was strongly pronounced in Lupold's work. The other feature of more direct interest in the present context was political: Lupold can well be said to have written the earliest work on German political ideas. For he was realist enough to view the identification of German kingship and Roman emperorship as a historical and ideological absurdity. He advocated a purely German Rulership. It was, he avowed, his zeal for his German fatherland (the *patria Germaniae*) which made him write the tract. Its significance was that it introduced the concept of sovereignty for Germany by shifting the imperial idea of universalism onto the narrower realm of royal-national dominion, and he did this much more professionally than Alexander of Roes had done a generation earlier.[3]

In regard to the concept of territorial sovereignty France had always been leading both in theory and practice, which is hardly surprising in view of French susceptibilities to the aspirations of the Western 'lords of the world' in the shape of the German emperors.[4] The statements by French jurists in the thirteenth century, the views expressed by John of Paris, the decision given by Clement V in 1313, and other testimonies persuasively proved this. This territorial concept had reference mainly to the intervention by another Ruler. In order to clarify the extent of French internal sovereignty, the king convoked an assembly at Vincennes

[1] Ed. and ET in L. Thorndyke, *University Records and Life in the M.A.*, 2nd ed. (1949) 202ff; 409ff (the third book only); further A. Pelzer and Th. Kaeppeli in *RHE* 45 (1950) 550ff (with extracts).

[2] *De iure regni et imperii*, ed. S. Schard, *De iurisdictione imperii* (Basle 1566) 328ff.

[3] Details by R. Most, 'Der Reichsgedanke des L. v. Bebenburg' in *DA* 4 (1941) 444ff.

[4] See also above, 103 n. 3, 104 n. 1.

in 1329. The royal spokesman Petrus Cugnerius, a counsellor at the court, advanced the view, based on political and legal considerations, that in regard to internal jurisdiction, taxation and related problems the king possessed the fullest power and sovereignty which was not to be impeded by ecclesiastical intervention: this would be nothing but interference. This source is especially important as it combines practical with theoretical exposition: the royal spokesman enumerated 66 items in which clerics had been wont to interfere with royal jurisdiction. For in regard to public matters supreme power was indubitably located in the king. To this the ecclesiastical spokesman in the person of the eminent Petrus Bertrandi replied at great length by once more regurgitating old and stale hierocratic arguments which now fell flat. These proceedings and speeches are sources of first-rate importance.[1]

Another source which reflects the French advance towards the modern concept of sovereignty (eventually formulated by Bodin) was a tract by Raoul de Presle, *De potestate pontificali et imperiali seu regali*.[2] It was originally written in French, which was significant: it is one of the first vernacular scholarly tracts. De Presle was a member of the court and later cabinet minister. In this work he wrote with characteristic French punch, incisiveness and erudition, and in almost classical form formulated the French king's sovereignty in internal and external respects. His main ideological support came from Aristotle, though by no means only from the *Politics*.[3] He also wrote between 1361–4 a compendium for the young French king which is the earliest call for the rebirth of the French State on entirely humanistic lines.[4] In close proximity to this source stood the *Somnium Viridarii* which followed the method of dialogue between a knight and a clerk successfully introduced at the beginning of the century.[5] It

---

[1] Ed. under the title *Actio coram rege habita de iurisdictione ecclesiastica et politica* in M. Goldast, *Monarchia* (Frankfurt 1668) II, 1361ff. Petrus Bertrandi was a canonist of the old stamp, cf. above, 173.

[2] Ed. in Goldast, I, 39ff.   [3] See esp. 45ff.

[4] Ed. W. Berges, *Fürstenspiegel* 350ff; personal details ibid. 266ff.

[5] Above, 260. The *Somnium* (or *Songe du Vergier* as the French translation, made soon after its appearance in 1376, called the work) ed. in M. Goldast, *Monarchia* I, 58ff. Details in Wilks, *Sovereignty* s.v.

presents the ascending theme of government in a very well argued manner: the Ruler's power was located in the people who elected him but who as the bearers of political power, could also depose him. No room was left for any papal or ecclesiastical interference. This author had therefore a number of important things to say on the vexed question of a Ruler's rights prior to his formal coronation.[1] This tract, which in its ideological substance reveals maturity of thought and a highly intelligent application of Aristotelian themes, also used powerful arguments to support the principle of inalienability: its disregard exposed the Ruler to deposition.[2] There is a freshness and directness in this tract which revels in demolishing 'historical' precedents so dear to hierocratic ideology. The work exercised a strong influence on the nascent Gallicanism[3] as well as on the tract by Jean de Terrevermeille (Johannes de Terra Rubea) who made the principle of inalienability of the French crown its main topic: no king was to be allowed to modify the established form of succession.[4]

There are numerous other minor works in the fourteenth century of which many are still not edited, while others were only of an ephemeral character.[5] That the second half of the century produced mainly works which can only with difficulty be called as sources in the present context is explicable by the

[1] Ed. cit., at I, 132ff, esp. 137.

[2] In this context see the exact contemporary statement by the parlement de Paris on royal rights and property: F. X. Leduc, 'Le droit du roi à donner la chose d'autrui à la fin du XIVᵉ siècle' in *RHDFE* 45 (1967) 612ff, with ed. of important texts, at 640ff.

[3] See F. Merzbacher, 'Das Somnium viridarii von 1376 als Spiegel des gallikanischen Staatskirchenrechts' in *SavZKA* 42 (1956) 55ff.

[4] He was royal counsellor at the turn of the 14th and 15th centuries. His tract *De iure legitimae successionis in haereditate regni Galliae* is ed. in F. Hotman, *Disputatio de controversia successionis regiae* (ed. Lyons (Frankfurt?) 1585) at 73–219. The latter made use of Jean de Terre Rouge's tract, see now R. Gisey in his Introduction to François Hotman, *Francogallia* (ed. and ET R. Gisey and J. H. N. Salmon, 1972) 97f, 101, 112; cf. text ibid., 462, 464ff. His son Jean was active at Oxford in the 16th cent. in promoting Roman law, see W. Holdsworth, *HEL* IV, 234f.

[5] See R. Scholz, *Unbekannte*, II, 576ff who has a very good survey of the authors in the first half of the 14th century, manuscripts and eds.

turmoil prevailing in Europe, a turmoil evidenced by the collapse of the papal leadership in religious matters, its sojourn at Avignon and the ensuing Great Schism, the Hundred Years War, the concomitant all-pervading decline in cultural and social standards, and in particular the effects of the working of the national monarchies with all the relevant attendant attributes of States which as yet had not produced their own theoreticians. In general it is true to say that the old was not yet old enough to be replaced by the new which was not yet strong enough to establish itself in the place of the old.[1]

Nevertheless, the writings of John Wyclif (1320–84)—a younger contemporary of Ockham—warrant some observations, as they constitute a source of a somewhat unusual character. He certainly was one of the most prolific of authors, and although he cannot rival Ockham in scholarly depth, vision, penetration and logical acumen, he left a mark not only in England but also abroad. His writings, as far as they are relevant in the present context, contain a great many political ideas. They are, however, indissolubly linked with his peculiar theology which had indubitably revolutionary facets. Nonetheless, three specific themes run throughout the relevant tracts of Wyclif: the basic humanistic conception of the individual as a fully-fledged, autonomous, independent member of society who had inherent, inborn rights: the idea of the individual as a subject did not form an operational element in his thought-processes. Intimately linked with this basic conception of the individual was Wyclif's notion of the nation-state: to him the nation-state was nothing but the citizen writ large. This point of view quite evidently made him an implacable adversary of the papacy which he attacked vigorously though not always consistently on the same grounds.[2]

[1] Petrarch's letter to Francesco of Carrara, *De republica optima administranda* (1373) (ed. V. Ussani 1922) was a mirror of the literary Renaissance rather than a serious contribution to politics or political science. The letter (which really is a tract) needs however closer study, esp. with reference to the rebirth of the citizen effected by the doctrinal evolution: this seems overlooked by W. Berges *Fürstenspiegel* 273ff.

[2] That he operated with hierocratic arguments in his early academic career has been shown by M. Wilks, 'The early Oxford Wyclif' in *SCH* V (1969) 69ff.

And thirdly, there was his theme of the Ruler's power expressed in terms of dominion which had a peculiarly wide connotation in the works of Wyclif: it enabled him to set forth the tutorial principle and consequently its perversion in the shape of tyranny.[1] But what above all made Wyclif especially important, if not seminal, was his aversion from the objective, collectivist-corporational point of view and his emphasis on subjective evaluation. In other words, the validity of law and of governmental actions depended on 'the moral worth' of the law-creative organ. The objective standpoint epitomized in the crucial concept of the office began to give way to the subjective-personal assessment of the governor.[2]

The Great Schism (1378-1417) almost suffocated constructive thinking in political matters. All intellectual energy was spent on efforts to bring this calamity to an end. Quite evidently, the Schism itself was to highlight grave deficiencies in the constitution of the Church: what, in brief, was to be done with a pope who was unsuitable? This was the case with Urban VI who was without doubt insane. But the constitution of the Church had never envisaged this contingency—though John of Paris had[3]—and on

---

[1] The most important tracts in the present context are: *De divino dominio*, ed. R. L. Poole (1890); *De officio regis*, ed. A. W. Pollard and C. Sayle (1887); *De potestate papae*, ed. J. Loserth (1907); *De compositione hominis*, ed. R. Beer (1884); *De civili dominio*, ed. R. L. Poole (1904). For modern lit. see, apart from H. B. Workman, *John Wycliff* (1926), M. J. Wilks' forthcoming study, and in the meantime his preparatory essays in *SCH* V (1969) cit, and 'Reformatio regni: Wyclif and Hus as leaders of religious protest movements' ibid. IX (1972) 109ff with copious lit. See also A. R. Myers in *EHD* IV, 646, 651 and J. Gilchrist, 'The social doctrines of John Wycliff' in *Hist. Papers* (of the Canadian Hist. Ass. for 1969) 157ff. For his influence on Hus cf. M. Spinka, *John Hus; a biography* (1968); also P. de Vooght, 'Obscurités anciennes autour de Jean Huss' in *RHE* 66 (1971) 137ff. For a rediscovered and now identified tract by a member of the Hussite circle and intended as a guide for the delegation at Constance, see F. M. Bartos, 'Das Reformprogramm des Magisters Johannes Cardinalis von Bergreichenstein, des Gesandten der Karls-Universität in Prag für das Konzil zu Konstanz' in *Festschrift H. Heimpel* (1972) II, 652ff.

[2] For some remarks and passages cited see *PGP* 103ff. The background of these views was the 'good' or 'bad' pope. Hus gave widest publicity to these theses. See also above for the reaction of Constance, 158.   [3] *PGP* 266.

the contrary had always asserted that the pope was not accountable to anyone for his official actions. The proposals to end the Schism of two (and later three) popes culminated in providing a constitution which prevented a recurrence of this situation. The problem itself was a blend of jurisprudence, theology and politics. The remarkable feature emerged that the ascending theme of government was now fully applied to the government of the Church: original power was now said to be located in the whole Church which acted through its representative organ, the general council, and its was to this (and thus to the whole Church) that the pope was responsible. The conciliarist idea was the very opposite of the descending-hierocratic theme: the pope, hitherto standing outside and above the Church in his official capacity, became a member of the Church to which he was accountable. Further, Aristotelian themes had hitherto not been favoured by the professional jurists but now were 'naturalized' in so far as some of his basic ideas were adopted, such as *epieikeia* (equity or fairness) which became an operational instrument in the interpretation of the otherwise intractable law of the Church. Jurists as well as theologians accepted this as the solvent. The literature of these 40 years is too vast to be enumerated in detail: in one way or another it exhibited three main strains: the Bartolist conception of the people's legal sovereignty, the Marsilian conception of the people's political sovereignty, and the canonists' conception of the Church as a corporation.[1] Only some specimens can be given here.

There were the already mentioned *Epistola Concordiae* (1380) by Conrad of Gelnhausen[2] and the *Consilium Pacis* by Henry of Langenstein (1381),[3] the beginnings of the large amount of literary production. But the overwhelming majority of writings belonged to the jurists: there was no jurist, notably canonist,

---

[1] See above, 157, 179.

[2] Ed. in E. Martène–U. Durand, *Thesaurus novus anecdotorum* (1717) II, 1200ff.

[3] Ed. in H. v. d. Hardt, *Magnum oecumenicum concilium Constantiense* (Frankfurt 1697) II, 3ff. About both see *Origins of the Great Schism* 176ff. ET of Henry's letter in *LCC* XIV (1963) 106ff.

who did not propound the conciliar theme in his lectures or commentaries. The classic exponent was (the later Cardinal) Franciscus Zabarella who was not only a brilliant scholar but also a most influential personage in the councils of the time. His programmatic tract *De schismatibus*[1] set forth the conciliar theme in cogent simplicity with a wealth of historical, Thomist, theological and juristic (canonistic and civilian) arguments: he shows that the emperor was fully entitled to summon a general council. Apart from the commentaries of the jurists, there were also numerous *Consilia* on specific questions.[2] A conciliarist of outstanding renown and influence was Panormitanus (Nicholas de Tudeschis) who was a directing force in the Councils after Constance, especially that at Basle.[3]

Among the conciliarist sources which were not juristic but which nevertheless exercised great influence, mention must be made of the tract by Dietrich of Niem, *De modis uniendi et reformandi ecclesiam in concilio generali* written in 1410.[4] In non-juristic terms it plainly stated that the monarchic plenitude of papal power was the root of all evil. Dietrich advocated the uncompromising implementation of the ascending theme of government, in order to prevent any further damage to the whole

---

[1] The full title is: *De schismatibus auctoritate imperatoris tollendis* ed. in S. Schard, *De iurisdictione, auctoritate et praeeminentia imperiali* (ed. Basle 1566) 688ff; also in his *Consilia* (Lyons 1552) fo. 90ff. He also dealt with the constitutional problem of the Schism in his lectures on the *Clementines* (ed. Lyons 1511).

[2] For some *Consilia* which have not attracted attention see W. Ullmann, 'Julius II and the schismatic cardinals' in *SCH* IX (1972) 177ff, at 180 n. 2, 185 n. 3.

[3] About him above, 187 and A. Black, *Monarchy & Community* (1970) esp. 9ff and 33ff, 136, 149; cf. also E. F. Jacob, 'Panormitanus and the Council of Basle' in *PICL* III (1971) 205ff. How much economic problems began to make themselves felt at Constance can be seen from Dominicus de s. Geminiano's disquisition; ed. v. d. Hardt (as 295 n. 3), II, 607ff. About this canonist see van Hove 497 with further lit.

[4] Ed. H. Heimpel (1933). ET in *LCC* XIV (1963) 149ff. To be consulted is also his history of the Schism, *De schismate libri tres* ed. G. Erler 1890, repr. 1972). In addition there is his *Viridarium imperatorum et regum romanorum*, ed. A. Lhotsky and K. Pivec (1956); his 'Invective against John XXIII' (ed. v. d. Hardt II, 296ff) has some good points concerning government.

of Christendom. Still greater influence, because coming from a celebrated teacher of the University of Paris, had the various tracts of Jean Gerson, then chancellor of the university, which argued in a subtle, Thomist-inspired way for the cause of conciliarism, on theological and partly also on juristic and political grounds. Most of these tracts were composed in the decade before the Council of Constance (1415).[1] Of no lesser significance was the view of Cardinal Peter d'Ailly, bishop of Cambrai, who mainly on Thomist lines (though relying also on historical and biblical material) set forth his plans for the reform of ecclesiastical government which in his opinion should no longer follow the rigid descending theme of government.[2] It will readily be seen that many of the tracts advocating conciliarism did so under the flag of 'reform of church government', obviously attempting to avoid the impression of radicalism. Yet in so doing they nevertheless set on foot a movement that was to continue well into the sixteenth century and past the Council of Trent—that Council which was to have dealt with the implementation of the battle-cry raised in the early fifteenth century: 'reform of head and members'. Virtually all the sources proposing 'reform' in the conciliar age had recourse to historical precedents and notably to early Church history which rapidly assumed the function of a pattern for late medieval conditions.[3] To this feature of 'historicism'

[1] *Opera omnia*, 5 vols. (ed. Amsterdam 1706) which also has the writings of d'Ailly and Almain; a new ed. is in progress initiated by P. Glorieux (*Oeuvres complètes*) (1960–); vol. V contains Gerson's writings relative to the Schism. For some details cf. J. B. Morral, *Gerson and the Great Schism* (1960).

[2] Esp. important is his *De materia concilii generalis*, ed. B. Meller in *Freiburger Theolog. Studien* 67 (1954) 290ff; some details in F. Oakley, *The political thought of Pierre d'Ailly* (1964).

[3] It should be mentioned that while the popes did not, on the whole, take the initiative for a 'reformatio in capite et membris' in the 15th century (see *SHP* 312ff), the secular side did, although the sources are not yet fully available. For this reform 'from above' cf. the stimulating contribution by H. Koller, 'Kaiserliche Politik und die Reformpläne des 15. Jh's' in *Festschrift H. Heimpel* (1972) II, 61ff. A vast research project is here in the making both in regard to opening up the sources and to interpreting them. The intellectual process well observed by D. R. Kelley (above, 110 n. 3) has at least some of its roots in the literature of the early fifteenth century.

too little attention seems to be paid in modern expositions of conciliarism, and it was the application of the ancient imperial prerogative to convoke a general council which ended the Great Schism—a remarkable revival of a principle that had been attacked so fiercely in antecedent ages.

What the sources of the fifteenth century reveal is a considerable widening of the mental horizon, prompted by greater experience, by greater facility to consult ancient authors and above all by the impact of humanistic theses concerned with citizenship and the citizens' full participation in public government. The emergence of the third estate was firmly embedded in this process.[1] The development could be particularly well witnessed in the North Italian city states in which the municipal statutes assumed major proportions as sources of political ideas:[2] so far, however, they have not been subjected to a close analysis. Although since the second half of the thirteenth century the North Italian cities had been in the foreground, the towns across the Alps in France and Germany came to adopt similar legislative devices in the fourteenth and fifteenth centuries.[3] These legislative measures too are to all intents and purposes virgin soil as sources and have yet to be explored from the political-ideological point of view.[4]

[1] The assumption by Gerda Koller, 'Was schuldet das Volk seinem Fürsten?' in *Festschrift H. Heimpel* II (1972) 815ff. that a new kind of literature emerged in the early 15th century is not warranted. Her discovered *collacio* is little more than an *exhortatio* couched in terms strongly reminiscent of much earlier similar products. This piece has all the appurtenances of the traditional descending theme.

[2] Cf. the eds. of municipal statutes in the *Corpus statutorum italicorum* (1912–1933). Particularly good examples are the statutes of Modena of 1327, ed. *Statuta civitatis Mutinae* (1864) or those of Parma, *Statuta communis Parmae* (1865) or of Piacenza (ed. 1860), esp. for the jurists (467ff), notaries (489ff), doctors (559ff).

[3] Cf. M. Gaupp, *Deutsche Stadtrechte des M.A.s* (1852–3); A. Gengler, *Codex iuris municipalis Germaniae* (1863); G. Espinas, *Recueil de documents relatifs à l'histoire du droit municipal: Artois* (1934–43). There are numerous eds. of individual municipal statutes.

[4] For an exhaustive presentation of the numerous legislative measures in the territorial kingdoms and communities, see A. Wolf in *HQL* 517–65 (admirable introduction to the jurisprudential problems) and 566–800 (details of regional legislation).

The emancipation of the third estate—the prosperous and educated bourgeoisie—appeared a menace to the established forces and produced a counter-reaction in the shape of alliances between the papacy and the kingdoms which took the form of Concordats. In these a number of issues came to be settled and arranged 'amicably' which had previously been explosive matter and had sparked off many a conflict. But it was now the threat perceived by popes and kings which joined old combatants together. These Concordats are very important sources which have not yet been studied from the angle of political ideology.[1] Further, the numerous diets in Germany in the middle of the fifteenth century overshadowed as these years were by the last quiverings of conciliarism (that is, the Council of Basle), served as platforms which produced speech after speech gloomily prophesying doom and disaster if the third estate (as allegedly observable in action at Basle) were allowed to enter the grand arena of politics.[2] And it was fear of the multitudes which persuaded erstwhile radical conciliarists to forsake their own so vociferously propagated programme and to embrace the very idea of monarchy which they had so fulsomely denounced only a short while before.[3]

If the English contribution to the growth of political ideas was, if not absent, at any rate small in comparison with the French and Italian, the explanation is not far to seek. The English soil had been thoroughly 'feudalized' which in practice meant that in contrast to the continental scene there never had been, certainly since the reign of King John in the early thirteenth century, the tension and alienation that characterized the relations between government and governed across the Channel.[4] The development of 'political' ideas in this feudal society of England took place within the constitutional framework and in an inconspicuous manner, not in learned tracts, of which there are in any case

---

[1] See A. Mercati, *Raccolta dei concordati* (1954) I, 144ff (with France, England, Spain and Germany) and 177ff (the important Concordat of Vienna, 1448).
[2] Cf. *Reichstagsakten* XIV–CVII (1935–63), esp. Mainz and Nurnberg, also Frankfurt. For some details see Black, *Monarchy* cit. 85ff.
[3] For further observations and materials see *SHP* 316ff.
[4] For this point see *IS* 84ff.

extraordinarily few. A further reason for the dearth of this literature in England was that the main legal system which nourished
so much political ideology on the Continent—the Roman law—
had virtually no practical significance here, with the consequence
that the study of canon law too suffered. There were no civilians
of calibre between the thirteenth and fifteenth centuries, though
there is unprinted material in College, University and cathedral
libraries which still needs exploration. In the course of the fourteenth century canonistic studies showed a revival—it was also
the time when Roman law studies began to attract attention again[1]
—as was evidenced by John of Athona and William Lyndwood.[2]

Of considerable importance as a source was the work of
William Lyndwood's exact contemporary, Sir John Fortescue,
a chief justice in Henry VI's reign. By any standards he can be
reckoned among the outstanding writers of the time. He attempted to clarify the difficult constitutional and legal position
in England by means of Thomist and other 'modern' arguments.
Not an academic jurist, yet with a thorough grasp of the political
ideas which gave birth to the law, Sir John's treatise (written in
English) on the governance of England is both a mirror of, and
a contribution to, the constitutional and political thought of the
time. It was indeed no mean feat to adopt—successfully—some
of the basic Thomist premises and accommodate them in the
English feudally inspired habitat.[3] This and the other tract (written
in Latin) *In praise of the laws of England*[4] (1469) were important
sources of political ideas in the fifteenth century: the tutorial

---

[1] See A. B. Cobban, *The King's Hall within the University of Cambridge in the
later M.A.* (1969) at 252f. Romanistic influences in Richard II's reign clearly
evident, cf. the documents assembled by E. C. Lodge and G. Thornton, *Engl.
constitutional documents 1307–1485* (1935), e.g. nos. 14–19, 21; for comments cf.
S. B. Chrimes, 'Richard II's questions to the judges' in *LQR* 72 (1956) 365ff,
esp. 374ff; also *PGP* 182ff. Hand in hand with this goes the conspicuous re-
surgence of the descending theme and the concomitant attempt at a more
effective theocratic kingship in the 15th cent.

[2] See above, 175.

[3] *Governance of England*, ed. Ch. Plummer (1885).

[4] *De laudibus legum Angliae*, ed. by S. B. Chrimes (1942) with a very perceptive
introd. by H. D. Hazeltine.

function of the king was brought out more clearly and tidily than in any other contemporary work.[1] The handling of the basic concept of *dominium* by him shows how much more mature this concept was in his system than in either Richard Fitzralph, archbishop of Armagh, or Wyclif two generations earlier.[2]

If ever there was a period of transition throughout Europe it was the fifteenth century. Literature proliferated to an extent that it had hardly done before, but quality did not keep pace with quantity. There was above all an intellectual restlessness which was clearly prompted by the crumbling of the foundations upon which European society was built. And the new landmarks were not yet discernible. A practical difficulty which this rich literature presents is the paucity of modern editions of a number of highly suggestive writers, such as Johannes de Ragusio[3] or Johannes de Segovia,[4] to mention just two outstanding thinkers. On the whole, the juristic writings exhibit an intellectual sluggishness if not torpor which makes their study sometimes a painful and unrewarding exercise. Admittedly, there were some fine juristic minds at work, such as the already mentioned Johannes de Turrecremata whose *Summa de ecclesia* constitutes a marvel of erudition and a highly intelligent adjustment of Thomist themes to contemporary ecclesiological problems.[5] Or there was the great Jason de Mayno (1435–1519)[6] whose quality of output as a civilian can at all events stand comparison with that of Bartolus or of Baldus. But by and large the juristic and ecclesiastical

---

[1] Cf. *PGP* 191f. Some of the statements cited here were quoted 150 years later by F. Hotman in his *Francogallia*, ed. cit. 306, cf. also 504.

[2] Richard Fitzralph, *De pauperie salvatoris*, ed. R. L. Poole in his ed. of Wyclif's *De divino dominio* (1890).

[3] About him and his works cf. A. Krchnák, *De vita et operibus Ioannis de Ragusio* (1961).

[4] For Johannes de Segovia see A. Black, *Monarchy*, cit. 18ff, 43ff, and excerpts from MSS, 141ff and esp. H. Diener, 'Zur Persönlichkeit des Johannes de Segovia: ein Beitrag zur Methode der Auswertung päpstl. Register des späten M.A.s' in *QFIAB* 44 (1964) 278ff (here further lit.).

[5] See above, 187f.

[6] For his works see Savigny VI, 397ff; esp. F. Calasso, *Medio evo* 585.

literature of this late period is not one that does credit to the age or the academic training.[1]

Similar observations can be made about the non-juristic literature which was also very bulky. But here too there were some works which deserve consideration in the present context. The strong advocacy of the monarchic form of government in the fifteenth century was no doubt a reaction to the powerful pressure which was exercised from below the surface, so to speak, by the third estate. One example of this kind was the long tract by Antonio Roselli, *Monarchia*,[2] written in the thirties of the century. Roselli was a jurist by training, but was above all a publicist of very considerable calibre. In his tract he operated with virtually all available arguments to prove the absolutist character of imperial rule—on a universal scale. The paternity of this idea belonged indubitably to Dante whose theme now began a new lease of life. The further significance of this work lies in that it postulated a form of monarchic government that took as its model the most extreme hierocratic theme. It was this which Roselli transferred to the emperor who in this fifteenth-century theory became what the pope was (or was to have been) in the high Middle Ages.[3] Indeed, the monarchic idea in its extreme form began now to be applied not only to the emperor but also to kings. By the end of the century the papal legate ordered this book to be burnt. Nevertheless, it had given rise to a number of other writings of a similar kind, such as to Aeneas Silvius' *De ortu et auctoritate imperii* (1446).[4] Here the idea of State sovereignty was considerably deepened in connection with a territorially conceived empire which to him was still 'Roman'.[5] About a dozen years afterwards

---

[1] As a deterrent example of this kind of literature may be cited the *Defensorium obedientiae apostolicae sedis*, ed. H. A. Oberman et al. (1968); cf. my review in *JTS* 20 (1969) 690ff.

[2] Ed. M. Goldast, *Monarchia*, cit. I, 253ff. The best account is still Klara Eckermann, *Studien zur Geschichte des monarchischen Gedankens im 15. Jh.* (1933).

[3] Eckermann 106.

[4] Ed. S. Schard, *De iurisdictione* (as above, 296 n. 1), 314ff (dedicated to Frederick III).

[5] Cf. also G. Kisch, *Enea Silvio Piccolomini und die Jurisprudenz* (1967).

the tract by Peter von Andlau (*Libellus de caesarea monarchia*)[1] continued the line begun by Lupold of Bebenburg and advocated a purely German empire. His editor called the work the first systematic exposition of German constitutional law. Nevertheless, it would be too much to claim originality for these works: by and large they contained stale matter expressed in different words. It would seem as if there had been certain signs of intellectual fatigue.

Nevertheless there were also men who were perfectly aware of the needs of the age and who put forward programmes for fulfilling them. Among the scholars who attempted a regeneration of contemporary social, political and ecclesiastical life was the bishop of Brixen, Cardinal Nicholas of Cues (Cusanus) (d. 1464). His *Concordantia catholica* (1432–4)[2] no less than his *De docta ignorantia*[3] are sources of major importance in the present context. Though still conceived within medieval cosmology, they point to new perspectives in both their analyses and syntheses. His variegated source material reveals the horizon of an exceptionally alert, erudite, reflective and responsive mind—it was juristic as much as Thomist, biblical and Aristotelian—which enabled him to construct a unity of the cosmos that welded together the triad consisting of God, the earthly universe and the individual personality. Even though his *Concordantia* had touches of unrealism —perhaps because in it spoke the youthful, idealistic author— there is no possible doubt about its potential, as instanced by his concept of representation, the principle of consent, the organological conception of the State, the antinomy of right and might (this is a specially fruitful recognition by Cusanus), the functional character of the law (in this there are points of contact between him and John of Salisbury), the tutorial structure of Rulership, the explanation of the numerical majority principle, to mention just a few of his more important ideas. But what raised him far

[1] Ed. by J. Hürbin in *SavZGA* 12 (1891) 34ff; 13 (1892) 163ff; cf. also *LTK* I, 509. He was the first vice-chancellor of Basle University.

[2] Ed. by G. Kallen (Heidelberger Akademie 1959–68). GT 1971.

[3] Ed. ibid. (1932); GT 1970. Selected passages in ET under the title *Unity and reform* (1962).

above his contemporaries was his critical acumen, his historical assessment of the sources and his highly developed juristic intellect. That he declared the Donation of Constantine apocryphal[1] (and not merely invalid on juristic grounds, as many of his contemporaries had done) was the result of an equally highly developed critical historical intellect.[2] But as so many of his contemporaries he cannot be said to have displayed the virtue of consistency in ecclesiastical-political matters;[3] nor did he heed his own 'reform programme', for he was a pluralist of considerable dimensions.

If most of the extant and available literature of the mid-fifteenth century does not yield much material that could be classed as original, the expectation that the commentaries on the *Politics* would advance political ideas, is not fulfilled either. There were some anonymous commentaries[4] which have not yet been edited. It deserves to be noted however that the translation provided by William of Moerbeke was now generally held in-

---

[1] Lorenzo Valla some seven years later came to the same conclusion, though his demonstration was perhaps not so elegant as that by Cusanus whose arguments he knew. See his *De falsa donatione*, ed. S. Schard, *De iurisdictione* (as above, 296 n. 1), 728ff; modern ed. by W. Schwahn (1928); also ed. P. Ciprotti, *De falso credita et ementita Constantini Donatione declamatio* (1967).

[2] For details see P. Sigmund, *Nicholas of Cusa and medieval political thought* (1963), and *Cusanus Gedächtnisschrift*, ed. N. Grass (1970) in which the contributions by P. Pernthaler, 'Die Repräsentationslehre im Staatsdenken der Concordantia' (45ff) and N. Grass, 'Cusanus als Rechtshistoriker, Quellenkritiker and Jurist' (103ff) are fundamental (here also further relevant lit.). See further the contributions to the fifth-centenary Memorial volume (*Nicolò Cusano agli inizi del mondo moderno* 1970), esp. F. Battaglia, 'Politica e religione' 49ff; J. Quillet, 'Le Defensor Pacis et la Concordantia de Nicolas' 485ff; P. E. Sigmund, 'The concept of equality in Nicholas of Cusa' 607ff. Cf. also E. Meuthen, *Nikolaus von Kues 1401–1464*, 2nd ed. (1964); N. Grass, *Cusanus und das Volkstum der Berge* (1972); and W. Krämer, 'Die ekklesiologische Auseinandersetzung um die wahre Repräsentation auf dem Basler Konzil' in *Misc. Med.* 8 (1971) 202ff; W. Mohr, 'Die Auswirkung des Gewaltenstreites auf die Entwicklung von Repräsentationsideen' in *Liber memorialis G. de Lagarde* (1970) 23ff.

[3] For which he was taken to task by Gregory of Heimburg in his *Invectiva in Cusanum*, ed. M. Goldast cit. II, 1626ff.

[4] See Grabmann, *SB Munich* (1941) cit., 63ff.

adequate. This gave rise to new translations in the fifteenth century. The translation by Leonardo Bruni[1] became the subject of specific commentaries, among which that by Ludovicus Valentia of Ferrara and Guilielmus Becchius as well as by the famed Donato Acciaiuoli (the great Florentine Aristotelian) have attracted attention.[2] But the present state of knowledge and the difficulty of consulting these sources—hardly any are edited— does not allow any comments on their quality.

As an example of a novel approach a source that is available in several recensions may be cited. This source breathes the spirit of the impending revolution to a far greater extent than other contemporary sources. It is the tract by John Wessel (d. 1489) who was a general theological writer of considerable repute, having had wide academic as well as literary and preaching experience. His tract *On ecclesiastical dignity and power* is a source of creditable dimensions.[3] It brings the double function of the individual as a Christian and a citizen into very sharp focus. The essential point in both is freedom of choice and will, and therefore consent to the laws is a vital operational element in his system. In regard to the laws of the State, whether in the religious or secular spheres, the judgment, assessment and evaluation is the individual's own. Linked with this is the other feature: the aversion from the objective, collectivist, corporational standpoint and the emphatic insistence on the individual-subjective conscience.[4] This can well be seen as the decisive turning point from the wholeness point of view to the individualistic standpoint. The revival of the right of resistance was consequently one more noteworthy item in his doctrine. No less significant was his exclusively teleological interpretation of the Pauline demand for

[1] Cf. H. Harth, 'Leonardo Brunis Selbstverständnis als Uebersetzer' in *AKG* 50 (1968) 41ff.

[2] Grabmann 76ff.

[3] Ed. M. Goldast, *Monarchia* cit., I, 563ff (together with the *Propositiones de potestate papae et ecclesiae*). Further texts ed. in G. A. Benrath, *Reformtheologen des 15. Jh's* (1968) 39ff. The tract is translated by J. W. Scudder, *Wessel Gansfort* (1917) 151ff.

[4] For earlier similar views (Hus), see *PGP* 103ff, 301ff; *IS* 143ff.

obedience to lawfully established authority: far from being un-
conditional it is severely narrowed in Wessel's programme by the
operation of the principle of consent and of the tutorial function
of the Ruler: he was held to have received power for positive,
constructive and never for a-social, unjust, selfish dynastic purposes. Thereby the right of resistance was given firm shape and
sharply-drawn contours. Wessel's political philosophy was
permeated with voluntarism.

The theses of John Wessel were therefore highly significant
from the evolutionary standpoint. For the greater part of the
Middle Ages religious, theological and ecclesiastical thinking had
determined the contents of the science of government. With the
appearance of the science of politics as an autonomous branch of
learning incorporating its own premises that were directly
applicable to social life, theology and its religious and ecclesiastical
companions were necessarily relegated to a place of secondary
importance as far as social norms went. They could no longer
raise a claim that their tenets be translated into law. Further, the
former collectivist point of view was replaced by the individual's
own assessment of a situation, and hence arose the necessity of
his consent to the law. But law and politics, by their very definition, presupposed a collective, if not corporate, entity, in which
even at the end of the medieval period religious issues still played
a vital part as matters of public law, though they were determined (not by the Church but) by the citizens' own body, the
State. The State began to be credited with the attributes that
formerly were assigned to the Church.

Select Bibliography

Apart from one or two exceptions only works not cited in the footnotes are here listed.

WORKS OF REFERENCE

Chartularium Studii Bononiensis: Documenti per la storia della Università di Bologna dalle origine fino al secolo XV (ed. by the 'Commissione per la storia dell' Università') (1907– in progress)

Chartularium Universitatis Parisiensis, ed. H. Denifle & Ae. Chatelain (1889–97); *Auctarium* (1894–1952)

Collectio bibliographica operum ad ius romanum pertinentium, ed. L. Caes (1971)

Dahlmann-Waitz, *Quellenkunde der deutschen Geschichte*, 10th ed. by H. Heimpel & H. Geuss II (1971), esp. nos. 414ff (Roman law); nos. 644ff (intellectual history and scholarship); nos. 936ff (medieval law); nos. 1841ff (political ideas)

Diplovatatius Thomas, *Liber de claris iurisconsultis*, ed. F. Schulz, H. Kantorowicz & G. Rabotti in *Studia Gratiana* X (1968)

Eichmann, E., *Quellen zur Kirchlichen Rechtsgeschichte* (repr. 1968)

Introduction bibliographique à l'histoire du droit et à l'ethnologie juridique, ed. J. Gilissen (1963– in progress)

IRMAE (relevant fascicles) (1961– in progress)

Mirbt, C., *Quellen zur Geschichte des Papsttums und des römischen Katholizismus*, 4th–5th ed. (1932) (for the less satisfactory 6th ed. by K. Aland (1967) see H. Fuhrmann, 'Der alte und der neue Mirbt' in *ZKG* 79 (1968) 198ff)

Panciroli, G., *De claris legum interpretibus libri quatuor*, ed. Christian Godofred Hoffmann (Leipzig 1721) (repr. 1968)

Repertorium bibliographicum institutionum et sodalitatum iuris historiae, ed. R. Feenstra (1969)

Select Bibliography

Santifaller, L., *Neuere Editionen mittelalterlicher Königs- und Papstur-kunden* (1958)

Sarti, M. et Fattorini, M., *De claris archigymnasii Bononiensis professoribus a saeculo XI usque ad saeculum XIV*, ed. C. Albicinus et C. Malagola (1888–96)

I

Besta, E., *Legislazione e scienzia giuridica della caduta dell' impero romano al secolo decimoquinto* (repr. 1969)

Dannenbauer, H., *Herrschaft und Staat im Mittelalter* (1960)

Duguit, L., *Les transformations du droit public* (repr. 1935)

Gierke, O., *Das deutsche Genossenschaftsrecht*, III (1885)

Jones, W., *Historical Introduction to the theory of law* (1940)

Pound, R., *Interpretations of legal history* (1929 and reprs.)

Strauss, L. and Cropsy, J. (eds.), *A history of political philosophy* (1963)

II

Hazeltine, H. D., 'Roman and Canon Law in medieval Europe' in *Cambridge Medieval History* V (1927)

Jolowicz, H. F., *Roman Foundations of modern law* (1957)

Jones, A. H. M., *The later Roman empire* (1964)

Koschaker, P., *Europa und das römische Recht* 2nd ed. (1954)

Stein, E., *Histoire du Bas Empire: de la disparation de l'empire d'Occident à la mort de Justinien (476–565)* (1949)

Vinogradoff, P., *Roman law in medieval Europe*, 2nd ed. (1929)

Wieacker, F., *Recht und Gesellschaft in der Spätantike* (1965)

III

Gilmore, M. P., *Argument from Roman law* (1941)

Fournier, M., *Les statuts et privilèges des universités françaises dépuis leur fondation jusqu'en 1789* (1890–2)

IRMAE (relevant fascicles) (1961– in progress)

Jolowicz, H. F., *Lectures on jurisprudence*, ed. J. A. Jolowicz (1964)

Jones, W., as under I

Paré, G., Brunet, A. et Tremblay, P., *La renaissance du XIIe siècle: les écoles et l'enseignment* (1933)

Stelling-Michaud, S., *L'université de Bologne et la pénétration des droits romain et canonique en Suisse au XIIIe et XIVe siècles* (1955)

Weigand, R., *Die Naturrechtslehre der Legisten & Dekretisten von Irnerius bis Accursius und von Gratian bis Johannes Teutonicus* (1967)

IV AND V

Le Bras, G. (ed.), *Histoire du droit et des institutions de l'église en Occident*
  I: *Prolégomènes*, by G. Le Bras (1955)
  II: *Les temps apostoliques*, by J. Dauvillier (1968)
  VII: *L'âge classique*, by G. Le Bras, Ch. Lefebvre et J. Rambaud (1965)
  XIII: *La période post-classique (1378–1500)*, by P. Ourliac et H. Gilles
    (1971)
Le Bras, G., *Institutions ecclésiastiques de la Chrétienté médiévale* (1959–64)
Plöchl, W., *Geschichte des Kirchenrechts* (1953–66)
Studia Gratiana (relevant contributions) (1953– in progress)
Weigand, R., as in III

VI

As an introduction may serve vol. I (1912) of the series called
Continental Legal History, especially for the Lombard kingdom (23ff);
the Germanic codes (45ff); feudal law (71ff); France (203ff); Germany
(311ff); Italy (87ff); Scandinavia (533ff); Spain (580ff).
Brissaud, J., *A history of French public law* (ET by J. W. Garner,
  1915)
Calisse, C., *A history of Italian law* (ET by L. B. Register, 1928)
Chénon, E., *Histoire générale du droit français publique et privé des origines
  à 1815* (1926–9)
Conrad, H., *Deutsche Rechtsgeschichte* (1962)
Gierke, O., *Der germanische Staatsgedanke* (1919)
Holdsworth, W., *Sources and Literature of English law* (repr. 1952);
  Some Makers of English law (1938)
Jolliffe, J. E. A., *Angevin kingship*, 2nd ed. (1963)
Kroeschell, K., *Deutsche Rechtsgeschichte*, 2 vols. (1972)
Leicht, P. S., *Storia del diritto italiano*, 4th ed. (1959)
Mitteis, H., *Lehnsrecht und Staatsgewalt* (1933)
Painter, S., *Feudalism and Liberty* (1961)
Paradisi, B., *Il pensiero politico dei giuristi medievali* (ed. L. Firpo, 1973)
Plucknett, T. F. T., *Early English legal literature* (1958)
Smalley, B., *The Becket Conflict and the Schools* (1973)

VII

Battaglia, F., *Lineamenti di storia delle dottrine politiche*, 2nd ed. (1953)
Carlyle, R. W. and A. J., *A history of medieval political theory in the
  West* (1903–36)

Figgis, J. N., *The divine right of kings* (repr. 1965); introduction by G. R. Elton

Gierke, O., *Political theories of the Middle Age*, ET and introduction by F. W. Maitland (repr. 1938)

Kantorowicz, E., *The king's two bodies* (1957)

McIlwain, C. H., *The growth of political thought in the West from the Greeks to the end of the Middle Ages* (repr. 1961)

Rehm, B., *Geschichte der Staatsrechtswissenschaft* (repr. 1956)

VIII

Battaglia, F., as under VII

Carlyle, R. W. and A. J., as under VII (vols. V, VI)

Franklin, J. H., *Jean Bodin and the rise of the absolutist theory* (1973), esp. ch. 1.

Friedrich, C. J., *The philosophy of law in historical perspective* (ed. 1968)

Gregory, T., *L'idea di natura nella filosofia medioevale* (1965)

Kantorowicz, E., as under VII

Limentani, U. (ed.), *The mind of Dante* (1965)

Lottin, O., *Le droit naturel chez s. Thomas d'Aquin et ses predécesseurs*, 2nd ed. (1951)

Oberman, H. A., *The harvest of medieval theology* (1963)

Rotelli, E. & Schiera, P., *Lo stato moderno: dal medioevo all' età moderna* (1971)

Schwöbel, H. O., *Der diplomatische Kampf zwischen Ludwig d. Bayern und der römischen Kurie* (1968)

Index

Index

Baldwin of Canterbury, 100
Baptismal rebirth, 39, 269f, 271
Bartholomaeus Brixiensis, 177
Bartholomaeus Salicetus, 116 n 1
Bartolus de Sassoferrato, 105 n 1, 107 n 2,
  108ff, 111, 112, 116 n 1, 186, 295, 301
Basic law, 206f
Basle, council, 157, 296, 299
  university, 303 n 1
Baumgarten Formulary, 202
Beaumanoir, Phillippe, 221
Becchius, Guilielmus, 305
Benedictus Levita, 130f
Beneficium, 123, 127
Benefit of clergy, 183
Bernard of Clairvaux, St, 98 n 1, 144, 255,
  257
Bernard Gui, 147 n 6
Bernard of Parma, 180
Bernard of Pavia, 169
Bernold of Constance, 139, 250
Bible, 32, 35, 39, 41ff, 54, 59, 119, 237, 242,
  245, 247, 251f, 254, 257, 297, 303
Bipolarity, 13, 270, 271
Bodin, Jean, 291
Body public concept, 28, 37, 40, 43, 47,
  120, 121, 140, 143, 199
Bologna, university, 66, 68, 69, 83, 87f,
  92f, 97, 99, 102, 106, 112, 129, 163, 164,
  166, 168, 169, 174, 176, 180, 184, 187 n
  11, 216, 287
Boniface St, 235
Boniface VIII, 106, 145, 168, 184, 211 n 3,
  255, 273 n 5, 276, 287
Bonizo of Sutri, 76 n 1, 136, 139, 250
Bracton, Henry de, 100, 220, 222
Bridgetine Order, 187 n 11
Bridlington Priory, 142 n 2
Britton, 221
Bruni, Leonardo, 305
Bulgars, 72 n 1, 177
Bulgarus, 98
Burchard of Worms, 132f
Buridan, John, 285
Burleigh, Walter, 284

Cambridge, university, 84 n 2, 174, 175,
  183 n 3
Canon law, 46, 72 n 1, 75, 83, 84, 85, 112 n
  1, 119ff, 161ff, 185, 284, 286 n 4
  collections of, 122, 127ff, 168f, 174;
    their influence, 133f
  study, 87, 90, 93, 101, 103, 163ff, 300

universality, 137, 154, 167
  and theology, 133, 178
Canonists, 108, 111, 165ff; *see also* under
  respective names
  laymen, 184f
  scholarship of, 46, 57, 79, 83, 163ff,
    168ff, 257, 281, 283, 295, 296, 301
Canossa, 239
Capella, papal, 170 n 1
Capitula Angilramni, 131 n 1
Capitularia, 153 n 2, 203ff
Cappa rubea, 263
Cardinalate, status, 159, 172
Cardinals, college of, 95 n 1, 149 n 5, 154f
Carolingians, 70, 73f, 152f; *see also* Re-
  naissance, Carolingian
Cathwulf, 235
Causae maiores, 122
Celestine II, 141 n 2; III, 144 n 5
Chalcedon, council, 122f, 151, 232
Chanceries, 44, 73, 95f, 125, 140, 148, 150,
  166 n 4, 170, 195, 196, 200f, 202, 209f,
  211 n 1, 212, 214, 228, 255, 259
Charlemagne, 96, 126, 127, 201, 203, 204,
  235, 239
Charles IV, 289 n 1; V, of France, 264 n 3
Charles of Anjou, 105 n 3
Charles the Bald, 205, 206 n 2, 207
Charters, 199, 200ff, 209ff, 214
Chaucer, 256 n 2
Childeberth I, 200 n 2
Chrism, 265
Christianitas, 271, 272
Christianity and law, 12, 32, 33, 34ff, 48f,
  60, 119, 126, 130, 143, 153, 227, 236, 237,
  306
Christus Domini, 209
Church, concept, 36ff, 121ff, 133, 134, 141,
  147, 150, 230, 231, 239, 246, 253, 256,
  270, 277, 280, 288, 294
Citizen, individual, 41, 219, 269f, 277, 278,
  280, 293, 298, 305
  will, 283
Civilian jurisprudence, 46, 55, 57 n 2, 79,
  83ff, 163, 164, 165, 168, 172, 175, 178,
  179, 180, 185, 212, 214, 216, 257, 269 n
  1, 281, 283, 295, 296, 301
Civilitas, 278
Civitas sibi princeps, 109f
Claudius of Turin, 242
Clement I, 119, 230; *see also* Pseudo-
  Clement; V, 146, 149 n 4, 186, 277 n 3,
  281, 290

312

Index

Index

Index

Mirror of Justices, 221
Missionaries, 54
Monarchy, concept, 35ff, 40f, 49, 56, 65, 70, 84, 94, 103, 120, 122, 134, 141, 151, 155f, 167, 182, 188, 209 n 3, 228, 229, 231, 233, 248, 257, 281, 285, 302
Monographs, 227ff
Monotheism, and monarchy, 34f, 46
Montluçon, Jean, 222
Montpellier, university, 84 n 2, 97, 100, 103, 106 n 2
Munt, 49, 196, 200 n 2, 205f

Nation states, 289f, 293, 303
National sentiments, 261
Nations, universities, 93 n 1, 261
Natural man, 39, 270
Naturalism, 188, 269ff, 276, 277
Nature, concept, 272, 282f
Negotia regni, 235
New Rome, 231; *see* Constantinople
Newton, Isaac, 285
Nicaea, council, 38, 151
Nicholas I, 72 n 1; V, 150 n 1
Nicholas d'Oresmes, 285
Nicholas de Tudeschis, *see* Panormitanus
Niem, Dietrich of, 296f
Normans, 71, 245
Notabilia, 86, 175
Notaries, 72f, 202, 209, 211 n 1, 298 n 2
Novellae, Justinian, 61, 62, 64ff, 69f, 217
Novitas vitae, 39

Oaths, 76, 249, 253, 264
Obedience to law, 49, 76, 92, 124, 158, 207, 233, 242, 248, 276, 305
Obertus de Orto, 217
Objectivism, 46, 48, 158, 229, 294, 305
Ockham, 282 n 3, 284, 287f, 293
Odofredus, 105
Office, and person, 35 n 3, 36, 47, 177, 229, 238, 294
Oldradus de Ponte, 106, 113, 186
Orléans, university, 84 n 2, 97 n 5, 103, 106 n 7, 107 n 2
Orosius, 232
Otto I, 209; III, 75
Otto of Freising, 95 n 1
Ottonianum, 247
Oxford, university, 97, 98, 104 n 2, 110, 169, 174, 175, 181, 183 n 3, 284, 292 n 4

Padua, university, 105 n 3, 106, 108, 112, 187 n 11
Pallium, 263
Panormitanus, 173, 176 n 1, 187, 296
Papacy, 38f, 40, 63, 71ff, 75, 77, 90, 91, 96, 101, 120f, 141, 152ff, 163, 168f, 182, 186f, 188, 212, 222, 228, 229, 233, 235, 240, 245ff, 256, 259, 261, 287, 289, 293
  and council, 156, 181 n 3, 281
Paris, university, 103, 173 n 2, 187, 261, 277, 284, 285, 297
  parlement, 222, 292 n 2
Pars sanior, 156 n 1
Paschasius Radbertus, 239 n 1
Pastoralis cura, 186, 290; *see also* Clement V, *and* Sovereignty
Patrimonies, Roman Church, 72
Paucapalea, 177
Paulus Castrensis, 116 n 1, 187
Paulus de Liazariis, 185
Pavia, university, 84 n 2, 112, 135 n 2, 197
People, law creation by, 109, 193, 204
  sovereignty of, 30f, 58f, 157, 291f; *see also* Ascending theme
Persona regalis, 238
Perugia, university, 84 n 2, 108, 112, 185
Peter of Auvergne, 272; Blois, 100, 257
Peter Damian, 247f
Peter Lombard, 273
Petrarch, 106, 181, 293 n 1
Petrinology, 144
Petrus de Ancharano, 185, 187
Petrus Blesensis, 100, 257
Petrus de Bellapertica, 107, 110 n 1
Petrus Bertrandi, 173, 291
Petrus Crassus, 77f, 251
Petrus de Cugneriis, 173 n 4, 291
Petrus Paludanus, 286
Philip II Augustus, 103, 218, 256 n 2; IV, 274, 277 n 3
Philip of Leyden, 114f
Phillippe Beaumanoir, 221
Phillipus Decius, 189
Pillius, 87 n 1, 100
Pippin the Short, 126
Pisa, university, 112
Pisana, 68
Pius II, 159
Placentinus, 97, 99f
Placidus of Nonantula, 76 n 1
Platonism, 32, 39, 40, 270
Plenitude of power, 123 n 2, 155, 296

317

Index